PROFESSING DARKNESS

CORMAC McCARTHY'S
CATHOLIC CRITIQUE OF
AMERICAN ENLIGHTENMENT

PROFESSING DARKNESS

D. MARCEL DeCOSTE

LOUISIANA STATE UNIVERSITY PRESS
BATON ROUGE

Published by Louisiana State University Press
lsupress.org

DESIGNER: Barbara Neely Bourgoyne
TYPEFACE: Whitman

Jacket image courtesy iStock/mammoth.

LIBRARY OF CONGRESS CATALOGING-IN-PUBLICATION DATA
Names: DeCoste, D. Marcel, author.
Title: Professing darkness : Cormac McCarthy's Catholic critique of
    American enlightenment / D. Marcel DeCoste.
Description: Baton Rouge : Louisiana State University Press, 2024. |
    ncludes bibliographical references and index.
Identifiers: LCCN 2023045243 (print) | LCCN 2023045244 (ebook) | ISBN
    978-0-8071-8153-9 (cloth) | ISBN 978-0-8071-8232-1 (pdf) | ISBN 978-0-8071-8231-4
    (epub)
Subjects: LCSH: McCarthy, Cormac, 1933–2023—Criticism and interpretation.
    | Catholic Church—In literature. | Theology in literature. | LCGFT:
    Literary criticism.
Classification: LCC PS3563.C337 Z646 2024 (print) | LCC PS3563.C337
    (ebook) | DDC 813/.54—dc23/eng/20231128
LC record available at https://lccn.loc.gov/2023045243
LC ebook record available at https://lccn.loc.gov/2023045244

for Katherine, Margaret, and Elizabeth,
lights always

CONTENTS

ABBREVIATIONS

APH   *All the Pretty Horses*
BM   *Blood Meridian*
C   *The Counselor*
CG   *Child of God*
CP   *Cities of the Plains*
OD   *Outer Dark*
P   *The Passenger*
R   *The Road*
S   *Suttree*
SM   *Stella Maris*
St   *The Stonemason*
TC   *The Crossing*

ACKNOWLEDGMENTS

This book owes its existence to author, teacher, and esteemed colleague Ken Mitchell. It was Ken whose passion for *The Road* brought me, some fifteen years ago, to my embarrassingly belated first encounter with the work of Cormac McCarthy. For this, I am forever grateful.

My gratitude is likewise owed to graduate and undergraduate participants in my 2012 and 2019 seminars on McCarthy at the University of Regina. As is often the case, these young scholars were as much teachers as students. This is particularly true of Carolyn Llewellyn who not only shone in the first of these offerings, but did so with an enthusiasm and intelligence that have stayed with me years later. Our discussions helped shape the thinking that yielded the present work. Similarly valuable were conversations with, and commentary from, Fr. Parker Love and Patrick Malone. Former students, dear friends, they were kind enough to read drafts of chapter 6 and the coda; for their generosity and acumen, as for their friendship, I am truly thankful. Thanks, too, to Kat Nogue for her editorial eye and timely encouragement; her rigor has helped make a book of a manuscript.

Thank you to Dr. William Arnal of the Department of Gender, Religion, and Critical Studies at the University of Regina. His kind invitation to speak to his department sowed the seeds of what is now chapter 4 of this book, and his expert guidance on matters Gnostic helped me define thinking documented in my Introduction here.

I wish also to express my gratitude to Baylor University's Institute of Faith and Learning, whose 2018 and 2019 Symposiums on Faith and Culture offered edifying venues for the debut of my thinking on certain McCarthy texts, including *The Crossing*. Thanks, also, to the Cormac McCarthy Society, who made me so very welcome at their 2022 conference. Their feedback on my presentation on *The Road* has strengthened the chapter 6 I present to readers here.

Finally, I must express love and thanks to my wife, Dr. Susan Johnston. More than a priceless critical interlocutor, she is my scholarly model and inspiration. A more generous, loving, and gifted teacher/mentor than I will ever be, she has unstintingly given me support, advice, and encouragement that are emotional, moral, and spiritual, as much as professional. Without her, this book would not exist; without her steady profession of light, I would be lost in darkness.

PROFESSING DARKNESS

INTRODUCTION

THE ONLY WORDS I KNOW ARE THE CATHOLIC ONES

McCARTHY'S CHRISTIAN CRITIQUE OF AMERICAN ENLIGHTENMENT

Cormac McCarthy's 2022 publication of *The Passenger* and *Stella Maris* brought to a close a novelistic hiatus of some sixteen years. What's more, it returned the 2007 Pulitzer Prize–winner to the literary spotlight. His new work praised, in such venues as the *Los Angeles Times* and *Time,* as "phenomenal" (Kellogg) and as "push[ing] his ambition to the very boundaries of human understanding" (Mancusi), the man himself became a subject of renewed interest, with a *New York Times* feature on newly discovered interviews from his early career (Harris). But if McCarthy, who recently died at the age of eighty-nine, had now re-emerged as a publishing event, this only marked a return to twenty-first-century form. Indeed, since the success of 1992's *All the Pretty Horses,* his work has enjoyed an increasingly wide readership and ever-intensifying critical attention. Its profile only grew in the first decade of the present century, with brisk sales for *No Country for Old Men* (2005) and *The Road* (2006), a wildly successful, Oscar-winning adaptation of the former, and a much-publicized televised 2007 interview with Oprah Winfrey in the wake of the latter. While McCarthy had garnered critical acclaim from the start of his career, and the first book-length study of his work, Vereen Bell's *The Achievement of Cormac McCarthy,* appeared in 1988, his rising popularity among readers has fueled a comparable growth in scholarly scrutiny over the past thirty years. Bell's pioneering work has been followed by scores of articles, critical monographs, and volumes of essays, and, in 2001, by the establishment of an academic journal devoted exclusively to McCarthy's work. Nor does such critical interest show any signs of flagging. The past decade alone has seen the publication of roughly two dozen books—monographs and essay anthologies—dealing with his oeuvre.

This scholarship has been diverse, ranging from introductory readers' guides to more thematic studies of McCarthy's engagement with philosophy, science, and genre, or of his ecological preoccupations, narrative technique, and treatment of gender. Still, it has been shaped by certain enduring debates. With Bell's work, McCarthy was first heralded by literary criticism as a literary nihilist. In both his 1988 monograph and the 1983 article that preceded it, Bell treats the fiction—with its penchant for depraved outsiders, murderous violence, and shocking taboo-breaking—as a relentless dismantling of transcendent values, truths, and purposes. McCarthy's world, then, is predicated on "no first principles, no foundational truth" ("Ambiguous" 32), but characterized by a "prevailing gothic and nihilistic mood" (*Achievement* 1), an ambience underwritten by an ontology in which "existence seems both to precede and preclude essence" ("Ambiguous" 31). Such assessments enjoyed considerable currency among the first generation of McCarthy scholars. Their echoes may be heard, for example, in Dana Phillips's influential reading of *Blood Meridian*, which deems that novel a "nihilistic" testament to "the equality of being between human and nonhuman objects" ("Ugly" 27, 29), as well as in John Cant's more recent declaration that, in McCarthy, the reader encounters an inverted Flannery O'Connor, a writer who, though given to religious symbolism, insistently demonstrates that "it is unbelief that is admirable" (30).[1]

Soon, however, others would take issue with such conclusions, arguing instead that McCarthy's persistent fascination with the problem of evil bespoke anything but an amoral worldview. Such early champions as Rick Wallach and Edwin T. Arnold, for example, insisted rather upon the writer's deep moral commitments. Wallach, maintaining that McCarthy's fiction "cannot be considered nihilistic" ("*Beowulf*" 199), presents even the carnage-laden *Blood Meridian* as a text that "cannot reasonably be interpreted as an amoral representation of violence for its own sake" (212). More affirmatively, Arnold identifies in McCarthy's work "a profound belief in the need for moral order" ("Naming" 46). Indeed, for Arnold, the canon testifies to McCarthy's status as an author whose work "venerates life in all its forms . . . who believe[d] in a source of being and order deeper than that manifested in outward show" ("McCarthy" 216). Such readings of McCarthy as a writer of a decidedly ethical bent have proliferated. Similar intuitions animate Steven Frye's 2009 declaration that McCarthy's work unfailingly "engages the ultimate questions—the nature of the real, the possibility of the divine, the source of ethics and identity" (*Understanding* 3), as well as Lydia Cooper's study of McCarthy's use of point of view in *No More Heroes* (2011). This latter work argues that "an examination of narrative perspective . . . suggests that [his] novels systematically privilege the heroic moral attitudes and actions of characters populating horrific and violent literary worlds" (13). Likewise a defense of the heroism of McCarthy's protagonists, Russell Hillier's *Morality in Cormac McCarthy's Fiction* (2017) holds that such characterization reveals the author to be "as intrigued by the mystery of goodness as . . . by the mystery of evil" and intent on producing a fiction that "conveys an impassioned and consistent moral vision" (6).

Such starkly arrayed theses and antitheses call for critical syntheses, and the latter were indeed forthcoming. Thus, in 2004, Farrell O'Gorman would contend that the allure of McCarthy's work lies "in the fact that it continually and brilliantly rearticulates religious questions without giving clear answers to them" (123), an account that allows the writer to have his parables and his threat of nothingness both.[2] More commonly, however, the marriage of these approaches has borne fruit in a focus on the fiction's critical stance on American culture and its Enlightenment underpinnings. Most evident in responses to McCarthy's Westerns, and so to his engagement with American history's animation by a national faith in Manifest Destiny, such interpretations vindicate the novels' seemingly nihilistic depictions of historical violence by allying them with an outraged and critical moral sense, one keen to arraign the destructive certainties of modern thought. Thus, even Bell treats *Blood Meridian*'s archvillain, Judge Holden, as "an only slightly demented revival of Enlightenment philosophy" (*Achievement* 124). More pointedly, Wallach argues that Holden exposes how the American dream has, in its historical enactment, been also "a nightmare of genocidal appropriation" ("Judge" 135). Such assessments proffer this diabolical figure as one whose own nihilism permits a critique of the Enlightenment tenets upon which his teachings, the westward expansionism of his day, and the materialist American culture of the author's own, all rest. They also inaugurate a long-standing critical tradition of reading McCarthy as

3

a relentless prosecutor of Enlightenment understandings of, and exhortations to, personal, scientific, and civilizational progress.

In David Holloway's work, such a tack helped define the direction of McCarthy scholarship in the new millennium. In *The Late Modernism of Cormac McCarthy* (2002), Holloway argues forcefully that McCarthy's corpus writes both from and about a world "in which the global market, and the neoliberal suppression of all alternative social and economic orders, [has] finally become a reality" (*Late* 19). Dramatizing its own imbrication in such a reality, McCarthy's fiction, on Holloway's account, nonetheless constitutes a powerful critical project, mapping out "the essential materiality of those more abstract Enlightenment doctrines on the rights of man or the sanctity of property which arise as bulwarks to the newly atomized world of the private bourgeois subject" (*Late* 65). Holloway's treatment of McCarthy's nightmare worlds as the graphic realization in art of Enlightenment ideals thus made susceptible to interrogation would find many subsequent adherents.[3] Picking up this same line of reasoning some fourteen years on, Monk also reads McCarthy's work as an extended critique of the West's "obsession with progress and the overarching will to control and rationalize, born of the ideas of the European Enlightenment" (xii). In particular, he sees the novels as preoccupied with the harm done to individual human beings, as well as to their social and natural environments, by that reduction of the person to Holloway's bourgeois subject and of that subject's reasoning power to pragmatic self-seeking: "The creation of the overarching *I*, the instrumental use of technology, the use of reason to justify even the most egregious aspects of capitalism, the banishment of the mediating aspects of the magical . . . and capitalism-modernity's resulting appearance of inevitability combine to produce what can be identified in McCarthy's work as Western civilization" (18). If, in other words, the fiction seemingly renders a world defined by valuelessness, it is, such critics argue, because it details the devastating consequences of a modernity defined solely by calculation.

But as Arnold's talk of veneration portended, critical concern with McCarthy's ethics has also produced studies seeking to define the writer's more specifically religious preoccupations, a project that has engendered its own synthesis of the nihilism/values binary. Thus, Arnold himself would maintain that not just moral, but spiritual concerns "have been an essential, though often disguised, part of [McCarthy's] fiction from his first book onward" ("McCarthy" 215), an argument seconded by Michael Crews's assertion of McCarthy's "fundamentally religious orientation" (159). Indeed, Manuel Broncano holds that the question of the author's religious commitments has, over the past decade, become "probably the most controversial issue in Cormac McCarthy studies" (1), a position bolstered not just by his own imputation to McCarthy of an "agonizing agnosticism," in lieu of any clear creed (3), but also by such critics as Matthew Potts, who while conceding that the work is "everywhere inflected by religion" (1), is hesitant to concede that McCarthy is best understood in the Christian terms such inflections invite (5). Such hesitancy has long found a home in the treatment of McCarthy as a Gnostic writer. Dating, at least, to Leo Daugherty's reading of McCarthy's first Western—"what [the Gnostics] saw is what we see in the world of *Blood Meridian*" (162)—as proof that "gnostic thought is central" to the writer's project (159), the identification of McCarthy with this ancient heterodoxy has had wide critical appeal.[4] Taken up by Dianne C. Luce, who argues that McCarthy's plots repeatedly enact "elements of the gnostic tragedy of the fleshbound human spirit" (*Reading* 66), this Gnostic reading receives its most thorough articulation in Petra Mundik's *A Bloody and Barbarous God* (2016), which judges McCarthy's work Gnostic for its "consistently anti-cosmic or world-rejecting attitude" (7). Defined, first, by "an unequivocally negative evaluation of the visible world and its creator" (Rudolph 60), and second, by the conviction that individuals can be ransomed from this world by secret knowledge of their truly divine nature, "an esoteric possession for the elect" (148), Gnosticism developed alongside patristic Christianity, but preached "a deliverance from the world and the body, not as in Christianity, from sin and guilt" (116). Yet wedding a profoundly anticosmic outlook with a commitment to humanity's spiritual essence, it represents a plausible means for reconciling the bleakness identified by a Phillips or a Bell to the clear moral and spiritual preoccupations highlighted by such critics as Hillier and Arnold.

Yet, as I have argued elsewhere, McCarthy's work seems explicitly to resist any easy application of this label.[5] Indeed, especially in those dramatic texts that, as Mary Brewer notes, betray "a distinct lack of ambivalence concerning the question of God's existence" (42), the author's portrait of the deity seems to wear a decidedly anti-Gnostic aspect. In his first play, in particular, McCarthy seems to speak directly to critical formulations of his Gnosticism and to counter them with a rather more Christian theism. *The Stonemason* (1994) functions, ultimately, as the tragedy of protagonist/narrator Ben Telfair, one characterized by his being, in his rather Gnostic pursuit of his mason grandfather's ancient craft, blind to "the necessary supremacy of ethos over gnosis" (DeCoste, "When" 139). Fixated on Papaw's possession of secret techniques, lore he identifies with the will of God (*St* 10), Ben presides over the catastrophic dissolution of his African American family, bearing considerable responsibility, in his neglect of his other kin, for the suicide of his debt-ridden father and the overdose death of his disowned nephew. What Ben comes to learn through these losses thus challenges the Gnostic teaching of salvation, through esoterica, of the elect and urges instead the cultivation of such traditional Christian virtues as humility and love. At play's end, Ben receives a revelation, one derived, however, not from the mastery of masonic or Gnostic secrets, but from the realization of simple human fraternity: "For we are all the elect, each one of us, and we are embarked upon a journey to something unimaginable" (132). In order to see himself as part of a humanity comprehensively called to redemption, Ben has had first to be humbled by his own moral failure, to be taught that progress in that spiritual journey is begun only "when you stop pretending that you know" (97). Indeed, as he comes to understand, God calls on him to be a learner, but of neighborly service, not esoteric lore: "What I need most is to learn charity. That most of all" (131).

What the Gnostic resolution of the controversy over McCarthy's religious commitments neglects, then, is the extent to which more orthodox Christian doctrine remains an open question in his work. Moreover, the whole debate over the specific cast of his spirituality has for the most part overlooked the degree to which the author's own religious background might have influenced his depictions not just of religion and ethics, but, indeed, of that modernity so many have seen him as critiquing. Though McCarthy himself minimized the importance of his Roman Catholic upbringing—"It wasn't a big issue," he insisted (Jurgenson)—the persistence of Catholic imagery, idiom, and theology in his work suggests that his avowed "sympathy for the spiritual view of life" (Jurgenson) remained informed by this specific tradition. Whether through Arthur Ownby's cup clasped like a Eucharistic "ciborium" in *The Orchard Keeper* (156), Culla Holme's gibbering like "a witless paraclete beleaguered with all limbo's clamor" in *Outer Dark* (18), *The Road*'s boy shining in his end-times wasteland like a host-bearing "tabernacle" (273), or the intriguingly Marian title of his final novel, *Stella Maris*, the McCarthy oeuvre, from start to finish, cued readers to its intent by explicit reference to specifically Catholic concepts, artifacts, and devotions. Yet despite long-standing critical consideration of his work's spiritual valences, the significance to the fiction of his family's faith has thus far, as James Watson observes, been decidedly underexplored (8). Indeed, Bryan Giemza's chapter on McCarthy's "unshakably Catholic worldview" (222) and Scott Yarbrough's recent emphasis on his use of Eucharistic imagery ("*Road*" 187–88) notwithstanding, the fairness of Watson's assessment stands. While there have now been several monographs—by Broncano, Potts, and Mundik, by Cooper, Hillier, and Hanna Boguta-Marchel—on faith and morality in McCarthy, there has not yet been a book-length study of how the Catholicism in which he was reared colors the rendering of such things in his writing. Indeed, when treated, it has most often been invoked as that which the fiction simply dismisses. Thus, for Luce, the eponymous protagonist of *Suttree* abandons his childhood church as "the remains of a dead religion" (*Reading* 256), and Potts reads in McCarthy's sacramental imagery only a "critique of Christianity" (19). And while Nicholas Monk has underscored how McCarthy's deconstruction of Enlightenment thought is itself grounded in "an ancient mysticism" and "broad spirituality" (116, 225), he nonetheless deems that spirituality to preclude Catholic thought. Indeed, Monk's McCarthy is roundly antipathetic to Christianity's putative hostility to the natural world (166).

It is just this enduring lacuna in the critical conversation that the present study proposes to address. Through an analysis of McCarthy's oeuvre both intensive and extensive, this book aims to establish the centrality of Catholic thought, symbol, and sacrament both to the spiritual outlook of the McCarthy corpus and, more specifically, to its critique of Enlightenment values and their realization in American history. In doing so, this project will undertake a substantial survey of McCarthy's fiction from both his Tennessee and Southwest periods, with chapters devoted to eight of his published novels: *Outer Dark* (1968), *Child of God* (1974), *Suttree* (1979), *Blood Meridian* (1985), the three volumes of the Border Trilogy (1992–98), and *The Road* (2006). Though the timing of their publication sadly precludes any substantial consideration here of *The Passenger* or *Stella Maris*, I will conclude with a coda that briefly analyzes their treatment of penitence in conjunction with that found in the literary work that, prior to these novels' appearance, stood as McCarthy's last: the 2013 screenplay for *The Counselor*. The argument to be advanced by these readings is twofold. First, they will demonstrate that, as others have remarked, McCarthy's work mounts a sustained assault on core Enlightenment values and on their bloody results in the American context: for Indigenous peoples, for ecosystems, for the viability of community, and for the possibility of a self that is something more than resource or commodity. Second, they will establish what has thus far gone unremarked, namely, that this enduring critical engagement with American Enlightenment is one empowered by, and consistently articulated through, specifically Catholic teachings—as to the goodness of Creation, the nature of evil, the insufficiency of the self, the preeminence of charity, and the radical invitation to conversion—and an essentially Roman Catholic sacramentalism, particularly as pertains to notions of Penance and Eucharist. My intent, then, is to offer a novel reading of two defining aspects of McCarthy's work, both his antimodern critique and his spiritual concerns.

As indicated above, the task here outlined is one unattempted by the critical literature as it stands. Holloway's *The Late Modernism of Cormac McCarthy*, Cant's *Cormac McCarthy and the Myth of American Exceptionalism*, and, most recently, Cooper's *Cormac McCarthy: A Complexity Theory of Literature* all trace how McCarthy's fiction undertakes a dissection of such Enlightenment American myths as radical individualism and Manifest Destiny, revealing their potential for dehumanizing violence and commodification. But none takes up the question of how the fiction's spiritual interests relate to this critical project: Holloway's approach is largely Marxian, Cant opens by declaring that "McCarthy's universe is without God" (7), and Cooper, though taking care to note the fiction's meditations on the divine, insists that "'God,' in McCarthy's lexicon, does not necessarily reflect a concrete, Catholic, or even monotheistic notion of deity" (23). On the other hand, while Broncano's *Religion in Cormac McCarthy's Fiction*, Potts's *Cormac McCarthy and the Signs of Sacrament*, and Mundik's *A Bloody and Barbarous God* all focus expressly on McCarthy's theological investments, none makes central to its analysis the question of how these inform the writer's stance toward Enlightenment thought. Moreover, Broncano's discussion of McCarthy's "apocryphal" narrative (2), Potts's elaboration of McCarthy's "sacramental ethics" (2), and Mundik's argument for the novelist's Gnosticism all largely neglect consideration of Catholic thinking on ethics, sacraments, or nature. The only book to make a case for the "deep Catholicism" of McCarthy's fiction is Giemza's *Irish Catholic Writers and the Invention of the American South*

(233), but this discussion is limited to one chapter and primarily to *Suttree*. Such constraints preclude anything like the extensive reading and synthesis of philosophy, history, and religious thought that the following pages pursue. In short, the chapters to come aspire, first, to bridge the gap between readings of McCarthy as a religious writer and those that focus on his critique of the Enlightenment, and, second, to address the relative absence from both of an engagement with those Catholic traditions to which the fiction so consistently alludes.

Now, to be clear, the present study makes no claims as to Cormac McCarthy's personal faith practice or confessional commitments. The arguments to follow neither presume to nor rely on any knowledge of the author's formal spiritual allegiances; though Dennis McCarthy is an avowed Benedictine oblate, his older brother Cormac was not noted for attending Sunday mass. My aim here, in other words, is not vicariously to profess McCarthy's faith. Rather, my project is to advance an argument concerning the work. This argument seeks to establish the link between the fiction's spiritual explorations and its unfailingly critical engagement with the American faith in progress through individual self-government, instrumental reason, and the expansion of territories, technologies, and marketplaces. The following chapters, that is, demonstrate how the McCarthy so widely understood to be a critic of Enlightenment thought advanced that critique precisely as part of his articulation of divergent moral, even spiritual commitments. Furthermore, this book argues that these alternative moral and spiritual premises are provided by Roman Catholicism, particularly that tradition's conception of the goodness of Creation, the nature and ubiquity of evil, the fallen and so inherently insufficient character of the human individual, the indispensability of charity as source of communion and hope, and the radical possibility of redemption through a penitential return to charitable communion. These are not simply Christian teachings, but more specifically Catholic ones, and as the following pages will demonstrate, they remain a persistent scaffolding for McCarthy's critical moral project over the full course of his career.

The making of this case will begin with a definition of terms. A short first chapter provides a philosophical and theological lexicon upon which subsequent textual analyses will draw. Specifically, chapter 1 works to elaborate, and to highlight disagreements between, Enlightenment and Catholic claims in a variety of spheres. Opening with recent arguments by such scholars as Charles Taylor, Michael Gillespie, and Ulrich Lehner as to the links between reforms in the Latin Church and the rise of Enlightenment thought, it nonetheless follows Taylor by articulating how Catholic doctrine and Enlightenment teachings diverge in their cosmology, anthropology, and ethics. Engaging a range of precursors to, and champions of, Enlightenment thought, the chapter identifies four core Enlightenment affirmations that recur as matters for interrogation in McCarthy's fiction. The first of these is the proclamation of a strictly materialist reality, comprehensively knowable to emergent modern science. The second involves the autonomy of the individual, who, given the opportunity to use her reason and pursue self-defined goods, will not just achieve self-realization, but advance the cause of Enlightenment itself. The third, related to this defense of individual self-sufficiency, is a modern faith in the reliability of instrumental reason as a route not simply to scientific truth, but to practical works and progressive and beneficent human mastery of nature. The fourth relates to the rise of contractual or marketplace relations as the accepted model for social intercourse between self-determining enlightened subjects.

Drawing on the work of such Doctors of the Church as Athanasius, Augustine, and Aquinas, the chapter then lays out four contrasting Catholic concepts I take to be operative in McCarthy's critique of the above tenets. First, it will define, and demonstrate as central to Catholic teaching, a sacramental worldview: that is, an affirmation of a cosmos which is the product of a benevolent Creator and so good in itself and a locus not simply of material objects, but also of the supernatural and the sacred. Next, I will discuss the Catholic understanding of the Fall as both a recognition of evil in the world and proof, for the Church, of humanity's inescapable moral and mortal frailty. Third, elaborating on these notions of sacramentalism and human insufficiency, chapter 1 articulates the double aspect of the Catholic notion of conversion: both its radical availability to all and its requirement of confession and atonement on the model of Penance. Last, the chapter elaborates the essential place in Catholic theology of communion, in terms both of charitable action and of more explicitly Eucharistic affirmations of community with God and neighbor, before concluding with the proposition that these four Catholic commitments, far from being dismissed by McCarthy, remain essential to his sustained quarrel with the disenchanting and dehumanizing tendencies of modernity.

Chapter 2 commences my analysis of the fiction itself with 1979's *Suttree*, easily the most autobiographical of McCarthy's works. One consequence of this trait is the novel's explicit treatment of the Catholic teachings in which Cornelius Suttree, like Cormac McCarthy, was educated. And while two stiff encounters with priests seem to offer a negative portrait of the Church here, the positioning of these episodes serves ultimately, I argue, to indicate how both Suttree's insistence on independence and his ongoing spiritual seeking are importantly framed by Catholicism's sacramental thinking. Such thought, indeed, animates the novel's critical depiction both of the materialism of the commodity-driven America against which Suttree rebels and the self-crippling premises of his rebellion itself. In its graphic depiction of the violence, pollution, and relentlessly mercenary obsessions that characterize its 1950s Knoxille, *Suttree*, I show, foregrounds how an America defined by atomistic individualism and a rising consumerism renders everyone and everything a commodity and a disposable good. As dramatized by the aspirations, pastimes, and grim fates of the dispossessed of McAnally Flats, the effect of such Enlightenment goods as individualism, calculative reason, and technological advance in McCarthy's postwar America is to marginalize, commodify, and finally erase society's most vulnerable, no matter how fierce their own commitment to personal autonomy and entrepreneurial self-seeking.

Suttree finds himself in this company of outcasts by virtue of his rejection of the prim materialism of his own, more privileged class. Yet like the hustlers of McAnally Flats, Suttree, even in his rebellion, only mirrors the atomistic ethos he reviles. Repudiating his caste, his church, his parents, his own wife and child for shackling him to a culture whose dehumanizing power he both intuits and resists, Suttree, I contend, nonetheless conforms to the core of that culture in his repeated running from any encroachment on his cherished independence. Yet the loneliness and the dread of his own mortality that result from this flight betray in him a profound insufficiency. This is a lack to which he tellingly responds with repeated spiritual quests: from furtive visits to his childhood church to life-threatening quests for visionary experience. Thus, in both the problem his protagonist shares with the culture he rejects and the manner in which he seeks to address it, McCarthy offers a spiritual rejoinder to the Enlightenment values of America. In the answers Suttree's seeking unearths, I argue, spirituality takes on a more clearly Catholic cast. For the Suttree who, in his flight from American materialism, cultivates a solitary disgust for the world begins, I demonstrate, to find healing when he embraces the goodness of the natural world and, through this sacramental experience, acknowledges his communion with other broken human beings.

Chapter 3 backtracks to take up the two novels that precede *Suttree*. More specifically, it argues that these two tales of human depravity—featuring incest and infanticide, serial murder and necrophilia—offer accounts not just of the dehumanizing fruit of Enlightenment thought, but also of human fallenness and possible redemption. Both novels, I argue, open with dramatizations of the Fall, in each case framed by grave sin, enacted by literal expulsion, and sustained by a fetishization of independence that puts commodities ahead of the person. For Culla Holme of *Outer Dark*, this takes the form of the perverse fruit of a radical self-sufficiency, the son he sires on his sister Rinthy, and even more powerfully, of his abandonment of that child to death by exposure; from these original sins follow a forfeiture of home and a life of itinerant wandering, subject to the dictates of an unfair marketplace and the violence of the murderous trio that dogs him. Orphaned Lester Ballard in *Child of God* experiences expulsion first through the sins of others, not just his parents but the community of Sevier County, which dispossesses him for unpaid taxes. This mercenary eviction begins a process of marginalization for Lester that sees him reduced to the status of cave dweller. Though one is thus initially cast as more sinned against than sinning, both characters, I contend, affirm an individualist American ethos. In this way, their experience of the Enlightenment ideals of self-government and self-interest is identified with fallenness itself. Both are jealously independent, seeking advancement as solitary economic agents by trading on their labor, their skills, and their capacity to dupe others. Yet they are both repeatedly losers in such exchanges, outwitted by authorities that exploit the weakness imposed by their cherished independence itself. This abjection, I show, is framed theologically as postlapsarian evil, not solely by means of the novels' openings, but also by the ramifying violence which the clinging to self-sufficiency engenders: for Culla through the unearthly trio whose crimes entrench his role as outcast, for Lester in his fall from trading for sexual favors to murderously reducing the living to sex objects.

In both cases, traditional American virtues are yoked to outrages whose framing works to identify those ideals as dehumanizing and sinful. This dehumanization is manifest in Lester's victims but also, I show, impacts Culla and Lester themselves. In Culla, it takes the form not simply of his own treatment as instrument, but of his final repudiation of his own kin, when he hands his child over to be slaughtered. Lester's debasement is captured not just in his troglodytic state, but in that loss of identity revealed in his masquerading in the clothes of his victims. Lester's case, I suggest, makes even more explicit the link between Enlightenment thought and such degradation, as he is consistently treated not as a partner in human community, but as the determined object of modern science. Yet these novels conclude by affirming something radically at odds with such an outlook. For both Culla and Lester, I argue, are taken seriously as children of God. Despite their horrific crimes, they are treated not just as human subjects, but as moral agents to whom the possibility of conversion is enduringly real and, indeed, explicitly extended. Offered the opportunity of genuine community at his novel's conclusion, Culla balks, but, I maintain, the ghoulish Lester does not; recalled to his humanity, he judges himself and turns himself in. Here, above all, McCarthy deploys a Catholic understanding—of the open offer of redemption—to resist what he depicts as modernity's fierce determination and dismantling of the human.

Tracking McCarthy's first foray into the Western genre, chapter 4 turns its attention to *Blood Meridian*. Seconding Robert Jarrett's classification of this historical novel as "a revisionary western" (*Cormac* 62), the chapter advances two main claims concerning McCarthy's rewriting of America's frontier: first, that it details the specifically Enlightenment roots of frontier violence; second, that this analysis is executed through the novel's presentation of Judge Holden as the damning avatar of American progress. As the novel's chief proponent of modern science and unfettered human autonomy, the Judge plays the part not just of teacher to his band of scalp-hunting mercenaries, but of advocate for modern humanism. More than this, Holden's world, I maintain, emulates Enlightenment *philosophes* through its assaults on faith and insistence that modernity install the human will in the place of a dethroned God. But if Holden is the novel's preeminent champion of Enlightenment ideals, he works, I argue, not only to highlight their role in the conquest of the American West, but to underscore the bloody violence of that role. Learned and modern, Holden rides with men whose trade is the murder of Native Americans. Urging them on, he is himself the deadliest of these riders: an eager scalp taker, murderous pedophile, and full-throated proponent of war as humanity's highest calling. Even the science he pursues is presented as death-dealing. In this way, Holden's participation in genocidal violence works to indict not just the history of America's western settlement, but the destructive effects of his Enlightenment creed.

This is an indictment, I contend, offered in Catholic terms. Pursuing a humanist progress through knowledge as power, the Judge presides over an eradication of peoples and species, over the brutalization of his comrades, that the novel presents as Augustinian in its evil. Diabolical in his longing to become God, Holden also enacts that unmaking war on an aboriginally good Creation that Augustine deems the essence of evil. By doing so, McCarthy's Judge is himself offered up for judgment and revealed as bound, by the logic of his Enlightenment desire for absolute human mastery, to the pursuit of evil as anticreation. Thus, this chapter argues that a Catholic view of Creation and of evil's belated and corrosive character is central to McCarthy's critique of American history and its Enlightenment grounds here. It concludes by demonstrating the role that Catholic teachings on the need for penitence play in articulating the novel's alternative to the Judge's worldview: the book's nameless protagonist, the kid. I read his trajectory as confirming both the novel's repudiation of Holden's Enlightenment and the specifically Catholic cast of this condemnation. Resistant to the Judge's gospel of absolute self-sufficiency and unbridled will, the kid ultimately pursues a different course, seeking out strangers whom he can serve and to whom he can confess. He thereby betrays a longing for communion through atonement indicative of an anthropology at odds with Holden's own. The kid never finds a confessor, but the fact that he never abandons this search works to ally the novel's moral ideal, as much as its critique of the Judge's monstrous Enlightenment, with Catholic thought.

Chapter 5 builds on the previous chapter by analyzing McCarthy's further exploration of the Western in the Border Trilogy. More specifically, it reads these novels—*All the Pretty Horses* (1992), *The Crossing* (1994), and *Cities of the Plain* (1998)—as together constituting a tragedy of the myth of American innocence and of the catastrophic undermining of faithfulness that myth facilitates. Carrying McCarthy's history of the Southwest forward to the mid-twentieth century of American ascendency, these novels trace the advance of Holden's ethos, charting the further progress of the dislocations, extinctions, and reifications of his nineteenth century. In the Comanche ghosts that captivate John Grady Cole, the vanished wolves that speak to Billy Parham's heart, and the ugly commodification of eros in *Cities of the Plains*, the trilogy emphasizes how America's

Enlightenment evolution involves serial depredations on life and human dignity. Yet these novels center on their protagonists' opposition to these deadly processes. John Grady and Billy both cling to a myth of the cowboy that lets them see themselves as rugged individualists and men of integrity, bulwarks against the corrosive tides of progress. But in their commitment to the role of frontiersman, they are, I argue, revealed to be complicit with historical forces they seek to repudiate. This complicity is not simply historical, but theological, for these are profoundly God-haunted novels. Believing themselves innocent victims of progress, these cowboys seek refuge in a Mexico they identify with a purer American past. But, as *Blood Meridian* has shown, the very losses these boys mourn are those effected by the American creeds to which they cling. The ranch life John Grady idealizes has been made possible by the extirpation of the Comanches he likewise romanticizes; Billy's wolves have been trapped to extinction by ranchmen like his father. Yet this is a kinship with progress neither boy recognizes. Instead, loyal to an American model of identity, they hold themselves innocent. Their thinking thus discounts a historical and spiritual fallenness that, I argue, McCarthy's tales insist upon. By so denying their own postlapsarian condition, however, they pursue courses that reenact the Fall through failures of faith.

Assured of the moral soundness of their self-determined missions, Cole and Parham refuse to recognize the limits imposed by their duties to others. In pursuing the goods to which they feel themselves entitled, they deny any need for communion or grace. As such, they each engage in over-reaching and doomed attempts at saving entities imperiled by their own culture. These gestures are sustained by a faith in their own innocence that Catholic lessons on human insufficiency deem false. Indeed, these quests tend toward moral disaster precisely as they refuse to recognize that fallen condition to which the trilogy's many Mexican tale-tellers testify. Married to their American dreams, both young men, I argue, enact that condition by breaking faith with kin, community, and God. The terrible consequences of this delinquency instill in both a sense of moral insufficiency and a need to confess their failings before a community and a God for whom they begin, at the end of each of the first two novels, to feel a genuine hunger. But their American setting, ideologically as much as geographically, works against these humbler quests, and the trilogy concludes with John Grady's catastrophic attempt to redeem himself and Magdalena through his own agency. Yet I conclude that the Border Trilogy does not, in denying readers a happy ending, lack a set of Christian criteria by which to find its heroes' American ideals tragically wanting.

My final chapter undertakes a reading of *The Road* that argues for its status as a still more explicit, and explicitly Catholic, critique of Western modernity. This status it secures by centering its tale on profane and sacramental communion. Opening with the novel's milieu, I argue that this apocalyptic setting is a telling endpoint for McCarthy's meditations on Enlightenment notions of progress. This is a world seemingly without a future, a world in which progress has been radically reversed and over which human science and technology seem to afford no power at all. Indeed, it is in their clinging to the practical reasoning and self-interest of Enlightenment thought that the novel's characters are most abjectly undone. I thus read the fate of the mother as indicating the profound threat to hope and love, indeed to life, posed in this novel by a strictly humanist outlook. Able to see no future in or beyond the world, she views her husband's love for her as meaningless because powerless. The fruit of this rational nihilism is her abandonment of husband and son in her taking of her own life. If the novel thus offers a powerful demonstration of the moral and practical limits of the Enlightenment exaltation of human knowledge-power, *The Road*'s more commonly depicted response to the end of things is even more damning. The flip side to the mother's suicidal pursuit of her interests is the brutish course charted by the marauders from whom her husband and son flee, a pursuit for sustenance that dissolves humane bonds as surely as does the mother's exit, but that effects a still greater dehumanization of self and other. Confronted with the disappearance of other foodstuffs, these survivors take to an anthropophagy that unmakes community by reducing human persons to mere appetite, on the one hand, and resource, on the other. These cannibals are presented, I argue, not simply as forfeiting their own humanity in the violent erasure of the other's, but as enacting a demonic Eucharist.

Eucharistic imagery abounds in this text, framing both the portrait of self-annihilating Enlightenment detailed above and the contrasting humanity preserved by the father and son. In their numberless acts of selfless love, this pair preserves genuine community and the possibility of a humane future, through their exemplification of an expanding Eucharistic ethos. This heroic persistence, I argue, is significantly framed by the pair's surviving, if tortured, faith. Indeed, the faith and sacrificial love at the heart of the Catholic sacrament of Eucharist are shown to be central to their rescue of humanity. To the extent that the father remains committed to prudential practical reason, he stands in the way not just of a widening community, but also of any real hope for that son who will outlive him. Despite his modeling of sacrificial love, his failure of faith and insistent self-reliance compromise his own moral standing and his child's future. In an unexpectedly hopeful ending, however, the father takes a leap of faith by committing to that Eucharistic promise he has consistently identified with the son. Indeed, I argue that the pair have, at this boy's urging, been pursuing an ever-widening Eucharistic communion based in love and faith: first, between themselves alone, then, in the abandoned shelter, with the dead and with God, then also with the living Ely. This expansion of faith and charity to include a properly human community finally trumps the father's fearful pragmatism and empowers his faith-filled release of his son into the hands of the adoptive family of the novel's conclusion. Thus, the dead end of a rapacious, self-seeking Enlightenment is presented as overcome by means of the faith, love, and sacrifice that lie at the heart of the Catholic Eucharist.

Professing Darkness closes with a reflection on the much-maligned screenplay for *The Counselor* and some preliminary thoughts on the novels that followed: *The Passenger* and *Stella Maris*. Taking issue with Peter Josyph's claim that *The Counselor* is "ethically and aesthetically bereft" ("What's Wrong" 203), I argue instead that this script is McCarthy at his most moralistic. Indeed, despite its contemporary setting, *The Counselor* enacts the same assault on American progress and call for atonement that animate the Westerns studied in chapters 4 and 5. Emphasizing the screenplay's dramatization of American culpability with respect to the cross-border drug trade, my coda focuses, first, on the place of sacramental confession in this work. Situating a visit to the confessional at the heart of his scenario, McCarthy underscores not just the blood-soaked guilt of his self-seeking investors or the radical chance at conversion for even the most depraved of sinners, but also the profound relevance of the Catholic confessional, and its testament to human frailty, to his ongoing critique of American Enlightenment. This insistence on Enlightenment's dark ends and how they counsel a penitent's path is, I show, central to McCarthy's final works, as well. Children of a Manhattan Project physicist, Bobby and Alicia Western are heirs to the catastrophic achievements of scientific Enlightenment, and their own pursuit of knowledge is depicted as doomed to moral, and not just epistemic, failure. This failure leads Alicia, unable to brook any limit on Enlightenment, to opt for suicide. Riddled with unsolved mysteries, Bobby's tale, too, is one of failed knowing, but burdened by grief and guilt, the fruit of his family's Enlightenment quests, he concedes that "in the end you really cant know" (P 279) and emerges as McCarthy's model penitent: accepting ignorance, lighting candles for his dead, and practicing prayer so as to offer penance for a truly Western hubris. Thus, these last texts only confirm what my study is at pains to establish, namely the ongoing relevance to McCarthy's literary project of the Catholic tradition in which he was raised.

In a 1992 account, Garry Wallace recalls the dismay with which McCarthy responded to his skepticism in the face of others' talk of visionary episodes: "he felt sorry for me because I was unable to grasp this concept of spiritual experience" (Wallace 138). Seventeen years later, McCarthy confessed in an interview that he "would like to be" himself a spiritual person (Jurgenson). *Professing Darkness* details the literary fruits of such wishing. First among these is a clear impatience with the strict materialism of Enlightenment cosmology. However naturalistically meticulous the fiction's descriptions of its environments, its world comprises more than dead matter or merely biological sentience; it is a cosmos in which something more than man "knows, and cannot be fled nor hid from" (*TC* 148). But more than metaphysical, the work's spiritual commitments are also ethical, and the result of their more than material vision is to disclose repeatedly the profound moral darkness of the world McCarthy's characters inhabit. Both this pushing beyond the Enlightenment's materialist ontology and this diagnosis of modernity's dark heart are, I submit, sustained in his oeuvre not by any authorial piety, but by McCarthy's abiding, specifically Catholic spiritual sense. The sacramental outlook of his Roman Catholic upbringing allows for the novels' disclosure of a living and sacred Creation in place of the Enlightenment's inert nature. More than this, however, that tradition's insistence on humankind's weakness and corruptibility, on the human need for communion both moral and spiritual, and on the radical reformative possibilities of penitential conversion animates much of the drama of McCarthy's work. Indeed, these fundamentally Catholic teachings form, as the following pages will show, the very core of his critical response to our culture's materialism and humanism, his profession of the darkness in which Enlightenment hubris has, on his view, entangled us and his faint delineation of a humbler alternate path.

CHAPTER 1

DISENCHANTMENT AND DEPENDENCE

THE CONTENDING CREEDS OF
ENLIGHTENMENT AND CATHOLICISM

The program of Enlightenment was the disenchantment of the world; the dissolution of myths and the substitution of knowledge for fancy.

—THEODOR ADORNO and MAX HORKHEIMER, *Dialectic of Enlightenment*

Every perfection and every virtue proceeds from charity, and charity is nourished by humility, which results from the knowledge and holy hatred of self.

—CATHERINE OF SIENA, *The Dialogue of Saint Catherine of Siena*

As stated in my Introduction, this book aims to establish that the religious questions that clearly preoccupy McCarthy's novels lie at the heart of his fiction's critical engagement with America's Enlightenment faith in progress through individual autonomy, technological innovation, and expansion of territories and marketplaces. Moreover, I will argue that the premises upon which this evolving critique is constructed are specifically Catholic ones, particularly teachings regarding the goodness of Creation, the fallen state of humankind, and the indispensability of contrition, charity, and communion to human flourishing. What this thesis presupposes is an actual divergence between Enlightenment and Roman Catholic worldviews, one sufficiently pronounced as to enable the latter to empower McCarthy's oppositional reading of the former. It is therefore the business of this first chapter to articulate the ways in which Enlightenment claims and Catholic doctrine do in fact differ in their cosmology, anthropology, and ethics. At root, this difference is the one indicated by my two epigraphs, one between a philosophy that excises any transcendent dimension from reality so as to enshrine and, through reason alone, to effectuate human sovereignty in this world, and one which insists upon a fragile humanity, dependent on loving communion with others and with the supernatural for its purpose and salvation.

Such a thesis might well be taken as read. Gillespie, for one, states that the view of modernity as "a secular realm in which man replaces God as the center of existence" (x–xi) has become our "conventional wisdom" (x). On Peter Gay's account, this antithesis between modernity and faith was axiomatic for Enlighteners. Gay's *philosophes*, then, "used their classical learning to free themselves from their Christian heritage" so as to become "modern pagans" (8); indeed, he dubs that touchstone of the Enlightenment, Voltaire's *Candide*, nothing short of "a declaration of war on Christianity" (203). Yet recent scholarship has argued persuasively against a simply antagonistic relationship between modernity and Christianity, even between the *philosophes* and Rome. Lehner, for example, has charted the history of a specifically Catholic Enlightenment, born of the Christian humanism of the Renaissance and effectively commissioned by the Council of Trent (14). For Lehner, most Enlighteners, moved by "the conviction that new discoveries in science and philosophy should renew the faith" (2), eschewed the warpath of Voltaire and sought not faith's defeat by reason but a synthesis of the two. Though discredited by a French Revolution which "disillusioned many Catholics who might have embraced the idea that modernity and Christianity were really reconcilable" (11), this global movement demonstrates, Lehner argues, that the narrative of antipathy between Catholicism and the Enlightenment is partial at best. Indeed, it is, for him, ideologically skewed, motivated by "a teleological view of history that sees religious commitments as deviations from the goal of human progress" (153), a view opposed by many historical Enlighteners (153).

Similarly, José Casanova has argued that the sources of modern secularism are to be found not solely in an Enlightenment dismissal of Christian thought and ecclesiastical authority, but in an ongoing, specifically Western relationship between the very notions of religion and secularity. Insisting that these are concepts "always and everywhere mutually constituted" (54), Casanova notes that they emerge in the Christian culture of medieval Western Europe, in its division of society into religious (monastic) and worldly vocations. Thus the narrative of the Enlightenment's guidance of humanity beyond belief and into a liberated secular modernity "needs to be understood as a particular reaction to the structuring dualism of medieval Christendom" (56). Though offering a more detailed account, Gillespie agrees that the putative secularism of emergent modernity must be understood in theological terms, as "a result of a titanic struggle between contradictory elements within Christianity itself" (xii). For Gillespie, the questions that gave birth to modernity and the Enlightenment derive specifically from the late medieval nominalist revolt against scholasticism, an upsetting of standard Church teaching that "brought to an end the great effort that had begun with the church fathers to combine reason and revelation" (14). Tracing the effects of this conclusion through the emergence of Christian humanism, Protestant Reform, and modern science, Gillespie underscores the extent to which even the ostensibly atheist materialism of scientific modernity has its genesis in this "nominalist revolution" in Catholic theology (36).

Most influential, perhaps, among these dissenting histories of the Enlightenment's Latin Christian pedigree is that offered by Charles Taylor in his magisterial *A Secular Age*. Taylor opens by asking how the West transformed itself in the span of five hundred years from a culture in which belief in the divine was near universal to one in which such belief is but one option among many (3). In his response, Taylor anticipates Casanova, arguing that it was the breakdown of the accepted complementarity between the secular and religious domains that "preceded and helped to bring about the secularization of public space" (50). On his account, the seeds of modern individualism and materialism are premodern and pre-Reformation; they begin, in fact, with movements for increased piety among the laity, an "internal crusade" carried out by the mendicant orders of the Latin Church (68). Far, then, from Adorno and Horkheimer's disenchantment of the world being something wholly divorced from Catholicism, it was, rather, the fruit of campaigns for that intensity of personal devotion expressed above by Catherine of Siena: "Disenchantment, Reform, and personal religion went together" (Taylor 146). Casting doubt on what he dubs the "subtraction story," according to which enlightened progress required only that the West unseat a repressive religious authority (253), Taylor's history of the Enlightenment tells of a modernity indelibly marked by the Christian traditions the Enlightenment's champions often refute.

These revisionist histories are to be welcomed for offering more nuanced and less self-congratulatory accounts of the present age's emergence, character, and challenges. Still, they do not alter the fact that the differences between a Catholic and an Enlightenment understanding are scarcely illusory. A chief motivator of Taylor's own project is a recognition of the gulf these differences represent, of the astonishing novelty, in terms of past times and even current cultures, represented by the West's contemporary secularity, in which a wholly humanist and materialist outlook is a widespread, frequently default, position. His quarrel with the "subtraction story" is that it "doesn't allow us to be as surprised as we ought to be at this achievement" (255). Likewise, though Gillespie insists upon the Christian roots of the defining currents of modern thought, his history of modernity nonetheless charts an epochal "transference of divine attributes to human beings . . . the natural world . . . and history" (273). The modern world shaped by Enlightenment ideals is thus a profound departure from any conformity to traditional Catholic teachings. Where, above all, they diverge is on questions of the presence and precedence of a supernatural order in the cosmos, and of the perfectibility and fitness for self-governance of human beings, both individually and in the aggregate. The chapters that follow will argue that Catholicism's answers to these questions inform McCarthy's critical analysis of American history. For now, I will elaborate briefly on four key, contrasting commitments of both the Enlightenment and the Catholic positions so as to lay the groundwork, and provide a lexicon, for those arguments to come.

DISENCHANTED SOVEREIGNTY

Perhaps the most salient feature of the Enlightenment thought with which McCarthy takes issue is that identified in my first epigraph. As Adorno and Horkheimer observe, the consensus world that emerges from the Enlighteners' championing of natural science is an emphatically disenchanted one. This means that the world people understand themselves to inhabit is no longer one populated by spirits and suffused by the supernatural; *the cosmology of our modern world is, rather, natural and material.* For the *philosophes,* cosmos and the nature perceived by such early modern scientists as Francis Bacon become virtually synonymous. The result is a world no longer abounding in angels and demons, or in sacred and hexed locales, and no longer understood to derive from the freedom of a providential God, an all-powerful divine person whose creative act has inaugurated, and whose ultimately benevolent regard oversees, human affairs and natural processes. For Gay, then, "the disenchanted universe of the Enlightenment is a natural universe" (148), and this represents, on Taylor's account, an "epochal change in our understanding of and stance towards nature" (113). Above all, it means that we now occupy a world in which we expect all things to be susceptible to explanation in terms of material causes, and even to be defined exclusively by such causes. As Adorno and Horkheimer put it, knowledge is defined in spatial, material, worldly terms: "multiplicity of forms is reduced to position and arrangement, history to fact, things to matter" (7).

This materialist cosmos is bequeathed to its Enlightenment advocates by an earlier generation of philosophers who argued both that truth was found through the observation of natural law and that such observation revealed a mechanistic universe. For Bacon, then, we are ourselves essentially natural beings. What we can ever be said to know is defined solely by what we learn from the regular and predictable workings of our physical environment: "man is but the servant and interpreter of nature: what he does and what he knows is only what he has observed of nature's order in fact or in thought; beyond this he knows nothing and can do nothing" (177). For Bacon's contemporary René Descartes, a more deductive analysis of the workings of this natural world likewise disclosed its wholly material, mechanical, and determined character. No enchanted world of spirits and miracles, Descartes' nature is one radically divorced from God, spirit, or even mind. Infamously, then, he declares animals themselves to be devoid of reason and little more than machines: "nature makes them behave as they do according to the disposition of their organs; just as a clock, composed only of wheels and weights . . . can count the hours" (43). Indeed, for Descartes, while our humanity lies in an immaterial reality, in our being "a thing or substance whose whole essence or nature [is] only to think" (25), the human body, as a natural entity, is best understood "as a machine created by the hand of God" (41). Baruch Spinoza rejects Cartesian mind/body dualism, but in his infinite substance or God, he likewise sees a cosmos governed by mechanical process and unshakable necessity. No freely creating, personal God (see 55–56), Spinozist substance, the source, existence, and truth of all that is, governs via strict determinism: "all things are determined from the necessity of the divine nature not only to exist but also to exist and to act in a definite way" (51). Everything that exists, including humanity and its affairs, does so untainted by contingency or free will. People think otherwise, for Spinoza, only because "they are conscious of their actions and ignorant of the causes by which they are determined" (86).

With Bacon and Spinoza in particular, we can see how early modern thought tends, as Michel Henry argues, both to promulgate a new way of looking at the natural world and to present this outlook not "as the delimitation of a specific domain of objects, but as the condition of all truth" (99). The effect of this universalized materialist epistemology is a disenchantment that works to sideline, if not to reject, divine agency and even existence. This is so because the philosophical materialism taken up by the Enlightenment defines the universe in profoundly horizontal and immanent terms. By this I mean that, for the early moderns canvassed above, knowledge of reality need have no reference to a transcendental or vertical dimension, to any cause or agency that exists apart from the natural world and its laws, as we human beings situated in a natural universe can uncover them by reason and experiment. The truth and sufficient causes for all things in nature are thus to be found within nature. As Taylor puts it, then, the "great invention" of Western culture during this period "was that of an immanent order in Nature, whose working could be systematically understood and explained on its own terms" (15). Within this order, the personal, freely acting, and omnibenevolent Creator of Judeo-Christian tradition recedes to the function of first cause or, indeed, altogether.

Certainly, Bacon's cosmos is one of efficient material causes, not of any ultimate purposes that supernatural agents or divine providence might be imagined to cherish. For Bacon, such final causes have no place in scientific inquiry, for they are alien to nature itself, "hav[ing] relation clearly to the nature of man rather than to the nature of the universe" (197). Spinoza puts this case more pithily still, defining God as nothing other or more than the totality of material and efficient causes: "God is the immanent, not the transitive, cause of all things" (46). Here, we can see how what Gillespie claims of Descartes is true also of his scientifically minded contemporaries. For all of them, the antithesis to doubt is not religious belief, but knowledge of the unvarying causal laws of the natural world: "Certainty and natural science thereby replace faith and theology" (Gillespie 199). As the scope, confidence, and technological efficacy of this new science grow over the next two centuries, a Creator's role in explanatory models steadily diminishes and the role of the supernatural in modern philosophy is dramatically curtailed. Indeed, Martin Heidegger insists that for his generation, heirs to the Enlightenment, the "suprasensory world of purposes and norms no longer quickens and supports life," but has "itself become lifeless" (98). As Gay would have it, then, the Enlighteners, with their "volatile mixture of classicism, impiety, and science" (8), helped forge a culture whose reality is immanent, materialist, and law- (not spirit- or purpose-) governed. As "modern pagans" (8), they helped fashion a modern cosmology powerfully independent of any belief in God or providence.

The second defining tenet of the Enlightenment follows in many ways from this first. If there are no a priori final causes in things and if God is either remote or nonexistent, then the question of the ends of human life becomes one to be decided by humankind itself, in the aggregate, but even more pressingly in the individual. Chief among Enlightenment ideals, then, is a proper pursuit of *sovereignty over one's beliefs and one's own interests.* For Gay's *philosophes,* "since God is silent, man is his own master" (419). In fact, this self-mastery is typically presented less as an opportunity than as an imperative. For Enlightenment thinkers, philosophy must be free of any direction or curtailment by authority or tradition: "philosophy was autonomous and omnipotent, or it was nothing" (236). Not just philosophers, but all true moderns were urged to think, to judge, and to decide for themselves both the truth of things and the kinds of life plans such self-won truth mandated. This involved a refusal of deference or conformity to the will of crowds, kings, or clerics, and the courage to govern one's self. Quite typically, as Craig Calhoun, Mark Juergensmeyer, and Jonathan Van Antwerpen observe, this was a matter of casting the turn to a more self-directed and secular life "as a kind of maturation . . . a developmental achievement" (20). To be enlightened, then, is to be properly grown up.[1] For Immanuel Kant, this was Enlightenment in a nutshell: "man's leaving his self-caused immaturity" by thinking for himself (132). Certainly, the eponymous comic butt of Voltaire's *Candide* is the long-suffering fool he is precisely because, having "been brought up never to judge anything for himself" (77), he fails ever to question the fatuous or self-serving teachings of authoritative elders. The "buffered self" of modernity is not simply, then, one "who no longer fears demons, spirits, magic forces" (Taylor 135); it is one that understands and conducts itself as a "rational autonomous free [agent]" (Casanova 68).

The Enlightenment subject is thus equipped and called to judge all things for itself. This applies equally to topics theoretical and political. This fitness and the autonomy it underwrites are powerfully evident as early as the Cartesian cogito. Not only does Descartes, through the independent exercise of doubt and reason, establish his own essence as a thinking being. He also thereby formulates the criterion that qualifies him to judge the truth of all things: "Since this truth, *I think, therefore I am,* . . . was so firm and assured that all the most extravagant suppositions of the sceptics were unable to shake it, I judged that I could safely accept it as the first principle of the philosophy I was seeking" (24). Empowered by a rational faculty capable of achieving, unaided, this bedrock principle, and vouchsafed in it with an exemplary instance of what certain judgment requires, Descartes proclaims a radical epistemological competence. He himself will decide what is true or false on the basis of a proposition's appearing to him as clear and certain as is the cogito itself; his inquiries can proceed, accepting nothing as true "unless [he] recognize[s] it to be certainly and evidently such" (15). This grants the self extraordinary epistemological independence; no longer seeking instruction from schoolmen, lawmakers, or priests, "we should never allow ourselves to be convinced except on the evidence of our reason" (30). For Spinoza, this capacity for self-governance has a more clearly ethical consequence. Possessed, like all entities, with a desire for self-preservation, a *conatus* that "is nothing but the actual essence of the thing itself" (109), human beings, Spinoza insists, are both impelled and entitled to seek what is best for themselves, that expansion of their own power which he equates with virtue (156): "it is by the sovereign natural right that every man judges what is good and what is bad, and has regard for his own advantage according to his own way of thinking" (176). Thus, the autonomy Descartes affirms in matters of reasoning is here enshrined as the inevitable compass for each individual's moral conduct.

Building on such advocacy for the individual's self-sufficiency in matters of theoretical and practical reason, Kant influentially defines Enlightenment as "the freedom for man to make *public use* of his reason" (134), to judge for himself and then to take his own judgments as guides to ethical and political action. Undergirding such calls for universal self-determination is a profound optimism in the power and acuity of human reason, as well as in the perfectibility by reason of the individual's moral sense. Indeed, Descartes, noting that our will seeks nothing but what seems to it good, sees the individual's exercise of her own reasoning powers as a sure road to her moral improvement, for "good judgment is sufficient to guarantee good behavior" (21). Similarly, Kant is assured of progress in scientific discovery and in human affairs, provided that Enlightenment, understood as that individual freedom to decide, is itself unfettered: "Men raise themselves by and by out of backwardness if one does not purposely invent artifices to keep them down" (138). Implicit here is a conviction that the individual's sovereign pursuit of truth and personal advantage will benefit not only the one, but the many, that from a regime of universal self-seeking may be expected a progress that will profit the polity, the race, as a whole. One might hear echoes here of Kant's contemporary, Adam Smith, and his notion of the market's benevolent invisible hand,[2] but also, once more, of Spinoza, who, like Descartes, is convinced that clear reasoning teaches that individuals' personal advantage is best secured by a state of harmony with their fellows (165). But this state is itself best advanced when we are each of us empowered to use our reason to pursue the good as we see it: "it is when every man is most devoted to seeking his own advantage that men are of most advantage to one another" (173).

The Enlightenment subject, then, is charged to deploy its sovereign judgment in pursuit of its own self-defined good. In so doing, it exercises a specifically instrumental reason to improve its lot. This takes us to the third core tenet of the Enlightenment that McCarthy's work will interrogate: namely, the commitment to a *human mastery over nature* by means of technological advance. Mastery of the machinery of nature was a primary aim of the early theorists of modern science so esteemed by Enlighteners. For Bacon, the value of his inductive method lay in its enabling humanity, through technological innovation, "to command nature in action" (167). Indeed, Bacon saw such sovereignty, not simply over one's own aims and conduct, but over the natural world itself, as the chief purpose of scientific endeavor. His new science was thus an enterprise whose end was an ever-expanding repertoire of means: "the true and lawful goal of the sciences is none other than this: that human life be endowed with new discoveries and powers" (222). Nor was Bacon alone in trumpeting both modernity's right to master nature through technology and science's essence as the means to such command. Promoting a deductive science no less committed to Bacon's "power and greatness of man" (250), Descartes also recommends his method as the path to "knowledge that will be of much utility in this life"

(Descartes 45). Again, as the enlightened individual is entitled both to define the nature of her own good and to pursue the practical means to her own advantage, so a science liberated from tradition and fruitless speculation is properly empowered to seek works that will secure material benefits for humanity as a whole. For Descartes, then, science's legitimate aim and ambition is to grant us such control over natural bodies that "we can employ these entities for all the purposes for which they are suited, and so make ourselves masters and possessors of nature" (45). Thus an early modern confidence in the individual's judgment goes hand in hand with a more comprehensive faith in humanity's right to remake its world through those practical works which are the fruits of true science.

This right of redesign, moreover, is taken by Enlighteners and their predecessors as effectively unlimited. As Gillespie demonstrates, the objectives of Cartesian science were nothing less than "to prolong human life (perhaps infinitely), to eliminate want, and to provide security" (190). Such lofty aims underwrite an absolute right to use and remake the naturally given. For Spinoza, we are not simply enabled by science to reshape nature to our purposes; we are, by our own natures, impelled to use, even exhaust, nature in pursuit of our own ends. Hence, "whatever there is in Nature external to man, regard for our own advantage does not require us to preserve it, but teaches us to preserve or destroy it according to its varying usefulness" (200). According to Gay, this was, virtually unmodified, the perspective of Spinoza's Enlightenment heirs. Not only did Gay's Enlightenment long "to conquer reality by thought" (134), securing for humanity a sovereignty over Creation akin to that rightly accorded the individual over his own affairs. More than this, the *philosophes* saw their mission as the realization of science's subordination of the natural world to human utility. Enlightenment empiricism thus sought "to translate into reality Bacon's and Descartes's grandiose vision of man controlling nature for his profit and delight" (182). Certainly, *Candide*'s earthly paradise, "the land where all is well" (45), is not to be found in a Europe ruled by Pangloss's fatuous speculations, but in that South American utopia, El Dorado, where craft aimed at human welfare has superseded empty cant: "Here the land had been cultivated as much for beauty as from necessity, for everywhere the useful was joined to the agreeable" (43). Indeed, what wisdom Candide finally achieves reflects this taste for practical works and cultivation of the naturally given; as Martin counsels at the tale's conclusion, it is such work, and not idle disputation, that makes life bearable (93). The consequence of this championing of utility is that, as Adorno and Horkheimer maintain, "Power and knowledge are synonymous" for the Enlightenment (4). Turning our instrumental reason to consider the clockwork of nature with our own convenience in view, we pursue science, and whatever practical means that works-seeking science provides, to refashion the natural machine to our advantage. For Heidegger, then, the world left us by the Enlightenment is one that defines "human capability as a domain given over to measuring and executing, for the purpose of gaining mastery over that which is" (132).

The last core Enlightenment concept I wish to discuss emerges logically enough from the previous two and has to do with the character not of nature, judgment, or science, but of the polity. As the individual is properly autonomous in her deliberation on, and active pursuit of, her own advantage, and as humanity's larger enterprise requires the (re)constitution, through science, of nature to human ends, so, too, does the individual enjoy a primacy relative to society, which exists and, with any legitimacy, endures only so long as its members see it as serving their own purposes. In short, from a commitment to individual autonomy and instrumental reason, the Enlightenment arrives at a vision of human associations as, at root, *contractual communities*. Certainly, for Taylor, modernity—from Locke through the Enlightenment to our own day—has imagined society as a secondary and elective phenomenon, an entity born of the self-interest and rescindable consent of preexisting individual subjects. Thus, "the picture of society is that of individuals who come together to form a political entity . . . with certain ends in view" (159); such a society exists solely as a means to these parties' disparate interests, "for the (mutual) benefit of individuals, and the defense of their rights" (160). This means that human community is not itself an end or a good, nor does it foster or realize some essential and shared human end or good. Rather, it is a means to the personal advantages of its members, whose autonomy and interests precede its genesis and ultimately legitimize its authority. Again, in Taylor's words, "political society is seen as an instrument for something pre-political" (170). This is corroborated by commentators on the American polity, in particular. For example, Thomas Paine looks ahead to a "CONTINENTAL CHARTER" for an independent and federated America (97), and what he envisions is a compact between equals aimed at preserving the inborn liberty and autonomy of each, a contract for "securing freedom and property to all men" and "the free exercise of religion, according to the dictates of conscience," itself sovereign (97). Such a constitution would in due course found a society in which, on de Tocqueville's view, all legislation necessarily "appeals to the interests of each individual" (94).

The primacy here accorded the individual implies also a distinctively modern anthropology. If human community is, as something contingent on the will of sovereign individuals, secondary, malleable, and revocable, then, the human subject who precedes and authorizes such a society must be posited as existing aboriginally without a necessary and enabling place within a community. Such a view, on Taylor's account, displaces the conviction that animates most cultures, "according to which a human being can only be a proper moral agent embedded in a larger social whole" (170). The autonomous self championed by the Enlightenment does not find itself, its notion of its own and larger goods, through relationships, commitments, and debts that precede and make possible its own emergence; modern subjects "are not agents who are essentially embedded in a society . . . but rather disembedded individuals who come to associate together" (447). Indeed, even in what might be understood to be its most intimate bonds, the modern self remains markedly self-referential and nonrelational. Spinoza defines love itself as something unrooted in notions of kinship or agape; inhering largely in the atomistic individual herself, it is simply "pleasure accompanied by the idea of an external cause" (113). And while he admits that the self can take pleasure in the pleasure of its love object (117), Spinoza struggles when it comes to a more disinterested charity or commitment to the welfare of the other per se: "As for pleasure arising from another's good, I know not what to call it" (117). The psychology advanced by philosophical precursors to the Enlightenment helps forge, Taylor argues, a Western ethos that all but jettisons belief in deep and binding communal relations: "communion itself has little or no place . . . : little enough even on the human level—the hegemony of atomist pictures of agency in modern cultures militates against this" (280).

To be clear, this is not simply a matter of polities' status, for philosophers and framers of constitutions, as creatures of a social contract between sovereign, antecedent individuals. It has to do, too, with the limited authority of such communities and with the translation of other relationships into contractual terms. This limitation and this translation follow naturally from the understanding of the subject at play in the core concepts I have already identified. If the self is properly sovereign, it cannot be compelled by any social obligation to forswear the pursuit of its own interests. As Spinoza puts it, "as an absolute rule, it is permissible by the highest natural right for everyone to do what conduces to his own advantage," and any brakes on such action society applies must be justified, ultimately, in terms of such advantage (198). The contract that founds the polity is not once and for all; we are not bound by the undertakings or traditions of our ancestors. Rather, society remains contingent, subject to the approval of individuals seeking their own profit. Thus, for Alexis de Tocqueville, governance in the American republic functions only by the ongoing consent of each American citizen, only "because he recognizes the usefulness of his association with his fellow men and because he knows that this association cannot exist without a regulating power" (77). Yet on such accounts, one might well exist in relation with others, even outside the political sphere, only insofar as these relations serve one's interests. Think of Spinoza on love. Less political communities, more intimate relationships, are entered into or exited by this enlightened self according to a utilitarian calculus and a transactional model of human relations. As Taylor puts it, for our modern secular age, "'Economic' . . . activity has become the model of human behavior" (167). From the discovery of a disenchanted, strictly material nature, then, the Enlightenment proceeds through the insistence on individual autonomy and a universal utilitarian ethics to arrive at modern societies defined in terms of voluntary, mutually beneficial contracts. Each stage in this development will come under scrutiny in McCarthy's fiction; each one is likewise starkly at odds with Catholic teaching on Creation, human perfectibility, and the nature and power of communion.

FALLEN COMMUNION

Catholic teaching proffers an understanding of the world and of human potential decisively divergent from those sketched out above. It does so, first of all, in terms of its cosmology. If it is true that, in Etienne Gilson's formulation, the scientific outlook discloses a universe "wherein everything can be accounted for by the geometrical properties of space and the physical laws of motion" (86), the Catholic Church professes, by contrast, a world not simply fashioned by a Creator, but sustained by his actions and intentions, in such a way as to make it the locus for encounters not solely with bodies and causes, but with the supernatural and divine. Core, then, to the Catholic thought I argue animates McCarthy's interrogation of Enlightenment doctrine is the notion of the universe as a *sacramental Creation*. As Roger Nutt states, "a vital sacramental spirituality constitutes the very heartbeat of the Church" (6). Far, then, from the Enlighteners' disenchanted clockwork, the Catholic cosmos is one animated by spirit and purpose. It is the site for discovering not only patterns of efficient causality, but also a reality that transcends the material and strictly temporal.

Foundational to this belief is a threefold conviction: first, that the natural world is itself the Creation of a transcendent and personal agent, one, like us, capable of free action and intentions; second, that nature is, therefore, only fully understood when the transcendent grounds of its existence are kept in view; and third, that the product of this creative act is a moral, and not simply physical, fact, that, in other words, it is good. For the Church, behind all that is lies a divine summoning into being of the physical and animate universe. According to the *Catechism*, then, all things are the result of God's free drawing of existence out of nothingness: "all existent beings, all of nature, and all human history are rooted in this primordial event" (98). That the natural world that surrounds us is—in its beauty, fecundity, and law-governed regularity—the product of a supernatural mind that infuses it with purpose is, for the Catholic tradition, an axiom that helps account for human experiences of epiphany and miracle, but one we do not need such supernatural aids to uncover. Indeed, Aquinas argues that the intelligibility of the cosmos leads reason, unaided by revelation, to affirm the existence of a Creator (116–17). For Ronald Knox, all truly persuasive proofs of God's existence are, in fact, arguments from nature, "prov[ing] the Unseen from the seen, the existence of the Creator from his visible effects in Creation" (*Belief* 43). This is so because, for this tradition, the intricacy and design of natural entities reflect mind and purpose, not hazard and mere mechanism, at the heart of things. The Catholic God, far from being divorced from the physical universe, leaves his imprint everywhere upon it. As Irenaeus puts it, "creation reveals Him who formed it . . . the world manifests Him who ordered it" (112). Nature's beauty and variety point to the infinite beauty of God (*Catechism* 99), and a Christian faith in divine benevolence mandates an understanding of the cosmos as itself good and aimed toward God's good purposes. For Boethius, then, "everything that exists [is] good" (94), a point seconded centuries later in Aquinas's assertion that "the existence itself of things is good" (159).

It is this status as an intentional act of a good Creator that affords nature its specifically sacramental character. Now, what I refer to by such language is something more than the seven acknowledged, largely clerically administered sacraments of the Roman Catholic Church.[3] In speaking of the world itself as sacramental, I mean to articulate how Catholicism, contra the Enlightenment, maintains a profoundly enchanted notion of the universe. Defining it in more specifically ritual and ecclesial terms, Aquinas describes a sacrament as "a sign of a sacred thing sanctifying men" (774). This accords, for instance, with a Catholic understanding of baptism, of the manner in which its ritual ablutions both signify and enact a spiritual cleansing of original sin. But the notion of the sacramental exceeds such prescribed ceremonies, however important these latter have historically been taken to be. The idea of sacrament itself indicates, the *Catechism* states, "the visible sign of the hidden reality of salvation" (222). It therefore affirms the intimate contact between God's intentions and goodness (crystalized in the notion of redemption itself), on the one hand, and the natural, even mundane reality human creatures occupy, on the other. As God's own presence is affirmed in the simple physical actions and constituents of the Eucharist, then, so is the divine will understood to be at work in the sensible world more broadly, sustaining God's Creation, directing it toward his purposes, and defining it as the site for his encounter with humanity. This intimate presence is most starkly revealed in the Incarnation itself, in the second person of the Trinity's assumption of humanity and entrance into nature and history. But, Athanasius maintains, even before the coming of Christ, the world was suffused with divine presence: "no part of creation [was] left void of him" (56). The Catholic world is sacramental, then, because it remains powerfully and enduringly sacred; for the Church, the supernatural "intersects and impregnates the world of sense" (Knox, *Belief* 153). This means that the transcendent is operative and encounterable in our everyday existence; in Luke Johnson's words, the body itself "becomes a place where the spiritual is revealed" (111).

What this means, in short, is a universe driven less by sheer mechanism than by the aims and concern of a divine Creator. Neither the cosmos generally nor human beings in particular are fashioned to be governed by the blind operation of natural law. As Catholicism's nature is sacramental, the Creator is ever at work and accessible through it. And, as the God Christian tradition takes him to be, he seeks the good, the good of each individual human person, in his action therein. Thus, the *Catechism* asserts, God does not simply create all things, but rather "at every moment, upholds and sustains them in being" (89). As Creator, he is, the Church maintains, also an attentive and assiduous caretaker; as Boethius affirms, "In fact I know that God the Creator watches over His Creation" (19). The universe becomes, on such a view, a matter not simply of existence, but of providence. It is sustained by God and so directed by him as to work toward his ends. Nothing that happens there, then, is a matter of necessity or simple chance. As Knox defines this Catholic perspective, "there can be no event, however insignificant, however apparently fortuitous . . . which does not demand, here and now, the concurrence of the Divine Power" (*Belief* 62), and that personal, caring, proximate power enacts a providential oversight such that "creation is geared to salvation" (Wawrykow 220). Nor is this salvation something, on the Christian understanding, abstract or impersonal. The objective of a personal God working through the sacrament of material Creation, it is concrete and particular, addressed in their worldly circumstances to each individual. In the words of Thérèse of Lisieux, "Our Lord is concerned particularly for every soul as if there were none other like it" (3). No mechanism awaiting our direction, then, the Catholic cosmos is the ever-open invitation for an encounter with a loving Creator.

On the Catholic view, our need for such an encounter is dire. As Nutt observes, "the sacramental life of the Church [is] unintelligible without recourse to the doctrine of original sin and its effects" (25). This points to the second of my four core Catholic tenets, namely, the insistence on *human fallenness*. Far from the autonomous agent of Enlightenment thought, the human person is, for the Church, defined by an essential brokenness and insufficiency, by the original sin Nutt cites, as well as by the limitations and moral imperfection which are the legacy of that sin. Following the biblical account of the expulsion from Eden, Catholicism teaches that the human character is forged in the beginning by an act of rebellion that lastingly deforms humanity's moral sense and agency. By judging for themselves, overturning divine law, and eating of the forbidden fruit, Adam and Eve inaugurate human sinfulness and define its essence as the assertion of human sovereignty itself. As the *Catechism* states, sin is from this beginning "humanity's rejection of God and opposition to him" (109), and "all subsequent sin would be disobedience toward God and lack of trust in his goodness" (112). On the Catholic understanding, then, sin is a matter of human beings insisting on a right to self-governance and their concomitant sundering of the relationship with God that an inherently sacramental Creation affords. As Hubert Van Zeller puts it, "Demanding autonomy, and rejecting the supernatural law that bound him to God, man was left with the self-determination which he had coveted" (49). This means that human sinfulness is itself a contingent fact, one brought into being not by the Creator, but by the will's insistence on its own sovereignty. Human evil is a misuse, and no necessary consequence, of a God-given human freedom, the "perversion of the will when it turns aside from you, O God," as Augustine puts it (*Confessions* 150). It is not, then, for Catholic teaching, a matter of our natural, but of our spiritual being, the fruit specifically of the latter's wish to be self-determining: "it is not by having flesh, which the devil has not, but by living according to himself" that Augustine's Adam falls (*City* 444).

In claiming for themselves this diabolical autonomy, Adam and Eve not only broke with God, but, on the Christian account, made both death and moral fallibility ubiquitous features of the human condition. This is, on the Catholic view, perhaps the single most consequential donnée of human history. In Nutt's words, the Catholic doctrine of original sin teaches that, far from human autonomy promising the perfectibility of the species, the proneness to conceive and commit evil is "a universal, existential condition from which each and every human being needs to be redeemed" (27). According to the *Catechism*, the sin of Adam "wounds man's nature and injures human solidarity" (510), in such a way as to powerfully constrain each human being's power of moral action and thus to reproduce such wounds within the individual and the human family both. The fallen state all participate in as a result of original sin has, the Church affirms, so maimed the human person, body and soul, that we are all now ineluctably "subject to ignorance, suffering, and the dominion of death; and inclined to sin" (114). This subjection and inclination to sin yield a self that, by its very insistence upon sovereignty, is incapable of governing itself, of reliably judging, willing, or acting truly. Not only is it the case, in the words of Francis de Sales, that "there is no natural temperament so good that it may not be made evil by vicious habits" (74); more, body and mind are now so disordered, and so

35

at odds, as to make ceaseless war on God and on our own God-given capacity to govern our thoughts and deeds. Because it chose to declare war on God's law, fallen humanity, Augustine insists, now makes war on itself with frequently ungovernable sinful and destructive desires (*City* 786), and because, in the Fall, it was the will that erred, that faculty alone remains insufficient to guide us to the good or to secure our salvation (Augustine, *Faith* 37). Though the efficacious, saving sacrifice of Christ offers humankind hope of the latter, it remains our lot as fallen, incapable, and self-divided creatures to "work out our salvation by sufferings and afflictions" (de Sales 118).

The most important corollary of this doctrine of original sin, for my purposes, is its portrait of human helplessness. Catholicism holds that, in the Garden and in the present day, it is precisely by pursuing autonomy that the self attains moral abjection. In proclaiming its sovereignty, it becomes utterly incapable of moral self-governance and dependent on God's grace to better and save itself. The chief lesson of the Fall, then, is properly that of humility and lack. As the anonymous author of the fourteenth-century *Cloud of Unknowing* instructs, "Everyone has something to sorrow over, but none more than he who knows and feels that he is" (112). For Catholicism, the subject that attains true self-knowledge is far from the lordly arbiter affirmed by Descartes and Kant; she is, rather, possessor of a profoundly impaired moral agency. And what holds true for fallen selves obtains also for the communities and histories they together constitute. Incapable of reliably discerning and willing, much less enacting, the good in their own lives, such agents, the Church teaches, cannot achieve a new Eden by means of social progress. For Knox, this is a key point of divergence between Enlightenment and Christian belief: "The moderns believe, the Church does not believe, in the perfectibility of the human character on a large scale" (*Belief* 214). Instead, spiritually impoverished and morally incapable, humankind stands, on the Catholic account, in need of supernatural rescue from the consequences of its own denial of any such dependence. A broken humanity, the Church maintains, can hope for such salvation only because of the exemplary, self-humbling sacrifice of the Cross, only insofar as it eschews pretensions to mastery and subjects itself, in its need, to that savior. As Catherine of Siena writes, souls can only trust in Christ, "Himself becoming as a servant to take [them] out of servitude, imposing on Himself obedience to do away the disobedience of Adam" (47).

This radical insufficiency points to the third of my four central Catholic teachings. Broken, fallen humankind has hope only in Christ; only by surrendering the willfulness which is the essence of sin and turning to God can the soul, through Christ's sacrifice, be saved. In other words, then, the Church teaches *moral progress through penance*. While the Enlightenment identifies progress with human achievement of greater technological mastery over nature, Catholic tradition insists human beings advance in spiritual perfection only by becoming penitents and petitioners, confessing their imperfections and seeking redemption through the lordship of Christ. Defining the human condition in terms of a universal propensity for evil that it is beyond any human agency finally to correct, the Church understands itself as minister to fallen pilgrims seeking health and hope in forgiveness. As Joseph Ratzinger writes, then, the church "is not a communion of the perfect but a communion of sinners who need and seek forgiveness" (64). This need begins to be met, though, only when each member of this body comes to recognize her own moral debts and her inability to discharge them, when she acknowledges her fallen state and, moved by contrite sorrow, turns not to human agency, but to God, for aid. This is a progress born, on the Catholic view, not of instrumental reasoning and its tools, but in what the *Catechism* calls a conversion of the heart, "a radical reorientation of our whole life, a return, a conversion to God [and] an end of sin" (399). By confronting its own insufficiency, the self can begin, with the help of Christ, to reverse the work of the Fall.

What this means, is that however much the individual, left to his own devices, is morally helpless, he is far from hopeless. In what will prove a persistent motif of McCarthy's own work, the conversion and rescue just described are, Catholicism insists, open to all, no matter how wicked or abject. The salvation made possible by penance is not something the Church sees God, or itself as minister, jealously hoarding. Rather, Ratzinger asserts, "the Church is founded upon forgiveness" (64); this is its mission. Penitent conversion, as a surrender of autonomy, trusts both in God's capacity and, even more, in his willingness to do for the soul what it cannot do for itself. It is, in other words, an act of faith in God's mercy. Such faith, on the Catholic view, is not misplaced. God, the *Catechism* states, wishes all to be saved (29); far from predestining souls to hell, he so desires their salvation that they must persist in rejecting it to the very end for it not to be granted (293). As Catherine of Siena writes, "while man lives is his time for mercy, but when he is dead comes the time of justice" (68). This means that there is always hope, even for the most wretched, while there is life; the intractable presence of evil in human history, in the human heart, in each individual's own moral resumé whose reality the Church affirms can nonetheless always be overcome by confessing its defining reality in one's own life and seeking for it a divine cure. The whole Christian story—Christ's Incarnation, Passion, and Resurrection—is aimed at making this remedy available to sinners, and the Church understands itself as a ready dispensary. On Knox's account, then, "the *instinct* of the Catholic Church . . . has always told in favour of leniency" (*Belief* 187). It asks only that the petitioner be penitent, frank, and remorseful with respect to his sins, earnest in a desire to forsake them. "Beyond that," Knox writes, "the Church will have nothing but tenderness for the sinner; she knows that we are dust" (*Belief* 188).[4] Thus, the exaltation of the human subject is located, in Catholic thought, not in the assertion of human powers, but in remorse and acknowledged need, the efficacy of which can thwart even the Fall: "Contrition and confession are so beautiful and sweet-smelling that they efface the ugliness and dissipate the stench of sin" (de Sales 67).

Yet while such regeneration is always available, it is also properly rooted both in the frank admission of sin and in the galling work of atonement. As Van Zeller declares, "We need to be penitent if we want to be saved" (55). The soul must, the Church teaches, admit its failures and request God's help and forgiveness. However essential, this conversion is dislocating, humbling, inevitably painful. That autonomy clung to in sin must be discarded and one's self-love undone, both by a humiliating confession of fault and by the agonizing work of moral reformation. As Augustine cautions, conversion may require nothing more than an act of faith in God's mercy, but this act demands a difficult resolve: "it must be a resolute and whole-hearted act of the will, not some lame wish" (*Confessions* 171). What must be willed is that God's will, not the penitent's, be done. This involves, the Church recognizes, a wrenching loss of self-mastery and self-ownership, indeed, the radical diminishment of the self. As Francis de Sales puts it, to partake of God's mercy, we must abjure that independence cherished by Enlighteners: "to receive the grace of God into our hearts, they must be void of our own glory" (121). As McCarthy's protagonists will dramatize, this surrendering of the self, particularly when wed to a confession of moral failure, is something charged with "repugnance toward the evil actions [one has] committed" and so "accompanied by a salutary pain and sadness" (*Catechism* 399). Such suffering extends beyond the moment of conversion. To return to God, the Church teaches, the penitent must pursue "a holy confession, contrition of heart, satisfaction, and purpose of amendment" (Catherine 144), and the work of repentance expressed in the last two of these is inevitably accomplished in hardship. Progress through penance requires we "accept the idea that our sins . . . need to be burned off us" (Van Zeller 55). For Catholicism, there is none so lost that she might not again be found, but redemption is an agonizing labor of self-judgment, self-surrender, and amendment. As Thérèse instructs, "*suffering alone* can give birth to souls" (197).

At the heart of this call to conversion, though, lies a conviction concerning the human person's need for relationship, not just personal acts of will. It is thus rooted in an anthropology strikingly at odds with that proffered by Enlightenment thinkers. If, on St. Catherine's account, only love can render penances worthy in God's eyes (10), then the soul can only be extricated from its fallen condition through others. Thus, we arrive at the last of those Catholic teachings that, I argue, resonate through McCarthy's oeuvre, namely, that human beings find *salvation in communion*. For the Church, the human person is never isolate. As creatures, we stand always already in relation to the Creator, but more than this, we inevitably come to be what and who we are in networks of community. Far from enjoying an original independence and only belatedly coming together to contract provisional associations, as on the Enlightenment's transactional model of social relations, human beings are always, in fact, creatures in communion with others like themselves and with God. According to the *Catechism*, "The human person needs to live in society. Society is not for him an extraneous addition but a requirement of his nature" (511). It is only, then, by way of violence against their own character that people estrange themselves from an embeddedness in spiritual and social relations that precede and enable any independent action whatsoever. More importantly, on the Catholic account, it is only in loving communion with God and neighbor that the human person begins to experience what salvation means. From their very beginnings, human persons are called to eternal life in and through an expressly twofold bond, that "love of God and of neighbor" the Church calls charity (*Catechism* 514).

In the Catholic context, such considerations of communion have decidedly sacramental overtones. On Nutt's view, then, "for Christ and his followers, the

Church and her sacraments are fundamentally sources of communion among friends" (1). But when it comes to the twofold character of the human being's call to communion as Catholicism conceives it, one sacrament is particularly instructive. For Catholic thinking on communion is, above all, informed by its understanding of Eucharist. The heart of the liturgy of the Mass, the consecration and sharing of bread and wine understood as truly the body and blood of Christ, the Eucharist not only memorializes Christ's words and deeds at the Last Supper; it also enacts the communion of the faithful, both with a truly present God and with one another as an ecclesial community. Such communion, Ratzinger writes, enables this oneness with coreligionists and with God "by breaching an opening in the walls of subjectivity," a breaking open of the communicant made possible by the self-opening and self-offering of Christ in his Passion (37).[5] That sacrifice, commemorated and made present in the Eucharist, provides for the revitalization of the soul's proper relationship with God and neighbor. For this reason, the Mass, on Ratzinger's account, "forever remains the place where the Church is generated" (37). In the words of the *Catechism*, then, the Eucharist is the "Sacrament of sacraments" (341), and all the rest of the Church's works "are bound up with the Eucharist and oriented toward it" (368). Similarly celebrated by de Sales as "the centre of the Christian religion, the heart of devotion, the soul of piety" (95), the Eucharist models communion as transformative and sacrificial love forging everlasting community with God and our fellow human beings both.

By founding a churchly society rooted in Christ's own sacrifice, the Eucharist is understood to empower an expansive sense of community to be regarded with and nourished by charity. As Peter Casarella notes, twentieth-century Catholic theology, in particular, insists that "thanksgiving that begins in the Mass ends in social responsibility" (428). With the sacrificial love made present in the Eucharist as its cue, Catholic teaching professes a duty to live "a life of self-giving" in communion with others, one animated by a charity cast as "the greatest social commandment" (*Catechism* 514). On the Catholic account, then, human beings are not simply by nature formed in and hungry for community; they are spiritually called to satisfy this hunger by means of their own Christ-like acts of giving and selflessness. Only in this are true human community and their own fully human flourishing advanced. Thus, as Aquinas puts it, "there can be no joyful possession of any good without sharing" (123). More than this, we are called to emulate Christ in sacrifice. "For it is a true sign of love to deprive oneself of something for the sake of the person loved" (de Sales 256), and people are called as creatures of communion to judge all beloved. As Catherine's interlocutor God instructs her, human beings have been fashioned as finite and needy so as to make such neighborliness both necessary and a path to sanctifying love: "I wish . . . that they should be My ministers to administer the graces and the gifts that they have received from Me" (18). Indeed, only in relationship can the human person pursue holiness and find her way to God, for only by living community as loving communion does she approach God's own gratuitous love.

But if it is thus true for Catherine's God that "there cannot be love of Me, without love of the neighbor," it is likewise the case that there cannot be "love of the neighbor without love of Me" (83). Fully realized communion, as the centrality of the Eucharist reveals, requires that the person exist in communion with God. Not only the satisfaction of her yearning for human community, but her realization of her own humanity, hinges upon her entering into relationship with her Creator. In the words of Irenaeus, "For, as much as God is in want of nothing, so much does man stand in need of fellowship with God" (330). Yet if there can be no such fellowship, as Catherine affirms, without love of neighbor, this is so, Catholic tradition teaches, because only an active charity allows us to approach God at all. Certainly, the Church enjoins regular prayer as a means to nurture this essential bond. For de Sales, it is a habit of faithfulness which, steadfastly maintained, deepens one's faith in God (86), while *The Cloud of Unknowing* emphasizes how prayer, as "a devout setting of our will in the direction of God" (106), can only work our reform, conforming our will to his. But pursuing a life of charitable self-giving in community empowers one's necessary connection to God, precisely because such loving itself lifts the soul up toward a God who, the Church teaches, is love itself. As Clement preached to first-century Corinthians, "It was in love that all God's chosen saints were made perfect; for without love nothing is pleasing to Him. It was in love that the Lord drew us to Himself" (Radice 43). By an emulation of God's own love have the saints participated in his ministry and been exalted; by following Christ's example of loving sacrifice they have, according to the Church, entered into communion with the saving power of that love. Indeed, this giving of self in relationship is the only path to eternal life, for "by love [God] can be caught and held, but by thinking never" (*Cloud* 68).

In the pages that follow, I argue that—through a variety of plots and characters and genres, over the course of eleven works published in seven different decades—McCarthy turns a consistently critical eye on the four Enlightenment doctrines detailed above. Depicting them as integral to America's understanding of nature, history, and personal identity all, he nonetheless presents their operation as tragic, for communities and individuals both. Moreover, the vantage point from which he portrays such an endarkened Enlightenment is, I contend, one profoundly informed by those Catholic commitments I have just enumerated. While his fiction does not lack for atomistic figures seeking profit through others and mastery over a natural world understood in deterministic terms, these exist alongside characters whose encounters with an awesomely animate cosmos, whose agonized search for forgiveness, and whose deep, often resisted, need for communion with neighbors, and even with God, suggest that McCarthy's heaven and earth contain more truths than his protagonists' own Enlightenment commitments can account for. As for the works, their own commitment to a spiritual life in both people and nature, to the recognition of the inescapable human propensity for evil, and to the corresponding need for human penitence and reconciliation suggests an antipathy toward key axioms of modernity powerfully animated by recognizably Catholic tenets. This is true, as the next chapter will demonstrate, even of the novel that seems most explicitly to exorcise its author's Catholic upbringing, 1979's *Suttree*, for Cornelius Suttree's self-destructive insistence on a very American independence and his ongoing search for transcendence both point, in the end, to rather sacramental critiques of his own Enlightenment outlook.

CHAPTER 2

IN THIS LUSH WASTE

COMMODIFICATION, COMMUNION, AND
THE SACRAMENTAL MARGINS IN *SUTTREE*

A spirituality that claims to be emancipated from creatureliness is no
Christian spirituality.

—HUBERT VAN ZELLER, *The Mystery of Suffering*

But suppose the highest good consists in communion, mutual giving and
receiving, as in the paradigm of the eschatological banquet.

—CHARLES TAYLOR, *A Secular Age*

Hailed by Wade Hall as possibly McCarthy's "most intriguing and successful
novel" ("Comedy" 53), *Suttree* has often been numbered among the writer's
finest works.[1] The longest of McCarthy's fictions, *Suttree* has also been widely
judged his most intertextual, with scholarly readers turning up a series of source
texts whose august stature has helped advance the novel's own claims to greatness. With its detailed evocation of mid-century Knoxville, McCarthy's novel is
routinely likened to Joyce's *Ulysses*—as in Giemza's discussion of "both books[']
attempt to 'preserve' cities by testament" (212)[2]—but *Suttree* has also been compared to a veritable canon of masterworks.[3] Yet I begin my study of the Catholic
cast of McCarthy's critique of Enlightenment with this text on account of another of its commonly identified features, namely its status as "McCarthy's most
autobiographical novel" (Beavers 96). Though it is, by publication, his fourth
book, *Suttree* is also, as Crews notes, the fruit of some twenty years' labor and so,

in a meaningful sense, the oldest of his novels (3). Indeed, tracing its origins to the period that saw the genesis of what would become his first published novel, 1965's *The Orchard Keeper* (*Reading* viii), Luce treats *Suttree* as an autobiographical *Künstlerroman*, in which congruities between the language used by protagonist and that deployed by narrator enable us to "read Suttree as an author-figure, even as the narrator of this book" (206). Certainly, the fact that *Suttree* is the tale of a literary young man who shares with his creator a hometown, a class, and a religious background, when combined with its status as that creator's earliest sustained attempt at writing himself into the role of novelist, invites biographical approaches to the text, and scholars have unearthed numerous links between the novel and McCarthy's young manhood in Knoxville.[4]

The novel's autobiographical character is relevant to my concerns and encourages my addressing it first in my reading of Catholicism in McCarthy, precisely because Cornelius Suttree's kinship with his author makes him (prior to the 2022 publication of *The Passenger*) the novels' only clearly Roman Catholic protagonist, one, moreover, with decided and seemingly hostile views of the faith. Thus, this text speaks more explicitly about the Church and its teachings than any other in McCarthy's catalog, and it does so through a character whose proximity to the biographical McCarthy might lend his thoughts on such matters considerable authority. What's more, if it is true, as Luce maintains, that *Suttree* consistently presents Roman Catholicism as "a dead religion" (*Reading* 256), and that Suttree is presented as heroically "repudiat[ing] and free[ing] himself from the hell of church doctrine" (267), then this novel poses a challenge for my thesis best met sooner rather than later. Luce is far from alone in reading the book as a rejection of its protagonist/author's childhood religion,[5] nor is the novel short on evidence that might seem to support such conclusions. For example, its italicized prologue describes European settlement of lands west of the Appalachians in terms of *"wave on wave of the violent and the insane"* driven by a Christianity enshrined in *"their abrogate semitic chapbook"* (4). In Cornelius Suttree himself, we find no pious churchgoer, but a man who happily confesses having "been defrocked" by the Church of his upbringing (191). Suttree reflects less than nostalgically on the "grim . . . orthopedic moralizing" of his Catholic educators (254), sharply contradicts one priest's claim that the Church of the Immaculate Conception is "God's house" (255), and rebukes another's presumption to understand his hard-won truths (462). Indeed, Suttree often seems as much in rebellion against Catholicism as anything, and so it is no surprise that he should so frequently be taken as an existentialist hero, opposing, through self-affirmation, the seeming nullity of a nonprovidential mortal existence. Thus, Frank Shelton dubs him "existential man . . . alien in a universe without meaning" (74), but reclaiming personal value "by asserting his freedom in defiance of death" (82).[6]

Yet while Crews is surely justified in speaking of *Suttree*'s "anticlerical bent" (64), it is also fair to observe, with Watson, that Suttree "does not approach religion with a dismissive and a priori repudiation" (13). However grim his Knoxville setting may prove, it is not, I maintain, an absurdist milieu best met by solitary assertions of hopeless, but heroic self-determination. Rather, the tale told by this first/fourth of McCarthy's novels is one that stresses, as does this chapter's first epigraph, the inescapably creaturely, material character of a still spiritual human reality, while insisting, too, in concert with my second epigraph, that human fulfilment is to be achieved not through existential independence, but in communion with other human beings and a transcendent reality. *Suttree*, whatever its leeriness of priests and dogma, remains profoundly invested in a sacramental, and therefore quite Catholic, view of nature and the person, and in a location of the human telos in communion with both the lowly and the most high informed, once again, by Catholic thought. Such thought, I argue, animates the novel's critical depiction both of the mid-century America materialism against which Suttree rebels and of the premises of his own self-crippling rebellion. To be sure, both novel and protagonist pass judgment on a postwar America that, in its ardent pursuit of progress and its atomistic, fundamentally transactional society, seems the apotheosis of the Enlightenment tenets detailed in chapter 1. Even among the social outcasts with whom Suttree consorts, each individual jealously guards his or her autonomy, while pursuing advantage almost exclusively through market-based calculations. But as the violence, misery, and sheer detritus of McAnally Flats make plain, these Enlightenment ideals establish a world of universalized, self-seeking consumerism, one which, far from enshrining the dignity of the sovereign individual, works to render everyone and everything, most especially the dispossessed, nothing more than fungible, disposable commodities.

It is from just such norms that Suttree recoils in his flight to a subsistence life on the Tennessee River. Son of privilege, he chooses a place among McAnally's pariahs as a rejection of the enlightened norms of his own class. Yet in this very repudiation, Suttree mirrors the atomistic culture he reviles. Though leaving behind a mainstream ethos whose dehumanizing power he both intuits and resists, Suttree conforms to that same culture in valuing independence above all, in his replacement of filial, spousal, paternal, even neighborly relations with transactional ones that afford him the autonomy he, too, desires. The freedom he finds, however, is a dubious one, and his jealous defense of the self's supremacy in fact threatens its existence; as Richard Marius observes, his rage for independence is "in itself a kind of bondage" (8). Indeed, his autonomy-seeking flight from others and from God binds him to a philosophical and practical materialism that helps make his existence absurd, undermining not just meaning, but his own bodily security, even his will to live. Thus, Suttree's revolt against modern America follows an essentially enlightened path to a discovery of the radical insufficiency of the solitary self and of materialist cosmology. His answer to this discovery is tellingly sacramental. Suttree responds to this lack in his elected independence with a search, first, for community and, then, for communion with the divine. However haltingly or inconsistently, he seeks to establish solidarity with modernity's castoffs, the broken, flesh-and-blood denizens of McAnally Flats, who are presented not as the material refuse, the worthless commodities, their culture judges them to be, but as sources of a value that exceeds materialist calculation. But Suttree also embarks on repeated spiritual journeys, seeking in churches, wilderness fasts, and visionary experiences contact with that which transcends the reified materialism of his culture and rebellion both. In both the problem he shares with the culture he rejects and the manner in which he seeks to resolve it, then, the novel frames a spiritual rejoinder to the Enlightenment ideals of America. This spirituality, I argue, is of a particularly Catholic cast. For the Suttree who cultivates, in his flight from American Enlightenment, a lonely disgust for Creation begins to find healing when he embraces the goodness of the natural world and, through this sacramental experience, acknowledges his need for a more than transactional communion with something greater than himself, signally including other needy and embodied human beings.

KNOXVILLE'S KINGDOM OF COMMODITIES

As Louise Jillett has suggested, then, "*Suttree* can certainly be interpreted as a critique of modernity" (147). This critique is, however, one rooted in the vividly depicted specificities of a particular setting, the Knoxville, Tennessee, of the early 1950s. As Giemza notes, McCarthy "creates a novel both steeped in place and highly critical of it" (200). And while Cowart insists that *Suttree*'s Knoxville "never becomes a symbol of America" (408), it is rather the case that the city emerges as the site at which both a national character and its broader Enlightenment underpinnings become objects of scrutiny. That McCarthy understands his tale to embrace more than just the peculiarities of life in mid-century East Tennessee is revealed by the novel's prologue. Having conducted the reader on a nocturnal tour of Knoxville, the narrator concludes by describing daybreak as "*a curtain . . . rising on the western world*" (5), thus framing the drama to follow in terms of a more comprehensive sense of the West and its progressive enlightenment. Knoxville can so dramatize an enlightened Western modernity insofar as it is presented as a community of fierce individualists. If a prizing of the proper sovereignty of each individual is a core commitment of Enlightenment thought and its American realization, then McCarthy's Knoxville, however benighted it may at times appear, functions as a symbol and embodiment of American Enlightenment. Such championing not just of class dignity but of one's own interests resonates, for example, in the advice Suttree's father has to offer. For Suttree Sr., it is past time for his prodigal son to forgo his dalliance with the lowly and to commence his proper business of directing the world to his advantage. Insisting that "there is nothing occurring in the streets . . . but a dumbshow composed of the helpless and the impotent" (14), he argues that "the world is run by those willing to take the responsibility for the running of it" (13), a prerogative that calls on Suttree to sever unseemly ties in favor of his own worldly advance.

Yet American individualism is not the exclusive domain of such privileged champions of enlightened self-interest as Suttree *père*. The hoi polloi whose irrelevance he condemns holds every bit as zealously to their solitary self-governance. Indigent and desperate, the denizens of Suttree's McAnally Flats—a district known for its racially mixed population, poverty, crime, and significant police presence (Rikard 92)—nonetheless jealously defend their right to stand alone and direct their own course. Suttree on his houseboat, the ragpicker squatting troll-like beneath a bridge, the "viperous evangelist" (106) in a house "shared with his soul" alone (66), Daddy Watson, stationed by his abandoned railroad tracks, country boy Gene Harrogate, turned "city rat" (115) and installed homeless beneath a viaduct: all are committed solitaries, living alone and as ready with invective as with solicitude for their brothers on the margins. Such community as exists among them is fleeting and begrudging. In fact, it takes the deadly cold of the novel's first winter to assemble these hermits, and even then, the result, as at the dosshouse where Suttree finds the displaced ragpicker, is uncomfortable, enforced proximity, not solidarity: a "congregation of the ravaged on their rickety chairs . . . old graylooking men crouched by the warmth in the barren room, nodding and muttering and hawking gobbets of spit" (174). The last image Suttree has of this place only underscores the in-turned and self-fixated nature of this unwanted convocation: "A thin little man was squatting by the window masturbating. He did not take his eyes from Suttree nor did he cease pulling at his limp and wattled cock" (176). The relentless and, even here, fundamentally solitary pursuit of one's own pleasures is thus disclosed as both the governing principle of Knoxville's streets, as much as its boardrooms, and something obsessive and obscene. That this last is so, that the novel questions the moral value of such self-seeking independence, is only underscored by the dissenting advice offered by Suttree's adopted McAnally father figure, Ab Jones, who decries onanistic self-sufficiency and tells Suttree to "look out for [his] own" (203), to stay true to community rather than to American dreams of personal success: "you dont never have it made. . . . Look up one mornin and you a old man. You aint got nothing to say to your brother" (203).

Such warnings notwithstanding, human interaction in McCarthy's Knoxville remains framed by the marketplace. If relations between his characters are intermittent, this is so largely because their commitment to a personal success defined by acquisition of consumer goods means that their encounters with each other are built primarily on that transactional model discussed in the last chapter. In this, however irrational or backward their acts may seem, they prove themselves proper moderns. On Taylor's account, definitive of the modern West is the fact that "'Economic' (that is ordered, peaceful, productive) activity has become the model for human behaviour" (167). The raucous, often criminal, conduct of Suttree and his peers may seem to diverge from this norm, but they remain nonetheless committed to the primacy of economic relations, particu-larly as these pertain to buying, selling, and consuming, rather than ownership and production. The latter are not wholly absent from the novel; modern indus-try encircles the seamy world of McAnally Flats. Suttree wakes to Monday on the river amid "the howl of the saws in the lumbermill [and] the intermittent scream of swine come under the knacker's hand at the packing company" (*S* 63) and can "hear everywhere in the hot summer air the drone of machinery, the lonely industry of the city" (63). But the heart of the novel's city comprises the diners, taverns, shops, and stalls of its market center, a forum teeming with people seeking not communion, but a trade in commodities. Wandering among its crowds, Suttree sees a "lazaret of comestibles and flora and maimed human-ity" (67), already identifying the market's usurpation of community with afflic-tion and dehumanization. Indeed, while this is where people interact with one another as sources of commodities, it is also where people are themselves com-modified, made less the agents than the objects of market transactions. Hence the novel's robust trade in human flesh, something seen in its many brothels (e.g., 76–79), in barroom prostitute Ethel—"She hiked her skirt up around her waist with one hand and cocked her leg forward" (75)—showcasing her wares for the regulars, in the "pale and pimpled part-time catamite" Leonard (241), and in the story of Suttree's lover, Joyce, on the run from Chicago for "selling [her] pussy" (394). A polity founded upon the fiercely guarded sovereignty of all, *Suttree*'s America is one where transactionalism leads to the displacement of relationship by commerce, of intimacy by consumption, such that the novel's loners themselves become salable items.

Again, this is a process the novel's outcasts are depicted as embracing, and not simply suffering. If it is true, as D. S. Buttersworth argues, that the novel "adopt[s] the project of recentering characters who have been marginalized . . . by the hierarchical economic structures of urban America" (95), then this fore-grounding takes care to detail their own participation in America's consumerist economy. For all their eremitical tendencies, *Suttree*'s marginalized do not iso-late themselves from the workings or the ethos of the market. Rather, they iden-tify it as the arena in which their sovereignly chosen goods may be secured and maximized. This being the case, what they most often seek is the money with which to become the buyers they long to be. Suttree's associates, then, com-monly figure not just as prodigious consumers—particularly of alcohol—but as energetic hustlers on the make. Thus, Reese sells Suttree on, and himself buys into, dreams of riches to be had through the harvest and sale of mussel shells and freshwater pearls. Further, he pledges allegiance to the almighty dollar as sole means to a properly American freedom, telling Suttree that, in this country, you can go wherever you want "when ye got the money to do it with" (S 337). Such devotion to the American dream of success through purchasing power is definitive, too, of Suttree's protégé, Eugene Harrogate.[7] "Convicted pervert of a botanical bent" (54), Harrogate is the hick melon-humper who tails his work-house protector to Knoxville on his release. While frequently obtuse, Harrogate is far from guileless or lacking in ambition, but as Potts notes, his "clever, technical knowledge is crassly materialistic" (83). His "strangely wizened childs-face rapt with larceny" (S 173), Harrogate dedicates himself to a series of illicit schemes, charting the shortest route to the swaggering independence money and the market can provide. Poisoning bats for the bounty on rabid specimens (214–19), tunneling through caves seeking access to bank vaults (259–70), and siphoning coins from Knoxville payphones (419), Gene finally, briefly, realizes his dreams with a personal success communicated by the fashionable goods he is able to purchase and flaunt, chomping on a cigar and sporting "a corduroy hat . . . and a black gabardine shirt with slacks to match" (418).

But if the residents of McAnally Flats thus submit, in their quest for self-sufficiency, to the logic of the marketplace, they also come to perpetuate and to suffer the commodification which is the lifeblood of such economics. That is, in accepting that people may be bought and sold, they work both to normalize dehumanization, their own included, and so to identify the reigning market-place ethos of America with predation and death. This translation of human persons into lifeless assets is made plainest perhaps in the fate of Leonard's father. Dead some six months, his passing has been concealed and his decaying body kept in the family home so that his welfare benefits may still be claimed by his widow. Eventually, with the smell "fuckin awful" (243), Leonard appeals to Suttree to help him dispose of this patriarch, "wrapped in the sheets he'd died in months before" (250), in the river. Here, then, the economic ordering of postwar America is starkly revealed as trading in blood money. Nor is this linkage of American progress and its economy with death limited to this one ghoulish enterprise. Harrogate, newly arrived in Knoxville, finds his first offer of paying work with the hungover junkman, his job being to wash up salvaged car wrecks for future sale. As the novel makes explicit, the junkman's business thus constitutes a trade in, and profit on, the maimed flesh and lost lives of those who suffered these accidents; scrubbing "deep burgundy black" blood that stains one such hulk (96), Harrogate is confronted by something "small and fat and wet with an umbilical looking tail" (96), a human eye left lying on the floorboards. Similarly, Ab Jones's tavern serves customers on tables formed from the scavenged gravestones of the displaced dead: "Whole families evicted from their graves downriver by the damming of the waters" (113).

If such touches highlight the predatory nature of America's devotion to industrial and technological progress, they also indicate how the economy sustained by such Enlightenment works to turn everything, including the marginalized themselves, into disposable, consumable goods. As Giemza rightly notes, then, McCarthy's Knoxville "consumes its poor as if they were consumer products" (215). This translation of persons and things into fungible commodities is, moreover, the main source of the novel's penchant for the grotesque and its characters' frequent abjection. Far from restricted to the black comedy of the burial of Leonard's father—recall the dosshouse onanist—the novel's grotesquerie, Cooper argues, works to foreground "depictions of human evil to confront readers with horrors from which they would otherwise avert their eyes" ("Tennessee" 41). While there is some truth to this, it seems to me that the evil at play here is frequently more systemic and suffered than this might suggest. Though the hapless, unruly denizens of McAnally Flats largely conform, in their independence and money-grubbing, to the norms of American modernity, it is also the case both that they live in circumstances straitened and degraded by these norms' commodification of all things and that they themselves suffer the consequences of this consumer culture. If, in Canfield's words, the people and environment of McAnally Flats proffer "an abjection so profound as to be apocalyptic" ("Dawning" 665), then, the resulting world of waste, disease, dead bodies, expelled bodily fluids, things that, in Julia Kristeva's formulation, undermine the self-contained subjectivity of the ego (Kristeva 3), is something that "disturbs identity, system, order" (4), but it does so as the perverse product of a system, an order, that McCarthy identifies with the modern West itself.[8]

Thus while *Suttree*'s grotesquerie may—as in the case of a legless Harrogate covered in his own vomit after filching Callahan's workhouse hooch (*S* 56–58)—sometimes skewer the peccadillos of McCarthy's outcasts, it more consistently demonstrates their rootedness in a deadly economy of purchase, consumption, and disposal. The novel's characters occupy a setting typified not just by sickness—the city's neon lights reflected "in the water like discolored sores" (212)—or death, but by detritus, human and nonhuman alike. Suttree traverses "a landscape of old tires and castoff watertanks rusting in the weeds" (64). The business of the ragpicker and junkman relies on a steady supply of just such trash. In this American environment, predicated on the individual pursuit of fulfilment through consumption, there is no shortage of such cast-away goods. Indeed, the keynote of the novel's portrait of Knoxville is its emphasis on pollution, above all of the "Cloaca Maxima" of the river (13). Noel Polk calls *Suttree*'s Tennessee River "more enervated and enervating than any other literary body of water . . . except perhaps the Thames of 'The Waste Land'" (18).[9] Certainly, it is the final destination of the bulk of the waste products of the novel's consumer polity. It is the city's toilet, awash with "gouts of sewage faintly working, gray clots of nameless waste and yellow condoms" (*S* 7), and its dump, site of "*ruined household artifacts*" and of "*beached and stinking forms of foetal humans*" (*S* 4). An American world of fulfilment purchased, enjoyed, and thrown away is revealed not simply as tainted, but as reifying human persons, even those committed to the solitary pursuit of their own success in such terms. Like the junkyard, the river is a domain of death, not just of unwanted children, their "bloated, pulpy rotted eyes in a bulbous skull" carried by its current (306), but of well-dressed failures like the suicide fished from the river at the novel's opening (9). The novel thus calls attention to the harms inflicted by the creed of self-sufficiency and the American reduction of relations to transactions and persons to goods. The emotional costs of these norms are written poignantly on the body, in the "light tracery of old razor scars on her inner wrists" (404) of prostitute Joyce. If the result of her sale of her body—a commodity, with its "scarred paunch" (404), of depreciating marketplace value—is attempted suicide, not self-realization, the fruit of others' pursuit of liberty in McAnally Flats is an ever-expanding body count. A thieving Callahan is shot down (375), the ragpicker is found having finally welcomed longed-for death (421), and "Clarence Raby [is] shot to death by police on the courthouse lawn" (416). Thus, postwar America, with its Enlightenment ideal of self-sufficiency and its faith in the boon of transactional relations, ends up portrayed very much as that "*Encampment of the damned*" (3) described in the prologue.

DOOMED DECLARATIONS OF INDEPENDENCE

Ironically, while Suttree has taken up residence in this encampment, he has done so precisely with a view to rejecting those American values to which so many of its denizens still subscribe. As Monk observes, Suttree is emphatically not a member by birth of the marginalized communities with whom he consorts and which society keeps sequestered in McAnally Flats (69). Indeed, as Vescio notes, if his cronies are depicted as outsiders struggling to find their way into the American mainstream, Suttree himself is "an insider desperately trying to get out" (78). Thus, if it is true, as Woods Nash argues, that Suttree's taking the part of society's outcasts against the authorities is "one of this novel's most obvious and persistent themes" ("Caravan" 81), this is, in fact, a dynamic fueled as much by antipathy to the latter as sympathy for the former. After all, Suttree has himself elected to take up residence beyond the pale; he has, in other words, had the luxury of choosing to occupy the social margins. As his father's letter indicates, he was born to another estate and a different set of opportunities and expectations than those associated with his shanty boathouse on the polluted Tennessee. A young man raised "on an allowance," he is, as his fellow workhouse inmates identify him, one of the "educated pisswillies" (*S* 47). The life he was groomed for was not that of subsistence fisherman and brawling drunk, but one lived in "the law courts, in business, in government" (14). His birthright was to join in the task of leading modern America, its progress and prosperity, forward. His very presence in Knoxville's grubbier purlieus is thus a matter of his disavowal of just that fate.

So Suttree has consciously rejected America's call to mercenary success and material progress, and chosen social obscurity over enlightened self-interest. This has taken the form of a series of radical severances, executed in hopes of freeing himself from a culture whose values he despises. Educated he has been, equipped to help guide America to new postwar heights he may be, but Suttree scorns both that training and that object, reflecting "from all old seamy throats of elders, musty books, I've salvaged not a word" (14). His rebellion against this past and the enlightened future toward which it beckons him takes the form of repudiation of kin. Young Suttree's alienation from his parents is emphasized from the outset, not just in his resentful recollection of paternal correspondence, but in his studied evasion of contact with either mother or father. In the workhouse, only he and Harrogate pass Sundays without visits from family (51), and when, on the Sunday after Christmas, this pattern is broken by a visit from Suttree's mother, guilty tears and flight are his only response; he flees the room saying, "I cant" (61). When hunted down by his maternal uncle, Suttree has John promise not to tell sister or brother-in-law where their son might be found (15). This pledge holds. When later they seek to share with Suttree news of his own child's death, they must send lifelong friend J-Bone as emissary (148). Indeed, while Suttree repudiates ties to his elders—shouting at John, for example, "I'm not like you. I'm not like [my father] . . . I'm like me" (18)—perhaps the most profound form his denial of his American inheritance takes is his desertion of his young wife and infant son. The cost of this refusal of American norms is revealed not simply in the "remorse lodged in his gorge like a great salt cinder" (150), or in his mother-in-law's assault on him (151), but in the image of this abandoned wife herself, a "madonna bereaved, so griefstunned and wooden" (150).

Luce is thus justified in her description of Suttree as "an alcoholic and soul-wounded man alienated from family, church, and twentieth-century American culture" (*Reading* 194), but it is clear that this is an alienation from origins and intimates resolutely chosen with an eye to rebelling against that national culture she cites. As John Vanderheide contends, Suttree's departure from parents, wife, and child is undertaken with a larger divorce in view; it "corresponds to the abandonment, partial if not total, of his class identity" (31). He determinedly flees the father, in other words, because he will not follow in his footsteps, will not live a life committed to vindicating Enlightenment values of material advancement he, in fact, reviles. He deserts the young woman, that daughter, in the town sheriff's words, whose "life [he's] ruined" (157), because to play the role of husband and provider would inevitably involve him again in his father's world, in a world of regularized, administered getting and spending. It is clear that the prodigal Suttree has no interest in playing any such cog's role in the machinery of American business or American progress. The novel's opening scene makes this plain enough. Learning from an acquaintance clearly concerned for his well-being that there is paying work available in men's shoes at Miller's department store, Suttree brusquely demurs, preferring "to stick to the river" and its dubious bounty "for a while yet" (10). This refusal of respectable work holds, as he prefers scraping by on catfish, mussel shells, and credit to taking up any settled situation in the American marketplace. This aversion to a regular job is matched by his distaste for the march of progress. It is noteworthy, on this score, that Suttree takes his leave of Knoxville when the forces of improvement are unleashed on his beloved McAnally Flats. As authorities undertake the slum clearance and highway construction aimed at such enlightened ends as expanding commerce and elevating standards of housing and health, Suttree sees only desolation—"nothing stood save rows of doors, some bearing numbers, all nailed to. Beyond lay fields of rubble, twisted steel and pipes" (464)—and takes the first ride out of town.

Thus, if Marius exaggerates when he claims "Suttree plays the role of the Nietzschean superman, the man who rejects all expectations handed onto him" (8), this is perhaps a hyperbole in tune with Suttree's own ambitions. Clearly, he wants no part of the American cult of wealth and progress, of its Enlightenment faith in material self-interest and technological advance. Yet McCarthy's text details Suttree's abiding implication in norms he has given up so much to escape. As Monk asserts, Suttree still "represents a symptom of modernity even in his response to it" (69). For all that he has abandoned both his upbringing and expectations, for all that he disdains the American cult of technical progress and material success, he remains bound both to the operation of the marketplace and to the enlightened American insistence on the sovereignty of the individual. First, as Christine Chollier observes, Suttree is far from having divorced himself from mercenary relations; as both subsistence fisherman and, given the chance, avid consumer, he is subject to the dictates of the Knoxville market ("I aint" 172). These ordinances seem, in fact, to have replaced for him the commandments of his childhood faith. Thus, as sartorially correct neighbors head to church on a "hushed and mazy Sunday," Suttree spends the Lord's Day at work, collecting fish from his lines in the river (*S* 13). The next day, he takes shelter from the summer heat in Miller's, embracing its "perfumed and airconditioned sanctuary . . . cool opulence available to the most pauperized" (69). That the department store has supplanted the cathedral, and labor the Sabbath, serves to indicate the extent to which Suttree's life remains oriented to market calculations and the pursuit of commodities. Indeed, trade in the latter is his very livelihood. He not only takes his catch to Monday markets and lives on the meager proceeds; in doing so, he even conforms to the racialization of the marketplace upon which 1950s America insists. Rebel Suttree not only has still to repair to the market for his living; he sells first, and offers his sought-after catfish, to the white fishmonger, only then offering the leavings to his African American counterpart, this even as the latter pays him eight cents more (67–69).

If Suttree's rebellion thus sees him still bound, as supplier, to an unjust economy, it likewise fails to free him from the role of consumer. Despite his adopted indigence, Suttree is pleased to play the buyer's part. The extent to which consumption governs his life is made manifest in the many blackout drunken binges that punctuate the narrative (see, e.g., 73–80, 338–43). Yet Suttree's purchases are not all disreputable. When, for example, he receives a $300 legacy, he embarks on a shopping spree to deck himself out in the costume of a fashionable moneyed man. He does not simply treat himself and J-Bone to "the biggest fucking steak" on offer at Regas (302); he further outfits himself, in a style to rival Harrogate's, with a camelhair sports coat (299), a pair of tailored mohair trousers, "a yellow gabardine shirt with handstitched collar and pockets," and a pair of zippered red shoes (300). "Looking rather affluent" (301), he then enjoys, rapt "in deep euphoria" (301), a shave, haircut, and shoeshine. For all his repudiation of his class privilege, then, Suttree remains an American consumer, one who allies, in part at least, the good with such goods as he can procure for himself in the modern marketplace. Nor, as such, does he balk at that economy's established propensity for the commodification and dehumanization of persons. He is eager to join J-Bone whoring at the Carnival Club (302), just as he later follows Reese to a disastrous drunk at a brothel called The Green Room (338). If the squalor of such carousals vindicates the dwarf preacher who, standing in the Knoxville market, proclaims "this aint where it's at," "not this buyin and sellin" (382), it is nonetheless clear that buying and selling are where the ostensibly iconoclastic Suttree remains stuck.

Yet Suttree is even more the exemplary American and man of Enlightenment in the obduracy of his declared independence from nonmarket relations or governance. Haunted by the spectre of a stillborn twin brother, his "mirror image," "like to the last hair" (14), plagued by the fear that the world might harbor "some doublegoer, some othersuttree" capable of supplanting him altogether (287), he recoils from the notion that his identity or fate might be encumbered by bonds of likeness, derivation, or duty. Hence the angry refusal of all familial likeness in his quarrel with Uncle John cited above. Hence, too, the jealously defended solitude of his retreat from class and kin. Like his McAnally neighbors, Suttree is a fierce individualist, living alone and literally off the grid on his shanty-boat, and continually rebuffing overtures of welcome and need both. Certainly, he repeatedly declines offers to break bread, to enter into that level of communion, with both family and his fellow outcasts. Despite their invitations, then, he refuses to partake of the ragpicker's potatoes (11), Harrogate's pigeons (117), and the goatman's fish (205), much less of the Sunday dinner offered several times by his Aunt Martha (125, 132).[10] Even on rare occasions when he does dine with others, a profound reserve persists, as at the workhouse, where meals pass with "no word spoke" (43), or at a lunch-counter Thanksgiving with Harrogate, during which "there was no conversation" (172). Similarly, Suttree, though not always averse to offering aid, will ignore the appeals of blind Richard, calling "supplicant" from the bridge and unable to find his own way down to Suttree's boat (373): "Suttree turned his back on him and his cries and went in and shut the door" (373). Likewise, a freezing Michael, one of his closer associates, knocks at Suttree's door with "a thin clatter of teeth" (404) only to go unheard and unhelped. As seen in his confrontation with his wife, then, Suttree is committed to his independence at the cost not simply of losing others, but of abandoning them to harm.

McCarthy's rebel is thus, in fact, a stout defender of values championed by the society he reviles. Hungry consumer and committed loner, he will, in American fashion, determine for himself his own goods and secure these in an economy in which others figure chiefly as means. This dual devotion to personal sovereignty and transactional relations is clearly evidenced in his time with Joyce. On the face of it, this "mock-bourgeois courtship" (Walsh 194) might seem to contradict what I have said about Suttree's independence-seeking refusal of intimacy. After all, over the course of this affair, Suttree abandons his basement flat and joins Joyce first in hotels and then in a shared apartment. Serving as her banker, he weds himself not simply to a common residence but to the enterprise of her sexual labor. But this last point is a telling one. Underwritten by Joyce's prostitution, this is a relationship predicated on Suttree's exploiting the market's dehumanizing translation of flesh into purchasing power and on his maintenance of the detachment this mercenary relationship fosters. From its beginnings in an evening of drinks at her expense, this is a "romance" in which Suttree plays parasite, accepting Joyce's treatment as a commodity at the hands of others in exchange for his own access to the consumer goods he, his slumming notwithstanding, still covets. He happily accepts from her largesse clothes more extravagant than past windfalls have afforded: alligator shoes, camelhair coat, and gabardine slacks (400). Undisturbed by scars on her wrists, by thoughts of the human cost of such gifts, Suttree nags her into buying him a 1950 Jaguar (407). Viewing her always only as a sexual commodity and means to other consumer goods, Suttree may become her "kept man" (Jillett 150), but he does not thereby cease to live by strictly market values or surrender his cherished independence. Unmoved by her tales of her past, her tears, her desire—not his—for a permanent residence, Suttree takes Joyce's gifts and maintains his distance from the emotional ties she yearns to forge. He remains "detached, a displaced soul musing on the hiatus between himself and the Suttree moving through these strange quarters" (S 402), until Joyce herself has had enough and attacks his loveless materialism, vandalizing the beloved Jaguar and tearing up the dollars she herself has paid so dearly for. Crying "It's just a car . . . It can be fixed" (410), Joyce ends their relationship by calling the reader's attention to Suttree's unrepudiated and American pursuit of self-realization through consumer goods purchased at the cost of the commodification of persons.[11]

Yet McCarthy's protagonist ultimately emerges as a truer rebel than all this might suggest. This he does insofar as his tale becomes, as Crews maintains, one of spiritual progress, "from death to life, fall to grace, sin to redemption" (120). Suttree's initial repudiation of American norms may well only rehearse them, but the untenable world to which this ongoing attachment to enlightened self-interest surrenders him leads him to endorse, by novel's end, a more religious and more Catholic view of the self's relationship with nature, with others, and with God. For Suttree's desperately defended independence, his insistence on his sovereignty and uniqueness, involves not just a rejection of humane relationships, but a refusal to accept, and an attempt to free himself from, the mortality he, in fact, shares with those whom he flees. Orienting this solitary course, then, is a revulsion in the face of the human limitation and insufficiency that mortality makes plain, a disgust that comes to embrace embodied others, material Creation, even his own flesh. From this loathing arises in him not simply a nihilistic conviction as to the worthlessness of all passing things, but also, paradoxically, a genuine death wish, a recurrent longing to be shut of a world that his own declaration of independence has helped frame for him as null and void. Thus, his flight to a lonely, consumerist autonomy, motivated by the desire to cheat the death he owes in common with those he abandons, leads him ultimately to court that same death. But precisely to the extent that his enduring allegiance to Enlightenment ideals makes his life unbearable, this spurious revolt urges him gradually to pursue alternatives in less simply materialistic and atomistic notions of nature and self.

That Suttree feels hounded by death, that he resorts to the margins in part to outpace it, is clear from the outset. The prologue concludes with an enemy prowling Knoxville, "*a hunter with hounds or do bone horses draw his deadcart*" (*S* 5). The recurrence of this "huntsman" and his hounds "ravening for souls in this world" (471) in the novel's last paragraphs helps confirm his embodiment of mortal peril and thus the extent to which Suttree's tale is framed by the problem of mortality. This problem, acutely felt by McCarthy's protagonist, in fact establishes his quintessential modernity. As Taylor argues, "Modern humanism tends to develop a notion of human flourishing which has no place for death" (320). Certainly, Suttree understands his flourishing as requiring escape from, rather than reconciliation with, this fell huntsman. For him, fully realized humanity requires an autonomy that overthrows death's dominion. Thus, he recoils from his own mortality, as an unconscionable proof of his subjection to a power beyond his consent or control. After a near-death experience, Suttree bridles at this intolerable dependence: "He felt his heart pumping down there under the palm of his hand. Who tells it so? Could a whole man not author his own death with a thought?" (295). His longing for that autonomy American Enlightenment so prizes motivates his living life as flight from an unacceptable death; it should therefore come as no surprise that this life mandates the severing of relationships with others subject to the unfreedom mortality represents. He flees family not simply as upholders of rejected norms, but as reminders of his own his own likeness to others doomed to die. He is haunted especially by knowledge of his stillborn twin, that "mirror image" (14) whose existence undercuts his presumed uniqueness and whose stillbirth argues that common humanity consists in nothing other than the affront of death. As Potts observes, the dead twin "binds him to death in a manner he cannot bear" (93). Indeed, kinship for Suttree can only be a kinship in death; it thus contradicts that ideal of personal sovereignty to which he clings. We see this in his study of Aunt Martha's photo albums. Their portraits of forebears constitute for him a repulsive "picturebook of the afflicted" (*S* 130), a testament to his own foreordained death, against which he asserts his independence: "Blind moil in the earth's nap cast up in an eyeblink between becoming and undone. I am, I am. An artifact of prior races" (129).

As detailed above, Suttree achieves that independence in some measure. But as his sovereignty is founded on the belief that humanity is in essence only its own vile dissolution, this achievement only delivers him up to a world of pervasive loss, of persons ephemeral and bereft of meaning. If Guinn is correct in locating the heart of Suttree in "the protagonist's struggle with nihilism" (112), then this struggle is predicated on the view of mortality that has fostered his retreat and on the radical divorce from human solidarity that his declaration of independence has necessitated. Haunted by dead twins, convinced kinship is untenable because it entails the common bondage of mortality, solitary Suttree is scarcely free from the annihilating presence of death. If anything, he has only more completely surrendered himself to death's power, its status as the unmaker of all value. Bell argues that death in Suttree "diminishes each particular being to pointless corrupting matter" (Achievement 69).[12] While this is not, I maintain, ultimately true for the novel itself, it is, for much of its course, true for Suttree, who continues to recoil from human persons as unacceptably mortal flesh. Sickened, as a youth, by "the slow seeping of life . . . running out like something foul, nightsoil from a cesspipe" (S 136), Suttree in his maturity still balks at the "mawky wormbent tabernacle" of the human body (130). Material reality, including the corporeality of his fellow human beings, is not simply fleeting, but, for Suttree, tainted by its subjection to material corruption. He comes, then, to view first his neighbors and then himself as things defiled and worthless. After Leonard's request for help in disposing of his father's corpse, Suttree looks upon McAnally "through eyes unscaled" and spies there nothing of value, only "clutches of the iniquitous and unshriven howling curses at the gates and calling aloud for redress of their right damnation" (246). Ultimately, though, he cannot maintain the distance upon which such fiery judgment rests. Understanding himself as just another of the "sad children of the fates whose home is the world, all gathered here a little while to forestall the going there" to nonbeing (386), Suttree sees his life as still subject to the death he flees in renouncing community and as worthless on that account. "My life is ghastly," he reflects after his failed enterprise with Reese (348), and he becomes as seized by self-loathing as by his prior disgust for others' too mortal flesh: "Am I a monster, are there monsters in me?" (366).

Suttree's refusal to accept the mortal state that binds him to others thus leads him to discover a world where death's dominion is so absolute that nothing, not even his refusal, can have value. His attempted flight from mortality consigns him to an existence so abhorrent that death itself becomes a temptation. As Prather notes, the novel's opening huntsman may threaten less as predator than as siren, representing "the allurements of escape and the consolations of death" (113). Significantly, McCarthy's narrator insists that this figure is "*not to be dwelt upon for it is by just suchwise that he's invited in*" (*S* 5), suggesting his danger lies in the attractive exit he offers from the ghastly reality Suttree's program of flight has established. Suttree may gainsay the ragpicker's death wish by insisting, "No one wants to die" (257), but his own conduct suggests he is less than confident even of his own preferences in this regard. When asked whether he would consider following the example of the suicide dragged from the river, Suttree manages only "I hope not" (12). In fact, the allure of this deadly example is demonstrated when, standing on the spot from which the dead man jumped, Suttree imagines sharing the suicide's fate: "To fall through dark to darkness. Struggle in those opaque and fecal deeps . . . to see that all is quiet for the advent of eternal night" (29). In the face of the repugnant life his will to sovereignty has crafted, Suttree comes paradoxically to assign value to the presumed nullity of death. As he reflects after his son's funeral, then, "the dead do not remember and nothingness is not a curse. Far from it" (153). Though he never makes a deliberate attempt on his own life, Suttree's drunken career in McAnally Flats clearly constitutes, as Shelton argues, an attempt "to blot out consciousness" (76). The novel details five such catastrophic sprees (see *S* 74–80, 184–88, 302, 337–41, 375–76), each concluding either in blackout or in death or near-death. The second, for example, has Suttree, in barroom melee, struck over the head with a floorbuffer: "He dropped like a zombie among the din and the flailing" (187). Along with his hospitalization for broken ribs and skull fracture (188), his aping of the undead here helps establish the destination toward which Suttree's benders tend. Less subtly still, the next will find him come to disoriented consciousness in a cemetery, "among the menhirs of the dead" (302), while the last culminates in the shooting death of crony Billy Callahan

(377). Having adopted his hermit's life in a jealous, and very American, defense of his independence—from social norms, community, even death itself—Suttree thus finds himself at an impasse, whereby his own refusal of untenable bonds and limitations imposes insupportable burdens that make even the alternative of death attractive.

SPIRIT, SACRAMENT, COMMUNION

Significantly, Suttree both declines that alternative and refuses to accept that death is the ultimate truth of the human person. Indeed, the abasement he suffers over the course of the novel seems less to confirm the absurdity of a wholly materialist universe than to push him toward the affirmation of transcendence. Echoing John of the Cross's teaching that the dark night of desolation and doubt can "enlighten the soul, giving it knowledge, not only of its lowliness and wretchedness . . . but likewise of the greatness and excellence of God" (32), Suttree also, in the face of ostensibly worthless matter and certain nullity, consistently seeks contrary spiritual truths. As Walsh observes, Suttree is no nihilist; rather his tale is more properly read as "a spiritual or quasi-religious quest" (188). To be sure, the novel shows its protagonist repeatedly undertaking such quests as a way of refuting the argument of nothingness his own pursuit of absolute sovereignty has made so cogent. In the wake of his most trying loss—the death of his son—Suttree receives from the sheriff both a warning to leave town and some fatherly advice: "Everything's important. A man lives his life, he has to make that important. . . . You might even understand that some day" (S 157). It is my contention that Suttree does, indeed, come to understand this, to refute the finality of death, the truth of modern materialism, and the tenability of atomistic autonomy, all of which have helped nearly make him a suicidal nihilist. That he refuses such nihilism is made plain in his response to the ragpicker's sorry fate. Checking in on this man's squat, Suttree finds but a corpse among the grubby, thief-strewn debris. Having long made a vociferous creed of his death wish, the ragman here "look[s] as if he had forced himself to death" (421). Yet Suttree, for all of his own courting of death, finds no solace in this man's success. Interestingly, he is moved both by a sense of a reality beyond the worldly present and by an outrage at his neighbor's embrace of a despairing and squalid end. "Hear[ing] dimly a shuffling and coughing beyond the painted drop of the world" (422), Suttree is filled with rage and denounces the manner in which the ragpicker's welcome of death debases the person, proclaiming a human worthlessness that Suttree cannot, in fact, endorse. "You have no right to represent people this way," he reproaches the ragman: "A man is all men. You have no right to your wretchedness" (422). Moved by an abiding belief in something more than meaningless material corruption, Suttree here refuses the allure of suicide, rejects the validity of nihilism, and establishes his own need for spiritual communion.

This late soliloquy, however, only articulates what his conduct has long made evident. As Shelton notes, Suttree is, from the start, a character moved by "an intense religious yearning" (74).[13] Though it is only late that the novel reveals that he is, by way of his mother's Christian name, quite literally "son of Grace" (*S* 432), Suttree, for all that he has fled kin, class, and church in pursuit of enlightened autonomy, is consistently drawn to the faith and preaching of others. The novel's early pages, then, have him watching from a distance as the African Americans of McAnally Flats assemble for Sunday worship, nor is this his first time doing so. Rather, this vicarious church going is something of a ritual for Suttree, "for even a false adumbration of the world of spirit is better than none at all" (21). Similarly, he is fascinated audience to, if no ready believer in, the sermons of "wild street preachers haranguing a lost world with a vigor unknown to the sane" (66). While Suttree's perspective here affirms the falsity of Black congregationalism and the madness of visions peddled by street-corner evangelists, that he continues to lend his ear indicates his intuition that a greater truth than his and modernity's own may be found in adumbrations of spiritual things. Thus he spends part of another Sunday observing bible-camp baptisms in the Tennessee. While he refuses communion with these believers—declaring he "sure as hell" will not be staying (124)—Suttree also encounters here another doppelganger, a seventy-six-year-old new convert who, until his late baptism, was as "awful bad about drinkin" as Suttree himself (123), suggesting that the needs and goals of these Protestant faithful are not altogether alien to him. Indeed, his spiritual searching gravitates to traditions beyond the Catholic, or even Christian, ones in which he has been raised. He regards the African American witch-cum-prophetess Mother She not just with fear, but "with a peculiar feeling of deference" (228). Likewise, he receives Michael's gift of a luck charm, "a small lozenge of yellowed bone" (239), with respect and happily claims a second such talisman, an ancient disc with "two rampant gods addorsed" (327), from the banks of the French Broad.

Of particular significance for my argument, however, is the fact that Suttree has not simply replaced the faith in which he was himself baptized with these alternate creeds. While Jillett maintains that his interactions with Catholic priests reveal "a fundamental rupture with any belief in the existence of, or redemption in, a hereafter" (160), it is rather the case that Suttree's ongoing sense that a beyond and hereafter do exist draws him repeatedly to the church of his childhood. As part of the novel's first drunken binge, Suttree has a dream that discloses both his feelings of guilt and dependence, and his identification of the Church as the site of possible absolution and support. This dream places him before a Catholic altar, kneeling "on the cold stone flags at a chancel gate where the winey light of votive candles cast his querulous shadow behind him . . . [bending] in tears until his forehead touch[es] the stone" (S 78). Defrocked he may be, but it is clear that the criteria by which he judges himself and others remain rooted in his ancestral faith. Hence his shock at Leonard's refusal to utter a prayer over his father's corpse—"I mean you're not going to bury your father without anything at all" (251)—and his drunken recourse, immediately after abetting in this watery interment, to the Cathedral of the Immaculate Conception, as though, still that "viceridden child, heart rotten with fear" once devout in his Sunday attendance (253), he feels the need to be forgiven this recent sin. Though he here declines the offer of confession, this nocturnal visit is not his last haunting of the Church. Following another blackout drunk, he finds himself returning to the now-abandoned "old brick house where he'd gone to school" (304), and while he never hails this figure, Suttree is captivated after his departure by an ordained custodian he disturbs by his visit, watching from the window "like a paper priest in a pulpit or a prophet sealed in glass" (305).

Suttree remains, then, even in his unintended mirroring of American materialism, a spiritual seeker shaped by his Catholic past, and his world is depicted as one in which belief in the supernatural is far from groundless. Apart from Mother She's widely conceded eldritch powers, there is also the example of identical twins Vernon and Fernon, capable of sharing one another's thoughts and unconsciously replicating one another's fate even at eight miles' remove (360).[14] This being the case, it is perhaps no surprise that Suttree, longing for the spiritual, should seek out and suffer at least three visionary experiences. The first of these unfolds over the course of some forty autumnal days in the Smoky Mountains (283–91), to which Suttree repairs with scant food, no water, and insufficient outerwear. William Spencer argues persuasively that this wilderness sojourn constitutes Suttree's attempt at "the Native American vision quest" ("Seventh" 100), one that sees him "rewarded with visions" (103). Certainly, this near-fatal trip, which has him searching for an alternate self in "this obscure wood" (*S* 287), is both purgative—"The first few dawns half made him nauseous, he'd not seen one dead sober in so long" (283)—and aimed at some more than simply naturalistic discovery. The second comes immediately after his crucial discovery of the ragman's body (423–29), with Suttree seemingly seeking answers to the problem of death in Mother She and her potions crafted "to read the weathers in your heart" (424); in an out-of-body experience (426) and vivid ghosts from his past (427–28), these tinctures deliver on their preternatural promise. The last, longest, and most decisive of these experiences derives from Suttree's climactic battle with typhoid fever (448–61), a phantasmagoria whose images of the dead, second ejection of soul from body, and inspection by an "eye at the end of the glass [that] would be God's" (461) again function, and are received, as forms of revelation of "the world beyond the world" (453). Thus, however much his repudiation of mainstream America alienates him from the Church, and however much his subsequent embrace of Enlightenment ideals might seem to consign him to a strictly materialist cosmos, Suttree remains motivated, not least by the despair such ideals stoke in him, to seek out and credit a more spiritually vital reality.

Significantly, too, these spirit quests prove efficacious. The epiphanies they yield save Suttree both from his own suicidal course and from the destructive forces of progress busy razing McAnally Flats at novel's end. Moreover, the ways in which they do so are rooted in the Catholic tradition in which both author and protagonist were raised. Desperate for reprobate Leonard to honor his father with a final prayer, Suttree confesses, "The only words I know are the Catholic ones" (251), and though he will, as his time in the mountains and at Mother She's indicates, explore non-Christian spirituality, the cosmology, anthropology, and theology that ultimately set him free remain animated by a specifically Catholic sacramentalism. Indeed, Watson argues that Suttree experiences a genuine Eucharist in the Smoky Mountains and, in the midst of his near-death experience of typhoid, offers a valid confession while receiving the Roman Catholic sacrament of Extreme Unction (17, 20).[15] Similarly, Crews asserts that the novel depicts his reception of baptism as well (32). Suttree's response to the seven instituted sacraments of the Roman Catholic Church is certainly ambivalent. For example, while he is described as resenting the presence at his hospital bed of the priest who administers the last rites for him—this "medieval ghost come to usurp his fallen corporeality" (*S* 460)—and feels himself helpless here, "like a rapevictim" (460), he also experiences with this anointing a less clearly malign "cold euphoria" (460). But while Suttree's relationship with clerical authority remains conflicted, Potts is correct in arguing that the outlook of the novel is, in the end, "largely congruent with the Christian theologies of incarnation and sacrament" (107). More particularly, I contend that the Catholic Church's teachings on sacramentalism and communion, more broadly construed, effect Suttree's ransom from the death that his own enlightened revolt against American Enlightenment has prepared for him.

This is demonstrated, first, in McCarthy's treatment of the natural world not simply as a source of beauty and consolation, but as a vital Creation and apt site for encounter with the divine. As Frye notes, McCarthy's fiction, for all its preoccupation with moral and physical ugliness, nonetheless consistently maintains "a focused attention on what makes the world beautiful" ("Histories" 10). Certainly, *Suttree* offers no contradiction of this claim. Though images of violence, decay, and death abound in the novel, its fecund nature persists in modeling rebirth and renewal, even in the most unpropitious of places. Thus, Harrogate, newly arrived in Knoxville, receives only indifference or venom from its residents, but is nonetheless welcomed by natural splendor, by "banks of honeysuckle dusted in ocher" near the river (*S* 91). In his early days in the mountains, Suttree, too, is awestruck by late shows of wildflowers and falls "into silent studies over the delicate loomwork in the moss" (284). Later, he beholds a resplendent night sky whose exquisiteness communicates to him a sense of rightness, goodness, and connection, all rooted in its clear status as Creation: "Halfmoon incandescent in her black galactic keyway, the heavens locked and wheeling. A sole star to the north pale and constant. . . . He closed his eyes and opened them and looked again. He was struck by the fidelity of this earth he inhabited and he bore it sudden love" (354). Though terms like "keyway" and "locked" evoke a mechanism, Suttree's loving, grateful response to the universe's perceived faithfulness suggests something more than the inert matter of Enlightenment science. Rather, his intense emotions here bespeak a sense of covenant with the natural world, a relationship between persons, not between detached subject and dead object. This being the case, the machine analogy works here, I suggest, to point to the cosmos's status as artifact. If, in other words, Suttree can stand in this kind of intimate personal relationship with nature, it is because, as the use of "loomwork" also indicates, it is understood as the handiwork of more than blind chance.

Far from dead, *Suttree*'s nature is represented as animate in the fullest sense. It both wars against the deadening forces of American modernity and opens onto the supernatural. Thus, it produces life even in the most degraded settings. In the midst of that emblem of consumer culture, the junkyard, it drops "hollyhocks . . . and dockweed blooming and begonias . . . sunflowers like some floral enormity in a child's garden" (269), flowers proliferating "everywhere in this lush waste" (93). If the subject- and commodity-centered modernity that Knoxville embodies and Suttree's rebellion replicates pursues barrenness and death, nature counters with seemingly indefeasible regeneration. And this indefeasibility derives from its status as something more than merely natural. Though Jay Beavers insists *Suttree* works "to foreground the utter transcendence of God," his absence from material Creation (97), the novel instead presents a cosmos that is clearly sacramental in the sense adumbrated in chapter 1: that is, understood as Creation and, therefore, good, but also as suffused with the divine and so as a site for encountering God. This latter sacramental role is most plainly detailed during Suttree's vision quest. Here, again, nature first offers itself as a gift of goodness and beauty. Mountain streams provide him waters of such exquisite cold and purity that they "[sing] in his head like wine" (286). As in the night sky above, here too he discovers "a world of incredible loveliness" (286). But surrendering himself to this gift, as well as to fasting and exposure, Suttree encounters a world that does not simply point to, but makes present, a supernatural reality. Soon, he can "hear the footsteps of the dead" and spies ghostly companions, "mauve monks in cobwebbed cowls and sandals hacked from ruined boots clapping along" (286). Nor does the text seek, by recourse to Suttree's physical extremity, wholly to dispel the spiritual significance of such experiences; rather, it insists upon granting them sacramental resonance. Thus when snow falls, it does so as benediction, even as Eucharist—"A delicate host expired on his filthy cuff" (289)—and his quest concludes with a vision both redolent of Catholic imaging of the Holy Spirit and explicitly resistant to strictly naturalistic explication. Almost free from the woods, Suttree comes upon a glade at evening to watch as "a white woodcock rose from the ferns before him and dissolved in smoke" (291). White like the pneumatic dove, this vanished bird is no apparition, leaving behind a "curling bit of down cradled in this green light for the sake of [Suttree's] sanity" (291). It is thus both natural and supernatural, an experienced fusion of matter and grace that Suttree, at least qualifiedly, hails as such, and for which he offers thanks: "Unreal and silent bird albified between the sun and my broken mind godspeed" (291).

Suttree's spiritual search discloses, then, a cosmos that refutes the Enlightenment materialism that elsewhere in the novel casts creatures only as commodities and persons solely as dying flesh. But as Suttree's avian epiphany indicates, it also affords him an alternative to his incipient nihilism in an available approach to God that offers instead, as Crews puts it, a death to self and spiritual rebirth (31). This alternative remains a live option long after his time in the mountains and notwithstanding spiritual backsliding. Thus, after his relationship with Joyce, arguably his most reprehensible immersion in the novel's reifying materialism, has come to an end, Suttree, formed by past sacramental experience, is able to detach from, judge, and amend his own self-seeking. In a crucial passage, he reflects: "I spoke with bitterness about my life and I said that I would take my own part against the slander of oblivion . . . and that I would stand a stone in the very void where all would read my name. Of that vanity I recant all" (S 414). It is worth noting just what this comprehensive recantation involves. Suttree here rejects the idolization of his own uniqueness and independence which has moved him, through much of the novel, to emulate the America he reviles; in doing so, he prepares himself for the saving forms of communion I detail below. But more than this, he repudiates the bitterness in the face of mortality that has helped stoke his attempts at self-sufficiency and the certitude of the individual's extinction that, in its turn, fed such bitterness. Having encountered a Creation sacramentally infused with eternity, Suttree is no longer certain of oblivion's dominion and so no longer desperate to outpace his own mortality through solitary, promethean self-assertion. The world and the flesh, in other words, cease to be infernal traps to be denied by flight or consumerist enactments of proprietary dominance; rather, such isolating and willful denials are themselves the road to nothingness. Once again, this is a realization as congruent with his Catholic upbringing as is his experience of a sacramental Creation. No less an authority than Augustine insists, "it is not by having flesh, which the devil has not, but by living according to himself . . . that man became like the devil" (*City* 444–45).

Suttree's reaffirmation of the flesh and the world empowers a transcendence of his modern project of living according to himself. What Crews treats as his death to self is almost literally achieved, and is sacramentally enacted, in his near succumbing to typhoid fever. Beset by visions of death and judgment, Suttree receives the last rites from a Catholic priest recruited by onetime fellow altar boy J-Bone. First anointed, he is then asked if he wishes to confess, and, after a fashion, he does, declaring simply, "I did it" (*S* 461). This might be read as irreverence still, yet it is not the simple refusal he has offered before (255). Significantly, it is followed by his asking for wine. For all his heroic bibulousness, Suttree has not once before been described as a wine drinker; in fact, the only "wine" he has previously consumed was the heady mountain water. Catechized as he has been, Suttree will know that the last rites follow anointing with confession and then the viaticum, a final administration of the Eucharist, in consecrated host and wine. The priest administering his last rites thus has wine on hand and provides it, and a knowing Suttree receives this sacramental drink with gratitude: "Suttree closed his eyes to savor it" (461). Further, as before in his study of wildflowers, his wonder at the stars, his address to the woodcock, he affirms its goodness and power: "That works" (461). This scene enacts a kind of death for Suttree, one ratified by his later discovery of the doppelganger corpse of a squatter in his houseboat (465), but this death is also significantly a return to an explicitly sacramental communion with Creation and even with God. As he tells the priest, he returns from death armed with visions, not of the void or of God's non-existence, but of His vital dynamism. "He is not a thing. Nothing ever stops moving" (461). This sacramental affirmation of faith in an immanent and not just transcendent spiritual life is, finally, also presented, in no uncertain terms, as rebirth. In the dreams that precede his anointing, Suttree undergoes a very carnal delivery into a new life that embraces more than the reduction of the self and body to dead matter: "He was being voided by an enormous liver-colored cunt . . . into a cold dimension without time and without space where all was motion" (452).

If Suttree is reborn through and for a sacramental reality, though, it is one which orients him not simply toward union with the creator God whose existence transcends time and space, but to communion with his worldly neighbors. For while Cooper has argued that penitence is the novel's chief theme (*Heroes* 65), the sacramental model that most clearly "works" Suttree's salvation is provided by the Eucharist he, analogically at least, accepts from his hospital bed. Nutt maintains that the Eucharist has a place of privilege among the Church's seven sacraments; as that which makes God substantially present and confirms communicants as the Body of Christ, it "stands at the center of the Christian spiritual life and the life of the Church" (192). Operating, as it does, horizontally and vertically, to bring the believer into communion both with God and his fellow worshipers, it provides, on Augustine's account, the template for all sacraments, which are all of them "about the formation or re-formation of genuine human community under and in God" (Ayres and Humphries 165). Similarly, Suttree's transformational encounter, first, with a sacramental Creation and then, through this, with a living God that is no mere object, goes hand in hand with a growing Eucharistic sense of his solidarity with other human beings. While a certain solicitude for his marginalized neighbors has marked McCarthy's protagonist from the start, this is, as Polk notes, somewhat mercurial, with Suttree "alternately engaged with and in retreat from the denizens of McAnally Flats" (20).[16] It is telling, in this regard, that Suttree, less than halfway through the novel, responds to Ab's telling him, "Look out for you own" (*S* 203), by insisting, "I dont have any own" (203). As we have seen, Suttree is, for much of the novel, jealous of his independence and ready to use others as much as serve them. But after his experiences in the mountains and his recantation of heroic individualism in the face of the void, Suttree shows himself capable of knowing his own and standing by none other than Ab Jones himself. When faced with police pursuing a drunken Ab with deadly intent, Suttree announces his solidarity with Knoxville's oppressed by stealing a patrol car and sending it into the river: "It tore across the field and ripped through the willows at the river's edge and went planing out over the water in two great wings of spray" (442).

Such lawless behavior may seem less than Eucharistic, but this is the moment, rivaled only by his rescue of Harrogate from premature burial (276), when Suttree most clearly stands with, and risks himself for, another. The epistle of Barnabas admonished early Christians thus: "you are not to withdraw into yourselves and live in solitude, as though God had already pronounced you holy" (Radice 162). Christian life, from the beginning, was a life lived in common. For much of the novel, whatever alms he might give, Suttree lives apart, in service to his enlightened valorization of autonomy and his flight from death's oblivion. In the end, though, he is called to communion with the lowliest in and under that divine reality to whose awareness he has begun to be reborn. Again, this conversion is most clearly effected during his sickness. Experiencing there a form of death, Suttree dreams of his day of judgment, of his standing to account for consorting with "derelicts, miscreants, pariahs, poltroons . . . murderers, gamblers, bawds, whores, trulls, brigands, topers" (*S* 457). Ultimately, however, his vision is of a God far less estranged from these fallen than the role of magistrate implies. No hanging judge, Suttree's God plays, in Catholic fashion, harrower of hell and redeemer. Thus, Suttree watches as "the archetypal patriarch himself [unlocks] with enormous keys the gates of Hades" (457), so that the oppressed, the outcast, the consumed and thrown away, may carry God himself into the here and now: "simmering sinners with their cloaks smoking carry the Logos itself from the tabernacle and bear it through the streets while the absolute prebarbaric mathematick of the western world howls them down and shrouds their ragged biblical forms" (458).

This is a vision of salvation as radical communion with spirit and with neighbor; the destitute and indigent are here cast as bearers of the Word, communicants with a higher truth rooted in their capacity for solidarity in an unforsaken Creation. Though the "mathematick of the western world" may recoil from their raggedness, a conventional Christian call to communion demands they not be consigned to oblivion, but embraced. Suttree, sharing with his priest what he has learned, articulates just this sacramental lesson: "I know all souls are one and all souls lonely" (459). As Luce glosses this insight, Suttree here "postulates in a new and more inclusive way the value of a universal kinship" (*Reading* 262). The sense of brotherhood this vision of the sacramental presence of the Logos among the lowly instills in Suttree allows him to affirm kinship with all souls. His recognition of the passion of souls in isolation, moreover, imposes a duty of caring communion with these suffering, something Suttree experiences in his recuperation, which has him "sharing his pain with those who lay in their blood by the highwayside or in the floors of glass strewn taverns or manacled in jail" (*S* 464). Thus, though *Suttree* closes with his departure from Knoxville, this does not represent a forsaking of community, but just the reverse. His un-characteristic acceptance of charity from others—from the boy who brings this stranger water in the heat, from the driver who stops for him (*S* 471)—shows him newly prepared for the eschatological banquet Taylor mentions. In leaving Knoxville, he abandons both the novel's embodiment of a degrading American modernity and the self-destructive pursuit of autonomy that has occupied him there, to embrace instead a sacramental belief in a divinity behind and within Creation, and in the necessity of worldly and spiritual communion.

Suttree, then, concludes by proffering a nondogmatic but still markedly Catholic sacramentalism as an answer to the Enlightenment values whose reign the novel treats as deeply problematic. Presenting modern America's pursuit of such ideals as serving only to despoil nature and objectify persons, McCarthy offers readers a protagonist whose true rebellion lies not in his initial repudia-tion of all faith and kinship, but rather in his readiness to engage in explicitly spiritual exploration. Such investigation yields a saving discovery of a nature unshorn of goodness, a cosmos unforsaken by God, and a self as capable and as in need of kinship with others as with Creation and Creator. In this way, Suttree ends up, whatever his conflicted relationship with the Church, siding with a Catholic tradition that empowers the novel's critique of, and his ransom from, the deadening tenets of American Enlightenment. His spiritual journey to rebirth affirms the goodness of a providential Creation, rather than a uni-verse of objects and commodities, the spiritual life and moral value of persons understood as more than just wormbent bodies, and the priority of communion over any individualist imperative to personal sovereignty. This final Eucharistic sensibility insists upon the saving Word's presence in the world and argues that salvation lies open to the world's most despised and even the most fallen. The radical implications of this Christian notion are at the heart of my next chapter, which focuses on the two novels that preceded *Suttree*'s publication. In their tales of human depravity, *Outer Dark* and *Child of God* offer not simply further diagnoses of the dehumanizing fallenness of Enlightenment ideals of self-sufficiency, self-interest, and scientific naturalism, but disturbing accounts of the radical reach of redemption even to the most ostensibly inhuman.

CHAPTER 3

A FIGURE OF WRETCHED ARROGANCE

REIFYING AUTONOMY, DEHUMANIZING SCIENCE, AND THE HOPE OF CONVERSION IN *OUTER DARK* AND *CHILD OF GOD*

For it is not by having flesh, which the devil has not, but by living according to himself—that is, according to man—that man became like the devil.

—AUGUSTINE, *The City of God*

The sinner confesses so that the guilt will be taken from him. He binds himself to this guilt so that he will be released from it.

—ADRIENNE VON SPEYR, *Confession*

If *Suttree* enacts its antihero's rescue from self-destructive autonomy by sacramental forms of communion with neighbor, world, and spirit, then the two Tennessee novels that precede this text foreground that self-subverting sovereignty rather than Suttree's brand of possible salvation.[1] Tales of men estranged from social and kin networks, *Outer Dark* (1968) and *Child of God* (1973) focus on the utter failure of communion and community. Further, these fictions convey the costs of such a miscarriage in terms more gruesome even than those used to detail Suttree's near-suicidal flight from need and obligation. Nash scarcely exaggerates in speaking of *Child of God*'s "nearly all-encompassing depiction of bodies as grotesque" ("Carnival" 88). Both books, in fact, tell stories not simply of dispossession, solitude, and suffering, but of profound deviance. Predicated on incest and suicide, respectively, they proceed to detail acts of desecration, necrophilia, murder, and infanticide, boasting, in Culla Holme and Lester Ballard, two of the most perverse protagonists imaginable. So unremittingly bleak are their careers that Bell has judged *Outer Dark* "as brutally nihilistic as any serious [American] novel written in [its] century" (*Achievement* 34). While this chapter will take issue with this verdict, it points to the undeniable brutishness of these men and their worlds. However, their degeneracy is cast as neither unaccountable nor incurable. Rather, McCarthy presents their crimes both as personal sins and as the dehumanizing result of their commerce with Enlightenment ideals of personal sovereignty, transactional self-interest, and scientific mastery. Indeed, identifying such goods as the substance of sin, these novels, I argue, eschew nihilism by holding to the promise of redemption through repentance.

In line with their shared concern with sin and salvation, both texts offer restagings of the Fall.[2] Neither novel is coy regarding the hamartiological framing of its tale. In its allusion to the Gospel of Matthew, *Outer Dark*'s title invites readers to situate its events in a landscape more eschatological than naturalistic, that outer darkness of exiled sinners that recurs in parables as a place of "weeping and gnashing of teeth" (22:13; 25:30). Similarly, despite Bartlett's dismissal of it as an interpretive red herring (3), the theological question concerning serial killer Lester Ballard that gives *Child of God* its title—"Saxon and Celtic bloods. A child of God much like yourself perhaps" (*CG* 4)—challenges the reader to think of Ballard's descent into madness and murder in other than strictly sociological terms.[3] In fact, the outlook in both novels is expressly lapsarian. Both tales open with their protagonists suffering an eviction into homelessness and want, an expulsion driven by a cruel severing of social or familial ties. Their subsequent wanderings see them traverse a landscape of ramifying criminality and bloodshed, whether their own, as in the case of Ballard, or that unleashed by their desires, as in the case of Holme and the murderous "grim triune" that dogs him over the course of his novel (*OD* 129). In other words, the setting in which they pursue the fulfillment, and flee the consequences, of their dark designs is not just associated with horrors and their own degeneracy; it is clearly identified with the fallen world of Christian teaching and Catholic thought.

As my title suggests, however, this is a domain McCarthy's characters embrace. Even in their abjection, they cling to an arrogant independence that permits only transactional, reifying dealings with others. Alienated from innocence and community, they seek to preserve the autonomy prized by the Enlightenment and enter only into mercantile relations; self-defeatingly, they sell their labor or collect and trade on other human beings as commodities. Yet putting their trust in the pursuit of sovereignty over one's person, environment, and ends, Holme and Ballard are routinely exploited, ever more radically marginalized, and ultimately dehumanized by their forfeiture of more humane relations.[4] Responding to their exile in the world by the solitary adoption of its values, they become ever more mired in monstrous crimes that undo them; in Augustine's terms, by living according to themselves, they become increasingly diabolical. In this way, these early novels make their own contributions to McCarthy's emerging critique of American Enlightenment. By identifying Holme's and Ballard's fallen worlds with the perspectives and norms of American modernity, McCarthy presents Enlightenment ideals as the essence of these novels' endarkened worlds. Most actively in play in the marketplaces wherein these men seek to trade to their advantage and in the forensic or zoological science that turns its objectifying gaze on Ballard, in particular, the Enlightenment is here enmeshed with the inhumanity these criminals both perpetrate and suffer. In fact, allied by McCarthy's Christian framework with original sin, it is exposed as a promise of liberating sovereignty that entails perdition.

Yet if this critique works by emphasizing the wretchedness of McCarthy's protagonists, its use of the Fall allows their tales to communicate something other than despair. Presented in terms of sin, and so of agency, Holme and Ballard are never simply fated; in fact, their novels mount explicit rebuttals of just this proposition. If their monstrosity stems from their culpable choosing of nonrelatedness, the framing story of the Fall affords the prospect of subsequent redemption, even for figures so depraved as they. As in *Suttree*, the dynamic at work in McCarthy's delineating such a prospect is not just Christian, but sacramental and Catholic. But if the sacramental idea key to Suttree's rehabilitation was Eucharistic, for Holme and Ballard it is rather penitential. As Van Zeller writes of Catholic teaching on contrition, "We need to be penitent if we want to be saved" (55). According to the demands of the sacrament of Penance, redemption requires both sorrow, and a frank admission of responsibility, for offenses committed (*Catechism* 404–6). As indicated by this chapter's second epigraph, the penitent must confess himself *as* sin in order to be redeemed *from* it, but can genuinely hope for such release: "The sinner is absolved from his sins. They are gone, are no longer there" (von Speyr 211). My argument is that McCarthy's theological framing of these narratives, while foregrounding his protagonists' guilt and associating it with Enlightenment anthropology, also presents these characters as redeemable, provided they can own and condemn their crimes. Culla Holme is repeatedly given opportunities to do just this and always he flees them, thus unleashing the terrible scourge of his alter ego, the "grim triune." Remarkably, it is Lester Ballard—necrophile and serial killer—who demonstrates the potency of this chance Holme scorns. As Crews suggests, *Child of God* can be read as a parable that concludes with the redemption, through penitence, of the ghoulish Ballard (283). In the end, if the enlightened world that is the landscape of their fallen exile is censured, Holme and Ballard remain something more than the fungible commodities or soulless specimens in which that world traffics; they are, indeed, children of God if they can confess themselves accountable as such.

LEGENDS OF THE FALL

Culla Holme and Lester Ballard spend most of their respective novels as solitaries: Holme roaming the byways of a spectral South, Ballard regressing from lonely squatter to hermitic troglodyte.[5] In both cases, their careers as outcasts are initiated by the decisive loss of an original dwelling place. Less than thirty-five pages into *Outer Dark*, Holme has left the cabin he shares with his sister Rinthy, never to return; *Child of God* begins with Ballard's dispossession by Sevier County. Both novels thus open with forms of eviction. Yet these expulsions are presented as something more than the working of individual restlessness or civic authority; both are framed as forfeitures deriving from crimes against kin, community, even God, and ramifying, post-eviction, in further such offenses. As such, they are restagings of the Fall that cue a reading of the narratives that follow in terms not just of losses, or even of crimes, but of sins that typify not solely McCarthy's protagonists, but the American world into which they are thrown. Thus, upon Rinthy's discovery of his crime against their son, Holme flees and consigns her, too, to a life of ceaseless searching for her lost child. Just as Holme is subsequently both tethered to "a dark stain in which he stood. In which he moved" (*OD* 13) and radically uprooted, going "Nowheres" for the rest of the novel (181), so Rinthy's homelessness betrays a lapsarian finality: "I don't lives nowheres no more," she tells a sympathetic doctor (156). Ballard's tale similarly opens with neighbors come "like a caravan of carnival folk" to celebrate the county's sale of his family home in lieu of unpaid taxes (*CG* 3), an unhoming framed by the narrator's consideration of Ballard's status as child of God and depicted as the start of an ever more heinous criminal career. Both texts, in other words, are at pains to examine characters and settings through a lens not simply theological, but Judeo-Christian.

Yet if both works offer retellings of the Fall, the nature of their respective original sins is neither identical nor straightforward. In the case of Holme, the obvious culprit is the incest with Rinthy that results in the birth of a son (*OD* 14). This is the scandalous sin with which the novel opens, not only by describing Culla coming awake "in the bed he shared with her and the nameless weight in her belly" (5), but by detailing the nightmare from which he wakes, one that has him begging a preacher for healing: "Me, he cried. Can I be cured?" (5). The acute sense of pollution communicated by this dream indicates Culla's sense of the gravity of his act, something from which, like the weight he will not name, he recoils with disgust, but which he views as a blight on him requiring a remedy beyond his power. In waking life, he never offers so clear an expression of his needs as this, but his conduct indicates a recognition of the shame attaching to his deed. Despite Rinthy's pleas, he refuses to fetch a midwife, not because of the cost, but because of the certainty of discovery: "I cain't. She'd tell" (10). Similarly, he warns off a passing tinker with talk of "sickness here" (6), lest the peddler discern his sister's state and infer its cause. If James R. Giles is correct that Culla's son must be understood as a child not just of incest, but of rape (97), then *Outer Dark* opens with a crime having already been committed, but the taboo nature of incest invokes for readers, as for Holme, a sense of something more transgressive than the merely criminal. Such an act, in violating foundational cultural covenants, involves just that sense of taint that "sin" and Holme's nightmare both convey. While Rinthy tells her doctor, "I wasn't ashamed" (*OD* 156), it is clear from the horror with which the tinker hears her confession—"That's a lie. . . . You say it's a lie" (193)—and Culla's own dream that incest is considered by her community a profound betrayal of social norms, and so a fitting candidate for this novel's dispossessing original sin.

Yet the timing of the Holmes' unhoming suggests otherwise. While it is hyperbolic to speak, as do Jonathan and Rick Elmore, of "the sinlessness of

Culla's incest" (121), it is worth noting that first brother, then sister, forsake their cabin only when Rinthy gains an inkling as to a later, more terrible crime: namely, Culla's abandonment of their child to die by exposure or predation. It is her discovery that the grave he claims holds their supposedly stillborn son is a sham that leads to Culla's first flight (*OD* 33), and his lie to her that he has traded their babe away, that prompts Rinthy's desertion of home in favor of her quest to find tinker and child. The novel thus indicates that the original sin that precipitates its Fall is not so much the sin against community and kin that is incest, but the still graver sin of infanticide. This act, it is clear, is far from impulsive. From the moment of its birth, Culla tells Rinthy lies that will facilitate his murderous disposal of their child. "I don't look for it to live," he tells her, and as she sleeps, he takes "it up in his arms and . . . cross[es] to the door and outside" (15). The novel presents this theft and deadly rejection of his child as the sin that effects Culla's expulsion not just from his rustic home, but from a rule-governed natural world. Leaving his son in a stand of cottonwoods, he flees into a stormy night that seems to undo the laws of nature themselves. Stumbling upon a creek, a breathless Culla spits and witnesses an impossibility: "His saliva bloomed palely on the water and wheeled and slid inexplicably upstream" (17). "In disbelief" (17), he repeats this act and has its violation of nature confirmed (17). So unnatural an occurrence underscores the perversity of Holme's act, presenting its lethal refusal of kinship as an upsetting of the natural order. Moreover, this phantasmagoric moment suggests that, with this crime, Holme effects his eviction not simply from his squalid shack, but from properly ordered Creation. This suggestion is only strengthened by the tinker's subsequent confusion over the cessation of Culla's tracks in the clearing in which he left his son, "as if their maker had met in this forest some dark other self in chemistry with whom he had been fused traceless from the earth" (20).

The supernatural elements of this scene point to a specifically theological, in fact, Catholic, reading of Culla's crimes, one which affirms that his truest sin is his denial of his guilt and so his rejection of any hope for forgiveness. While Luce asserts that, "in his unameliorated shame over his incest, [Holme] takes on the blame for the darkness of the universe itself" (*Reading* 79), it is rather the case that he steadfastly refuses to acknowledge, or accept blame for, any of his misdeeds. This, indeed, is the substance of his gravest sin. In abandoning his child to death, Holme seeks to obliterate the sin of incest, so that no one can ever uncover it, proclaim it, or task him with it. This disowning of his fault, a perfect inversion of von Speyr's confessional dynamic, is what leads to the damning sin against his son. While Rinthy is eager to claim her child—"I just want what's mine," she tells the tinker (*OD* 186)—Culla refuses, for to do so would mean owning the deed that child literally embodies. This later transgression is graver than the first but is presented as deriving from a still more grievous spiritual offense. As Ann Fisher-Wirth observes, the novel's opening nightmare discloses not just Culla's shame, but his despair of forgiveness (129). Despite the preacher's assurances, no healing dawn arrives. Instead, a mob of the afflicted turns on Holme: "he tried to hide among them but they knew him even in that pit of hopeless dark" (*OD* 6). This dream hints that Culla's characteristic acts of flight and denial, murderously wedded in his abandonment of his son, derive from the conviction that he cannot be healed. His course is thus that of despair, the sin Catholic tradition identifies as "the blasphemy against the Holy Ghost [that] shall not be forgiven" (Matthew 12:31).[6] *Outer Dark* twice ties Holme's fallen state to this sin. First, in his peregrinations, he collapses in another forest, kneeling "like something broken or penitent among the corrugate columns. A dove called softly and ceased" (90). Holme here fails to repent, but his need to do so is indicated, as is the link between his failure and the Holy Spirit, whose emblem, the dove, is stilled by his mute presence. In more explicitly Catholic idiom, the Spirit is invoked in Culla's disposal of his son. Circling confusedly in the dark, Holme finds himself returned to the abandoned child. Granted an opportunity to repent and undo his crime, he seeks only to blot out a sin he will not own or seek forgiveness for: "he lay there gibbering . . . his hands putting back the night like some witless paraclete beleaguered with all limbo's clamor" (18). His refusal is here cast as a parody of the Spirit's sapience and locates the source of Holme's crimes in that blasphemy which is despair.

Thus, the outer dark in which Culla incurably wanders is presented in terms of election, his refusal of the possibility of mercy, and so echoes Irenaeus's account of the fate of the damned: "those who fly from the eternal light of God, which contains in itself all good things, are themselves the cause to themselves of their inhabiting eternal darkness" (421). Cave-dwelling killer Lester Ballard's end is still darker than Holme's, but his text complicates the extent to which he himself is cause of his Fall. As Cant notes, despite the vileness of his crimes, Ballard never wholly alienates readerly sympathy (89).[7] One reason for this is

that his expulsion seems less the fruit of his sins than the work of those responsible for providing for him. Ballard has, in a sense, been ousted from home long
before the county auctions off his land. If the sin that dispossesses Holme is
not the incest his novel refrains from narrating, but the attempted infanticide it
does describe, in Ballard's case the most consequential transgression may have
been committed long before *Child of God* opens. Moreover, it is one he suffers,
not one he commits. The novel informs us that Ballard, only "nine or ten year
old at the time" (*CG* 21), has been left orphaned by his father's suicide. Thus,
Ballard is himself the abandoned child of this version of the Fall. Having been
disowned even prior to this desertion—"The mother had run off, I don't know
where to nor who with" (21)—he is marked for life by this bloody and final
paternal rejection. Finding his father hanged, watching as neighbors cut him
down like "meat" (21), Ballard has been barred by the sins of his parents from
any true home or hope for a normal life: "They say he never was right after his
daddy killed hisself" (21). That this original trauma, fruit of the father's sin, still
resonates in Ballard's final dispossession is further indicated by the fact that, on
the day his family's land is sold, the rope with which the father killed himself
still hangs from the barn loft (4).

This delinquency on the part of his parents is only compounded by the ostracism enacted by the county, which renders Ballard not simply homeless, but
bereft of community. The county takes no more heed of Ballard's welfare than
have mother and father, and not content to sell off his land, meets his protests
with violence. He is subdued by a blow to the head with the broadside of an axe,
an act whose legacy testifies to the consequence of this eviction. "Lester Ballard
never could hold his head right after that" (9), and this lasting impairment signals the enduring penury this dispossession inflicts, leaving Ballard homeless
and resourceless in the Appalachian wilds. Yet, though unhoused, he is not
unregarded. Excised from their community by the indifference of his neighbors,
he remains nonetheless policed by them. Before his offenses have graduated
beyond voyeurism, he is arrested, falsely accused of rape by a woman he finds
unconscious at the Frog Mountain turnaround (51). Even after he has become
a necrophile, an oblivious county disowns him for less taboo crimes. Brought
in for questioning on the burning of the derelict cabin he has been occupying,
Ballard is told "you are either going to have to find some other way to live or

some other place . . . to do it" (123). Again, his expulsion is actively sought by a community that refuses him membership or aid, such that his ultimate fate as itinerant criminal seems the work of other hands, other sins, than his own. Ballard's presentation as victim of others' withheld charity is clearest in his rejection by Sevier County Christians. Seeking communion, Ballard arrives late for services at Six-mile Church, but though himself offering, "with his hat in his hand" (31), gestures of respect, none is extended to him, as he enters unhailed, even unrebuked. This lack of welcome derives not from an unawareness of his presence, but from the congregation's conscious refusal to admit him to their ranks: "Ballard had a cold and snuffled loudly through the service but nobody expected he would stop if God himself looked back askance so no one looked" (32). Ballard's ultimate state as depraved outcast here seems the result less of his deeds than of the sins of kin and community.[8]

However, though his fall into darkness is more clearly initiated by the sins of others than is Holme's, the novel never presents him as blameless. Even before his decline from squatter to necrophile to murderer has commenced, the text is at some pains to mitigate too sympathetic an impression of Lester. Thus, while he is driven from his first home and hunted from later lodgings by a hostile community, he is also presented as mirroring its traits and so participating in his Fall. Defined from the first by "a constrained truculence" (4), Ballard is ever belligerent. He rushes out to meet the auction with a greater readiness for conflict than for communion, with a greater appetite for violence against his neighbor than the crowd itself exhibits. He confronts them "holding a rifle" and spewing obscenities (7), inviting the blow that will maim him. He is consistently characterized by fury and aggression, both before this expulsion—as in his childhood bullying of a younger boy (17–18)—and afterward, as in the violence he visits upon a dog that invades his squat one night: "Ballard flailed blindly at it with his fist, great drumlike thumps that echoed in the near empty room" (24). Though he repeatedly attempts to forge a community for himself, Ballard is more commonly scornful of amicable intercourse, meeting others with execrations, cursing and spitting at passing cars (41). This emphasis on Ballard's cursing is significant. Just as his having to clear the abandoned cabin in which, post-eviction, he takes shelter of its resident "blacksnake" evokes a forfeit Eden (16), so do Ballard's many blasphemies—the litany of "goddamns" with which he peppers the auction scene (7), his "muffled curses at the bullbriers and blackberries" as he moves into his squat (14)—establish his repudiation of God as well as man, his own status as sinner, and not just victim.

Indeed, the lapsarian nature of these characters' respective evictions is indicated not only by the fact that their subsequent exiles situate them in a world of ever-ramifying sin, but also by their texts' insistence on their implication in this further corruption. While both are exposed to ever-more-hostile environments, they are presented not as victims, but substantially as creators of these grim milieus, precisely as their narratives take care to trace their assent to ever-graver depravity. This is amply evident in the steady escalation of Ballard's crimes after his expulsion. Lester opens the novel characterized by an eagerness for conflict that alienates him from his community, but that violence, in defense of what he views as his property, is illegal without being beyond the pale. Once ousted from his family's lands, however, Ballard swiftly embarks on a career of evermore-taboo offenses. First, he plays Peeping Tom, spying on, and masturbating to, backseat lovers on Frog Mountain. This habituated sexual deviancy has him haunt this spot in search of gratification (see 41, 85). In the course of these visits, Ballard's scopophilia becomes ominously tied to his love of trophies. Just as he persists at a fairground shooting gallery until he is barred, emerging the proud owner of two "ponderous mohair teddybear[s]" and a stuffed tiger (64), so his mountain prowling soon has him claiming prizes from women he does more than simply spy on. Finding a nearly naked woman unconscious one morning, Ballard rouses her and responds to her violent reaction not just by slapping her, but by making off with the last of her clothing: "Ballard seized a fistful of the wispy rayon and snatched it" (43). In short order, then, he moves from belligerence through voyeurism to assault and theft, and the linking of violence and fetishization to sexual desire points to more aberrant acts to come in his descent into necrophilia and murderous harvesting of sexual objects.

The novel features characters who understand this arc as determined, something beyond Ballard's personal, or the local community's collective, responsibility. This is the view of the aptly named Fate, "high sheriff of Sevier County" (48). Heading out to bring Ballard in for questioning, Fate tells the story of Bill Parsons's failed hunting dog, Suzie: "I said: Suzie was sick yesterday. Suzie has always been sick. Suzie will always be sick. Suzie is a sick dog" (49). As Suzie is a born incurable, so Ballard, for Fate, is a natural deviant, whose criminality can be predicted—"I guess murder is next on the list ain't it?" (56)—and punished, but never prevented or rehabilitated.[9] Some critics have agreed, with Luce suggesting Ballard's fate is set by parental neglect and communal ostracism ("Ballard" 101) and Cant viewing him as "driven by the irresistible appetite of sexuality" (91). McCarthy's text, however, suggests otherwise, presenting Ballard's degeneration in terms of morally meaningful decisions. That Ballard remains a figure capable of moral deliberation and restraint, and so of perversity and sin, is indicated both early and late. New to his role as hungry itinerant, Ballard raises his rifle to a bluebird, but "something of an old foreboding [makes] him hold" (*CG* 25). Later, driven by homesick rage to spy on the man who bought his land, Ballard has Greer in his sights, but again refrains from shooting: "His finger filled the cold curve of the trigger. Bang, he said" (109). That Ballard remains a moral agent is clearest in the most decisive of his crimes, the commencement of his necrophilia. Coming across lovers asphyxiated in their backseat, Ballard ends up claiming the ultimate sexual trophy, carrying off the woman's body as prize (91). But this deepening of his deviance is detailed as a series of smaller decisions that emphasize Ballard's agency. Noting the dead couple, Ballard first walks on, before recalling the helplessness of the dead—"A pair of eyes staring with lidless fixity" (86)—and returning to exploit it, "a crazed gymnast laboring over a cold corpse" (88). The text underscores this act's status as decision by rehearsing the walk-away/return dynamic fully four more times. Ballard again departs before returning to reclaim incriminating evidence left at the scene (89), then to rifle a wallet, purse, and glove compartment (89–90), and next, to sit briefly listening to the car radio (90). He is almost "at the foot of the mountain" (91), and has had several chances to walk away, when he finally decides to claim the corpse and affirm his identity as necrophile.

Ballard's criminality ultimately extends, with his shooting of Ralph's daughter (118–19), to the murderous collection of sex objects, but these later crimes are framed by an initial presentation of him as agent. However mad and monstrous the world he occupies after his eviction, then, it remains one parsable in terms of those ideas of sin and its dominion supplied by the narrative of the Fall to which *Child of God* initially alludes. While the evil that eddies around Holme may seem largely the work of other hands, the same title of fallen sinner applies to him. As noted, his attempted infanticide has seemingly cosmic ramifications, but the results of his self-exile are also revealed in his own person. If the loss of his home condemns him not simply to sleep rough at the roadside, but to wake "to such darkness he did not trust his balance" (*OD* 37), this darkness in which he travels is clearly shown to reflect a malignant inner murk. This is established, for example, in a passage that externalizes as shadow Culla's rage at a squire who exploits his labor: "Their shadows canted upon the whitewashed brick of the kitchen shed in a pantomime of static violence in which the squire reeled backward and [Holme] leaned upon him in headlong assault" (47). If such rancor finds no open expression against this target, it is nonetheless communicated, not simply in narratorial touches like this, but in the evicted Holme's persistence in petty sinfulness; if he forgoes assaulting the squire, he does make off with his fine boots (49). But his crimes extend beyond such relative misdemeanors. Later, he will watch idly as swineherd Vernon, "borne on like some old gospel recreant" (218), is swept to his death by stampeding hogs. The ramification of his sin culminates in his final participation in the death of his son. Culla himself hands his child over, "like a dressed rabbit" (235), to be murdered by the novel's sinister trio: "Holme saw the blade wink in the light like a long cat's eye slant and malevolent and a dark smile erupted on the child's throat" (236).

That the trio consummate Holme's original murderous intent is only fitting, as it is they who perpetrate most of the tale's evil, making of the outer dark through which Holme wanders that fallen domain adumbrated by the novel's opening pages. Introduced as moving with "*implacability*" (3), the trio first seem an embodiment of motiveless malevolence. On Giles's account, they "kill at random and for no comprehensible reason" (103). Certainly, they seem to relish unleashing mayhem and bloodshed wherever they go. Thus, unsatisfied with having themselves left "*old man Salter . . . Dead. Stobbed and murdered*" (*OD* 95), they turn next to rousing a mob to hunt down likely suspects, their bearded leader exhorting others to "*findin the man that done it*" (95). The fruit of his labors is the summary execution of two men, strangers to him, as to the lynching crowd: "*In the cool and smoking dawn there hung from a blackhaw tree . . . the bodies of two itinerant millhands*" (95). This scene follows swiftly on the heels of another that establishes the dark troika's delight in violating taboo and spreading panic. The bearded one addresses his vigilantes wearing "*a shapeless and dusty suit of black linen that was small on him*" (95), for the trio have just come from scandalizing the town of Cheatham, where they have desecrated the churchyard, disinterred "them old dead people" (86), and left a corpse wearing a "white shirt and a necktie but no coat or trousers" (88).

Yet the profanations of the triune are not so gratuitous as they seem.[10] While they are, in Evenson's words, "palpable embodiments of evil" ("Uses" 58), their malice is neither motiveless nor freestanding; rather, it is intimately linked to the crimes of Culla Holme. Their ghoulish work in Cheatham immediately precedes Holme's arrival there and serves to make him, as outsider, target for just that mob justice we see them foment elsewhere. On account of their deeds, he must flee for his life (*OD* 88). Moreover, relentlessly tracking Culla, they bring ruin to virtually everyone he meets. It is they, "*armed with crude agrarian weapons*" stolen from his own barn (35), who put an end to the reviled squire: "*the next one came up . . . swung the brush-hook . . . and took him in the small of the back severing his spine*" (51). Culla having taken his leave of an old snake trapper who treats him to water, the trio descend and leave him "*disemboweled*" at his door (129). Similarly, Clark, who, in his "filthy white suit" (139), toys with Holme before setting him to work as gravedigger, ends up, at the trio's hands, adorning that same hanging tree, "from which hung the bodies of three men. One was dressed in a dirty white suit" (146). These murderers not only dog Holme, then; they coldbloodedly leave carnage in his wake. Indeed, by killing those against whom Holme harbors ill will, they seem to fulfill his own wishes, realizing murderous acts he imagines but does not execute.[11] This is clearest in their murder of his child; as Bell notes, this only completes the deed Holme intended but left undone in his abandonment of his son (*Achievement* 36). Thus, the trio express the indelibility of Holme's original sin and the encompassing nature of his Fall. Emerging on the novel's first page, while Holme dreams his despair and conceives infanticide, they pursue him until that child is, with his consent, their cannibalized victim. As Fisher-Wirth notes, then, "the more he runs, the more his transgression pursues him" (130). What's more, in their decidedly diabolical mien—Holme sees their leader at a campfire seeming "to be seated in the fire itself, cradling the flames to his body as if there were something there beyond all warming" (179)—they underline the moral and theological dimensions of Holme's ruin.[12] Their career not only mirrors his; by rendering the world a dark reflection of his soul, they reveal that soul's fallenness and sin's power to ramify in corruption.

DARKNESS OF ENLIGHTENMENT

But such darkness and sin, in their being externalized, make of these narratives something more than theological parables. Indeed, as the fallenness of Holme and Ballard taints their worlds, it comes also to be associated with hallmarks of American modernity. In this way, both these texts cast America's Enlightenment values as themselves fallen, as, in fact, the very substance of these characters' lapsarian condition. The debased world into which they are, by sin, ejected is one defined by Enlightenment ideals. This is demonstrated by the fact that Holme and Ballard both live out their post-exilic descent into further depravity as, in part at least, a zealous pursuit of such quintessentially modern and American goods as personal autonomy, self-interested, transactional relations, and scientific materialism. While Hawkins argues that violence, in *Outer Dark*, "can halt modernization, creating space for something else" (116), both Culla and Lester serve to indicate the intimate connection between their own violent careers and the modern norms of the societies from which they are ostensibly barred. Certainly, both men are pronounced individualists, jealously guarding their independence and shying away from debts or duties that might come from community membership or the acceptance of gift or charity.

This is plainly the case with Holme, who, even before his expulsion, has clearly sought to stand alone and live beholden to none. Thus it is that Rinthy can say, in response to his admonition that she admit no strangers in his absence, "They ain't a soul in this world but what is a stranger to me" (*OD* 29). Indeed, Holme's denial of relationship with the most intimate others is amply demonstrated by the simple fact that he has, in the tinker's words, "thowed away" his own child (22). This refusal of kinship and his steadfast defense of his self-sufficiency are maintained throughout his subsequent travels. While he at times claims that he wanders the roads in search of his sister (81, 126), what he above all seeks to maintain is his freedom to come and go, to govern himself as he pleases. For example, he seconds the snake collector's claim that "kin ain't nothin but trouble noway" (126), and later avers "I ain't got sign one of kin on this earth" (207). This assertion he bloodily confirms, when he declares of his soon to be slaughtered son, "It ain't nothin to me" (233). But this refusal of relatedness extends beyond this renunciation of blood ties. For Holme, the human world is largely null and can assert no legitimate claim on him. Thus, he tells the murderous trio, "You ain't nothin to me" (234), and abjures even the violation of his autonomy that others' welcome or kindness might entail; as he tells a teamster from whom he seeks paying work, "I ain't lookin for nobody to be sorry for me" (136). Similarly, the even more abject Lester Ballard repeatedly scorns the company or regard of others. Outcast, starving, homeless, he seeks neither charity nor paying work, but only angrily proclaims his independence. "A man much for himself" (*CG* 41), Ballard is that "figure of wretched arrogance" of my title (41), clinging to his misery, so long as his sovereignty is uncompromised. Cant is right, then, to dub him a parodic version of that American ideal, the self-reliant frontiersman (95), for Ballard, just as much as Holme, both jealously guards his solitary liberty and, by so doing, indicates how even his most depraved acts tread on firmly established American ground.

The modern cast of this duo's crimes is further established by their embrace of only one form of human interaction: that suitable to buyers and sellers. Abjuring kin and community, they have recourse only to those transactional relations recommended by Enlightenment thought to the sovereign, self-seeking subject. Certainly, Holme's travels center on his dealings in the marketplace. The first place he visits after deserting shack and sister is the general store, counting out his coins for a "dime's worth of cheese and crackers" (*OD* 38). But Holme is more typically a seller than a buyer, attempting to secure his subsistence by hiring himself out as a casual laborer. Before making his purchase, then, he chats up a wagoner, asking if he needs help unloading. As becomes clear, this is not an offer of help but a request for paid work. Rebuffed, Holme makes his intentions plain: "Well, you don't know where a man might find work hereabouts do ye?" (40). Following the wagoner's suggestions takes Holme to his first contract, cutting up firewood for a local squire who "look[s] him over with those hard little eyes as he would anything for sale" (42). The squire offers, and Holme accepts, a single meal in exchange for a day's hard labor. In addition to establishing the pattern of selling himself cheaply, this scene underscores how Holme's expulsion and subsequent defense of his independence surrender him to a world in which human relations are always provisional, mercantile, and commodifying. Looking to others only as temporary sources of income, Holme himself becomes only a commodity to be purchased and exploited. This is, then, that domain of transactionalism, governed solely by the best interests of each atomistic party, detailed in chapter 1. Nor does it obtain only in this early contract. In Cheatham, too, Holme gravitates first to the town store, before contracting himself out to paint a barn roof in the summer's heat for a dollar a day and the privilege of sleeping under that same roof (91). He subsequently accepts a commission as gravedigger, again for the princely sum of one dollar (144). Holme thus continually petitions others not for charity, but for piecemeal work that will not establish any enduring tie to others. Seeking to preserve his autonomy, he presents himself as a good for sale so as to serve his own ability to be a purchaser of such goods.

If Holme's itinerant existence is lapsarian, then, his experience of fallenness is identified with the commodifying atomism of the market. Indeed, both this marketplace and the essentially Enlightenment anthropology that undergirds it are assimilated to the darkness in which the sinful Culla and the malignant trio move. Thus, at the Cheatham general store he finds a space as endarkened as his own inner landscape: "Shadows washed across the yellow light in the storewindows, spilled through over the merchandise" (85). *Child of God's* Lester Ballard likewise seeks to be a man sufficient to himself by defining his exile in terms of similarly suspect market relations, yet if Culla is typically a poor seller, Ballard more frequently plays the part of buyer. For while both Lancaster (146) and Gamblin (33) argue that even his murders derive from his longing to establish human community in the face of his rejection by Sevier County,[13] it is also the case that Ballard's overtures are most commonly matters of exchange and tend, in the most literal way, to the objectification of others as goods for his enjoyment. It is true that the ostracized Ballard does seek out the company of others; not long after the auction itself, he visits the home of Fred Kirby. However, what draws him is the hope less of companionship than of a taste of this bootlegger's wares; Ballard is hoping to buy a jar on credit, if he can, or to trade for one, if he can't (*OD* 10–11). Similarly, his other two named acquaintances—Reubel and Ralph—are valued solely for the prospect Ballard cherishes of trading for their daughters' sexual favors. Dumpkeeper Reubel's home beckons due to a daughter who "used to sit with her legs propped so that you could see her drawers" (28). But Ballard's sexual designs extend beyond free voyeuristic pleasures; the dump is a place where sexualized bodies are to be bargained and paid for. When Ballard asks a daughter to show him her breasts, she replies, "Gimme a quarter," before teasingly telling another man, "He's done looked a halfdollar's worth now" (29). Later, Ballard seeks to ingratiate himself to Ralph's daughter with a gift of a still-living bluebird he has captured (77), thus rendering one living thing a commodity in hopes of securing for himself access to commodified sex.

Indeed, Ballard's imperviousness to nonmercantile considerations of value and relationship is strikingly communicated in his visit to the local blacksmith. Having found a "rusty axehead" (70), Ballard presents himself again as buyer, hoping to hire the smith to give him a usable axe. "I allowed I'd just get it sharpened for a quarter or something" (71), Lester says, in response to the tradesman's telling him the axe could be fully restored and fitted to a handle for two dollars. The smith, though himself a shopkeeper, is interested in the axe as something more than the cheapest possible tool, and in Ballard as something more than a bill of sale. Instead of seeking just to sell his skills at a premium, the blacksmith offers Ballard a free lesson in how to do for himself that for which he must now pay another. Guiding him through the process of tempering, reshaping, and honing the blade, teaching him to watch for the color that indicates the steel is ready to come off the fire, the smith graciously provides Ballard with more than a two-dollar axe; his own expertise, his regard for Ballard as something more than a customer, are offered as gift. "Reckon you could do it now from watchin?" (74), he asks, clearly hoping Lester will take away not just a purchase, but a valuable skill. Treating Ballard as a person, in other words, the smith disturbs the strictly economic dynamic that governs Ballard's other interactions and seeks to forge a more human relationship with him. Yet such intercourse is beyond the fallen Ballard's ken or ambition, as he replies, "Do what" (74), revealing his lack of interest in nonreifying relations.

Thus, in his pursuit of human relations focused solely on the cheap procurement of consumer goods, Lester is, as Stilley argues, "both reflective and symptomatic of an American culture of materialism" (98). That this reflection serves to indict the values that underlie that culture is indicated by the extent to which Ballard's profound aberrance involves his wholesale embrace of consumerist thinking, his literal reduction of human interaction to the acquisition and enjoyment of mere things.[14] In this regard, it is important to note the extent to which his crimes are money-making ventures, aimed at empowering him as a consumer. During the pivotal scene that sees him turn necrophile, Ballard returns to the car to clean out the dead man's wallet and claim his undrunk whiskey before he thinks to carry off the dead woman's body (CG 90). It is this first theft that allows him next day to play boyfriend, buying his trophy lingerie and a new dress (97–99). Likewise, Lester's later victims serve as emporia or low-cost wholesalers. When he visits another store "wearing black lowcut shoes that were longer than he should have needed" (129), the reader is alerted that Ballard is claiming more than sex from those he kills. This scene underlines the point, as Ballard tries to undersell the store's stock of wristwatches with three he has acquired in the commission of his crimes (129–32). But his necrophilia itself is, as Luce argues ("Cave" 178), a grotesque literalization of the materialist ethos of the world into which he has fallen, one that involves a deadly confusion of person and commodity. First, Ballard treats the corpse as a living beloved. Thus it is that, in his violation of the found dead girl, he "pour[s] into that waxen ear everything he'd ever thought of saying to a woman" (88); hence his careful dressing of the body for a ghoulish date and whispering, "You been wantin it" (103). In order to continue enjoying this illusion, however, Ballard must soon become a killer; in order to go on pretending the corpse is a living lover, he must begin making dead possessions of living women. Certainly, he treats his first "conquest," much as the first squire treats Culla, as a possible purchase to be scrutinized for quality: "He took off all her clothes and looked at her, inspecting her body carefully, as if he would see how she were made" (91–92). Subsequent lover-trophies—such as Ralph's daughter (118) or the girl in the pickup truck (151)—will need to be bloodily harvested so that they can become, through their reduction to the status of objects, eligible for the only form of human interaction his fallen world seems to afford.

In so allying Ballard's monstrous crimes to the norms of the marketplace, McCarthy crafts not simply a parable of his unique fall, but as Hawkins holds, a critique of modernity itself (120). Given the similarly taboo-breaking nature of Holme's pursuit of market relations, the same can be said of *Outer Dark*. Yet if these novels use Christian subtexts to indict American society, this indictment is intensified by the way Holme's and Ballard's embrace of Enlightenment ideals of autonomy and material advancement works to their disadvantage. Gary Ciuba asserts that Lester's crimes are in fact empowering: "Just as [his] murders make him lord of the living, his sexual violations make him master of the dead" (80). Yet both Ballard and Holme are repeated losers in their pursuit of agency through reifying market relations. Such is certainly the case with Culla. His preferring the itinerant sale of his own labor over residence, community, or charity not only proves consistently profitless, but continually draws others' suspicion, proclaiming the guilt he has taken to the roads to outpace. First, Culla's homelessness, his status as solitary stranger, disadvantages him in his search for work and leads always to his selling himself at a bargain. His first job sees him working half a day chopping deadwood in return for a single meal. The squire himself marvels that Holme rates himself so cheaply: "Still ain't said nothing about breakfast. Let alone a place to sleep. Not even to mention money" (*OD* 46). When he is hired to paint the barn roof, he negotiates payment, but so far as a place to sleep goes, he is offered only space with the livestock: "You can stay in the barn if ye ain't proud" (91). Nor, indeed, does he ever collect. Both in this case and in his stint as gravedigger, Culla does the work unpaid: in the first instance, as he must run for his life from the Cheatham mob (92), in the second, as the triune's murder of Clark deprives him of his employer (145–46).

This pursuit by the good folks of Cheatham is instructive. As noted, Holme clings to his independence and, in service to this quintessential American ideal, sets down roots in no town and fiercely rebuffs any relationship beyond the strictly contractual. Yet this independence not only facilitates the ramifying evil of the triune and the repeated diminishment of his economic options; more than this, it repeatedly renders him a suspect and scapegoat. This is evident from his first job. Baffled that Holme should ask so little for his work, the squire rightly concludes him guilty of some crime: "What is it you've done. Where are runnin from?" (46). Likewise, arrived in Cheatham on the day desecrated graves are discovered, Holme is an immediate object of suspicion; once he runs, he is convicted by the crowd that chases him. Similarly, his lack of a community to vouch for him exposes him to mortal threat in his encounter with the hog drovers. Having watched from the sidelines the stampede that claims young Vernon, Culla the stranger is soon identified as cause of this tragedy: "That's all right about him settin on some rock, who was it got them hogs started in the first place?" (220). Soon the focus of talk of hanging (221–25), Holme finds himself once again running for his life. Indeed, so complete a failure is his flight from his original sin and toward marketplace self-sufficiency that he ends up yearning for the servitude of the convicted man. Taken before a second squire for the itinerant's crime of squatting, Holme is unable to pay the five-dollar fine and so must work ten days to earn his liberty. While the value of his (unpaid) labor has fallen to fifty cents per day, the fact that this sentence includes room and board moves Holme to petition for its extension: "I'll stay on just for board if you can use me" (208).

Ballard's efforts to be a "man much for himself" achieve comparably ruinous results. While his pursuit of people as commodities succeeds in making him the subterranean proprietor of "seven bodies" dead at his hand (*CG* 196), his career in a human world reduced to buying and selling sees him perpetually play the loser. From his early visit with Kirby, Ballard is a failed buyer. Penniless, he is denied credit, and though willing to engage in an unequal trade, Ballard comes away empty-handed as the bootlegger cannot find his stock (11–12). When he escalates to trading living things for human flesh, offering the captured bluebird to impress Ralph's daughter, the result is more gruesome failure. Made gift to the house's disabled son, the bird repulses the girl as it becomes quite literally a consumer good: "He's done chewed its legs off, the girl said" (79). Ballard's purchasing failures extend to more licit and public markets, as well. In Fox's store, he tries to charge $5.10 worth of perishable goods, only to be told that, with his tab already at $34.19, his credit is exhausted. When Ballard offers to pay $4.19, Fox makes plain the hopelessness of his standing in the market; if it's taken Lester his twenty-seven years to earn that much, Fox calculates, "it's goin to take a hundred and ninety-four years to pay out" the outstanding sum (126). Yet if his attempts at being the shrewd consumer produce only debt, his efforts as salesman prove no more profitable. Arrived at a store that charges eight dollars each for its wristwatches, Ballard seeks to undercut the competition by selling the three his killings have yielded for five apiece. Yet clearly a trader in suspect goods—"I'll give two and won't ast where ye got it," says one potential buyer (131)—Lester is forced not only to sell his entire stock for what the store gets for a single timepiece, but also to witness his buyer immediately sell the watches at a dearer price (132).

Yet Ballard's faith in the empowering promise of the market leads him not only to losses as buyer and seller, but as subject. If the proud Holme who shares that faith ends up craving indenture, Ballard's career as would-be trader and consumer leads to the near dissolution of his identity altogether. Arrogant and independent he may work at being, but only at the cost of an increasingly forfeit humanity. This loss is perhaps first demonstrated in an encounter with the man who has dispossessed him, John Greer. Running into him on the road, Ballard responds to Greer's calling him by name with, "No, I ain't him" (114). Such self-estrangement is less deliberate in a subsequent moment of nonrecognition. Bending to a pool to drink, Ballard, an anti-Narcissus, seems baffled by the reflection he sees: "He halfway put his hand to the water as if he would touch the face that watched there" (127). As his descent into his fallen world of radical self-reliance and deadly commodification deepens, Ballard, far from empowered, is fundamentally unmade, emerging as a ghastly pastiche of his crimes and victims, cloaked not simply in their clothing but in their objectified flesh. Late in the text, he seems little more than a mannequin for the accessories of the dead: "He'd long been wearing the underclothes of his female victims but now he took to appearing in their outerwear as well" (140). And when Ballard is shot, Greer discovers what he took to be a wig on Ballard's head is instead "fashioned whole from a dried human scalp" (173).

Ballard's fallen world is thus one not just of his deepening criminality, but of his dehumanization by the objectifying ethos to which he and his culture adhere. It is with some justice, then, that Alexandra Blair claims that the novel depicts Lester and his neighbors "as if they were filthy creatures or mere animate matter" (92). Ballard's reduction to matter is abetted by his participation not just in the reifying world of the market, but in the materialist discourse of Enlightenment science. For while Cant is, I think, mistaken in deeming *Child of God* McCarthy's least metaphysical, most naturalistic text (89), it is nonetheless true that the novel enacts the diminishment of its main character by repeatedly presenting him through forensic and zoological lenses. From the start, by its very title, the book presents Ballard and his outrages as an etiological puzzle. What accounts for the monster he becomes? If he is, indeed, a child of God, if he is the reader's brother, then how to square this status with the evil he commits? Part I of the novel has Ballard's neighbors seek to sidestep the latter question by proffering answers to the former, attempting explanations for Ballard's deeds that place him beyond the pale of kinship, in the domain of natural objects and scientific determinism. Thus, as noted, his crimes are variously attributed to sufficient physical causes (see note 9). Finally, these accounts conclude that his crimes are a necessary effect of breeding, the Ballards having always been prone to violence. The good people of Sevier point to the fate of a grand-uncle, executed as an outlaw in neighboring Mississippi: "Goes to show it ain't just the place. He'd of been hanged no matter where he lived" (*CG* 81). What this community lore underlines, then, is how the forensic deployment of the Enlightenment's materialist cosmology works to otherize Lester, indicating how the modernity to which his fall delivers him works to facilitate his dehumanization.

Such erasure of his humanity is only exacerbated by his frequent treatment as strictly an anatomical or zoological object. If, for Descartes, the causation that reigns in the physical universe is such that the human body must be understood "as a machine created by the hand of God" (41), then the customary reduction of Ballard to bodily functions helps, again, to rob him of human dignity and personal identity. As Cooper notes, "Throughout the novel, the narrator emphasizes all things bizarre, scatological, and deformed" ("Tennessee" 46). This degrading emphasis is evident from the outset. Lester is introduced having just relieved himself outdoors, buttoning his jeans after having "made in the dark humus a darker pool" (*CG* 4). Once housed in Waldrop's abandoned cabin, Ballard again establishes his residency in the most undomesticated way: "he trod a clearing in the clumps of jimson and nightshade and squatted and shat" (13). Likewise, the open-air masturbation that caps his mountainside voyeurism offers some support at least to Bell's contention that Ballard "is ruled at every turn . . . by unspeakable appetite" and so is much more an expression of brute instinct than a morally reasoning child of God (*Achievement* 61). This portrait is further developed in the text's insistent reduction of Lester and others to the status of animals. When the onanistic Ballard, discovered, takes flight, he is described as "a misplaced and loveless simian shape scuttling across the turnaround" (*CG* 20). The detached narrator's translation of Ballard the man into a lesser primate becomes, in fact, something of a leitmotif. Thus, when he attempts in his cave to warm his near-frozen feet, he lets loose with moans "that [echo] from the walls of the grotto like the mutterings of a band of sympathetic apes" (159). Later, leading a group of vigilantes through his subterranean realm, Ballard crawls forward, "his bare toes gripping the rocks like an ape" (184). Yet this zoological perspective on the man, one that will see him finally "found dead in the floor of his cage" at the state hospital (194), does not always involve assigning Ballard such elevated taxonomies. At other times, he will be described "peer[ing] about like a groundhog" (155), or as in his flight from the turnaround, "scuttling" like a crustacean or insect (154).

That such bestializing descriptions are to be understood as more than mere similes, that they rather demonstrate for us the potentially brutalizing effects of the Enlightenment's scientific, as well as its economic, understanding of homo sapiens, is underlined by the reinforcing example of the dumpkeeper. Certainly, Reubel's domestic situation is brutish enough. Described as having "spawned nine daughters" (26), and himself sufficiently ruled by impulse as to rape one he catches with a younger partner (28), Reubel might seem to ratify the thoroughgoing, not to say misanthropic, naturalism discerned by Cant. Yet that this bestialization has as much to do with culture as with instinct is indicated by the role scientific discourse itself plays in this degraded *ménage*. The nine daughters, ostensible embodiments and victims of sexual compulsion, are themselves scripted not simply by biology, but by the text of modern medicine. Named "out of an old medical dictionary" (26), they are, through this imposition of an Enlightenment episteme, reduced from whole persons to parts of dissectible bodies: "Urethra, Cerebella, Hernia Sue" (26). This suggests, then, that it is the mapping of objectifying modern science onto human beings, and not an entrenched authorial perspective, that works to dehumanize Lester Ballard and his victims. If Holme and Ballard are cast in the role of fallen man, in such a way as to identify their American milieu as a locus of sin and human loss, then *Child of God* argues that the modern readiness to reduce all things to matter is not just a means for describing, but itself a source of the degradation of, villains and victims both. The novel's conclusion, in particular, emphasizes how Ballard is not simply one who objectifies others, but himself a specimen dehumanized by science's way of knowing. Once dead, he is wholly surrendered to the forensic and anatomizing gazes that have fixed on him throughout and, in the process, utterly obliterated as a human entity: "He was laid out on a slab and flayed, eviscerated, dissected. His head was sawed open and the brains removed" (194). If Ballard ends up so much tissue to be "scraped from the table into a plastic bag" (194), this is less a matter of his innate animality than of the modern epistemology directed toward him. Thus is demonstrated once more how their embrace of an Enlightenment outlook works to disempower McCarthy's protagonists and to endarken their worlds.

THE PENITENT'S HOPE

Yet, as the framing of their tale in terms of the Fall would indicate, neither Holme nor Ballard is presented as fated to such disempowerment at the hands of Enlightenment ideals of science and self-sufficiency. As Evenson says of *Child of God*, McCarthy's fiction "points to the failure of both epistemology and science to offer answers, and suggests that human nature exceeds" both ("Uses" 61). If the clearly elected character of the evil perpetrated by McCarthy's antiheroes frustrates such deterministic accounts, so too does their enduring capacity for reform. And the path to the realization of this capacity follows, like the Fall which so degrades them, a decidedly Christian, indeed Catholic, course. This it does by making central to the failed conversion of Holme and the ultimate redemption of Ballard the Catholic understanding of penance and absolution as agencies efficacious in the face even of the grimmest circumstances and the darkest sin. While Spinoza, prophet of Enlightenment, scorns penitence as an imperfection in a properly sovereign human subject—"he who repents of his action is doubly unhappy or weak" (185)—the faith in which McCarthy was raised understands it not simply as central to personal salvation, but as the essence of the Church's ministering mission. As Anthony Akinwale states, "the sacrament of reconciliation is what the church is and what the church offers" (553). Moreover, in Knox's words, "the *instinct* of the Church," in this matter of reconciliation and forgiveness, "has always told in favour of leniency" (*Belief* 187); it has never taught that sins cannot be forgiven, but rather that absolution and salvation are always open to the blackest reprobate should she sincerely adopt the role of penitent (187–88). Just this perspective, I argue, animates the respectively tragic and comic rendering of the gruesome careers of Culla Holme and Lester Ballard. Cast by their novels' lapsarian imagery in the role of moral agent and sinner, they are also presented, to the end, as eligible for the salvation promised, on the Catholic view, by confession of, and sorrow over, one's sins.

While he obdurately refuses this deliverance, Holme nonetheless journeys through a landscape that makes plain that his wretchedness is no necessary doom, but rather a condition he himself chooses, precisely by rejecting every opportunity to own his wrongs and reforge those bonds his insistence on autonomy have sundered. For while Bell maintains that the world of *Outer Dark* is one "bereft of God, or at least of grace" (*Achievement* 52), the novel in fact takes care to detail a contrasting path to Culla's own, one marked by just those things—light, hope, relationship—his disavowal of kin and sin has cost him. This is most plainly illustrated in the travels of his sister. Rinthy enacts a decidedly less atomistic ethos than does her brother and is animated by a love for her child that involves admission of her sins, repeated encounters with charity, and her consistent depiction as a figure of grace. Indeed, with a name likely drawn from the Pauline epistles (Arnold, "Naming" 48), Rinthy exemplifies the supremacy of charity, not autonomy, outlined in I Corinthians 13: "And now abideth faith, hope, charity, these three; but the greatest of these is charity." She is accordingly motivated throughout by love, duty, and a thirst for nontransactional relationship; in Julia Harper's words, she "actively looks for human connection where Culla cannot" (10). Guided by the need to rescue and nurture what her brother has condemned to die—"I just go around huntin my chap" (*OD* 156)—Rinthy, unlike Culla, confesses her incest both to the tinker and to a small-town doctor (193, 156). The fruit of that sin being still worthy of her devotion, she denies neither the act nor its consequence. So moved by love, she repeatedly receives charity and concern. Welcomed, fed, and housed by the first family she encounters (59–77), she is routinely met with kindness: from the old couple, so wracked with hatred for one another that the last Rinthy hears of them on her departure is "crash on crash . . . of shattered glass" (108), from the snake-hating old woman who offers her food and shelter without barter (111), from the astonished doctor, who offers her, at no charge, his expertise and a salve for her cracked, miraculously still lactating, breasts (154–55). For all her travails, then, she moves in a world of light, walking "into the sunshine" (53), and not her brother's darkness, and is possessed of a certain sanctity, an "air of staid and canonical propriety" (64). In her stark contrast with him, Rinthy thus indicates the contingent, elected character of Culla's grim course, as well as the possibility of an alternative path, even for him.

For if Culla never takes Rinthy's road, it is not because such routes are barred to him, but because, in his flight from sister and son, he refuses to play the penitent's part and acknowledge his sin. While Frye characterizes his wanderings as a "seemingly futile quest to find redemption" ("Life" 5), it is rather the case that he flees every chance for confession and forgiveness. Yet these opportunities are far from scarce. As Walsh notes, "Culla is subjected to a series of mock trials and judgments" (103), each of which calls on him to confess a guilt he never concedes. The first squire he meets asks what crime he has left home to outrun, only to be told, "I ain't runnin from nowheres" (*OD* 46). When the snake trapper inquires why Rinthy ran off, Culla again lies: "I don't know" (126). Asked by a second squire, "What did they run you off for" (201), Holme prevaricates: "They never run me off" (201). But the chief magistrates before whom he refuses to incriminate himself are the sinister trio. As Spencer notes, these three seem, in their encounters with Holme, "to act as judges" ("Unholy" 69), their aim being, in Luce's words, "to challenge or trick him to acknowledge his crimes" (*Reading* 96). This role is signaled in their second meeting by the murdered tinker's gear, off which firelight glints "like the baleful eyes of some outsized and mute and mindless jury" (*OD* 231). Their arraignment of Culla begins with the relatively trivial, as their leader remarks, "That is a jimdandy pair of boots you got there" (173), and asks about their provenance. True to form, Holme insists these stolen goods were a gift (177). If the trio's rehearsal of Holme's theft suggests they are undeceived, this holds true in other matters as well. When Holme denies knowledge of Rinthy's reason for leaving home, the bearded leader replies, "That ain't the way it is" (178); when pushed to acknowledge his incest and attempted murder—"That ain't all, is it?" (181)—Culla refuses to name his sin. This refusal to name is, as the bearded one observes, a refusal to own, but also the forfeiture of a chance to mend, the harm thus disavowed. Speaking of his own decision to leave a son nameless, he explains, "if you cain't name somethin you cain't claim it. You cain't talk about it even" (177). It is this refusal to name and claim his own infant, or the dual sin it embodies, that has motivated Culla's flight, and his Fall into a hopeless Enlightenment milieu, throughout. If his persistence in this denial has so consigned him to the darkness in which he moves, it finds its most damning realization in his final rejection of his child. Disclaiming any relationship to son and sin both—"He ain't nothin to me" (235)—Holme hands the toddler over so that the trio might consummate the act he has both desired and denied: "The child made no sound. It hung there with its one eye glazing over like a wet stone and the black blood pumping down its naked belly" (236).

Holme's status as unnatural criminal is thus confirmed, but neither his surrender of his child nor his refusal to acknowledge and repent of the act that leads to that child's death is itself fated. In this scene, he is afforded the opportunity to claim his sin, and by such penitential means, to save his son and his soul. It is his refusal of the penitent's part—of the "contrition, confession, and satisfaction" of the sacrament of Penance (*Catechism* 404)—that enables this monstrous crime and his final degradation. If he is doomed to the debasement his pursuit of self-sufficiency has been shown to entail, then, this is the result of his denying his own culpability and his embracing Enlightenment dreams of perfection. Yet even years after this grisly climax, Holme is granted another chance to repent of his crimes against charity and community, but while Frye contends that his travels culminate "in a realization, albeit a weak one, of his own error and a muted attempt to correct it" ("Histories" 8), *Outer Dark* instead concludes with Holme affirming both his refusal of relationship and the guiltlessness of that choice. His encounter with a blind man offers him a moment in which he may both heed the gospel of forgiveness and perform an atoning altruistic act. "Ragged and serene" (239), this sightless itinerant hails the passing Culla, attempts friendly conversation, and extends concern: "Is they anything you need?" (240). He denies the title of preacher, asking "What is they to preach? It's all plain enough. Word and flesh" (240). He then shares a tale of a failed faith healer and expresses the desire to find that man and relieve him of whatever guilt he may yet feel: "If somebody don't tell him he never will have no rest" (241).[15] While the blind man offers welcome, models solicitude, and implies that the Incarnation expresses both a duty to succor others and universal access to divine solace, Culla wants none of it. In keeping with his mercenary outlook, he assumes this evangelist's overtures are those of a salesman and seeks to move on. Doing so, he finds that the road terminates in an impassable swamp, "a landscape of the damned" (242). Returning, he spies the blind man still coming and passes by him without a word, reflecting "did he know how the road ended. Someone should tell a blind man before setting him out that way" (242). Even here, Holme might be the Samaritan to offer this warning, to recognize as his own the duty to extend the same concern that has been shown him. But having spent the novel betraying—in his lies and rejection of kinship—both word and flesh, Holme once again refuses the call to speak truly or forge a saving fraternity. Seeing in this refusal no sin he is empowered to commit or to forbear, he balks at that recognition of moral responsibility for and before others that is the essence of penitence, and persists in his benighted roving.

That this penitent's hope remains open even to so perverse a figure as Culla Holme might well surprise, but the ultimate fate of Lester Ballard enacts even more forcefully Knox's Catholic notion that no sinner is irredeemable, provided he takes the path of contrition and surrenders an enlightened insistence on his perfect sovereignty. In his lurking in the shadows and retreat to subterranean haunts, Ballard typically flees the scrutiny and judgment of his community.

Indeed, once arrested, he is as quick with denials of guilt as Holme himself. Convinced early on of his blamelessness before the law, Ballard tells Sheriff Fate, "I ain't done nothin. . . . You just got it in for me" (*CG* 56). After the commission of his many murders, he again denies any fault, telling the vigilantes who have released him in hopes of finding his victims' remains, "I ain't killed nary'n" (177). But like Holme's, his tale not only establishes his grave guilt, but hints repeatedly at the possibility of his redemption. The episode with the axe already points in this direction, its description of the reclamation of a worn-out implement offering an effective parable of how the seemingly ruined might still hope for rescue. Saving the rusted blade from uselessness and from "heatin to perdition" (72), the smith not only returns it to Ballard good as new, but does so by taking his cue from "the color of grace" it reflects in the forge (72). Ballard's insensibility to this lesson might suggest that he is not as salvageable as this discarded tool, but even after his ghastly crimes have begun to erode his humanity and identity both, Ballard remains less than wholly estranged from potentially redemptive longings.

If nothing else, it is true, as Bell notes, that he is moved by an abiding longing for a less troglodytic home (*Achievement* 60). Both before and after the commencement of his killing spree, he is drawn toward reintegration with the community that has shunned him and that he, in his proud assertions of independence, frequently shuns in his turn. This is manifest in his failed attempt to join the congregation at Six-mile Church. Later, when he is so lost to himself as to wear his victims' clothes and skins, Ballard still reaches out toward a more humane past, embarking on daily visits "to his old homeplace where he'd watch the house, the house's new tenant" from afar (*CG* 109). While such surveillance, and the "queer plans" that accompany it (140), reveal his growing desire for vengeance against usurper Greer, this ritual also clearly speaks to Ballard's longing for rescue from his degraded, postlapsarian condition. Indeed, the rugged independence that coincides with his status as fallen outcast, however much an ideal of America's Enlightenment creed, is, for him, fundamentally untenable. For all his jealous guarding of his solitude, for all his pursuit of the autonomy he thinks strictly market relations afford, Ballard, even in his most degraded state, yearns for a return home and a resumption of humane relations. Thus, watching from his mountainside perch as vernal renewal comes to his former lands, Ballard is shaken by loss and longing: "Squatting there he let his head drop between his knees and he began to cry" (170). In his underground dominion, he is not yet bereft of humanity, but subject still to "some old shed self that [comes] yet from time to time in the name of sanity, a hand to gentle him back from the rim of his disastrous wrath" (158). Even his murders betray a desperate desire for forfeit community. While his consumerist understanding of relationship drives a deadly objectification of persons, those persons, once reified, are not treated altogether as chattel, and certainly not like the disposable commodities of the modern market. Rather, in his own perverse fashion, he seeks a community of persons with them, preserving them and treating them with care, even reverence: "Here in the bowels of the mountain Ballard turned his light on ledges or pallets of stone where dead people lay like saints" (135).

If such evidence testifies to Ballard's enduring capacity for human feeling, the novel's climax insists upon his potential, too, for moral reclamation through contrition and confession. Having been freed by men seeking a guide to the missing bodies of his victims, Ballard leads them underground only to elude them. As these vigilantes themselves recognize, they have afforded Ballard the opportunity to resume his predation on Sevier County: "We've rescued the little fucker from jail and turned him loose where he can murder folks again" (186). Yet this is not at all what transpires. Seemingly safe and free in his caves, Ballard feels himself a prisoner, and longs for release cast tellingly as a delivery: "He'd cause to wish and he did wish for some brute midwife to spald him from his rocky keep" (189). This rebirth is, in fact, realized, but once Ballard is again on the roads, it becomes clear that more than his physical liberty has been resuscitated. In an uncharacteristic moment of empathy and self-reflection, he undergoes a Damascene experience that facilitates his spiritual reclamation. Newly returned to the open air, Ballard walks at night down a country road and is overtaken by a passing bus, out of whose rear window peers a small boy. Spying this young face and its readiness for wonder—"There was nothing out there to see but he was looking anyway" (191)—Ballard returns his gaze and experiences the novel's first moment of genuinely reciprocated, nonmercenary relationship: "As he went by he looked at Ballard and Ballard looked back" (191). This moment of recognizing the other swiftly becomes something more. In the innocence, potential, and humanity of this child, Ballard recalls something of himself: "He was trying to fix in his mind where he'd seen the boy when it came to him that the boy looked like himself" (191).

Now, on Luce's account, "this is as close to epiphany as Ballard comes, yet he refuses it" (*Reading* 167). *Child of God,* however, powerfully suggests otherwise. This moment of genuine, if fleeting, human connection returns to Ballard that sense of identity that his solitary course in sin has largely eroded. Here, in the other, he finds that reflection he could not recognize in his watering pool. Moreover, the self he sees and affirms is one defined by the innocence and potential of the wondering child. What he rediscovers, I argue, is a sense of moral capacity and hope, and he does so, not by clinging to the Enlightenment's fallen veneration of autonomy, but through the experience of his insufficiency and fallenness themselves. This brief vision is, indeed, epiphanic, then, and it moves Ballard to choose for himself what Holme never does, namely the saving path of the penitent. Afterward, Ballard follows the road into town and presents himself to the hospital from which he has been sprung: "his eyes were caved and smoking. I'm supposed to be here, he said" (*CG* 192). While certain critics have dismissed the moral significance of this voluntary surrender,[16] it strikes me as a moment of profound conversion. Through intercourse, not commodified commerce, with another human being, Ballard responds to that repressed need for genuine community his homesickness has already indicated. Avowing this insufficiency in himself, he achieves an understanding both of his own fallenness and of the rightness of his standing to account for his crimes. Free to persist in them, he instead chooses to acknowledge his guilt, abandon his criminal course, and offer satisfaction for his offenses. In the end, then, he confirms his status as a child of God by voluntarily playing the penitent's part and surrendering the modern ideals that have marked his fall. In enacting such an end even for so ghoulish a figure as Ballard, McCarthy not only punctuates the novel's critique of the Enlightenment, but adopts a radical, very Catholic stance on the question of the agency and hope for redemption of even the most depraved of sinners.

Describing the power of penitence, de Sales writes, "Contrition and confession . . . efface the ugliness and dissipate the stench of sin" (67). If Culla Holme resists their attractions, his tale nonetheless underscores both his need for repentance and the self-destructive consequences of his contrary allegiance to ideals of autonomy and self-interest. Few protagonists rival the ugliness of Lester Ballard, but McCarthy insists that even his humanity may be saved if he pursues the course not of modern markets and science, but of the penitent, conceived in Catholic terms. A similar deployment of contrition as an alternative to Enlightenment values is evident in *Blood Meridian*, the book I turn to next, but such contrition will not mark the character whose villainy rivals Ballard's own. Rather, Judge Holden, McCarthy's fullest embodiment of Enlightenment discourse, will reveal both how, for McCarthy, such thought has shaped American history's bloody course and how that course is to be understood, in Augustinian terms, as a diabolical unmaking. Yet through the figure of the kid, the runaway Holden seeks to claim as protégé, *Blood Meridian* suggests that the word of the Judge, while nearly final, is not all-powerful. In his own seeking after confession and atonement, the kid not only models a morally potent response to America's Enlightenment history, but reveals again the extent to which his creator's moral compass remains compellingly Catholic.

CHAPTER 4

PROPERLY SUZERAIN OF THE EARTH

AUGUSTINIAN EVIL AND THE UNMAKING OF
DIABOLICAL ENLIGHTENMENT IN *BLOOD MERIDIAN*

The curse of irresistible progress is irresistible regression.

—THEODOR ADORNO and MAX HORKHEIMER, *Dialectic of Enlightenment*

Murder is negative creation, and every murderer is therefore the rebel who claims the right to be omnipotent.

—W. H. AUDEN, "The Guilty Vicarage"

Despite the critical and commercial success of *All the Pretty Horses* and *The Road*, McCarthy's *Blood Meridian* has retained a privileged place in his catalog. Bloom calls it "the ultimate Western, not to be surpassed" (1), and such praise is not rare. As Hage notes, McCarthy's first foray into the Southwest is commonly deemed his "masterpiece" (43).[1] But such widespread admiration has not resulted in critical consensus as to the novel's significance or even its form. While Jarrett's identification of *Blood Meridian* as "a revisionary western" has won considerable support (*Cormac* 69),[2] others have proffered different generic tags. Denying its kinship with the Western, Josyph, for example, considers it "the achievement of epic prose" (*Adventures* 57, 63).[3] Jason P. Mitchell, by contrast, judges it "in structure, style, and subject, a fairly traditional nineteenth-century novel" (295), whereas John Sepich styles it an "historical romance" ("Dance" 27).[4] Discerning a more modernist model, Cooper dubs it McCarthy's American *Heart of Darkness* (*Heroes* 55).[5] Yet if critics have turned up a diversity of narrative templates, their disparate readings have tended to agree upon one thing, and that is the essential godlessness of the novel's universe. However they have defined its form, they have largely concurred that its content amounts, in Broncano's words, to a world "abandoned by a God that may have never existed to the chaos of deadly violence" (3).[6]

Central to such construals of the text's metaphysical commitments is the role played by the character Dorson identifies as *Blood Meridian*'s most central: Judge Holden ("Demystifying" 107). This towering figure has captivated and appalled, and has consistently been identified as the novel's interpretive hinge. In fact, the Judge's dominating rhetorical presence has led to his identification as the authoritative voice of the novel. For Jarrett, he "personifies the law of the narrative's events" (*Cormac* 78), while for Ellis, the kinship between his own magniloquence and the style of *Blood Meridian*'s narrator allies the Judge's perspective with McCarthy's own (*No Place* 1). Shaviro goes so far as to argue that author and character share a common project, insofar as the act of writing, for both, constitutes a war on the real (155).[7] But while I agree that the Judge's assault on Creation lies at the heart of this novel, he figures so prominently, I argue, not as McCarthy's surrogate, but as his chief object of criticism. The Judge does, as Jarrett suggests, articulate the principles behind the novel's infamous gore, but he does so primarily as the representative of an Enlightenment "progress," enacted through America's pursuit of her putative Manifest Destiny, that McCarthy presents in terms of Adorno and Horkheimer's "irresistible regression." Indeed, Holden may be taken as embodying—as Adorno and Horkheimer say of Sade's Juliette—an "*amor intellectualis diaboli*, the pleasure of attacking civilization with its own weapons" (94). Such a formulation is apt, for what I see McCarthy as undertaking in *Blood Meridian* is a critique of Western modernity as, in fact, a diabolical thirst for godhead that plays out in an Enlightenment pursuit of knowledge as power and of human suzerainty as the unmaking of Creation.

For Judge Holden most certainly is "an Enlightenment encyclopedist" (Cant 169), and in his binding of scientific progress not just to his own murderous appetites, but to the bloodthirsty exploits of historical scalp hunters and their quintessential American push to the Pacific, he functions as the novel's damning presentation of a brutish modernity. As Moos argues, Holden "represents the ideological skeleton of a new imperialist scientific world order sprouting

from Enlightenment rationality" (28).[8] He is a man of great learning and culture, but even more, a man of modern science; in addition to being an accomplished linguist, musician, and dancer, then, he is, further, a chemist and naturalist, geologist and paleontologist. Above all, he is, as knower, emphatically
a doer, an agent in history, both natural and geopolitical. In step with Francis
Bacon, the Judge holds that "those twin objects, human Knowledge and human
Power, do really meet in one" (Bacon 177). Like Bacon's cotheorist of modern
science, Descartes, Holden pursues a learning aimed at making human beings
"masters and possessors of nature" (Descartes 45). It is, after all, the Judge,
cultured spokesman of Enlightenment, who claims to be "suzerain of the earth"
(BM 207), acknowledging no power or authority superior to his purposes. Yet
if such an ambition to enthrone an omnipotent human reason is married for
Kant to the conviction that "men raise themselves by and by out of backwardness if one does not purposely invent artifices to keep them down" (138), for
McCarthy, it is instead mired in a bloody war not just on nature, but on any
potential Creator. This, in turn, means that Enlightenment progress, that "attitude of modernity" (Foucault 38) at work in Blood Meridian forging America's
new republic, is at root implicated in an evil whose essence is, as per Augustine
and Catholic tradition, a deliberate pursuit of annihilation for any good alien
to the ego's governing will.

For if Bacon located the truth of his methods in their fruitfulness, in their
generating practical works "for the benefit and use of life" (164), Judge Holden
and company are, like Auden's murderer, notable instead as negative creators,
asserting knowledge as power through a comprehensive unmaking of their
world that coincides with the Augustinian teaching that "evil . . . is not a substance," but rather the push toward nonbeing of created substances (Confessions
148).[9] While Moos claims his Enlightenment rationality empowers Holden to
be one who "manufactures, rather than just rearranges, meaning" (31), what his
science repeatedly effects is an assault on the already created, an eradication of
artifacts and cultures, of persons and peoples, not as progress, but as the self's
zero-sum war on anything beyond or prior to itself. Precisely as he presents
the modern ethos of ever-expanding human suzerainty as quintessentially the
practice of "the ultimate trade," war (BM 259), Holden establishes not just that
ethos's implication in colonialism, but also its coincidence with diabolical and
dehumanizing forms of violence. McCarthy's placement of Holden in the midst

of Glanton's gang and at the forefront of the reader's experience demonstrates, first, that the bloodshed upon which America was founded is not incidental, but altogether essential, to the Enlightenment thought that sustained that founding. It further indicates that this thought constitutes in its crimes that wilful rejection of the Creator, and unmaking of Creation, core to Catholic understandings of evil and sin.

Thus, Patrick Shaw's description of *Blood Meridian* as "a text where violence is pandemic but blasphemy scarce" is off the mark ("Kid's Fate" 108). The novel is preoccupied with nothing other than blasphemy and with presenting it as the source of modernity's scourging of the peoples and landscapes of America. Judge Holden is the perfect embodiment of this sacrilege. Preacher of Enlightenment reason, science, and autonomy, he reflects the operations of Manifest Destiny and modern science's mastery of nature in seeking to claim for himself lordship over all things. In this project of "uncovering the deity within himself" (Parrish, "Killer" 35), he enacts modernity's push to replace God with a wholly sovereign human agency. But confronted on all sides by histories, cultures, creatures that exceed and precede his will, Holden's striving for godhead is met with the constraining evidence of his dependence on another providence, a Creation he has not authorized. His pursuit of godlike suzerainty, then, can only take the form of belated assertions of mastery over that which surpasses him; he can only seek lordship by conquest of what he has not created, making it his through obliterating violence. Only by unmaking what he has not authored can he secure the autonomy he seeks. In this way, he becomes an exposé not just of the historical crimes of the Enlightenment in America, but of an unmaking evil at their root. If this Augustinian critique works to undercut Cant's claim that McCarthy's oeuvre "rejects a religious vision of the world" (112), then the novel's presentation of its alternative to the Judge's annihilating progress only bolsters this rebuttal. In the unlettered kid, the novel offers not just a foil to the enlightened will of the Judge, but the text's "most persuasive manifestation of the possibility of a moral ground" (Hillier, *Morality* 53). That possibility lies in the abandonment of Enlightenment hubris in favor of Christian admissions of fault, need, and dependence, through acts, specifically, of penance and charity. Not just by rejecting the Judge's vision, but by seeking an authority beyond himself whom he can serve and before whom he can atone for sins committed in Enlightenment's name, McCarthy's kid serves to ratify the novel's indictment of Holden's worldview and to establish how this indictment derives from an essentially Catholic outlook.

ENLIGHTENMENT'S DIABOLICAL SUZERAINTY

Judge Holden's centrality to the project of the novel may be seen, first, in the way its setting reflects his Enlightenment aims. This congruence between the philosophy he embodies and the history in which he participates is perhaps clearest in his enacting the fulfillment of America's Manifest Destiny to span and to "civilize" the continent. For America is, in its republicanism and colonialism both, at root an Enlightenment enterprise. On Taylor's account, the Declaration of Independence offers an archetypal expression of "the Modern Moral Order," in its imagining of the social only in terms of the free, autonomous, and self-governing subjects of Enlightenment thought (447). Writing more than a decade before the Mexican War that forms the background to McCarthy's novel, Tocqueville would likewise treat the American character in such terms, depicting its democracy as the reign of the individual's self-sufficient judgment. If, for Kant, "Have the courage to use your own intelligence! is . . . the motto of the enlightenment" and surest path to the progress which is our "the original destiny" (132, 136), then Tocqueville's America would appear the vanguard of such progress. Nowhere else, he insists, are men so convinced that "at birth each person has received the capacity for self-government" (439). More than this, Americans are convinced of the infallibility of this autonomy, cherishing "a lively faith in human perfectibility" (439). This is a faith not simply in the power of unfettered individual reason to guide citizen or state to prosperity, but in that capacity to master the environment championed by Bacon and Descartes: "Nowhere do [Anglo-Americans] see any limit placed by nature on man's efforts" (475).

This conviction as to the individual's supremacy impacts not just America's popular government, but also its geographical expansion. Recognizing no limits on progress in their New World, Tocqueville's Americans subscribe to a vision of western territories as free to be claimed by a colonization which is both an instance of and a portal to the freedom the nation proclaims as its own unique achievement. Having been told that prosperity lies westward, Americans "rush to catch up with it" (328). Tocqueville thus anticipates Frederick Jackson Turner in seeing that America "has had a colonial history and policy from the beginning of the Republic" (Turner 127), a colonialism rooted in the "selfishness and individualism" that pioneer living fostered in the American people (32). Derived from Enlightenment values, America's colonial mission unfolds in the inexorable advance to the Pacific of the western frontier. Indeed, so powerful a force has this project been that Turner deems it definitive: "Up to our own day American history has been in a large degree the history of the colonization of the Great West" (1). The significance of this claim, as Richard Slotkin shows, is both ideological and historical. Speaking of a Frontier Myth he terms "arguably the longest-lived of American myths" (*Fatal* 15), Slotkin details how identification of western settlement with the progress not just of borders, but of liberty and civilization, fueled expansion as much as it emerged from historical frontier experience. This myth thus functioned as a commission, justifying pursuit of a shared destiny in which "conquest of the wilderness and the subjugation or displacement of the Native Americans who originally inhabited it have been the means to . . . achievement of a national identity, a democratic polity, an ever-expanding economy, and a phenomenally dynamic and 'progressive' civilization" (*Gunfighter* 10).

Blood Meridian isn't simply set in a sparsely populated Southwest; it is so constructed as to make its readers aware of this larger mythic context and of the bloody particulars of American expansion into territories only lately surrendered by Mexico. As Ken Hanssen notes, "we are never allowed to forget how the Glanton gang rides through landscapes ravaged by the violent displacement of American Indians and the Mexico-American War" (184). But in foregrounding the historicity of his southwestern wilderness, McCarthy also stresses its dynamism, its steady movement to the end of the frontier. Thus, his tale narrates the execution of that colonial mission authorized by America's Enlightenment Frontier Myth. This is explicitly proclaimed, early in the text, by Captain White, who sees his unauthorized foray into Mexico as sanctioned by just this mission; his invasion is unimpeachable, as it will enable "Americans . . . to get to California without having to pass through our benighted sister republic" (*BM* 37). Further, as Cant remarks, the peregrinations of McCarthy's kid—from Tennessee through Texas, Mexico, and Arizona to California—chart "the mythic journey across the continent that led to the establishment of the United States as a transcontinental entity, the very heart of the project of Manifest Destiny"

(158). Yet in tracing this path, the kid is himself followed by the Judge, who tracks him from Nacogdoches, Texas, to the town of San Diego, and back east to their fatal encounter at Fort Griffin in the year 1878. In other words, Holden, too, exemplifies Manifest Destiny, but much more than the kid, he also articulates its Enlightenment underpinnings. Certainly, it is he who understands their travels and their bloody deeds as a nation-founding enterprise aimed at the triumph of the most "advanced." It is part of a historic collective "work" (*BM* 319), one he accuses the kid of betraying by harboring "clemency for the heathen" (312). On Holden's account, as his scorn for the "heathen" indicates, Glanton's men are agents in an evolutionary contest, outriders for a Western culture before whom their victims, and even such advanced Indigenous peoples as the Anasazi, are judged both superseded and "primitive" (152).

As such dismissals of "primitive" cultures would suggest, the Judge here embodies the notion of civilizational advance through conquest of "lesser" races that underwrote America's own colonial efforts. By so doing, he works to expose the terrible violence this enterprise authorized. As Slotkin argues, the Frontier Myth that emerged from America's belief in its role as agent of progress understood such enlightenment as requiring the extirpation of other, "backward" races, signally America's own Indigenous peoples. Written as a necessary advance into a wilderness that only the white race could redeem, "the story of American progress . . . thus took the form of a fable of race war" (*Fatal* 53), one in which, Slotkin asserts, "the war of extermination [becomes] the central theme" (528). Given this national myth's belief in "the principle that violence and savage war were the necessary instruments of American progress" (*Gunfighter* 77), it is perhaps unsurprising that McCarthy's commitment to rendering the prosecution of such warfare should result in what Pilkington calls "one of the bloodiest books ever penned by an American author" (316). As the novel's chief theorist of the violence that Glanton's gang visits upon Mexicans and Native Americans, Holden looms not only, in Parrish's terms, as "the most violent character in American literature" ("History" 71), but as a character whose violence itself qualifies him to represent the work of the cult of progress in America's closing of the frontier. In speaking of Glanton's butchery in terms of "holy" war (*BM* 319), the Judge is an able advocate for a Frontier Myth that, as Slotkin states, "represented the redemption of American spirit" as something achieved by a "*regeneration through violence*" in the American wilds (*Gunfighter* 12).

Yet Apaches and Mexicans are far from the only targets, and Manifest Destiny far from the only instrument, of Holden's less than regenerative violence. The setting of the novel reveals his Enlightenment aspirations in its detailing the displacement not just of the "heathen," but of the Church. As Luce notes, *Blood Meridian*'s landscape is one dotted as much by "ruined churches" as by mesas, camps, or cantinas ("Trail" 847).[10] These ruins may certainly bespeak, as in chapter 5, Apache or Comanche depredations (*BM* 63–64). They also bear witness to that recently concluded episode in America's Manifest Destiny, the American-Mexican War (1846–48). The text's very first church is one ravaged by Americans: "The facade of the building bore an array of saints in their niches and they had been shot up by American troops trying their rifles . . . a carved stone Virgin held in her arms a headless child" (28). Such exterior vandalism, and even more the dishonored civilian dead within, testify to the violence with which progress makes its advance. But that bastions of Christian faith are so consistently targets of this violence is also consonant with Holden's Enlightenment creed. As Gay defines it, "the Enlightenment was a volatile mixture of classicism, impiety, and science; the philosophes, in a phrase, were modern pagans" (8). Their thought was "a declaration of war on Christianity" (203), whose call to belief and obedience they scorned as a "collapse of confidence in man's unaided intellect" (231). While Taylor traces how the novelty of "a purely self-sufficient humanism" arose from long-standing movements of reform within Christendom itself (18), he, too, presents the Enlightenment as conceiving a nature "whose working could be systematically understood and explained on its own terms," without recourse to a Creator-God (15). For Enlightenment thinkers, then, progress required the displacement of the Christian authorities that still governed Europe; this campaign against ecclesial power and supernatural thinking was deemed essential to the liberation of man's knowledge and person. This is a program to which the Judge explicitly subscribes. Lecturing his bewildered class of bounty hunters on palaeontology and comparative morphology, Holden concludes, "Your heart's desire is to be told some mystery. The mystery is that there is no mystery" (*BM* 263).

The barrens through which Holden and his pupils roam seem often enough to support this claim, at least if the mystery in question has anything to do with the vitality of the Christian, and more expressly, the Roman Catholic Church. While Spurgeon overstates things when she declares the Christian God and

Christian morality altogether absent from the novel ("Sacred" 81), the prophets, preachers, and chapels that, in fact, pepper its narrative are remarkable for being uniformly inoperative. Precisely as such, these traces of a Christian worldview are instructive: epitaphs for faith and cues to the novel's understanding of Enlightenment culture. The obsolescence of belief is gruesomely conveyed by the churches in which McCarthy's characters seek, but fail to find, safe haven. Far from gateways to eternal life, these desecrated structures are assimilated to the novel's relentlessly mortal world. Wakening "in the nave of a ruinous church" (27), then, the kid finds its parishioners have been likewise laid waste: "along the back wall lay the remains of several bodies, one a child" (28). Stormed by Comanches, a second church is likewise but a congregation of the dead, its interior piled high "with the scalped and naked and partly eaten bodies of some forty souls who'd barricaded themselves in this house of God against the heathen" (63). Powerless to protect such petitioners, the God putatively housed here has himself failed to escape profanation: "The altars had been hauled down and the tabernacle looted and the great sleeping God of the Mexicans routed from his golden cup" (63). Glanton's men also demonstrate the futility of sacred space, as they turn to storming village chapels and leaving helpless believers "slain and scalped in the chancel floor" (189). Perhaps the most final vision of the Church in ruins comes near the novel's end, when the twenty-eight-year-old "kid" finds himself moved to track a procession of penitents, including "a hooded man in a white robe who bore a heavy wooden cross" (326). When he catches them, he discovers only a hopeless passion: the pilgrims left "hacked and butchered" around a fallen cross (327). As Diana Curtis contends, "that the penitents [have] not been saved by the cross suggests that the kid has found no refuge in religion" (113), whatever hope of such salvation he may have harbored.

In addition to these ravaged sanctuaries and slaughtered devotees, *Blood Meridian* offers an impressive array of failed pastors and prophets, who offer warnings against the evils of this new frontier but no belief in or hope for Christian redemption. The earliest of these is the "old anchorite" the kid meets in chapter 2 (*BM* 17). While this title identifies him with a tradition of Christian piety, this hermit has no good news to proclaim. Though he offers the kid water and shelter, his bleak gospel—"You can find meanness in the least of creatures, but when God made man the devil was at his elbow" (20)—is matched by his own sinister intent. Far from safeguarding the kid's welfare, he is only barely prevented from sexually assaulting the boy (21). This solitary shepherd with no faith in, and little capacity for, goodness is not alone in heralding the passing of Christianity's graces. Other despairing prophets include the "old disordered Mennonite" met on the eve of the kid's departure for Mexico with Captain White (42). He, too, would be a voice crying in the wilderness, but he has no vision to offer but that of sure doom south of the border (43). Mexico itself abounds with hopeless preachers. Thus the old barfly of chapter 8 who confesses his abandonment of Catholic devotion—"What I need to talk to them dolls there?" (108)—encourages Glanton's gang in their hunt for the Apache "barbaros" (108), but denies that project any spiritual fruit: "This country is give much blood. This Mexico. This is a thirsty country. The blood of a thousand Christs. Nothing" (108). Yet the most prominent of the novel's failed prophets is the so-called "expriest" Tobin (97),[11] who serves as Holden's rival as would-be teacher to the kid. As such, he shows himself capable of testifying to a God not yet wholly routed from man's dominion on earth; he insists that "God speaks in the least of creatures" and warns a skeptical kid of the terrible fate of falling deaf to that providential voice (130). Yet Tobin never openly disputes the Judge's teachings, and his epithet reveals him to be bereft of any compelling alternative creed. His participation in Glanton's un-Christian work, as Holden argues, exposes his own apostasy: "For the priest has put by the robes of his craft and taken up the tools of that calling which all men honor," namely war (262).

The world of *Blood Meridian* is thus one which seems, in line with the *philosophes*, to have cast aside an archaic Christian past to uncover a world without God or God-fearing men. Moreover, it has found a new creed, one rooted in Western civics, science, and conquest. The kid's first expeditionary leader, Captain White, is cast in the role of Messiah, not as a witness to a kingdom beyond this world, but as preacher of a gospel of progress through America's colonizing efforts. A somewhat premature filibuster mustering a private militia to seize Mexican lands,[12] White sees his raid as a mission on behalf of civilization against benighted backwardness. "We are to be the instruments of liberation in a dark and troubled land," he tells the kid (37), bringing to "a people manifestly incapable of governing themselves" the boon of enlightened American rule (36). Such zeal is not his alone. The man who recruits for the Captain's cause waxes still more rhapsodic, identifying White as his savior: "he come along and raised me up like Lazarus. Set my feet in the path of righteousness" (32). If White's fate—as a disembodied head, plaything for his enemies (73)—allies him more with the Baptist than with the role of a secular Christ, he does prepare the way for a still more compelling incarnation of modernity in the Judge. Spurgeon insists that "McCarthy consistently presents the judge as a priest, a mediator between man and nature" ("Sacred" 78); it is certainly true that he and his teachings come to dominate this tale bestrewn with the detritus of superseded faith. Indeed, that such wreckage conforms to his wishes is the first thing we learn about him. His debut in the novel has him bringing ruin on yet another of the novel's failed Christian shepherds; Reverend Green of Nacogdoches falls victim to the mob after Holden mendaciously denounces him as a fraud and pedophile (*BM* 7). Thus, if McCarthy's Southwest has waged successful war on belief, it has, by so doing, conformed to the aims of the Judge's own humanist philosophy of disenchantment.

As his role in the novel's historical setting and that setting's portrayal as a graveyard to faith both demonstrate, then, Holden embodies a larger cultural process playing itself out on the frontiers of the New World: an Enlightenment displacement of any epistemology that affirms a divinity that transcends material reality. With such belief in abeyance, the explicit question of McCarthy's American history becomes the degree, and the ends, to which humanity can take God's power and authority upon itself, to become its own creator and master of Creation. As the narrator describes his milieu, "not again in all the world's turning will there be terrains so wild and barbarous to try whether the stuff of creation may be shaped to man's will or whether his own heart is not another kind of clay" (5). In other words, this unchurched, ostensibly godless world provides a perfect testing ground for Enlightenment humanism itself, a space bereft of operative legal, ecclesial, or conventional authority in which may be measured man's capacity, à la the *philosophes,* to define himself and refashion the earth, or conversely, to demonstrate his enduring status as God-shaped clay, an object, not an agent of creation. This sets the book up as nothing less than a trial for the premises of Western modernity. Certainly, for Bacon, the natural world was an inert object to be anatomized, understood, and thereby mastered, so as to confer on humanity worldly omnipotence; as formulated in *The New Atlantis,* his empiricism has as its ultimate aim "the enlarging of the bounds of Human Empire, to the effecting of all things possible" (297). *Blood Meridian* presents its wilderness as the realm in which such a secular conquest might be attempted and the moral consequences of that attempt clarified.

Ultimately, it is Holden, not White, who most seriously makes this attempt and discloses such consequences. As Cant argues, the Judge represents the replacement of deference to the Christian God with the reign of empirical reason (174). This process of substitution, and the sort of redemption in which it deals, is nowhere clearer than in the tale of Holden's first encounter with Glanton, related in chapter 10. As told by Tobin, this account is etiological, the story of the origins of a new savior, and a new faith, in a science cast as the path to human self-creation and worldly lordship. McCarthy's source for Holden, Samuel Chamberlain's *My Confession*, describes the Judge as "by far the best educated man in northern Mexico," "in short another Admirable Crichton" (309). Tobin concurs, acclaiming Holden as a polymath of the first order: "I've never seen him turn to a task but what he didnt prove clever at it" (*BM* 129). As he first appears to a defenseless Glanton gang harried by Apache pursuers, the Judge reveals himself as even more: a man of learning and science capable of wedding knowledge with works both life-saving and death-dealing. The ambivalent fruit of this marriage of culture and power is revealed by the weapon he bears, a rifle inscribed with classical wisdom as to death's ubiquity: *"Et In Arcadia Ego"* (131). Yet it is precisely modern reason's generation of such mighty works as the rifle represents that allows the Judge to take on that role of redeemer that Sepich justly assigns him; Holden does, indeed, "[save] the gang from certain death" (*Notes* 119).

But this salvation is altogether in and of the world, reliant on his role as applied scientist. It is his mastery of zoology, geology, and chemistry that allows him to harness for the bounty hunters a new power over men and nature in this wilderness testing-ground of human suzerainty. First, his observations allow them to track bats to a cave rich in guano (*BM* 133). Then, his chemical knowledge permits the precipitation from this harvest of "eight pounds of pure crystal saltpetre" ready to be mixed with charcoal he has also prepared (134). His knowledge of geology leads them to the crust of an ancient lava stream and thence to "the dead cone" of an old volcano, where sulphur is collected (137). Finally, enjoining the gang to urinate on these ingredients, the Judge, "a bloody dark pastryman" (138), kneads his "foul black dough" (138), before leaving it to dry on the rocks. The resultant gunpowder, fruit of Holden's science, proves

efficacious; Tobin reports "not a misfire in the batch" (141). This scientific remaking of the naturally given becomes the source of the gang's salvation and
triumph: luring the Apaches near with a white flag, the Judge calls on the mercenaries to open fire, initiating a massacre: "there was fifty-eight of them lay
slaughtered among the gravels" (141). Yet while deadly for their pursuers, this
episode is cast in salvific terms by Tobin; his Judge looms large, in Spurgeon's
words, as "the spokesman of what is presented as a sort of new religion—science"
("Sacred" 79).[13] Perched on a pile of rock, Holden delivers his Sermon on the
Mount, if "no such sermon as any man of us had ever heard before" (BM 136),
proclaiming the sufficient geological riches of an earth that "contained all good
things within her" (136). Awestruck, Glanton's men, reduced to twelve, follow
"behind him like the disciples of a new faith" (136). The Judge bears a gospel
of the truth to be found, the powers to be unlocked, in the stony heart of this
world, powers mighty enough to make men masters of the earth, clay formed
by no will but their own. This Enlightenment creed yokes empirical reason
to practical works, and those awesome works save. Indeed, they effect a new,
wholly human sacrament. Thus, when Holden calls on his followers to fill their
powderhorns, they come "one by one, circlin past him like communicants"
(140). If the old faith has seemingly failed, what the Judge offers in its place
is human dominion through science, a power rooted in, and exercised over, a
material world whose secrets Enlightenment philosophy has helped unlock. It
is worth noting, however, that this communion is founded in bloodshed, not of
the self-given sacrifice, but of Slotkin's genocidal race war.

Though often bloodstained, Judge Holden, "European Enlightenment made
flesh" (Monk 37), is presented as the incarnation of a scientific endeavor that
enables an ever-expanding human agency. His embodiment of humanist values
is scarcely limited to this scene nor to natural sciences; he is ever the novel's
man of learning and refinement *par excellence*. He is, in Hage's words, "a para-
gon of high culture . . . multilingual and socially gracious . . . a keen historian"
(99). Much like the *philosophes*, for whom the road to advancement in science
and liberty "lay through the ancients" (Gay 69), Holden weds classical and
modern history, social and natural science, liberal and applied arts. Custodian
of Western culture, he maintains a position throughout as pedagogue to Glanton's ragged group, his nimble oratory ranging the full spectrum of human ac-
complishment. Thus, negotiations with an arms trader find him explaining the

presence of the Black John Jackson in a lecture that cites biblical tales, classical authors, the newest findings of anthropology, and the power of climate (*BM* 88–89). A geologist, he is an avid collector of specimens, scouring abandoned mines for rocks "in whose organic lobations he purport[s] to read news of the earth's origins" (122). Eager naturalist, he assiduously sketches, catalogs, and stuffs new species of birds the gang's travels uncover (206).[14] His erudition encompasses more human sciences, as well. He discourses on vanished Indigenous cultures, whose artifacts he studies and whose accomplishments he explains (145; 152), as well as on Western jurisprudence from Anaximander and Thales to Coke and Blackstone (250).

THE BLASPHEMOUS UN-CREATION OF AMERICAN PROGRESS

As evangelist of the Enlightenment gospel of knowledge and works, then, Judge Holden is, as his seven-foot, twenty-four-stone frame indicates (6; 135), the towering figure in this frontier test of humanity's capacity for self-fashioning. In him, the attainments of Western culture and the newest accomplishments of science outstrip faith in superhuman authorities; in him, scientific progress serves to found a truly new world. Yet such a characterization sits ill with the company Holden keeps, with the kinds of works his form of salvation enables, and with that "terrible covenant" that binds him to the scalp hunter John Glanton (132). This grim pact—which terminates only with the death of every member of Glanton's party but Holden—powerfully suggests that the Enlightenment American progress Holden represents is itself a profound force for evil and is so in just such terms as might in fact vindicate the seemingly obsolete old faith and its teachings on Creation, God, and the sources of sin. For the Judge's disciples, far from founding a new republic based on the sovereignty of human reason, pursue instead an inhuman butchery and an irrational license that effect only destruction, dehumanization, and murder. As all the bloodied churches cataloged above demonstrate, the landscape Holden's party works to define is given more to savagery than to science, more to kinship with the "300,000-year-old fossil skull . . . show[ing] evidence of having been scalped" (n. p.) of the epigraphs than with some utopian future.

Now, such radical violence may seem first to be the preserve of the Native Americans Glanton and company hunt. White's promise to bring light and liberation to Mexico runs, after all, into a Comanche war party of horrifying ferocity: "a fabled horde of mounted lancers and archers bearing shields bedight with bits of broken mirrorglass that cast a thousand unpieced suns against the eyes of their enemies. A legion of horribles, hundreds in number, half naked or clad in costumes attic or biblical or wardrobed out of a fevered dream with the skins of animals and silk finery and pieces of uniform tracked with the blood of prior owners" (54–55). This army descends with merciless fury on White's troops, cutting them down, scalping them, falling "upon the dying and sod-omiz[ing] them with loud cries to their fellows" (56). The terrific inhumanity of this scene might thus seem to vindicate McGilchrist's claim that McCarthy dehumanizes his Native Americans, presenting them more as brutal forces of nature than as peoples or cultures (151). Yet such unbridled warcraft does not distinguish them. It is not merely the case that the book is punctuated by mas-sacres visited upon, rather than perpetrated by, Indigenous Americans. This passage itself presents the Comanches as reflecting, in their bloodlust, both White's "civilizing" mission and the whole cultural history that undergirds it. It is by offering these putatively enlightened warriors a mirror that the Co-manches bedazzle and disarm them, and the bloodied trophies in which the victors are clad include not just a collage of nineteenth-century fashions, but costumes reaching back to the biblical and Attic foundations of the West. If these are the "barbarians" of this frontier, then, they seem to fill that role by reflecting important truths about the would-be emissaries of enlightenment; if they represent a primitive past that White's West insists needs surpassing, that past is revealed in its violence as markedly occidental and contemporary.

White's own appetite for Mexican blood in service to America's Manifest Destiny indicates that this Western culture sits at the vanguard of the novel's violent progress, something only more starkly underlined by the Glanton gang. Now, on the face of it, the historic Glanton seems odd company for a progres-sive figure like Holden. According to Sepich, Glanton contracted as an Indian hunter with the government of the Mexican state of Chihuahua on June 27, 1849, his commission being to kill as many of the Apaches and Comanches har-rying Mexican settlements as possible ("What Kind" 127). As proof of such kills, Glanton was to collect and present scalps which could garner as much as $200 (126). His, then, was not just a bloody, but a profoundly dehumanizing trade, reducing the lives and persons of Indigenous Americans, by gruesome synecdoche, to tradable commodities. As described by Chamberlain, the historical Glanton was a man well suited to such work. Chamberlain's first encounter with Glanton in a San Antonio saloon is with a man eager to face down pistol-toting antagonists with his Bowie knife (61). On Chamberlain's account, this knife did its work indiscriminately, collecting not just Indian, but also Mexican, scalps for payment from duped Mexican governors (310), and so indicating how the bloody reification involved in this trade brooked no lawful limits. McCarthy's Glanton cleaves close to this source. But the novel's rendering of its scalp collector serves both to stress the licitness of his venture—he is doing the work of "civilization," at the behest of duly constituted authorities—and to disclose it as radically dehumanizing, not only for those identified as legal quarry, but for agents of the Enlightenment themselves.

For McCarthy not only refuses to spare his readers the graphic details of this work on behalf of civilized authority; he insists upon its fundamentally inhuman character. While Glanton, Holden, and company may be feted heroes when the kid first lays eyes on them in Chihuahua, they are nonetheless described in terms evocative of the war party described above. They are "a pack of viciouslooking humans mounted on unshod indian ponies . . . bearded, barbarous, clad in the skins of animals" (*BM* 82). If their plundered mounts and rough garb recall the war dress of the Comanche raiders, their loot bespeaks an even bloodier theft of other men's costumes: "the trappings of their horses [are] fashioned out of human skin and their bridles woven up from human hair and decorated with human teeth and the riders wearing scapulars or necklaces of dried and blackened human ears" (82). Trading on human lives reduced to body parts reduced to currency, these agents of progress are revealed as proud collectors of macabre tokens, and they are themselves, it seems, in the process of disassembly, their status as civilized men lost in the badges of their bloodlust. Indeed, in their strikes against the Apaches, they mirror their supposedly "primitive" quarry almost perfectly, descending with terrible ruthlessness: "some of the men were moving on foot among the huts with torches and dragging the victims out, slathered and dripping with blood, hacking at the dying and decapitating those who knelt for mercy" (162). And, like the Comanches, these deputies of Western culture use phallic sexuality to debase the foe; their slaughter of a sleeping encampment concludes not only with a grim harvest of "receipts," but with hunters "coupled to the bludgeoned bodies of young women dead or dying on the beach" (163). The Enlightenment call to power is here revealed, then, as having less to do with the advance of civilization than with the licensing of brutishness.

Thus, as pursued by order of the civil authorities, Glanton's trade is from the start revealed as "merely carnage, without any rejuvenating or civilizing component" (Moos 24). In legitimizing such mayhem and murder, the project of "civilization" unleashes a violence that swiftly scorns its own parameters, fueling an insatiable rapine that targets all others not simply as enemies to be subdued, but as raw material to be rendered profitable commodity. In the raid quoted above, Glanton's men are already killing and scalping not just Apaches and their Mexican captives, but fallen Mexican comrades (*BM* 162; 165); soon they turn to bar fights and attacks on Mexican villages for more "receipts" (188; 189). After an earlier sojourn in Chihuahua descends into such havoc that the governor's own people scrawl "Mejor los indios" on the city's walls (178–79),[15] the gang returns, riding into the city "reeking with the blood of the citizenry for whose protection they had contracted" (193). Here, the process of brutalization plainly encompasses its agents themselves. If the Comanches' depredations link them to a distant occidental past, so Glanton's butchery in the cause of Enlightenment returns his men to a primordial, prehuman state. Tracking their prey, they ride "like men invested with a purpose whose origins were antecedent to them, like blood legatees of an order both imperative and remote" (158). Deputed champions of modernity, they loom as iterations of a bloody ancient script beyond their authorship or ken. Fleeing Mexican authorities, they arrive at Tucson like paleolithic throwbacks: "Save for their guns and buckles and a few pieces of metal in the harness of the animals there was nothing about these arrivals to suggest even the discovery of the wheel" (242). If their work in the cause of progress thus subverts progress and civilization both, it is further true that their assertions of suzerainty serve to unravel their own humanity. This is indicated both by their spiraling bloodlust and by the names they bear. Not only is the novel's seeming protagonist denied any humanizing proper name; as Hillier notes, bestializing monikers abound among his comrades (*Morality* 39), who boast such handles as Toadvine (*BM* 9), Grannyrat (81), and Bathcat (91).[16]

The Judge's elect, then, like the landscape they traverse, are steeped in blood and dehumanizing ruin; far from agents of scientific progress or proofs of man's self-mastery, they seem only to enact man's reduction to savage animal or dead, tradable thing. As McGilchrist puts it, "humanity here has become feral, less than feral . . . : reduced to some depraved state which mimics the wild, but lacks the dignity of the natural world" (122). Indeed, in its wildness, it works ultimately to produce a humanity reduced to matter, something as ruined and scattered as the novel's ravaged Church. Yet this diminishment of the human is, as McGilchrist also notes, gleefully "led by the avatar of science, the Judge" (122), in ways that indicate that his Enlightenment, far from securing human advancement, is itself servant to humanity's most destructive instincts. As William H. Goetzmann says of Holden, he figures as Glanton's "intellectual alter ego" (4), not his antithesis. Far from scorning Glanton's bloody bacchanal, the Judge is indeed the second of his party to claim a scalp (*BM* 117). Though happy to discourse on cutting-edge science, he is at one with the bounty hunters in their murders and their sprees alike. He, too, runs riot, baring his naked form to the elements as he shouts down the night's thunderstorms (124) or outfaces, "like some great balden archimandrite" (284), the setting sun. As much as he is presented as scientist and pedagogue, spokesman for the Enlightenment, Holden is also something both pagan and fearsome. Thus, we see him described not only as the hierophant named above, but as, "naked to the waist, himself like some great pale deity" (97).

What, then, are we to make of the novel's marriage of Holden and Glanton, of Enlightenment humanism and the bloodlust of lawless frontiersmen? First, this marriage speaks to McCarthy's revisionist aims, his seeking to document the violence unleashed by America's program of enlightened Manifest Destiny. Further, that the Judge, who seeks to make the New World subject to man's agency, is happy not just to serve, but wholeheartedly to spur, Glanton's crimes indicates his function in *Blood Meridian* as a critique of Enlightenment thought as ultimately antihumanist. More even than this, though, Holden's words and works reveal that thought as quintessentially evil, in a Christian and Catholic sense, insofar as, through him, it wages a war on Creation, on the very existence of beings alien to the ego, so as to secure for the latter the supremacy that the modern philosophy of knowledge-power mandates. In his uniting modern, secular reason with annihilating violence, Holden enacts the deformative consequences of the agonistic structure of the Enlightenment's equation of knowledge and power. As we have seen, the novel presents itself as the testing of human sovereignty against humanity's subjection, as simple clay, to a nature indifferent to our ends. As such, it establishes as its subject a contest more fundamental than Glanton's campaign against the Indians, a war whose basic architecture is determined by an Enlightenment outlook that demands the progressive expansion of human dominion over Creation. To pursue scientific knowledge, Descartes writes, "is really to engage in battle" (49). As Heidegger glosses this outlook, "through this uprising, all that is, is transformed into object [and] swallowed up into the immanence of subjectivity" (107). Similarly, the Judge, both in his choice of allies and in the practice of his science, reveals Enlightenment progress as deadly warfare, not simply between cultures, but between individual knowers who would be master and everything else, reduced to the merely knowable. Holden thus incarnates something close to what Adorno and Horkheimer identify as the dialectic of Enlightenment, modern thought's aptitude, even as it yields ever-new powers, for "sinking into a new kind of barbarism" (xi). As the Enlightenment program of advancement through reason reduces the individual to detached, self-sufficient knower and the world to inert, manipulable object, so, for Adorno and Horkheimer, it does violence to self and environment, precisely as it reduces them to the roles of mismatched combatants. With its aim of a rational human suzerainty over all that may be known, their Enlightenment represents a "sick" reification that "contains the despotism of the subjective purpose which is hostile to the thing and forgets the thing itself, thus committing the mental act of violence which is later put into practice" (193).

Certainly, Holden, both in his mode of inquiry and in his celebration of warfare, cleaves to Enlightenment norms so understood. He and his comrades literally trade on the reification of other human beings and the surrender of their own humanity. But even more clearly in his discourses on science and war does Holden claim for himself a fusion of power and knowledge whose aim is mastery but whose realization may be known only in destruction. Indeed, as others have noted, the Judge pursues Enlightenment ends through rather Nietzschean means;[17] for him, as for Nietzsche, "life itself is *essentially* appropriation, injury, overpowering of what is alien and weaker" (Nietzsche 203). Both his practice and his defence of science affirm the overpowering, assimilation, and destruction of the object of inquiry as a proper will to dominion over all that is external or antecedent to the knowing self. Collecting specimens and taking notes, the Judge is a student of artifacts, fossils, and living creatures, but this diversity of subjects is bound by a consistency in method. He collects so as to claim, takes his scientific notes so as to destroy, the objects of those observations, so that nothing external to his knowledge or will remains. As Moos contends, "in his desire to catalog the world, the judge seeks to destroy that world" (29). So, while he copies prehistoric pictographs in the desert, he seals his conquest of the known by the effacement of the thing itself: "he rose and with a piece of broken chert he scappled away one of the designs, leaving no trace of it" (*BM* 180). Likewise, his harvest of Spanish and Native American relics, all carefully entered in his ledger, concludes with their consignment to flames: "When he had done he took up the little footguard and . . . crushed it into a ball of foil and pitched it into the fire. He gathered up the other artifacts and cast them also into the fire" (146). Even the birds he sketches and stuffs must be killed to be mastered by this scientific knower (206). As he explains, "The freedom of birds is an insult to me. I'd have them all in zoos" (208).

My point is that such destruction is not accidental, nor is it some alien addition of Holden's to the Enlightenment's call to make the world subject to human sovereignty. The brand of humanism promoted by his modernity will brook no rival governor, no evidence of any other creative or controlling power. But Holden's program of unmaking—of the civilization and even humanity of Glanton and his victims, of ancient artifacts, of living birds and beasts—works both to involve his Enlightenment in a specifically Augustinian species of evil and to expose the modern outlook he embodies to a decidedly Catholic critique. Thus, while Parrish declares *Blood Meridian* a text decidedly "beyond good and evil" ("History" 77), it is rather the case that it is, as Mundik states, a novel "primarily concerned with evil" ("Terra" 29), an evil it identifies above all with its Enlightenment spokesman. Moreover, though Hawkins argues that McCarthy "insists on a positive ontological status for evil" (8), I maintain that what is most striking about the novel's rendering of the malevolence it ascribes to Western modernity is its ontological dependence and ultimate nullity. This fundamentally insubstantial, indeed, antisubstantial evil pursued by Holden is best understood in terms of the thought, not of the *philosophes*, but of Augustine of Hippo. As Augustine recognized, Christianity's portrait of an all-good, all-powerful Creator yields a daunting moral question: "Where then does evil come from, if God made all things and, because he is good, made them good too?" (*Confessions* 138). Two significant and abiding Catholic teachings are embedded in this query. First, there is the assertion of the goodness of Creation, corollary to God's own goodness. As expressed by the *Catechism*, this is the conviction that, "because creation comes forth from God's goodness, it shares in that goodness" (88). Second, and consequent on this, is the insistence on both the priority and relative fullness of the good. What exists before all else is an infinite and perfectly good being who, in the first instance, creates that which is good. What this means is that being and the cosmos are, at root, coincident with the good; as Aquinas later puts this, "the existence itself of things is good and any created thing, insofar as it exists, is good" (159).

This means that evil must be conceived not just as secondary and inferior, but as antithetical to being, as an unmaking of an aboriginally good Creation. That which is less than perfectly good is, Augustine notes, susceptible to defect and corruption. Significantly, this very vulnerability testifies to the initial goodness of such beings, since "if they were entirely without good, there would be nothing in them that could become corrupt" (*Confessions* 148). But corruption represents a loss of that original fullness of being which is goodness. Far from enjoying positive ontological status, evil, for Augustine, is rather a kind of nothingness, an uncreated lack: "What is that which is called evil, but the privation of good?" (*Faith* 18). On this account, "to lessen the good is to give rise to evil" (19), and since evil is loss and lack, and good coincident with a being derived from a benevolent Creator, then evil can only be understood as a belated corrosion of being, an unmaking of Creation. In the words of Aquinas, "since evil is a privation it is a kind of non-being" (572), one that threatens creatures with the loss of perfections and ultimate annihilation. Human evil, for Augustine, is the privation attendant on the perversion of the will, on its making idols of lesser goods at the cost of communion with the greatest good: God (*Confessions* 150). Nonetheless, key to his theodicy is an understanding of evil, first, as unmaking work rather than actual creation, and second, as something that can only arise in response to an antecedent good: "Evil things therefore had their origins in good things, and unless they reside in good things, they do not exist at all" (*Faith* 22). The goodness of Creation and its Creator, in other words, both precedes and exceeds the unmaking power of evil.

Holden's pursuit of human sovereignty through scientific conquest and martial unmaking can thus be read as an Augustinian indictment against Enlightenment aims, condemning both their motives and their methods. The Judge's scientific record expressly seeks the obliteration of the original specimen, for such annihilating violence is the means by which the knower's status as lord may finally be proved. He presents his destructive science as the elevation of the investigator to the status of godlike power; indeed, such usurpation of godhead is its goal. After tossing artifacts into the fire, "he [sits] with his hands cupped in his lap and he seem[s] much satisfied with the world, as if his counsel had been sought at its creation" (*BM* 146). Knowledge, for him, is about the expansion of dominion, the reconfiguration of the existent as the personally willed and thus the assumption of the Creator's role. As he says of the birds he kills in science's name, "whatever in creation exists without my knowledge exists without my consent" (207), and the fulfilment of his enlightened mission is to have Creation itself limited to that to which he does consent. If we are to progress by conquering nature, then all Creation must become, as known, subject to and product of, our attention and our will. This mandate itself, however, works against the existence of other entities and toward the deification of the human knower. As Brown puts it, in his destruction of objects of knowledge, Holden seeks "to instate himself as the ultimate referent—the transcendental signified—of all meaning" (75). His enlightened science constitutes an attempt to obliterate any other creator, a decisive turning of the human will away from relationship with the God Augustine proclaims our highest good.

Yet the terms of this project betray its ultimate futility. Creation, Holden's own empiricism reveals, exists prior to his consent, to his creative or destructive act; its mere existence refutes the absolute reign of human purposes which is his Enlightenment's goal and promise. Significantly, the novel is at pains to emphasize the inherent mystery and fullness of the natural world that the Judge seeks belatedly to claim through unmaking. Thus, for example, nighttime prairie skies are described as "so sprent with stars that there is scarcely space of black at all and they fall all night in bitter arcs and it is so that their numbers are no less" (*BM* 16). Much later, the kid, lost in the wintry desert night, beholds a lone blazing tree offering life-saving warmth and convoking a veritable Noah's ark of uncaged and luminous creatures: "A constellation of ignited eyes that edged the ring of light all bound in a precarious truce before this torch" (225). Wallach suggests this scene is meant "to parody the biblical burning bush" ("*Beowulf*" 205), but the simple awe which this tableau generates works, I contend, to stress the wonder of created being, its flamboyant outstripping of human knowledge and design. Thus, Holden's insistence on creative priority is undercut by the text and can, in fact, play out only in terms of conflict, of that petulant insistence on consent detailed above; if this is to be upheld, it must, then, take the form of the human will's war on the existent. As an Enlightenment thinker on Adorno and Horkheimer's model, Holden exists in antagonistic relationship with a world presented as beyond his ken and power. To be a true knower, he must, post facto, bring that world under his control and make it identical with himself; as he says, "in order for it to be mine nothing must be permitted to occur upon it save by my dispensation" (*BM* 207). Yet relative to a geology, an ecology, even a human history that precede his ability to define them, the only way knowledge can be validated as power, the only way to make the known subject to his will, is through acts of conquest. Only when that which exists by some agency beyond his own has been unmade and absorbed wholly into his ego has the Judge proved himself as scientist; only by destroying can he be modernity's self-determining will. His sole path to suzerainty, then, is to deny the manifest fact and binding precedent of nature, something he can pursue only by means of war on Creation and Creator both. His enterprise is revealed as a substitution of nothingness for being, that reversal of creation that Augustine terms evil. In his embodiment of Enlightenment progress, then, Holden reveals its work as fundamentally diabolical.[18]

If such evil is the pith of his scientific project, the affinity of this humanist polymath with Glanton's savagery becomes clearer. Ceaselessly at war with the cosmos, Holden is a champion of self-validating and other-obliterating violence in the human domain. Not just as knowers, but as social beings, human individuals are, for him, wills seeking autonomy and mastery. He understands the antagonistic model of Enlightenment inquiry as something bound to be enacted in social relations; this is not simply inescapable, but ennobling. For Holden, war is the badge of human freedom, just as wreckage is the warrant of true science. In his words, "if war is not holy man is nothing but antic clay" (319): created and determined, not the Enlightenment's self-governing rational will. War, then, is the one god the Judge avows (261); it must be so acknowledged because it is, on his view, who properly suzerain human beings are. As Holden's scientific method demonstrates, knowledge, for him, is existential contest; what enlightened inquiry teaches best, then, it teaches about us, and that is that we must be warriors, that through strife alone will we author and empower ourselves. In the Judge, then, the Enlightenment serves to validate the bloody economy of this bloodiest of texts. But in this pursuit of war on being as human empowerment, Holden and his confederates achieve, as noted, only the reverse of exaltation. In constant warfare, the human person, as much as the scientist's specimen, must be conquered, its own being and integrity unmade, if human preeminence is to be established. Holden's modernity thus devolves into a doctrine of ceaseless and corrosive violence, whose end is only the final annihilation of any other's will or work: "War was always here. Before man was, war waited for him. The ultimate trade awaiting its ultimate practitioner" (259). In defining war as the definitive human vocation, the Judge seeks to effect that unseating of the Creator that is his consistent diabolical aim, by claiming for war's own radical unmaking absolute primacy. In this, his Enlightenment binds him to Glanton's campaign, another attempt at radical autonomy through the negative creation of conflict. Inarticulate though he is, Glanton's thoughts resonate with the Judge's own pronouncements. Like Holden's, his violence is an assertion of radical independence and self-mastery: "allowing as he did that men's destinies are given yet he usurped to contain within him all that he would ever be in the world and . . . be his charter written in the urstone itself he claimed agency and said so and he'd drive the remorseless sun on to its final endarkenment as if he'd ordered it all ages since" (254).

My argument, then, is that the Judge, in his unmaking science, reveals how the Enlightenment pursues such endarkenment as Glanton represents. Holden's humanistic modernity is disclosed finally as a deadly and dehumanizing force, as, in fact, evil on the Catholic understanding. Despite his grounding in the core philosophies of American progress, then, Holden preaches no future; his thinking can image no generation of futurity, because it can conceive no development beyond the single, agonistic will. For Holden, man's "spirit is exhausted at the peak of its achievement. His meridian is at once his darkening and the evening of his day" (153). As an avatar of Enlightenment, the Judge undermines, as Adorno and Horkheimer would have us expect, such key Enlightenment ends as works and progress. If, for Bacon, modern science represents maturity, a movement beyond a puerile classical speculation that "can talk, but . . . cannot generate" (156), Holden's enactment of Bacon's assault on Creation proves signally barren. Both he and the warring world he celebrates traffic in exterminations, not engenderings of better, more humane futures. That this is so again testifies to the fundamentally Augustinian evil the novel ascribes to the Enlightenment he champions, the radically unmaking power it must claim for itself so as to be free of any higher or prior Creator. But this makes of Holden's brand of human empowerment, then, something not simply anti-God or anti-nature, but diabolically antihuman.

Thus, the tale over which he presides is driven everywhere by genocidal, rather than generational, impulses. McCarthy's Southwest is a graveyard for vanished peoples like the Anasazi and bestrewn with the wreckage of cultures unmade by bloody wars of extermination. If the Comanches, caught up in this colonial history, wipe out villages, such acts are anticipated by earlier Mexican massacres (94–95) and eclipsed by the work of the novel's instruments of modern progress. Glanton's indiscriminate assaults on Apache encampments and Mexican villages work to extend this economy of extermination under Holden's supervision and with his enlightened imprimatur. And such projects of extirpation encompass more than that eradication of peoples to which the Judge is merry party. As the example of his ornithology suggests, the establishment of modernity's empire of human ends underwrites the unmaking of nature, a war not just on cultures but on life. Hence the eerie landscape of the book's conclusion, a Texas of the 1870s in which established American rule, expansion of the age-defining technology of rail travel, and so "progress" through ascendant human agency in Enlightenment terms make a literal boneyard of the world. The novel's final chapter depicts the kid in middle age surveying the results of the great buffalo hunts that cleared the West for Anglo-American settlement: "The bones had been gathered into windrows ten feet high and hundreds long or into great conical hills" (331). As an old hunter explains, this is the perverse fruit of a cull awesome in its scope and terrible in its finality. He reports that "between the Arkansas River and the Concho there was eight million carcasses" (330), and that this is but one killing ground of a comprehensively annihilating program: "Ever one of them that God ever made is gone as if they'd never been at all" (330). This modern America whose laws the Judge embodies is one not of creation, but of its precise Augustinian antithesis, an unmaking of peoples and species on a massive scale.

Further, McCarthy's text makes clear that such negative creation is not to be understood as the Enlightenment's means to a more humane future predicated upon the works of empowered reason. Indeed, it is not the case that

Enlightenment, here, only contingently fails to secure that better world Captain White promises. Rather, by its core ambition to undo to human specifications the givens of the natural and social worlds, such thought works essentially to preclude any human progress at all and to dictate rehearsals of atavistic violence, in which the Judge and the principle of annihilation he represents will be the only things sure, as he chants at novel's end, never to die (348–49). In its pursuit of human supremacy and God's overthrow, then, the Judge's enlightened call to arms can achieve only destruction masquerading as godlike Creation and a worldly suzerainty seeking through its violent displays of power to disguise its own forfeit humanity. This negation of humanity and futurity is underscored by the common character of the prime targets of Holden's violence: namely, children. That this is a world without generation, without hope for a future that might grow beyond that bloody meridian of human ascendancy Holden announces, is made plain by the fact that virtually no children get out of its narrative alive. As George Guillemin notes, "Crimes committed on and by children abound" ("See" 242). This grisly theme is established early on, when the kid and Toadvine, following in the Comanches' bloody wake, come upon "a bush . . . hung with dead babies" (*BM* 60). But if these poor victims are, indeed, the strange fruit of Native American violence, this destruction of the promise children represent is more characteristic of their Euro-American enemies. The scalp hunters stumble across the remains of Mexico's infanticidal attacks on its Indian peoples, another boneyard scattered with "the tiny limbs and toothless paper skulls of infants" (95), before themselves energetically joining this dark trade. Their own massacre of a sleeping Apache camp sees babes bashed "against the stones so that the brains burst forth through the fontanel in a bloody spew" (162).

Yet the novel's prime consumer of children is Judge Holden himself. As Wallach notes, Holden's hairlessness serves to make his very person "suggestively penile" ("*Beowulf*" 206). But this phallicism is scarcely Baconian; his sexuality is notably issueless, only a further means to power through the unmaking of young life. Chamberlain's judge is identified as the author of "horrid crimes" against "a little girl of ten years . . . foully violated and murdered" (309). So, too, is McCarthy's Holden, Sepich's demurrals notwithstanding, presented as a voracious sexual predator, destroyer, not source, of generation.[19] His first victim is "a Mexican or halfbreed boy maybe twelve years old" found with a group of squatters at an abandoned copper mine (*BM* 122). As the bounty hunters prepare to depart, Holden appears "picking his teeth with a thorn as if he had just eaten" (124), right before the murdered child is discovered, naked and with his neck broken (125). The Judge, it is clear, is not just a child-killer, but one who feeds upon the young. Nor is this a singular instance; his victims punctuate the text. Five more, male and female, disappeared or found dead, follow on this first. There is the young boy preserved from the massacre of the Gileños to be Holden's plaything before ending up dead and scalped (170), the girl discovered missing soon after the Judge and company arrive at Jesús María (200), and the young girl kidnapped after their arrival at Tucson, her clothes "found torn and bloodied under the north wall, over which she could only have been thrown" (250). Later, left in charge of the Yuma ferry, Holden claims a more lasting prize: "A young Mexican girl was crouched naked under the shade of the wall. . . . She wore a rawhide collar about her neck and she was chained to a post" (284). After yet another girl goes missing at Fort Griffin (347), the kid himself, though taken belatedly in manhood in the outhouse of a Fort Griffin bar, might well be counted the Judge's seventh child victim: "[Holden] was naked and he rose up smiling and gathered him in his arms against his immense and terrible flesh" (347).[20] Here, as with the "halfbreed" boy, Holden seeks to assimilate and unmake his prey, just as he does the stones, artifacts, and specimens of his science; by doing so sexually, as well as murderously, he reveals the ungenerative character of his power-seeking epistemology. In him, we see a stridently godless modernity made sterile by its own warlike nature and servant, in its ostensible humanism, to a dehumanizing will to power.

THE MORAL GROUND OF CONTRITION

If the abhorrence of such crimes is not sufficient to establish the monstrosity of Holden and his philosophy, the fact that his incarnation of Enlightenment ambition so conforms to an Augustinian account of the nature of evil helps cue us to pass moral judgment on Holden's character and the historical works his teachings underwrite. That this moral assessment is significantly empowered by a countervailing Catholic understanding is indicated, however, not just by the formulation of evil at play in the text, but by the alternatives to that evil to be found there. These alternatives center chiefly on McCarthy's nameless protagonist, the kid. Holden himself accuses the kid of offering a unique resistance to his philosophy and its bloody enactment in Glanton's work; "each was called upon to empty out his heart into the common and one did not" (319), he tells the kid in his San Diego prison. Yet the extent to which this far from guiltless, ultimately doomed, figure serves as a moral foil to the Judge has been a matter of critical controversy, with many echoing Potts's assessment that, "against the absolute moral horror perpetrated by the Glanton Gang, [the kid's] minor mercies simply do not suffice" (65).[21] Still, in so ruthless a world as *Blood Meridian* details, such mercies are more than rare and certainly oppose, as Holden sees, the Judge's modern gospel. Thus, I concur with Joshua Masters that the kid does indeed represent "a moral possibility existing outside the judge's ego" (33). Nor is the text chary in offering evidence of the kid's antipathy to the total warfare Holden's program of unmaking demands. In contrast to the radical evil of the Judge, McCarthy's brutalized runaway retains some measure of innate goodness. Despite a paternal neglect that results in his being an illiterate son of a schoolmaster (*BM* 3), he preserves, even after many violent incidents, a "face . . . curiously untouched behind the scars, the eyes oddly innocent" (4). This potential for something more than the "taste for mindless violence" (3) his experience has cultivated is indicated even in the aftermath of a barfight that sees him kill a man. The terrible morning after has him wading "into the river like some wholly wretched baptismal candidate" (29).

While the wretchedness of his moral state, his need for absolution and reform, is underscored here, so, too, is a longing for and even the faint possibility of just such conversion. Though the kid will never realize that possibility, neither does he ever simply foreclose upon it. Significantly, the kid is not present when the Judge makes disciples and communicants of the Glanton gang. Rather, associated, as above, with more Christian sacraments, he remains true to his refusal of what he calls Holden's "craziness" (343). It is noteworthy that McCarthy's detailed renderings of the gang's assaults on their victims include no report of the kid's own acts; disappearing from the narrative at these points, he seems almost one who, in Holden's words, "broke with the body of which you were pledged a part" (319). Certainly, his final confrontation with the Judge indicates the kid's enduring refusal to pledge himself to Holden's bloody Enlightenment. At Fort Griffin, he insists, "I aint with you" (341). In the face of Holden's insistent prompts both to acknowledge his bloody deeds and to celebrate them as

triumphs, not sins requiring baptismal ablutions, the kid, now thirty years removed from his Glanton years, both refuses and incisively diagnoses the Judge.
As Holden proclaims God's death—the "gods of vengeance and of compassion
alike lie sleeping in their crypt" (343)—and trumpets the bloody suzerainty this
enjoins upon the human ego, the kid persists in his dissent before offering his
final judgment on the Judge: "You aint nothin" (345). Despite the implications
of his idiomatic double negative, McCarthy's protagonist is clearly condemning
the Judge's diabolical humanism and, I submit, defining his evil in Augustinian
terms. Thus, he not only rejects Holden's deification of bloody will to power,
but adopts a rather traditional moral perspective in doing so.

If the kid reveals here, in Brown's words, "that the judge's . . . power is
incomplete" (74), he does so by offering a rival moral outlook, one which his
own early deeds and later spiritual searching cast in Christian terms. Though
made party to the terrible violence of the frontier, the kid is most typically described, after the first two chapters—after, indeed, his wretched river bath—as
offering compassionate service to others, not seeking to vanquish, assimilate,
and annihilate them. There abides in him, in other words, traces not just of
innocence, but of charity, of that Samaritan compassion whose scornful eulogy
Holden delivers above. Indicated by his early work "in a diptheria pesthouse"
(*BM* 5), this readiness to serve and not enslave the other endures in him. Thus,
while Sepich notes in the whole of the novel but seventeen instances of helping
behavior, fully nine of these belong to the kid (*Notes* 181–82). These include his
refusal, despite the latter's telling him to save himself, to abandon the gravely
wounded Sproule, fellow survivor of the Comanche rout of Captain White's filibuster (66–71). Similarly, he moves, after the gang's first assault on the Apaches,
to help a comrade struck through with a lance before Glanton orders him away
and puts a bullet in the hapless McGill's head (163–64). Given the treatment
of the wounded so normalized, it is little wonder that the mercenaries, even
ex-priest Tobin, refuse to help David Brown with the arrow lodged in his thigh,
yet the kid comes to his aid and successfully removes it (168–69). Left to kill
Shelby, another wounded confrere Glanton will not have hampering the gang's
work, the kid balks and instead hides Shelby as best he can before moving on
(217–18). Such merciful gestures and refusals of needless violence extend even
to the Judge. After the massacre at the Yuma ferry, the kid refrains several times,
and despite Tobin's urging, from shooting an unarmed Holden. As the Judge

says, "you've not the heart of a common assassin. I've passed before your gun-
sights twice this hour" (311). Though this refusal of the Judge's ethos will doom
the kid to die at Holden's hands years later,[22] it conforms, in fact, to a consistent
pattern in his conduct: a growing reluctance, not Holden's eagerness, to assert
the self in deadly violence, and more, a capacity for mercy and fellowship that
binds the self to service, rather than calling it to lordship.

The kid thus seems, in the Judge's words, "mutinous" indeed (312), striving
when possible to uphold a standard of compassionate charity, not murderous
assertion of the self's primacy over God and neighbor both. But it is in his
efforts after his time with Glanton to offer not just service, but confession and
atonement that the kid's ethical alternative to Holden takes on a more patently
Catholic cast. Practiced by Christians since the first century, normalized by
the twelfth century, in its private, auricular form, as a sacrament of the Latin
Church (Coolman 211), and reaffirmed by the Council of Trent as a Christ-
founded work of that Church (Walter 322), Penance, or confession, has long
been a distinguishing feature of Roman Catholic life. Requiring of the penitent
the oral enumeration of faults before a priest, as well as penitential good works
to atone for those sins, confession is an act that defies Holden's Enlightenment
on at least two counts. First, it demands submission before a higher authority—
both priestly and divine—that the confessant understands to be not just legitimate, but absolutely necessary to his or her own ultimate good. Second, it posits
fellowship, not sovereignty, as essential to self-realization. Also known as the
sacrament of reconciliation, it seeks the self's return to relationship with its
Creator and with human beings both: "the goal of sacramental reception and
celebration of reconciliation is to bring the sinner back into communion with
God and into unity with all men and women" (Akinwale 545). In its accepting
a higher authority and striving for community, as well as in its proclamation of
a God other and greater than the human will, confession is antithetical to the
philosophy Holden represents. As Akinwale puts it, the Christian life to which
it bears witness "is the absolute negation of all forms of self-sufficiency" (556).

Importantly, though he never finds an alternate judge before whom he
can make his confession and from whom he can receive absolution, the kid
clearly seeks just such an authority in the novel's final chapters. Though initially fiercely independent and scornful of the divine—he believes he neither
hears nor needs God's voice, for example (*BM* 130), and denies any bond with

a Creator he feels never "much had [him] in mind" (20)—by the time he has freed himself from Glanton and the Judge, he seems hungry both to confess and to atone. Thus, while Carson sees his volubility, first, before his jailers and, then, before the eldress in the rocks as an attempt at self-justification (33), it is clear that these moments involve rueful self-judgment and a need to make amends, to be forgiven and reconciled on the sacramental pattern. As Knox notes, the confessant need bring only two things to the sacrament: "sorrow for sin combined with a purpose . . . of avoiding it in the future" (*Belief* 188). Certainly, the first of these is indicated by the kid's conduct after his Glanton travels. Under arrest in San Diego, "he began to speak with a strange urgency of things few men have seen in a lifetime and his jailers said that his mind had come uncottered by the acts of blood in which he had participated" (*BM* 317). This sounds less like boasting or self-exoneration than unburdening. Both the purpose and the equipage of the travel he undertakes upon his release underscore his seeming need for a confession of guilt and for a path to reconciliation through penitential works. After having a wound attended to, "he inquire[s] at every door for news of the expriest" with whom he arrived at the coast (323). Though he never finds Tobin (325), it is clear that he maintains this search for some time, a search not simply for a comrade, but, I argue, for a confessor. Two talismanic items he bears with him throughout the remainder of his life likewise testify both to his readiness to own his crimes and to his longing for an auditor competent to forgive them.

Tellingly, he purchases with the last of his money "the scapular of heathen ears that Brown had worn" (324), and he carries away from a mining camp a bible "no word of which could he read" (325). That he preserves the former might seem to indicate pride in, or fondness for, bloody days spent with the now-executed Brown. More obviously, however, this grim accessory, worn openly, serves as a public proclamation of his violent past. As the scene with Elrod demonstrates, he is prepared to tell anyone who asks of its origins and does so plainly, with neither glee nor menace (333). Thus, it becomes an invitation to confessors. That a desire for absolution is at work here is indicated not only by his attachment to a Christian good news left sealed to him, but even more by the other major encounter narrated from the roughly thirty years that separate San Diego from Fort Griffin. Sighting a procession of penitents, "men naked to the waist in black capes and hoods who flailed themselves with whips of braided yucca" following another "who bore a heavy wooden cross on his shoulders" (326), he traces next morning their bloody footprints, as though not just condemned to, but actively seeking, his own penitential path. That he is moved by such longing is demonstrated by the fact that, once he finds them murdered, he turns to offer his story and his service to an old woman, a seeming survivor, kneeling nearby. As Broncano notes, what follows bears striking parallels to sacramental confession (41). While no priest, the woman, clad in a shawl adorned with "the figures of stars and quartermoons and other insignia of a provenance unknown to him" (*BM* 328), is, as Sepich states, evocative of Our Lady of Guadalupe (*Notes* 123), and so a fit tribunal before whom to state one's need for forgiveness. This the kid does, telling her his life story, including that he "had been at war" (*BM* 328), before offering, in Samaritan fashion, to "convey her to a safe place . . . for he could not leave her in this place or she would surely die" (328). Once again, then, the kid is ready to confess his crimes and to undertake good works that manifest sorrow over, and a willingness to do penance for, such acts. As such, he reaffirms both his ethical alternative to the power seeking of the Judge and that alternative's investment in a Catholic imagination antithetical to the unmaking Holden champions.

Yet what I am here treating as the kid's penitential quest proves, in the end, a failure. This wayside confessor proves incapable of absolving his sins or esteeming his charity. As he moves to help her up, the kid discovers that "she [is] just a dried shell . . . dead in that place for years" (328). With this act of confession, this reaching out for communion, proved futile, the kid spends the rest of his life a wanderer, unable, as his shooting of young Elrod reveals, even to put his killing days behind him. Having found, despite seeking, neither community nor congregation, he is inexorably drawn back to Holden and a grisly end in a saloon jakes (347). Nor do I agree with those, like Hamilton (143), who read the novel's epilogue as undermining this apparent victory for the Judge and the brand of progress he represents.[23] Describing "a man progressing over the plain by means of holes which he is making in the ground" and followed by "wanderers in search of bones" (*BM* 351), this vignette offers us a portrait of the same subdued wilderness—its bison annihilated, its Indigenous peoples extirpated— through which the kid travels en route to his meeting with Holden. A scene of America's settling of the West, it seems governed by the same tyrannical knowing and relentless unmaking that define the Judge's Enlightenment. Thus, the man is driven by "the verification of a principle, a validation of sequence and causality" (351), and the bone gatherers seem as soulless as their gleanings, moving "like mechanisms" with a "prudence or reflectiveness which has no inner reality" (351). There seems little warrant here for thinking the American future Holden's Enlightenment invites will be less dehumanizing than the landscape in which he enjoys his closing dance. As Dorson contends, "the sacrilegious creed of progress and effectivity . . . remains victorious" ("Demystifying" 109).

And yet, by virtue of the Catholic touchstones deployed in the depiction of the kid and Judge both, this death-dealing creed does not go unopposed. This is true even diegetically. The kid, his failure to find peace and grace notwithstanding, resists the Judge to the end. What's more, that his attempts at goodness through confession and service finally fail to achieve their ends—his mercies no more save Sproule or Shelby than his longing to repent rescues him—itself offers a metric of goodness independent of human success, the effectivity that Holden preaches. This last is perhaps most to the point. Though the kid does not prosper, his countervailing example empowers readers to take the moral measure of Holden's cult of human lordship which, as *Blood Meridian* makes graphically plain, has unleashed such ruin on the New World. As I have argued, this novel reveals how a modernity that pursues the triumph of the human will through a science wed to domination becomes itself mired in bloody evils and historic crimes. So far as it remains centered upon an agonistic quest for dominion over its strictly material world, Enlightenment thought is, on *Blood Meridian*'s account, barred from meaningful progress in human terms. Holden's worldview wages war on humanity, nature, and futurity, securing the proper suzerainty of Enlightenment thought only in a program of radical unmaking. Yet McCarthy's text underwrites an ethical condemnation of that program by way of its deployment of Christian concepts at odds with the creeds of modernity. In its use of Holden to unpack this modernity in Augustinian terms and its presentation, in the kid, of a powerfully confessional response to the challenge of our history, *Blood Meridian* offers a critique of the Enlightenment that is steeped in Catholic tradition. While this morally challenging work need not be taken as an authorial confession of faith, it does establish a rather Catholic refusal to subscribe to Holden's combative metaphysics.

CHAPTER 5

LA FE ES TODO

FALSE INNOCENCE AND BROKEN FAITH IN THE BORDER TRILOGY

Not only does democracy make men forget their ancestors but also hides their descendants and keeps them apart from their fellows. It constantly brings them back to themselves and threatens . . . to imprison them in the isolation of their own hearts.

— ALEXIS DE TOCQUEVILLE, *Democracy in America*

Faith always implies the surpassing of a limit; it presupposes movement toward others and from others, which then points to the origin from *the* other, the Lord himself.

— JOSEPH RATZINGER, *Called to Communion*

The 1992 publication of *All the Pretty Horses* marked a watershed in McCarthy's career. Capturing the National Book Award while selling nearly half a million copies in two years (Jarrett, *Cormac* 6), the first volume of the Border Trilogy won McCarthy's work a much expanded audience it has yet to lose. What permitted his second foray into the Western a commercial success that eluded *Blood Meridian* is unclear, but surely part of the answer lies in the fact that the trilogy's central figures, John Grady Cole and Billy Parham, offer readers more sympathetic footholds in the novelist's imagined worlds than do the demonic Judge Holden or the minimally delineated kid. Parrish argues that these twentieth-century cowboys represent a new brand of protagonist for McCarthy, in that they "are honorable and traditionally heroic" ("History" 71).[1] Yet despite such innovations, there are clear continuities between these texts. Set, as Broncano notes, almost exactly one hundred years after (57), and on much the same terrain as, the main action of McCarthy's first southwestern fiction, *All the Pretty Horses* invites readers to situate its narrative in relation to that earlier work. In fact, James Lilley contends that the trilogy "begins where *Blood Meridian* ends" (273). This it does, I submit, by tracing the continuation of those processes my last chapter revealed to be central to Holden's assault on the nineteenth-century frontier, charting the further advance of the kinds of commodification, extirpation, and dislocation exemplified in *Blood Meridian*'s scalp trade, bison slaughter, and final closing of the frontier. Thus, in the Comanche ghosts that haunt John Grady, the vanished wolves that call to Billy's heart, and the reduction of romance to sex trade in *Cities of the Plains*, the trilogy emphasizes how American progress involves serial depredations on life and human dignity.

These novels, then, extend the critique of Enlightenment that animated McCarthy's first Western, dramatizing how America's faith in human mastery over self and nature historically effects a profound unmaking. While bringing the story begun in *Blood Meridian* into the postwar age of American hegemony, the trilogy once again questions the national ideals that have driven this ascent, ultimately echoing Turner's own fears that American democracy, "strong in selfishness and individualism . . . and pressing individual liberty beyond its proper bounds, has its dangers as well as its benefits" (32). Yet it is this question of benefits that distinguishes these novels of the 1990s from their predecessor. As noted, the trilogy centers on the most attractive McCarthy protagonists to date. Clinging to a cowboy lifestyle that progress has rendered anachronistic, to ranches being lost to oil companies and military expropriation, John Grady and Billy experience themselves as victims of modernity and dissident champions of a nobler past. Indeed, it is by casting themselves in this underdog's role that they remain, in their own eyes and many readers', righteous figures. In love with America's frontier history, and the pioneering self-reliance that shaped it, they seem to embody that tradition as a virtuous counterpoint to a degraded modernity. Put simply, they understand themselves to be not just at odds with their world of regnant industrialism and commercialism, but innocent of its crimes.

It is in this presumption of innocence, however, that they reveal their debt to the destructive Enlightenment they wish to escape. As Hawkins notes, McCarthy consistently demonstrates "that belief in American innocence is a particularly dangerous aspect of American mythology" (34). Certainly, John

Grady's and Billy's belief in their own righteousness, their insistence on a rightful sovereignty over their destinies, exposes this duo and all they love to considerable danger. First, far from resisting the faults of their historical moment, both their self-elected quests and the traditions they seek to cleave to in following them are revealed to be predicated on the same Enlightenment values—personal autonomy, progress through mastery of one's environment, purely elective, contractual bonds—that produce the modernity from which they recoil. Just as the frontier past they seek has eradicated the very exemplars of wildness they romanticize, so their attempts to recapture that lost America see them enact its suspect values. Assured of their own innocence, they insist upon the right to go their own way and claim their own goods, and ignore the extent to which they are, by virtue of their own sense of such rights, implicated in the crimes of American history, past and present. By so doing, they persist, as I have elsewhere argued of Billy, in "attempts [at] a self-authored return to Eden" (DeCoste, "One Among" 441). Yet if it is true, as Alan Bourassa maintains, that Westerns are fundamentally "about the American Garden of Eden" (440), then in McCarthy's hands, the genre becomes a testimony to human fallenness and so to the folly of the quintessentially American mission the trilogy's protagonists undertake. Indeed, their thinking discounts a fallen state that McCarthy's rather more Catholic texts insist upon. By so denying their postlapsarian condition, Cole and Parham end up pursuing courses that reenact the Fall through failures to keep faith with neighbors and to maintain faith in God.

Thus, despite Mundik's claim that these novels ultimately rebuke "the harshness of some traditional Catholic dogmas" (*Bloody* 220), the trilogy deploys Catholic understandings of faith and fallenness to indict the Enlightenment ideals that underwrite attempts to escape the tainted modernity such ideals have fashioned. The boys' quests become tragically self-critiquing insofar as they dramatize that sundering of solidarity that de Tocqueville deems a characteristic American malady. Assured of the moral soundness of their self-elected course, John Grady and Billy refuse to honor limits imposed by duties to others. Repeatedly, they abandon, neglect, or even betray family, friends, and benefactors. They not only deny any need for community or communion; they catastrophically reject the obligation to keep faith with their neighbor. More, as revealed by the novels' intensifying attention to religious questions, this pursuit of innocence involves what is presented as a lamentable loss of that dependence on a divine other that Ratzinger details above. The trilogy dramatizes how notions of the sovereign individual effect a tragic abandonment of faith as unnecessary to a self conceived, in Enlightenment terms, as sufficient and unfallen. Cole and Parham both engage in doomed attempts at playing savior to entities imperiled by their Enlightenment culture. Yet their refusal of obligation to God or neighbor leads them to exacerbate sins they seek to oppose and to accelerate the loss of goods they yearn to defend. These ill-fated projects are sustained by an American faith in their own innocence that a more Catholic perspective on human insufficiency operative in these texts—particularly in their interpolated parables[2]—deems false. Indeed, these cowboys summon disaster by refusing to avow that fallen condition and to pursue the faithfulness such a condition urges, revealing how central to McCarthy's critique of the myth of American innocence Catholic concepts are. Unlike *Blood Meridian*, however, the trilogy does not abandon hope for its heroes. If not in John Grady's violent end, then certainly in Billy's final surrender to loving kinship, there remains a chance that McCarthy's characters might yet be saved, not by a mythical American past or dubious Enlightenment ethos, but by faith.

MODERNITY'S COMPROMISED MAVERICKS

Yet however divergent their endings, McCarthy's protagonists begin their respective tales facing a similar American donnée. Each volume of the trilogy opens by establishing a Southwest defined by an encroaching modernity. Their mid-century milieu is one defined by just those Enlightenment tenets canvassed in chapter 1; it is a world in which technological dominion over nature, faith in personal autonomy, and contractual, marketplace relations govern. If, in Gillespie's words, "modernity has two goals—to make man master and possessor of nature and to make human freedom possible" (42), then John Grady and Billy inhabit a decidedly modern environment. Such suzerainty over nature and sovereign possession of oneself have not, however, conduced to emancipation. Here, as in *Blood Meridian*, the advancement of the Enlightenment project involves an unmaking of the natural world and a commodification and diminishment of the human person. As Cooper argues concerning *The Crossing*, the trilogy concerns itself with "the ways that men seize, claim, and profit from the violent acquisition of the bodies of human and nonhuman others" (*Cormac*

57). The deadly nature of this process is indicated by the experience of old Mr. Johnson, a man whose life effectively bridges the world of the kid and that of Oppenheimer: "In his time the country had gone from the oil lamp and the horse and buggy to jet planes and the atomic bomb" (*CP* 106). As the rendering of progress in terms of unprecedentedly deadly weaponry indicates, though centered on more appealing characters, these novels detail the same bloody costs of American Enlightenment as form the focus of McCarthy's first Western.

These costs are most evident in postwar America's obliteration of the continent's ecology and Indigenous peoples. If, for Bacon, the aim of his new science was to inaugurate the modern by being a means through which "nature may be commanded and subdued" (230), then the Border Trilogy repeatedly foregrounds how American modernity has assumed just such command. Certainly, whatever in nonhuman Creation was once wild and free is presented as emphatically tamed or extinct. This is demonstrated first by the completion of that fencing of the frontier with which *Blood Meridian* concludes. Though Billy can recall the Hidalgo County of his early childhood as an untouched expanse—"You could ride clear to Mexico and not strike a crossfence" (*TC* 3)—Cooper's dynamic of seizure and profit soon parcels out the lands conquered and annexed by the United States to craft a series of borders out of the mastered wilderness. Some twenty years later, John Grady and Lacey Rawlins find their flight to Mexico amply impeded by fences and wire. "How the hell do they expect a man to ride a horse in this country," Rawlins asks, to which Cole replies simply, "They dont" (*APH* 31). Further, the novels make clear that this process of enclosure and discarding even of that first engine of pioneer enterprise, the horse, involves, as much as jet fighters and Manhattan Projects, a real measure of harm and loss. Thus, Billy, returning from his first Mexican sojourn, traces "the shadow of [a] fence crossing the land in the moonlight like a suture" (*TC* 164).

These pastures have not just been bounded; they have been substantially cleared. The program of extinction chronicled in *Blood Meridian* reaches here beyond the bison. It extends first, and most obviously, to the wolf. Though six-year-old Billy wakes of a winter's night to howling and gazes, rapt, at "wolves twist[ing] and turn[ing] and leap[ing] in a silence such that they [seem] of another world entire" (4), ten years later wolves have been uprooted from his world altogether. "There aint no more wolves but what they come up out of

Mexico" (24), he concedes as a teen, the nuisance species having been hunted to extinction for the benefit of a ranch economy. For Mr. Johnson, memories of the wolf are even more remote: "I aint heard a wolf howl in thirty odd years. I dont know where you'd go to hear one" (CP 126). But America's progressive mastering of nature eradicates more than this predator. Remaking the wilds as pasture means unmaking much more native life and aboriginal culture. Thus, the stray Mexican wolf that Billy tracks finds a landscape made lean by a voracious modernity: "Most of the game was slaughtered out of the country. Most of the forest cut to feed the boilers of the stampmills at the mines" (TC 25). Where trees once towered, there remains only a massive stump "upon which in winters past herders had pitched a four by six foot canvass supply tent for the wooden floor it gave" (5). This assault on teeming wildlife persists postwar, as indicated by Troy's tale of speeding in a new Oldsmobile only to discover at a fuel stop the grille of the car "packed completely full of jackrabbit heads. I mean there was a hundred of em jammed in there" (CP 22). Here, that emblem of American ascendancy, the automobile, becomes the vanquisher of nature par excellence, a role it rehearses scant pages later when a backroads collision leaves a "large owl [lying] cruciform across the driver's windshield" of the truck in which Troy has shared his story (34).

Yet perhaps the most poignant equation of progress with loss has to do with peoples, not beasts or forests. The trilogy's first two volumes are haunted by ghosts of America's first peoples and so by reminders of what the enlightened mastery of nature has involved for the Indigenous cultures that westward expansion found occupying the supposed wilds. In the Southwest of The Crossing, Native Americans are as removed from the land as the wolf. The Indian the Parham boys disturb at his hunting is, in Billy's words, "just a drifter" (14), solitary, displaced, and indigent: "He wore an old tattered blanketcoat and an old greasy Stetson . . . and his boots were mended with wire" (6). Yet, however disinherited by modernity, this figure remains, quite consequentially, on the land. Less than a decade later, John Grady will be able to meet Native Americans only in fantasy. Mourning his grandfather, he rides out "where the western fork of the old Comanche road coming down out of the Kiowa country to the north passed through the westernmost section of the ranch" (APH 5). In 1949, no Comanches remain to roam this settled land, the remnants of this powerful nation having long since been removed to reservations.[3] Thus, Cole can only imagine the spectacle of their passage, "nation and ghost of nation passing in a soft chorale across that mineral waste . . . bearing lost to all history and all remembrance like a grail the sum of their secular and transitory and violent lives" (5). If John Grady envisions this people as an avatar of the fierce and unbroken, the fact that he must conjure such a vision testifies that their dominion is itself concluded, a victim of American progress.

But if America's mastering of nature thus involves not just the reshaping, but the erasure of much that is native to its lands, this does not halt at aboriginal cultures. The first settlers' pastoralism, too, is presented as a victim of, and not just a stage in, progress. Guillemin argues that the trilogy concludes with a final foreclosure on the pastoral itself ("As of" 95). Certainly, it opens with John Grady described as "like a man come to the end of something" (*APH* 5), and what seems to be ending is an eighty-three-year-old family ranch. In an America seeking ever-greater power from and over nature, these lands, which have "barely paid expenses for twenty years" (15), are of value not for the cattle they can feed, but for the fuel they might provide an automotive economy. Nearby San Angelo features not horses, but "oilfield scouts' cars parked along the street that looked like they'd been in a warzone" (11). These buyers find a receptive audience in John Grady's mother, who sells the ranch he deems his just inheritance. That these agents are linked to warfare indicates the inimical aspect they wear in his eyes, but also the kinds of power definitive of his historical moment. The economic expansion and technological advance that disinherit John Grady are both rooted in recent military success and linked to America's superpower ambitions. Thus, when, years later, he has found work on Mac's ranch, he knows this is no lasting sanctuary. These lands, too, are set to be condemned for weapons testing; as Cole concedes, "We'll all be goin somewhere when the army takes this spread over" (*CP* 50). The pastoral life that he, a boy convinced "that God had put horses on earth to work cattle and that other than cattle there was no wealth proper to a man" (*APH* 127), embodies must make way for progress, as have the wolves and the hunters before it. Indeed, he and his father discern this repetition and identify with Native Americans' loss of their way of life. In the words of Mr. Cole, "We're like the Comanches was two hundred years ago. We dont know what's goin to show up" (*APH* 25–26).[4]

Modernity's depredation embraces more than an increasingly antiquated pastoralism. As the Enlightenment call to master nature serves the obliteration of pre-Columbian life, so does the mid-century marketplace increasingly render all intercourse a process of commodification. Arnold calls attention to the "diminished world" McCarthy offers readers in the trilogy's last volume ("Last" 222), a shift signaled by Billy's reduction to a "coarse cowpoke joking about fucking fat whores" (232). But this dehumanizing trajectory impacts more than just Parham or *Cities of the Plains*. Rather, as Holloway argues, the whole trilogy is predicated on the view that World War II reshaped American society "according to the diktats of an intensified logic of commodification" (*Late* 106), a process which effected an "unprecedented extension of exchange value into all areas of human life" (117). Though this last claim may sound like over-reach, it does not exaggerate the role played in these novels by those contractual communities discussed in chapter 1. In the Border Trilogy, everything is for sale. Its world matches that definition of a healthy society proffered by a Mexican cabbie, one where "choice should always be the prerogative of the buyer" (*CP* 56). In fact, the Juarez of *Cities* seems nothing more than a bazaar catering to empowered American shoppers. As McCarthy's ranch hands walk its streets, they run a gauntlet of sales pitches: "Shopowners called to them and streetvendors with jewelry and serapes sallied forth to attend them" (7). The trilogy's merchandise comprises more than trinkets, however. As Billy learns from a Juarez bartender, jobs, too, are for sale—"do you know what it costs to buy a job like this?" (128)—and Cole discovers that discharge from Mexican prisons is a matter less of law than of lucre when Dueña Alfonsa purchases his release (*APH* 209).

The reduction of the human person to saleable commodity is, however, most starkly revealed in the fate of women.[5] Having already witnessed the she-wolf he struggled to save transformed into a ten-centavo sideshow (*TC* 104), Billy recoils from witnessing a traveling diva's similar fate as a peepshow siren, angrily refusing a barker's offer of a free peek: "No quiero verlo, me entiende?" (377). Yet in *Cities*, he is not just content to go whoring in the Juarez brothel in which that novel opens, but revels in the dehumanization of its prostitutes, telling John Grady, "Get that one I had. She's five gaited or I never rode" (*CP* 6). This treatment of the young and vulnerable as so much livestock is no simple matter of profane idiom. The sex worker that here captivates John Grady, "[a] young girl of no more than seventeen" (6), has been first consigned to sexual slavery at thirteen to settle a gambling debt and is thereafter sold and resold, by pimps, nuns, and police, into the most brutalizing abjection: "When [the officers] were through with her they sold her to the other policemen. Then they sold her to the prisoners for what few pesos they could muster or traded her for cigarettes" (139). Thus in Magdalena is intensified that radical commodification of persons McCarthy detailed in *Suttree*. In her experience, a society predicated on the empowered consumer, on the unfettered right of the individual to name and procure his own goods, emerges as a predatory marketplace in which people become fungible commodities.

Yet the enlightened mastery of environment and ends achieves its most profound undoing of nature and humanity in the historic event that resounds through McCarthy's tale: World War II. Billy insists "the war changed everything" (78), and the trilogy seems to bear this out. John Grady's father has been broken by service in the Pacific. Though he has survived Japanese POW camps, he tells his son, "I aint the same as I was" (*APH* 12); indeed, before the first novel closes, he is dead. But it is, above all, in the atom bomb that human dominion over nature, on Enlightenment lines and through Enlightenment means, is revealed as an unprecedented unmaking. The birth of the nuclear age lies at the heart of the trilogy, providing the conclusion to its second installment. Utterly orphaned in the world, Billy is roused from slumber in a derelict waystation by the terrible dawning of a new epoch, what Knox, in 1945, termed "a catastrophic leap in the history of human achievement," in our "efforts to gain the mastery over brute nature" (*God* 12). Billy wakes to "the white light of the desert noon" in the predawn hours of a summer's morning (*TC* 425). This unnatural midday emanates not from the east, but from the north, and though brilliant, is nothing solar: "there was no sun and there was no dawn" (425). Quickly dissipating, leaving behind "an alien dusk" and "an alien dark" (425), this mysterious illumination is, as Arnold affirms, the first atomic detonation of the Trinity Project.[6] This marks more than a new command of nature that allows for the vaporization of flora, fauna, and landscape; it inaugurates a power aimed at a destruction of human life so colossal as to threaten its wielders themselves with extinction. Its baleful character is communicated both in the idiom used in its depiction and in the abject sobs to which it reduces McCarthy's protagonist. Here, the trilogy dramatizes both the modernity his cowboys occupy and the radical menace of its form of Enlightenment.

Such, then, is the moment in which John Grady and Billy find themselves: one of tamed wilderness, dehumanizing mercantile relations, and profoundly destructive scientific advance. Yet, as Chollier notes and *Suttree* has shown, McCarthy is drawn to "individual rebellion against market economies which involve the commodification of animals and human beings" ("Autotextuality" 17). It should come, then, as no surprise that the trilogy's protagonists live, in Ellis's words, "in defiance of their actual technological moment" ("Science" 187). John Grady and Billy begin by repudiating their present and identifying with an idealized frontier past. This is communicated in the former's dreams of vanished Comanches, but it resonates more broadly in his romanticization of wildness and the rancher's life. The first of these, *All the Pretty Horses* makes plain, is the matrix of his self-conception: "All his reverence and all his fondness and all the leanings of his life were for the ardenthearted and they would always be so" (6). Cole resists modernity by seeking to tap into the premodern power of nature itself. This passionate identification with the untamed underwrites his love of horses and his longing for immersion in their experience. His bond with these creatures is such that "if he were begot by malice or mischance into some queer land where horses never were he would [find] them anyway" (23). In moments of distress, he is sustained by dreams of communion with them, of moving "in a resonance that was like a music among them . . . they ran in that resonance which is the world itself and which cannot be spoken but only praised" (161–62). Thus holding the horse—and the life of the horseman—sacred, John Grady recoils from his automotive present and seeks a return to that past the horse symbolizes. Because, in the words of his killer, Eduardo, he "cannot bear that the world be ordinary" (*CP* 253), at least not in twentieth-century terms, his aspirations fix on a past defined by the ranching life his own age denies him. He heads to Mexico, as Lilley observes, in an attempt to travel back in time to "a place where the codes of the Old West are still valorized" (274). His contentment upon arrival south of the border is derived from a belief that, in Rawlins's words, "this is how it was with the old waddies," and expressed in a wish to remain in here for "about a hundred years" (*APH* 96).[7]

Though warned that "the past cannot be mended" (*TC* 202), Billy, too, dreams of travel to a better time. His Mexican sojourns in *The Crossing* represent nothing other than serial attempts to reclaim some forfeit treasure: the wildness of the wolves routed from his land, his murdered parents' stolen horses, the person of his lost brother, Boyd. His attraction to a pre-Columbian past is indicated in his ultimately disastrous readiness to feed the solitary Indian hunter of the novel's opening pages, notwithstanding Boyd's qualms: "Everthing you can do it dont mean it's a good idea" (9).[8] But Billy's romance of the wild is most forcefully conveyed in his relationship with the displaced wolves of the Southwest. The most powerful of his childhood experiences is a first encounter with wolves in the wild. As noted, he is called by nocturnal wolfsong to communion with the untamed: "He could hear their breath. He could feel the presence of their knowing that was electric in the air" (4). So sacred is this memory that he will not tell his brother what he has seen: "He never told anybody" (5). When, long after wolves have been cleared from his county, a pregnant she-wolf from Mexico starts preying on Parham herds, he is galvanized less by the prospect of killing this threat to his family's livelihood than by the opportunity again to commune with lupine purity. As Raymond Malewitz states, Billy responds to this predator "as a symbol of wildness" (549), a wildness he yearns to access. Despite Don Arnulfo's insistence that "no man knew what the wolf knew" (*TC* 45), Billy, like John Grady with his horses, longs for just such knowledge. Tracking her, he repeatedly "trie[s] to see the world the wolf saw" (51): "He closed his eyes and tried to see her. Her and others of her kind . . . running in the whiteness of that high world as perfect to their use as if their counsel had been sought in the devising of it" (31). This is a vision of a wilderness defined by freedom and belonging. In his desire, then, to communicate with the trapped wolf—time and again, he will speak to her (56, 77, 105)—Billy seeks not only to occupy the wolf's vantage point, but to experience that fundamental communion with Creation he understands the wolf to enjoy.

If both Billy and John Grady long to escape into an imagined past, they do so in dreams not just of totemic animals, but of themselves as old-time waddies. Guillemin argues that the trilogy upends the Western by presenting the frontier "not [as] the beachhead of civilization in a howling wilderness but a last stronghold against civilization" ("As of" 93). Whether or not this is how McCarthy imagines the Old West, it is certainly how his protagonists do. For them, a historical dynamic which pits a fallen modernity against a past defined in terms of freedom, vitality, and harmony mandates an affinity not just to a certain time, but to a certain identity: that of the cowboy maverick. For Tom Pilkington, John Grady is defined above all by his faith in such quintessential Western virtues as "individualism, free will, volition" (320). Certainly, he is more than ready to play the genre's ruggedly self-sufficient, even outlaw, hero. Teased by Billy for posing as "the all-american cowboy" (*CP* 3), Cole does a credible job of filling this role as "an expert horseman, able gunman (when needed), and lover of the most beautiful girl at the ranch" (Kiefer 28).[9] Like Rawlins, he happily plays at "desperado" (*APH* 36) and recites an outlaw's lines to cow young Jimmy Blevins (40).[10] But his investment in this identity goes deeper. When he crosses into Texas on horseback, he truly embodies this American icon: "He must have appeared to [bystanders] some apparition out of the vanished past" (287). The national ideal of the cowboy is already an archaism superseded by the modernity he disdains, yet not just in his travels and work, but in his person, he pledges allegiance to the values associated with this time-worn archetype.

Above all, he incarnates an all-American independence, a determination to decide and do for himself. Less teasingly, then, Billy speaks of John Grady's "outlaw heart" (*CP* 218), expressed in a resolve to reclaim a putatively superior past by steadfastly pursuing his own path. If this makes him, for Billy, "bull-headed" (174), this trait does nothing to disqualify Cole as beloved exemplar of American tradition. Luce speaks critically of his being motivated by a "disappointed sense of entitlement" after the sale of the Grady ranch ("When You Wake" 155), something evident still in his decision to engage in banditry to rescue his and Blevins's seized property: "The hell with it, he said. I aint leavin my horse down here" (*APH* 257). That this bullheadedness leads to gunplay, grave wounds, and his own cruelty toward Blevins's killer might well indicate the unacceptable costs of his entitlement, but this is neither his view nor that of his peers. As Troy says of his own self-destructive brother, another Johnny, while he courted tragedy precisely because "you couldnt head him" (*CP* 28), it was still the case that everyone loved him: "You couldnt not" (29). Billy himself is both attracted and prone to this same unbending independence. He is not simply driven to defend the wildness he sees in the wolf; he enacts the same fierce insistence on his rights as marks Cole's life. In almost the same words, he heads to Mexico, and away from kin and community, so as to serve that unique calling the she-wolf represents: "Damn all of it, the boy said. Just damn all of it" (*TC* 63). Later, his search for his father's stolen horses will lead him, like John Grady, to play horse thief and gunfighter, risking not just himself, but his brother, to his commitment to the long-ago. In the end, having lost Boyd in his pursuit of a cowboy's life, he crosses into New Mexico having become, in his allegiance to such self-determined quests, the embodiment of his idealized past: "The people looked back at him through the rolling dust as if he were a thing wholly alien in that landscape. Something from an older time of which they'd only heard" (334).

The uncanny character of Billy's appearance here—alien, yet familiar— conveys the ambivalent nature of his relationship to the cultural mainstream. Both he and John Grady understand themselves, in their individualist ethos, as opposing the destructive tide of an enlightened American modernity. But, as Phillip A. Snyder notes, "McCarthy critiques and renovates, at the same time as he reaffirms, the cowboy codes" of his protagonists ("Cowboy" 201). Thus, if Cole and Billy retreat from something problematic by assuming antiquated wrangler roles, they remain implicated in that same American malaise to the extent that they align themselves with so quintessential an American identity. This is to say that, much like Suttree's, the premises of their rebellion are questioned throughout. This interrogation centers most fundamentally on their faith in their own innocence. However Edenic the American past they imagine, however righteous they understand their missions to be, John Grady and Billy are repeatedly presented, in their pursuit of such things, as fallen creatures. If, in his family's forfeiture of the ranch, John Grady deems himself blamelessly evicted from paradise, *All the Pretty Horses* quickly offers a dissenting gloss on this self-estimate. Laid low by the local alcohol, John Grady and Lacey begin their Mexican adventure with a self-inflicted sickness that underscores their less than spotless character: "those retchings seemed to echo like the calls of some rude provisional species loosed upon that waste. Something imperfect and malformed lodged in the heart of being" (*APH* 71). These boys are not alone in such imperfections. As Alfonsa tells John Grady, the past offers unvarying testimony to humanity's fallenness: "What is constant in history is greed and foolishness and a love of blood" (239); even Mr. Johnson affirms as much, responding to Cole's questions about the good old days with memories of "lots of people shot and killed" (*CP* 185). Nor is Billy denied such teaching. His last return from Mexico in *The Crossing* occurring on Ash Wednesday, "the first folk he saw were Mexicans with sootmarks on their foreheads" (421), penitential mirrors not simply to his mortality, but to his moral frailty.

Indeed, Billy receives perhaps the trilogy's most plangent articulation of humanity's fallen lot. Quijada, manager of the Nahuerichic division of the sprawling Babícora ranch,[11] tries to dissuade him from repatriating Boyd's remains, questioning both the reparability of the past and the acuity of humankind's notions of its place in the scheme of things. Speaking of the latter, he tells Billy, "The names of the cerros and the sierras and the deserts exist only on maps. We name them that we do not lose our way. Yet it was because the way was lost to us already that we have made those names" (387). Billy and John Grady proclaim both their certainty as to the path they must follow and their inalienable right to chart for themselves such courses. They do not simply romanticize a lost frontier past that their texts, as much as *Blood Meridian*, insist on rendering in a much less flattering light. They further claim for themselves a perfect autonomy and righteousness in their pursuit of that ideal. In both of these gestures, they oppose not so much the dreams of their suspect American present as the testimony of wiser elders and the tenor of their own tragic tales. Indeed, in their insistence on their right to pursue an idealized past, Cole and Parham emulate much that defines the modernity they wish to oppose. Their performance of the outlaw-rebel, in fact, substantially conforms to what Taylor terms the "Romantic protest" against post-Enlightenment modernity (315). Animated by the intuition that "in closing ourselves to the enchanted world, we have been cut off from a great source of life and meaning" (315), the Romantic rejects Enlightenment by seeking a fundamentally subjective transcendence of modernity's wholly material cosmos. Yet this rebellion, Taylor notes, in its own aversion to religious tradition and elevation of the sovereign self, derives from and remains defined by the "entirely anthropological" outlook of the properly enlightened subject (356). Both Billy and John Grady are, in their disdain for the contemporary, just such Romantics. While sure of the righteousness and dissenting character of their rejection of modernity, they remain products of that same culture, defined by the faults they see themselves blamelessly opposing.

That the idealized past they treasure is entangled with just those forms of destruction they flee in their present is repeatedly driven home. Would-be heirs to a ranching life, John Grady and Billy are not just shaped by, but long to perpetuate, a world predicated on the erasure of the wild and indigenous. If the once pristine lands of the Southwest are scarred by fences, it is America's Gradys and Parhams who have done this wounding work. The lands they have parcelled out into range and pasture became eligible for such use only through a wholesale displacement of the Native American populations of which Cole wistfully dreams. "Twenty-three hundred acres out of . . . the Fisher-Miller grant" (*APH* 6), the Grady ranch is born of a colonizing enterprise of the Republic of Texas and so of a program of dispossession vis-à-vis the Comanche nation and others. Likewise, if wolfsong has become mere memory, this is the result of programmatic efforts by such trappers as *The Crossing*'s Echols, whose labors aimed at enabling the Parhams' livelihood and whose hunting methods Billy and his father themselves adopt. Men like Mr. Parham have settled upon these lands, from the lupine perspective McCarthy's narrative briefly adopts, as a scourge, a "malignant lesser god come pale and naked and alien to slaughter all . . . A god insatiable whom no ceding could appease" (17). Even in his attempt to preserve the she-wolf, Billy rehearses this same process, not just in removing his captured prize from American territory, but in forcefully denaturing the wolf's character. As Holloway observes, in repatriating the wolf, Billy is "repeatedly forced into an antagonistic relation with the animal" ("Modernism" 191). Far from preserving her nature, his intention requires that he muzzle, leash, and tame that wildness with which he identifies: "He pulled the rope tighter . . . until he'd shut off her air and then he jammed the stick between her teeth" (*TC* 55). As Malewitz remarks, for Billy, "to free the wolf requires that he first violently enslave it" (553); thus, like the modernity he reviles, Billy unmakes the wildness he longs to conserve.

This status as tamer and colonizer is something shared both with John Grady and with that American history both cowboys romanticize. That Cole does not shrink from the bloody extirpation of the wild is demonstrated in *Cities of the Plain*, when he joins Billy in "the fun" of a gruesome cull of feral dogs (164): "The slack of Billy's catchrope hissed along the ground and stopped and the big yellow dog rose suddenly . . . taut between the two ropes and the ropes resonated a single brief dull note and then the dog exploded" (167). Such violence is the essence of the history these men cherish. As Turner himself concedes, "the first ideal of the pioneer was that of conquest" (269), and in seeking a return to a pioneering past as a defense of their own purity, Billy and John Grady reenact the less than innocent role of conquerors. Woodson reads Cole as an imperial figure who "assumes that he can move into Mexico and take control of whatever he desires" ("Leaving" 272). *All the Pretty Horses* uses much the same language. Seeking a return to a pastoral age he imagines as Edenic repository of the wild and the good, John Grady views Mexico as both an earlier time and a Terra Nullius. South of the border, his roadmap reveals, "all [is] white" (*APH* 34), and confident that it remains to be claimed as his chance at a better life, he makes for Mexico with a colonizer's intent. Thus, he and Lacey head south at night "like young thieves in a glowing orchard" (30), and they cross the Rio Grande, "making for the alien shore like a party of marauders" (45). Arrived at the Hacienda de Nuestra Señora de la Purísima Concepción, John Grady does indeed, as Lacey intuits, have "eyes for the spread" (138), but his faith in his right to these lands is still more comprehensive, darkly recalling Judge Holden himself.[12] Gazing at the Mexican night sky, John Grady feels the very life of this land to be his to grasp: "he put his hands on the ground at either side of him and pressed them against the earth and . . . he slowly turned dead center to the world, all of it taut and trembling and moving enormous and alive under his hands" (119).

This echo of Holden's absolute claim to lordship serves, along with their affiliation with historical processes of violent subdual and displacement, to foreground how John Grady and Billy remain, despite their Romantic self-understanding, agents of the unmaking they decry in their present. If their protests are thus compromised by rehearsing the past's own crimes, they are likewise vitiated by these cowboys' participation in the contemporary market-place. Though Billy repeatedly insists that he cannot sell his catch (TC 70, 90, 110), that he is "custodian to the wolf" and no mere peddler (118), he finally submits to the law of exchange and trades his father's rifle for her carcass (124). More strikingly, John Grady's attempt to rescue Magdalena from sexual slavery relies throughout on his acceptance of the john's role. Their relationship starts in a Juarez whorehouse and is consummated in a more upscale brothel. "Es muy caro," Magdalena cautions, when John Grady asks to spend the night (CP 69), but he insists, paying fifty dollars for this first tryst. Their romance, then, is shot through with the dehumanizing effects of the consumerism Cole sets himself against; indeed, by wooing in this way, he sustains its inhumane economy and profits Magdalena's pimp-captor. Far from transcending commodifying com-merce, his turn at knight-rescuer has him capitulate to its brutalizing terms. His first plan for Magdalena's redemption thus involves validating her status as prop-erty. By directing Billy, as purchasing agent, "to go to a whorehouse in Juárez Mexico and buy this whore cash money and bring her back across the river" (118), John Grady affirms both her commodity status and his role as customer, not lover. The costs of these affirmations are dear, including the death of Mag-dalena and John Grady both. The trilogy ends, then, with McCarthy's protagonists having facilitated, in their pursuit of a dissident cowboy persona, just that unmaking they sought, through that role, to oppose. Though Billy, in the wake of Magdalena's death, curses Eduardo—"Damn you to hell, he said. You and all your kind" (241)—his tale demonstrates that Eduardo's kind can exist only because of the market Billy, John Grady, and their choices provide.

FALSE INNOCENCE, BROKEN BONDS

Yet despite such evidence of how their maverick roles and the traditions they seek, through such identities, to preserve are implicated in a destructive modernity, Parham and Cole cling to a sense of themselves not just as innocent, but as fit saviors. Yet as Boguta-Marchel observes, in McCarthy, "power and the desire to act out one's fate are . . . inextricably linked not with creation, but with destruction" (87). His cowboys' rebellion in the face of a degraded present proves not just unhappy, but hubristic. Both Billy and John Grady are cast as over-reachers, pretending to an innocence beyond them. Such messianic presumption thus serves only to underscore their own unacknowledged fallen state. An obvious instance of such doomed playing at redeemer is Billy's quest to save the she-wolf. Though Arnulfo's caregiver warns him against the Don's "sin of Satanás. The sin of orgullo" (*TC* 48), assuring him that the Don's sad fate "could happen to you" (48), Billy remains committed both to finding the wolf and to knowing as she knows. Ignoring talk of sin and consequence, he proceeds first to capture the wolf, and then, so as to claim a knowledge even the Don insists is properly beyond him, to master it and adopt it as his charge. As noted, though, this adoption effects no liberation, but an enslavement of the creature Billy styles himself as saving, and though he tries repeatedly to commune with the wolf, she remains terrified quarry beyond his reach: "he could not calm her and she did not stop trembling" (77). Ultimately, his efforts prove him a failed savior, delivering her up to debasing torment in a dog-fighting pit: "her head lay in the dirt and her tongue lolled in the dirt and her fur was matted with dirt and blood" (122). The only salvation he can offer, then, is the same eradication of the wild he's fought to oppose, as he ends her misery with a bullet to the head.

As many critics have noted, John Grady's assumption of the savior's role is even more pronounced.[13] But while Broncano speaks of "the passion and death of the Christlike John Grady Cole" (91), his efforts to rescue Magdalena prove him more reckless than redeeming. Certainly, the part of savior/protector is one near to his heart. Recalling his love for his first colt, Cole sees himself "a young lord" (CP 204), moved always by one dream: "Something was afraid and he had come to comfort it. He dreamed it yet" (204). In pursuit of this dream's realization, nineteen-year-old John Grady is prepared to struggle, to suffer, and to sacrifice. So as to have his first night with Magdalena, he secures and exhausts an advance on his meager pay (59). To continue courting, he sells a stallion he has been at pains to break and pawns his gun for a paltry thirty dollars (149, 94). He is ready to pledge $2,000 for her release, despite having, as Billy points out, no reasonable means to such cash: "You dont make that in a year" (120). Finally, he earns the enmity of the dangerous Eduardo by working to steal her away. Yet the virtue of these efforts is dubious. As in his childhood reveries, there is a presumption of lordship, of sure right and competence, in his pursuit of a fairytale ending with Magdalena. It is not simply the case that his efforts fail, but that they do so for his beloved and despite his having been warned of such consequences. Billy tells him Eduardo "will kill you graveyard dead if you mess with him" (137), and the maestro refuses to abet the planned wedding because he knows what her departure will mean: "I believe he will kill her" (197). Yet confident in his lordship, in his rightness and not just his ability, Cole persists, bringing about Magdalena's death—"Her face so pale. The severed throat gaping bloodlessly" (229)—and demonstrating a damning blindness to his fallibility and her danger.

The suspect character of these cowboys' pursuit of their American dreams is further revealed in their relations with horses. Monk argues that the trilogy's animals function "as bridges, links, or even hierophants, mediating between the material and the mystical" (127). Cole and Parham would concur; for both, horses, particularly, figure as loci for reclamations of purity in the face of a fallen modernity.[14] They do so, however, in ways that demonstrate these protagonists' participation not just in a destructive American Enlightenment, but in a more universal fallenness on whose denial their cowboy quests and such Enlightenment are predicated. John Grady's spiritual identification with horses has been remarked, but his kinship with these creatures involves an insistence on their subdual. Thus, seeking notice on the hacienda, he sets himself the task of breaking sixteen animals brought down from the highlands. Here, he functions not as comforter, but as conqueror. While Luis tells him "the horse shares a common soul" (*APH* 111), Cole's work aims at the shattering of that communion. His success is depicted as an act of violence against creatures left disoriented by "this rendering of their fluid and collective selves into that condition of separate and helpless paralysis which seemed to be among them like a creeping plague" (105). In four days, John Grady refashions wild nature into utile commodity, but has achieved thereby no intimacy with the sacred he takes the horse to embody. Having left the herd with "all communion among them broken" (105), he has effected the ruin of an original harmony.[15] He has done so, moreover, for self-seeking purposes, securing for himself a place of privilege in Don Hector's scheme for breeding workhorses. Thus, his embodiment here of the cowboy ideal casts him not as savior, but as the haughty master he proclaims himself to be to Hector's new stallion: "Soy commandante de las yeguas . . . Sin la caridad de estas manos no tengas nada. Ni comida ni agua ni hijos" (128).

The cost of Billy's attempts at horse mastery is still higher. Committed, after the murder of his parents, to the rescue of six stolen horses, Billy identifies these animals with the restoration of a violated past. Yet confident in the righteousness of his pursuit of endangered creatures, he falls victim to a pride similar to, but more ruinous than, John Grady's own. Only sixteen, Billy hastily removes his orphaned fourteen-year-old brother, Boyd, from foster care so that they may cross into Mexico to track and reclaim the lost horses. Assured of the justice of his ends and the innocence of his means, Billy is nonetheless as reckless with others' lives as is Cole. Ignoring his brother's "uneasy feelin'" about this enterprise (*TC* 179), and deaf to elders' warnings that "death often leads [men] to attribute great consequence to trivial things" (186), Billy launches his brother and himself into a genuine cowboy adventure. Sustained by his idealization of a frontier history and an unstinting confidence in his ability to redeem it, Billy has them hunt these horses as the prizes whose possession will vindicate that confidence and restore that past. In hazarding his brother in this enterprise, Billy clearly mistakes the trivial for the grave, but this confusion will itself be of great consequence. Indeed, his pursuit of the rescuer's role involves his moral diminishment from the start. Thus, they depart from the foster family's home as thieves, taking "a shotgun [and] nineteen dollars in coins and small bills" (171). In order to recapture the lost horses, they must act as rustlers, seizing property from those who have duly bought and paid for it. While this affords them, in chases and gunfights, an opportunity to play outlaw, Billy's stubborn pursuit of this self-elected ideal fails to secure his return to an Edenic past. Rather, it brings only further loss, the near-fatal shooting of his brother: "[Boyd] put up one hand as if to reach for the first of the horses . . . and then his shirt belled out behind him redly and he fell down on the ground" (269).

What becomes clear, then, in these protagonists' adherence to an imagined past and an Enlightenment ideal of personal autonomy is that such loyalty is ultimately disastrous. Thinking they can themselves redeem what has been forfeit, Cole and Parham incur greater losses yet. Even so, they will not be swayed from walking alone down their self-elected paths. They are unyielding in this regard, no matter the cost, finding room among the ranks of Dueña Alfonsa's proud parabolic minters: "we are all like that myopic coiner at his press . . . all of us bent so jealously at our work, determined that not even chaos be outside of our own making" (*APH* 241). John Grady and Billy initiate and suffer such chaos so as never to surrender their American ideal of self-determination, but the dreadful consequences of this steadfastness, borne by Magdalena and Boyd especially, indicate that, in the Border Trilogy, "to order the world purely in human terms . . . is an insanity, one reflecting (and creating) a profound disorder" (Scoones 134). Indeed, as Monk argues, the tales that circulate in the trilogy serve to detail "the dangers that reside in attempts to form an identity constituted solely in an *I* sealed hermetically against God and community" (140). Nor is such a demonstration one to which the reader alone is privy. Both of McCarthy's cowboys are offered repeated warnings against their commitment to Enlightenment notions of self-sufficient identity and contractual, disposable community, warnings which take on, as Monk's language implies, an increasingly spiritual, ultimately Christian, savor.

Such cautions first emanate from those closest to the protagonists, figures owed their attention and care. In the concerns raised by Lacey Rawlins and Boyd Parham, the trilogy interrogates the moral status of its cowboys' quests, posing, in Keegan's words, such questions as, "what are the individual human's responsibilities to his fellow creatures? To his fellow humans? To God?" (44). Certainly, Rawlins, though devoted to Cole to the point of haring off to foreign lands, works to keep ties to their homeland in view. Before they enter Mexico, he prods John Grady in this direction by asking, "Wonder what all they're doin back home" (*APH* 36), and after they cross the Rio Grande, he muses, "What do you reckon they're sayin at home about now?" (51). Though John Grady is dismissive in both instances, it is clear that, for Rawlins, home still exists north of the border. What's more, it has a claim not just on his imagination, but on his moral sense. What they are saying at home, how they are suffering or judging his absence, matters to him, and that he repeatedly poses such questions indicates that, loyal friend though he may be, Rawlins feels such things ought to matter to Cole. Hence his increasing readiness to challenge this comrade to whom he typically defers. When John Grady admits to designs on Alejandra, Rawlins seeks to recall to him what he owes his best friend, if not his employer: "What I see is you fixin to get us fired and run off the place" (138). Once this romantic pursuit results in their arrest, Rawlins rebuffs belated appeals to solidarity, responding to Cole's insistence that they stick together to get out of this mess with, "You mean like we got in it?" (155). Such cautions and rebukes articulate a moral alternative to, and judgment on, the ideal of personal sovereignty John Grady embodies to his and others' harm. This they do by speaking to the greater claim obligations to kin and community, even to God, should have on Cole's conduct. Thus it is that Rawlins becomes the first volume's unlikely theologian, keeping what might be owed God in view by raising questions concerning divine judgment (61), the afterlife (91), and providence: "You think God looks out for people?" (92).

Boyd is similarly inquisitive, consistently questioning Billy's dogged pursuit of lost wildness. Troubled by the itinerant Indian's questions concerning the saleable contents of the Parham home, Boyd condemns Billy's putting this stranger ahead of their family's safety: "We ought not to of gone out there to start with" (*TC* 12). When Billy repays the kindness of the larger community with injury, stealing from Boyd's foster family, the younger Parham calls attention to this offense: "Even a outlaw dont rob them that's took him in" (172). While Billy remains faithful only to his cowboy's notion of the good, Boyd warns against such disregard of duties owed to family and community, denouncing from the start Billy's single-minded course as culpable outlawry, not noble, saving work. This cautionary role persists during their Mexican hunt for the Parham horses. When they follow the evidence to a trader in Casas Grandes, Boyd, like Rawlins, urges restraint in place of his brother's obsessive commitment to his self-determined path: "You dont think we might be better off to just keep ridin?" (198). Even prior to this, Boyd is predicting the bloodshed with which Billy's cowboy quest will conclude, insisting, after they abscond with the first rescued horse, "They're goin to shoot us" (183). Though Billy remains unmoved by such warnings, the brother who will most suffer the costs of this deafness has clearly understood the wrongheadedness of their course throughout. Thus, when the chase that leaves him with a bullet in his chest commences, Boyd states simply, "We were in it when we left home" (245), affirming, like Rawlins, how their ruin stems from his companion's valuing of autonomy over obligations to any home or brother.

But as the example of Rawlins indicates, these warnings against faith in oneself alone swiftly assume a more than consequentialist cast. As Mark Busby argues, by its second installment, if not before, the trilogy begins to foreground more expressly theological questions, including "especially the existence and purpose of God in a violent and inhumane world" (237). Billy, in particular, becomes the target of parables seemingly aimed at dissolving his privileging of personal sovereignty over solidarity with human and divine others. Thus, after the failure of his savior's mission with the she-wolf, a famished Billy is himself saved in the wilderness by a kindly band of Indians, an elder among whom seeks to minister to more than bodily needs. Addressing him as "huérfano" (TC 134), this old man sees in Billy a boy threatened not by hunger, but by the disregard for communal bonds that has underwritten his pursuit of idealized wildness. The threatened loss of such ties is made clear not only in his truly orphaned status—his parents are, by now, dead at another Indian's hands—but also in the condition of Billy's heart: "His home had come to seem remote and dreamlike. There were times he could not call to mind his father's face" (135). Such ceding of communion, the elder insists, entails costs other than heartbreak in a gaming pit or starvation in the desert. Rather, Billy's essentially American cult of radical self-ownership risks final self-forfeiture. He must, therefore, return to the home he has scorned, "because to wander in this way would become for him a passion and by this passion he would become estranged from men and so ultimately from himself" (134). If he is not, in other words, to lose his soul, he must "live with men and not simply pass among them" (134).

If this mentor offers more spiritual counsel than Boyd, other teachers seek to remedy Billy's unbending individualism with more explicit reference to God. Such is the case with the old revolutionary, source of one of Arnold's three "interpolated narratives" in The Crossing ("McCarthy" 224).[16] Gruesomely blinded by the enemy, this veteran relates the despair that first accompanied his descent into darkness before turning to address the blindness of the sighted. Those who see, he says, are themselves prone to forget their own dependency, empowered, as they are, to direct their gaze and so to encounter only those facets of the world they choose to consider: "men with eyes may select what they wish to see but for the blind the world appears of its own will" (*TC* 291). The sighted enjoy both a lordly capacity to choose what the world will be for them and the possibility of remoteness from its entanglements. Taken together, these two traits allow the sighted to misapprehend the world and their own place in it, to view the latter, in particular, in terms of sure knowledge and goodness. Hence, the blind man is skeptical of the righteous, insisting that they themselves do harm on account of their partial outlook and confident imposition of subjective ends on the world at large. The righteous man presumes to "call upon the world itself to testify as to the truth of what are in fact but his desires" (293), in the process entrenching himself in error and enforcing a distance from others. By contrast, truth is to be found not in detached entitlement, but in the humble, community-forging posture of attention: "Ultimamente sabemos que no podemos ver el buen Dios . . . Debemos eschuchar" (292). Only by listening, only, that is, by establishing an intimate relationship with and reliance on the other, ultimately on God himself, can anything be known about one's right place in Creation. The individual, then, finds herself not by pursuing her own path, but by existing as one who listens to, and so serves, the other. All persons stand in need of such communion, because we are all, even when most sure of our vision, blind: "Somos dolientes en la oscuridad. Todos nostoros" (293).

This increasingly Christian catechism of community finds its culmination in exhortations to prayer in *Cities of the Plain*. Cole does not want for warnings against his courtship of Magdalena. She herself repeatedly dissuades him, avoiding contact with him because it is "too dangerous" (*CP* 80), and telling him she fears Eduardo will kill her before he lets her go (103). But the most eloquent of such cautions comes from John Grady's confidante, the blind maestro. Convinced of Magdalena's spiritual worth—"She does not belong here. Among us," he asserts (81)—the maestro believes in goods beyond the human and material world of Enlightenment thinking. Affirming moral laws that transcend the determinations of individuals, he speaks of a cosmic conscience that "may stand alone and each man's share . . . but some small imperfect part of it" (193). Like the veteran, he sees a humanity whose vision and knowledge are imperfect, and that needs not to follow its own maverick course, but to take instruction. Incompetent both morally and epistemologically—"Our plans are predicated upon a future unknown to us" (195)—we must, he insists, listen to the Creator: "We have only God's law, and the wisdom to follow it if we will" (195). And as Catholic tradition teaches that "prayer is nothing else than a devout setting of our will in the direction of God" (*Cloud* 106), so does the maestro finally advise Cole against his deadly course by urging him to pray, to listen and conform his will. Certain of Eduardo's murderous intent and less sure than John Grady of his power to protect Magdalena, the maestro instructs Cole to "pray to God" (197), to forsake his autonomy and be governed by the divine will for the good of the beloved. As Mundik notes, this is advice aimed not at Cole's contriving surer means to his ends, but at his finding the courage to abandon Magdalena for her own sake (*Bloody* 219). While John Grady refuses to pray, precisely because he cannot brook surrendering the object of his desire (*CP* 198), it is clear, first, that he has been offered a path away from his and Magdalena's bloody ends and, second, that this path veers from his Enlightenment conception of his rights and toward belief in the wisdom of others and the proper sovereignty of God.

Now, de Sales enjoins the devout to regular prayer, even in periods of desolation, as it sustains faithfulness to God (86). Despite consonant warnings, Billy and John Grady abjure such faith, disastrously breaking the bonds of community and prayer in pursuit of their own goods as self-determining modern agents. That said, McCarthy's protagonists appeal to the extent that they do precisely because they are capable of fidelity, to certain causes and persons at least. Thus, while Canfield reads the trilogy's conclusion as bathetic, *Cities of the Plains* "replay[ing] John Grady's and Billy's tragedies as farce" ("Crossing" 263), Hillier is right to affirm the cowboys' enduring virtues, discerning in this final volume a "more selfless and magnanimous" John Grady than that of *All the Pretty Horses* (*Morality* 139). Indeed, his capacity for selflessness predates his love for Magdalena and, frequently enough, takes the form of gestures of loyalty and care to those in desperate need of both. As he tells Rawlins, "all I know to do is stick. . . . I dont believe in signing on just till it quits suitin you" (*APH* 155). His willingness to stand by his neighbor is evident in his attempts to look out for the hapless Jimmy Blevins. A thirteen-year-old runaway from an abusive home riding a suspiciously fine horse, Jimmy is, to Lacey's eyes, nothing but trouble. Confessing to "a uneasy feelin about that little son of a bitch" (43), Rawlins wants nothing to do with him: "I aint takin no responsibility for him" (69). Nonetheless, Cole will not abandon Blevins to face a world marked by such perils as wax-camp workers ready to use him as a sex slave (76). When, terrified by a thunderstorm, Blevins hares off, unhorsed and nearly naked, then, John Grady does indeed stick, telling a reluctant Rawlins, "I don't believe I can leave him out here afoot" (71). Similarly, as Blevins readies himself for the ill-fated recapture of his horse, Cole's loyalty is unbroken; he rebuffs Rawlins's appeals that they leave Blevins to it with a simple "I cant do it" (79).

But his commitment to Blevins is nothing compared to his steadfast pursuit of Magdalena. After first spying her at La Venada, he is unwavering in his search for her, spending money he can scarcely afford for word of her new placement at the costly White Lake and, as noted, effectively bankrupting himself in his efforts to secure her release so that she might come to America as his wife. His willingness to sacrifice for the sake of this love extends to those things dearest to his own ardent heart. To help fund his trips to the White Lake, he pawns his gun and belt for thirty dollars. As he informs the broker, this kit "belonged to my grandfather" (*CP* 94). Thus, by placing it in hock, Cole is showing his readiness to surrender not just the tools associated with his jealously maintained cowboy identity, but an heirloom that is his last material tie to that past he has heretofore cherished above all else. This gesture, as much as his promises to Magdalena that he will love her always, "para todo mi vida" (206), indicates the extent of his commitment to this beloved. Indeed, as he tells Billy, his faithfulness in this matter brooks no possibility of surrender. Despite Billy's enumeration of the obstacles and perils that attend this star-crossed love, despite even the maestro's warning that this "love has no friends. . . . Perhaps not even God" (199), John Grady insists his mind is "done made up" (121). Having fallen for Magdalena, he must be faithful in his seeking her good and devoting his life to that cause. As he says, when Billy emphasizes the threat Eduardo represents, then, "I cant help it" (120).[17]

Billy, too, shows himself capable of genuine fidelity to projects and people. While Kiefer simplifies matters when he states that Billy "does not shirk his responsibilities even when faced with . . . dire consequences" (29), Parham is steadfast in his pursuit of certain goods and in his commitment to certain comrades. The former is demonstrated in the hunt for the Parham horses. Despite Boyd's misgivings, despite their vulnerability in Mexico as "two pale and wasted orphans from the north" (*TC* 192), despite horse-trader Gillian's prescient warnings—"I see great trouble in store" (202)—Billy is undeterred in this act of filial loyalty to his late parents. But Billy can also keep faith with the living. *Cities of the Plains* sees him playing "Samaritan" to a party of Mexicans with a flat tire (33), a gesture of solidarity with Mexican strangers who once drove a wounded Boyd to safety (see *TC* 272): "They didnt have no reason to stop for us. But they did" (*CP* 36). Yet Billy's fidelity to something more than a cowboy's love of independence is most evident in his relationship with John Grady. Though happy enough to tease this protégé—"John Grady Cole was a rugged old soul . . . With a buckskin belly and a rubber asshole" (76)—and ready to protest Cole's ill-fated courtship, Billy works to advance this project and, so far as he is able, to protect the young lover. Despite deeming plans for Magdalena's rescue "completely crazy" (118), Billy agrees to act on John Grady's behalf in the attempt to purchase her freedom and, when challenged by Eduardo with the folly of John Grady's hopes, is reluctant to admit his agreement for fear of disloyalty: "It seems like a betrayal of some kind" (134). After Magdalena's murder, Billy is again willing to risk himself for loyalty's sake, when he confronts Eduardo over Cole's fate: "if you've harmed a hair on his head you're a dead son of a bitch" (239). No fair-weather friend, Parham stands by John Grady in dire circumstances; as the captain of police perceives, he is someone who would not turn on this comrade "even if his hands were dripping. Especially not then" (245). Indeed, Billy stands with John Grady to the death, bearing his body through Juarez streets in mournful testimony to his faithfulness: "He was crying and the tears ran on his angry face and he called out to the broken day" (261).

These instances of doomed fidelity are, however, framed by a larger pattern of breaking faith with God and man in the independent pursuit of suspect goods. Both characters, despite their initial confidence in the unfallen nature of their quests, are depicted as betraying the texts' ideal of human solidarity. Notably, such commitment to one's neighbor, like Billy's Samaritanism, is a Christian, indeed, a Catholic commandment. As Catherine of Siena's divine interlocutor informs her, "I could easily have created men possessed of all that they should need both for body and soul, but I wish that one should have need of the other, and that they should be My ministers" (18). As Cooper notes, this call to care for one's human community lies at the heart of the trilogy's own ethics; here, as she states, "relationship, in the sense of a responsibility to the other, is that which mitigates death and offers a sense of hope" (*Heroes* 104).[18] Both John Grady and (as seen in his recollection of Boyd's rescuers) Billy are frequent recipients of others' charity: in advice offered, food shared, and services rendered. Strangers, in other words, frequently adopt toward them that stance of responsibility of which Cooper speaks, and the novels explicitly describe such gestures as placing a burden of reciprocity on McCarthy's protagonists; they, too, are called to be faithful to the trilogy's ministry of care. Thus, departing from one of the many meals freely offered him in *The Crossing*, Billy is described as beholden to his humble benefactors, "carrying in his belly the gift of the meal he'd received which both sustained him and laid claim upon him. For the sharing of bread is not such a simple thing nor is its acknowledgement" (161). Heedless of this claim, he demonstrates the price of such disregard. When he discovers Boyd decamped, Billy is presented as both desolate and exemplary, embodying the sad lot of those who have forfeited human communion: "For the enmity of the world was newly plain to him that day and cold and inameliorate as it must be to all who have no longer cause except themselves to stand against it" (331).

That McCarthy's heroes court such enmity by breaking faith with their fellows is made plain from the trilogy's outset. John Grady may well, as David Gugin holds, end up "a quintessential, twenty-first-century nomad" (93), but this is an identity crafted by his own dismissal of family ties and of the regard owed friends, benefactors, and lovers. His maverick's search for a putatively innocent American past requires his abandonment of parents whom he will never again see. But this abjuring of community is mere prelude to a series of betrayals of those owed his friendship. If, as Trenton Hickman argues, the trilogy's bloodshed "occurs because of intimacy" (29), this seems enabled by its protagonists' disregard for the most intimate of bonds. Certainly, Cole proves careless of the welfare of his best friend, Lacey Rawlins. Having resolved to flee modernity by journeying to Mexico, John Grady is cruel in his bullying of Rawlins to join him: "What the hell reason you got for stayin? You think somebody's goin to die and leave you somethin?" (*APH* 27). Projecting his own disinheritance on a Rawlins who, as Andrew Husband observes, comes from lesser means (62), Cole succeeds in recruiting a sidekick, but does so by exploiting a friend's unreciprocated loyalty. Though Rawlins believes in such reciprocity—"I wouldnt leave you and you wouldnt leave me" (*APH* 79)—John

Grady fails to justify this faith. Unresponsive to the homesickness audible in Rawlins's repeated queries concerning those left behind, John Grady ultimately deserts both bunkhouse and friend when Don Hector offers him a role in his horse-breeding scheme. Though Cole insists on his fidelity—"You just say the word and I'll tell him no" (116)—Rawlins's own loyalty precludes barring his friend's path. The consequences of such faithfulness, however, are grave. On account of John Grady's dishonesty with the Don, Rawlins ends up a prisoner at Saltillo, where he is a target for beatings that leave him bloodied and ultimately for assaults by knife-wielding assailants: "the lowest cut was the deepest and it had severed the outer fascia" (189).

A less compelling obligation for John Grady than the search for what he deems his due at the hacienda, Rawlins finally takes his leave, but only after having nearly given his life for his friend. Importantly, this suffering, too, is the fruit not just of Cole's pursuit of the cowboy ideal, but also of his disloyalty to a trusting benefactor. After his success with the wild horses, John Grady is invited to meet with the hacendado himself. The purpose of this interview is twofold: to make that offer of promotion that separates Cole from Rawlins, and to discover whether the young American has anything to do with Blevins's crimes. The Don twice asks whether Cole crossed the Rio Grande with Rawlins alone; twice John Grady breaks faith with his employer by falsely asserting this to be so (116). His faithlessness in pursuit of his self-chosen goods is demonstrated in his further betrayal of the Don with Alejandra. Smitten, John Grady ignores not just Rawlins, but Alejandra's grand-aunt, Alfonsa, in his pursuit of Hector's daughter. Having heard of their riding together, Alfonsa asks him "to be considerate of a young girl's reputation" (136), but John Grady prevaricates to Alfonsa and Rawlins both in pursuit of a consummation whose appeal for him lies, at least in part, in its duplicity. Their first lovemaking is described as "sweeter for the larceny of time and flesh, sweeter for the betrayal" (141). Cole here betrays more than just the Don and Dueña. It is the discovery of this treachery that leads Hector to hunt and nearly kill the Americans, before surrendering them to the authorities; thus, this is a wrong that extends to Rawlins, as well. More poignantly, it is a betrayal of his love for Alejandra, as their affair effects the devastation of her relationship with her father: "I didnt know that he would stop loving me. I didnt know he could. Now I know" (252). Reflecting on Rawlins as a man "who'd come to ruin no man's house. No man's daughter" (255), John

Grady comes to see the gravity of his assumed innocence and enacted faithlessness. As he later admits, his own acts have engendered the violence suffered in prison, even the Don's nearness to murder: "I was the one that brought it about" (291). As Cooper asserts, then, Cole's growth as a character is revealed "in the sense that his appreciation of his own culpability deepens" (*Heroes* 85).[19]

Yet, ironically, John Grady most profoundly abdicates his duty of care in that relationship to which he proves most loyal, namely his romance with Magdalena. Though he recognizes his ignorance of her situation in Juarez—"He could not even imagine her life" (*CP* 85)—and so of the risks his attentions might mean for her, he nonetheless ignores her warnings. For a month, he haunts the White Lake despite pleas that he should stay away, her protests that "Estamos perdidos" (103), that they are doomed. Instead, vowing that he will love her "para siempre" (205), promising that "no harm would come to her" (206), he succeeds with Magdalena, as earlier with Rawlins, by winning her commitment to his vision of the future. Thus, she offers vows of her own: "she said that she was his and that she would do whatever he asked her if it take her life" (139). Her fidelity will cost her just this, and the fact that Cole's single-minded pursuit of his own intent leads to this end underscores not just his failure, but a carelessness with her life that disproves the fidelity he professes. Indeed, that he is less committed to Magdalena's life than to his own dream of a home with her is revealed in his refusal to have his ignorance about her experience remedied. When she tells him of past abuse at the hands of parents, police, and pimps, he is reduced to "weeping" (139), and significantly, acts to silence her: "She would tell him more but again he placed his fingers against her mouth" (140). As Potts argues, this is itself an act of infidelity: "He wants her promise of marriage but not the burden of the history she desires to share with him" (144). This refusal to hear of her sufferings facilitates a culpable blindness to her peril, one that will cost Magdalena's life. Indeed, it is an imbalance of faith that ensures her demise, for she has a chance at another rescue prior to her murder. Returning to the White Lake after a seizure lands her in hospital, Magdalena is found on the streets, "half naked" (*CP* 210), by a woman who offers, in Samaritan fashion, to save her from exploitation: "She said that she could come with her and live in her house" (211). But Magdalena's faith in Cole's blind confidence forbids this. Telling her would-be benefactor that "in three days' time the boy she loved would come to marry her" (211), she returns to Eduardo's domain and her death.

Billy, too, repeatedly breaks faith with those most owed his loyalty. As noted, the proper solidarity of humankind is a leitmotif in *The Crossing* and a lesson frequently expounded for his benefit. Thus, the ex-priest he encounters on his way home from his first Mexican sojourn insists, "All men are one and there is no other tale to tell" (*TC* 157). Yet this is a story Billy seems unable to assimilate. Despite Hall's suggestion that the novel concludes with Billy's having "learned the importance of compassion for all forms of life" ("Hero" 194), Luce writes with greater justice of his "rejection of faith in life and other men" ("Road" 201).[20] Certainly, his self-appointed mission to save the wolf involves abandonment of his family and any sense of responsibility toward them. Not only does he depart for a foreign country without a word of goodbye; by having led the Indian, eager to find "somethin maybe [he] can sell" (*TC* 10), to their home, Billy exposes his kin to harm. Indeed, having taken the Parhams' sole weapon—"The only gun on the place was a forty-four forty carbine and I had that with me" (167)—he has left them defenseless in the face of a threat he has conjured. Returned to discover their murders, Billy takes his younger brother, still "a juvenile" (169), with him on a second journey south, but despite an elder Mexican's exhortation to them "to care for one another in the world" (186), Billy is less concerned with being Boyd's caretaker than with becoming redeemer of the Parhams' lost horses. The fruit of such disregard is gunplay and a near-fatal wound for the minor in his charge, "a small round hole a few inches above and to the left of his left nipple" (310). Ultimately, however, the wages of Billy's faithlessness to family are higher still. First abandoned, in his turn, by the brother he himself deserted, he later learns that, schooled by his own example, Boyd has died a teen-aged outlaw. "He killed two men in Galeana" (384), Billy hears, before being himself shot down.

The force of this loss moves Billy, like John Grady vis-à-vis Hector, to consider his guilt in this matter. As he confesses to strangers, "he should not have abandoned [Boyd] but he did" (359). Indeed, this recognition seems a powerful motivator in his dealings with Cole in *Cities of the Plain*. But if Billy adopts the younger man as a surrogate Boyd by whom he can more faithfully stand, it is also true, as Hawkins observes, that this later allegiance leads to a rehearsal of, and no reparation for, his failure to protect his actual brother (53). Certainly, Billy understands himself pledged to Cole, whom he dubs "as good a boy as I ever knew" (*CP* 244). Yet much as John Grady's faithful courtship effects Magdalena's undoing, so does Billy's loyalty to Cole facilitate the latter's ruin. This it does by moving Parham ultimately to support the fairy-tale plans of a friend he himself says has "lost [his] rabbit-assed mind" (119). Despite his vociferous protests, he serves as go-between in John Grady's dealings with Eduardo and helps prepare an abandoned adobe to serve as a marriage home. More than this, he joins three generations of American cowboys in endorsing John Grady's pursuit of his self-determined good, no matter the cost. Thus, old Mr. Johnson says of getting married, "I think you ought to follow your heart" (188); Mac himself goes further, to pledge his assistance to this purpose: "if you got it in your head to go on, then go ahead. I'll do whatever I can for you" (144). Though he knows what these men do not, that Magdalena is a sex slave and a wedding requires that Cole cross a murderous criminal, Billy joins this same chorus and so, far from protecting his adopted brother, abets his destruction more culpably than Mac or Johnson. Like them loyal to American notions of the sovereign self, Billy ultimately lets this allegiance override his duty of care to a headstrong boy of nineteen.

AMERICAN INDEPENDENCE AND THE WAGES OF FAITHLESSNESS

Significantly for my argument, their failures to keep faith with neighbors coincide with these protagonists' loss of faith in a God their stories take as a matter of abiding importance. While Jarrett is right to observe that the Border Trilogy depicts modern American experience as "detached from the sacred" ("Sense" 322), it is also true, as Arnold contends, that these volumes confirm McCarthy himself as "a writer of the sacred" in specifically Christian terms ("McCarthy" 215). So while Cole and Parham pursue, in their commitment to an Enlightenment model of selfhood, increasingly profane paths, the trilogy itself foregrounds the question of God so as to highlight that model's deficiencies. The latter are manifest in the disastrous lapses in human solidarity detailed above, but they are fueled by these cowboys' refusal to submit to anything other than their own sovereign wills. This tragic defiance is expressed and cemented in their abandonment of Christian belief and that humble deference to a higher power that such faith entails. Certainly, John Grady is hesitant in affirming any creed. Though questions about God's existence dog his tale from the outset, these consistently emanate from others and meet, in him, with equivocation. Thus, when Rawlins asks whether he believes in God, the Cole who is certain of his right to pursue self-elected goods, whatever the costs for community, is rather evasive: "I dont know. Yeah, I reckon" (APH 61). After their first brush with violence in Mexico, a rattled Rawlins inquires whether John Grady believes in a heavenly afterlife and receives, as a response, "Yeah. Don't you?" (91). Yet this answer proves less firm than it seems, for Cole immediately amends this affirmation, pledging loyalty instead to that belief in personal autonomy which is, in fact, his highest ideal: "I guess you can believe what you want to" (91). Finally, when Rawlins professes belief in divine providence, stating that, absent God's "look[ing] out for people" (92), "I dont believe we'd make it a day" (92), John Grady is decidedly lukewarm in response: "Yeah. I guess" (92).

Such evasiveness should not surprise. The young maverick who revels in his lordship over the powerful stallion, who feels he holds the life current of the cosmos in his hands, is scarcely inclined to take direction from or conform his will to any higher authority, whether that be his mother, Alfonsa, the maestro, or God. He, in fact, embodies that gringo hubris that the papazote of Saltillo prison, Perez, thinks makes of Americans "a godless people" (194). Echoing the blind veteran's lesson, Perez describes an American character blinded by its insistence on its mastery over itself, its life, and its world: "It is not that he is stupid. It is that his picture of the world is incomplete ... He looks only where he wishes to see" (192). By doing so, the American sees only himself and his personally determined destiny, and remains oblivious to any other claims or powers. This diagnosis is confirmed, two volumes later, by the testimony of an El Paso shoeshine boy: "If there's something I want to be a different way from what it is then that's how I say it is" (CP 97). This is a creed the boy's auditor, John Grady, can neither fault nor gainsay. They are, indeed, words he lives by, in his desertion of kin and country to find an idealized American past, in his illicit wooing of Alejandra, in his exposure of Rawlins to deadly peril, and in his perilous plans for Magdalena. In each case, he breaks faith with those whom he should honor for the sake of asserting his sovereign right to command the world to be only what and as he says it must.

Such a perspective affords little room for a providential, judging, or merciful God, for a divine power to whom belief, obedience, and penitence might be owed. Thus, as Cole doggedly pursues his own ends, even that tenuous faith he expresses to Rawlins seems to dissipate. As Cooper states, by the end of *All the Pretty Horses*, John Grady "does not . . . know where to find God or where to find absolution" (*Heroes* 94).[21] Indeed, though eager to play the quester, he proves quite reluctant to seek God, belief in whom might require some curtailment of liberty or admission of fault. Though Mexico, if not America, offers him instruction in faith, he is loath to heed it. Released from prison and determined still to win Alejandra, John Grady shares his tale with a group of Mexican children who offer him advice at odds with the El Paso boy's American dream: "The girl said that he needed to find some wise man with whom he could discuss his difficulties . . . and the younger girl said that he should pray to God" (*APH* 244). But such submission to the counsel of another is no fit stance for an American maverick. Indeed, as Cole admits to Rawlins, he has "got kindly out of the habit" of prayer (214). If he cannot confess his need of supernatural direction or aid, still less can he admit that his proper pursuit of his ideals, of the world as he wishes it, has been anything but innocent or righteous. Thus, when Rawlins asks him to name his most shameful deed, John Grady is typically evasive: "I guess if I done anything real bad I'd rather not tell it" (214). Refusing to admit wrongdoing, he is far from placing himself before God or neighbor in search of correction. Indeed, nearer the novel's end, he proclaims to Blevins's killer that he has nothing to fear in God's judgment, but instead has judgments of his own to render: "I got no reason to be afraid of God. I've even got a bone or two to pick with Him" (272).

That such pretensions to suzerainty are untenable, however, John Grady himself makes plain. Though he persists in Enlightenment claims to self-authorship, his doing so only reveals his insufficiency, in moral as well as practical terms. Despite professions of innocence, he is, as Cooper implies, plagued by a sense of his culpability, haunted by failures he experiences as sins. As he tells a Texas judge, "I dont feel justified" (290). In this interview, Cole confesses to his betrayal of Hector's trust and to his killing of the prison cuchillero in self-defense. Clearly burdened by these acts, he is even more troubled by sins of omission. While he is first to intuit that their captors "aim to kill Blevins" (170), Cole fails to raise a voice against this murder: "John Grady said nothing at all" (176). Whether or not he fears God's judging such faults, it is clear enough, first, that he judges himself—"I stood there and let him walk that boy out in the trees and shoot him" (293)—and, second, that he yearns for a power beyond himself to absolve him. As Broncano states, the judge fills "the role of the priest in this apocryphal reenactment of the Catholic sacrament of penance" (71). But its apocryphal character is important. If Cole's search for a competent confessor leads him uncharacteristically to surrender claims to autonomy and to submit his crimes against fidelity to a judgment other than his own, he has, in this secular authority, an interlocutor too American to recognize his failures as sins at all. Faithful, like Johnson, Mac, and Billy, to a right to self-determination he takes to be faultless, the judge can only affirm what Cole feels moved to confess: "There's nothing wrong with you son. I think you'll get it sorted out" (*APH* 293). Having given up on a faith that would constrain his self-seeking, John Grady, like *Blood Meridian*'s kid, cannot find the forgiveness he knows he needs.

Billy Parham is similarly lost, but not for want of guides. Indeed, *The Crossing* often seems a serial catechesis staged for his benefit and aimed at ideals other than his cowboy's independence. Billy is born to a family of faith, to a mother who rebukes him for plans to continue hunting on a Sunday: "I dont know how you think the Lord is goin to bless your efforts and you dont keep the Sabbath" (*TC* 34). If this American home seeks to curb his self-determination, it is nonetheless the case that the bulk of Billy's instruction in this regard derives from more Mexican and Catholic sources. Thus, Arnulfo's nurse warns against the proud self-sufficiency that has robbed the old man of "parentesco" or kin (48), insisting, in the words of this chapter's title, that faith, not autonomy, is everything (49). Throughout three Mexican journeys, Billy is repeatedly offered examples not just of charity, but of inclusive human community, in the form of Catholic intercessions. The traveling diva grants him her blessing—"May God go with you" (230)—an oxen-driver offers his prayers on Billy's behalf (236), and a shopkeeper gifts him with a "milagro" as token of her prayers for Boyd's life (298). However solitary a figure he insists on being, then, Billy traverses a land where a religious belief that founds human solidarity is ubiquitous and vital. Thus, Boyd's novia kneels in the dirt of the road to give thanks to God when her beau survives his gunshot. She literally abases herself to acknowledge what she understands as the providential source of her being and her blessings both. Telling Billy that "one must put oneself in the care of God" (324), she affirms "that God look[s] after everything and that one could no more evade his care than evade his judgment" (325). Even the ex-priest has not lost such faith, testifying to the primacy of a living God to our essential humanity: "In the end we shall all of us be only what we have made of God. For nothing is real save his grace" (158).

Thus, Billy receives ample instruction in his own dependence on divine gifts and in how this obliges him to have faith in God and show fidelity to his fellows. Yet like John Grady, he is no more ready to bend his knee before providence than to bend his will to what he owes his neighbors. Indeed, as Mundik observes, by the time of Boyd's wounding, Billy "[has] lost faith in the idea that an omniscient, omnipotent, and benevolent God looks after this world" (*Bloody* 176). Certainly, by *Cities of the Plain* such belief is an object of his ridicule, not reverence. Hence his mockery of Travis's piety, noting that neither he nor his "Christian dogs" will "hunt on a Sunday" (*CP* 157). Even earlier, he struggles with the humility and gratitude in which mentors attempt to school him. Though he twice cries "Oh God" when Boyd is shot (*TC* 270), he finds himself incapable of following the shopkeeper in praying to God for his brother's life: "he tried to think how to pray. Finally he just prayed to Boyd. Dont be dead, he prayed" (274). Despite his many teachers, Billy can conceive of no power higher than the human to which to appeal and ultimately resorts to asking his brother to will his own survival. As Billy confesses in response to the testimony of Boyd's novia, then, "he himself had no such idea of God and . . . he'd pretty much given up praying to Him" (325). Yet putting his faith in his own purity or Boyd's fierceness does little to heal the rift his zeal for self-determination has created between the brothers and little to salve the wounds his failed turns at savior have inflicted. Days after his words to the novia, Boyd and she have departed without a farewell, never again to be seen alive. This loss, like others before it, imposes its own burden of guilt. Just as he reacts to the death of the she-wolf with a punishing sojourn in the wilderness that Hall deems an act of penance ("Hero" 192),[22] so Billy responds to his failure with Boyd by pledging himself to the task of safeguarding Cole. But in doing so, he rehearses not just an outcome—the death of the brother figure—but the prelude, in that, trusting in no God to care for or forgive either of them, he relies exclusively on himself and only abets John Grady's American folly.

If Billy Parham once again fails, then, he does so to the extent not just that he breaks faith with those owed his regard, but also that he abjures, along with the Catholic God preached by would-be guides, the gratitude, humility, and steadfastness faith in that God demands. In these twinned derelictions, doubles to John Grady's own, Billy renders himself a tragic figure and powerfully invokes the alternative outlook that reveals these cowboys' attempted repudiation of a debased modernity to have fallen short. As de Sales articulates it, Catholic tradition teaches that "humility perfects us in regard to God, and gentleness in regard to our neighbor" (134). Such a stance toward God remains alien to the Billy who offers Cole's body as an indictment of providence: "he called to God to see what was before his eyes. Look at this, he called. Do you see?" (*CP* 261). Yet if Billy fails in humility and even gentleness, his tale features a perfect exemplar of such virtues by which to weigh his American ideals. Returned a third time to Mexico, Billy encounters in a derelict church an old woman at prayer. Her faith unshaken by the flight of priests, the ruin of buildings, or her own seeming abandonment, she continues offering petitions to God on behalf of humanity: "She said that she left it to God as to how the prayers should be apportioned. She prayed for all" (*TC* 390). Humble dependence on the divine here underwrites selfless care for the other, qualities thwarted in McCarthy's protagonists by the Enlightenment notion of the self to which, above all, they remain faithful. While the woman's petitions might be read as being mocked by their seeming fruitlessness, the narrator rather emphasizes in her a nobility that does not flatter Billy and his more American idols: "still who could say what worse wastes of war and torment and despair the old woman's constancy might not have stayed. . . . Unmoving, austere, implacable. Before just such a God" (390).

Yet it is in *Cities of the Plains* that the trilogy's deployment of faith as a means to critique its protagonists' enlightened commitments takes on its most Catholic cast. Most explicitly concerned of the three with matters of sin and forgiveness, this last installment also features the most fateful abjuration of trust in God. Now, Potts maintains that this novel reveals religion to be "either irrelevant or insufficient to the moral demands" of Cole and Parham's world (127), and Owens maintains that these cowboys' tales conclude with "no Christ, no salvation, no other possibility except certain death" (111). It is true that *Cities* confirms the Border Trilogy's status as tragedy, certainly so far as John Grady is concerned. However, the Christian God is more a subject for open discussion here even than in *The Crossing*, and John Grady's own dying words proclaim the centrality of faith, or lack thereof, in God's mercy to his, Magdalena's, and Eduardo's fate. Indeed, that his faith in this sense is insufficient is altogether relevant to his bloody failures in terms of more human fidelity. What's more, through the important role played by Magdalena herself in this final act, these considerations become more explicitly framed by Catholic notions of human sinfulness, efficacious confession, and God's grace than ever before, signaling the extent to which the trilogy's critical treatment of American ideals of self-sufficiency rests upon an effectively Catholic anthropology.

Certainly, Magdalena's Catholicism is as salient an aspect of her character as is her status as prostitute or as John Grady's beloved. In fact, it is through her faith that central questions concerning humanity's need for relationship with a God who can forgive and redeem human weakness come to be articulated. As Jarrett observes, her discussions with Cole "continually evoke the sacred" ("Sense" 328), and they do so in the language of her Catholic faith. For Magdalena remains faithful not just to Cole, but to the Catholicism of her culture. This is so notwithstanding all she has suffered at the hands of pimps, police, and even the Church, the last of which has, in the form of venal religious, sold her back into sexual slavery: "The procurer himself appeared on the convent steps . . . and in the pure light of day paid money into the hand of the mother superior and took [her] away again" (*CP* 139). Nonetheless, Magdalena offers blessings in the name of the Catholic God, telling John Grady, "Vete con Dios" after their first night together (70). Interrogated by Eduardo, she admits she still prays to this God, even when she feels that "Nadie," no one, is answering (183). But her faithfulness has to do with more than just habitual prayer, idiomatic benedictions, or devotion to the "crude carved santo" she insists on taking with her from the White Lake (220). It includes also an acute awareness of human imperfection and the burden of obligation this imposes vis-à-vis both neighbor and God. She has had ample experience of others' sinfulness, but she is also aware of her own weakness and of how she must guard against breaking faith with others. Thus, before first spending the night with John Grady, she asks if he is single, and takes comfort in hearing that he is, for, she tells him, "it would be a worse sin if he were married" (70). Though herself ill-used, then, she remains motivated by a desire to betray God and neighbor as little as she might.

Indeed, it is through her scrupulousness in this regard that the question of fault and forgiveness that proves decisive in Cole's end comes to the fore. While John Grady first understands this query as expressing a romantic interest in his availability—"He asked if her if that was really why she wished to know" (70)—the seriousness of this matter for Magdalena is communicated in her return to it on the eve of her planned escape, when she asks him whether he believes in the forgiveness of sins. Though John Grady has lost the habit of prayer and outright rejects the maestro's recommendation that he turn to God, for fear of the answer such submission to a divine will might yield, here he offers a considered and rather orthodox response: "he said that he believed in God. . . . But that a God unable to forgive was no God at all" (206). Indeed, he maintains, when she presses, that this applies to all sins, "Con la excepción de desesperación" (206); despair, he concedes, cannot be forgiven, as it is itself the surrender of hope for forgiveness. This last, as noted in chapter 3 (see note 6), is traditional Catholic teaching. These are, then, answers that a faithful Magdalena knows and that, burdened by her own shame, she longs to hear confirmed by this man in whom she has placed her trust. But while Cole knows well enough what he has to say here, the rest of his tale makes plain that these are words in which he will not believe. In fact, after Magdalena's murder, he is motivated by nothing other than a despair that finds its roots in a renunciation of faith in God's authority and mercy, and its fruits in a bloody refusal of moral limits to his self-determination.

Catholicism teaches that forgiveness of sins is to be found through the sacrament of confession; more than this, it highlights two preconditions for the absolution this rite promises. As de Sales writes, sinners, though discouraged by their repeated failures, must retain a faith in God's goodness and turn to the confessional "with great courage and confidence in his mercy" (139). Such a turning requires, as von Speyr notes, not just faith, but genuine surrender of the self before the divine other; thus, it "wants nothing more from a person than that he absolutely own up to his sin and that he do so in truth" (201). All-American cowboy to the end, Cole remains incapable of such faith and humility. It is true that his final moments feature his only recorded prayer. Bleeding to death from the many knife wounds inflicted by Eduardo, he finally petitions an authority higher than himself or a small-town judge: "Help me, he said. If you think I'm worth it" (CP 257). Yet this act of surrender is tellingly conditional and bespeaks that inability to trust in another's guidance that has already cost his own and Magdalena's life. So far as the former is concerned, it is clear that John Grady has deliberately thrown his life away precisely because he cannot credit God's mercy. As he admits to Billy, he never fully believed what he said to Magdalena on this score: "I thought maybe she wouldnt go to heaven because, you know" (259). Judging his beloved beyond redemption on account of the dehumanization forced upon her, he opts for a violence that is both self-assertion and self-destruction. "I didnt want to be forgiven if she wasnt" (259), he insists, and so chooses the course of vengeance against Magdalena's killer in place of faith in her salvation or humble prayer for himself. Despite his appeal for divine assistance, it is clear that Cole's refusal to submit to God's law holds to the end. The John Grady so hungry for a confessor at the end of *All the Pretty Horses* here knows, by virtue of the catechism Magdalena has offered him, where to look for absolution, but lacking the necessary faith in God's forgiveness and willingness to be governed by another's judgment, he cannot pursue it. Insisting to the last that he "aint sorry" for killing Eduardo (259), Cole insists upon his sovereignty unto death.

In all of this, John Grady insists not just on Eduardo's demise, but on his own spiritual ruin. His rejection of humble trust in God's goodness leads him to that crime against human solidarity which is murder, to the loss of his own life, and to his embrace of the sin he himself has confessed to be unforgivable. Now, Cooper reads Cole's fatal duel with Eduardo in heroic terms, as, indeed, a kind of self-sacrifice in which "he faces evil, names it, condemns it, and offers himself as a gesture of expiation" (*Heroes* 98). Though less celebratory, Hillier, too, argues that Eduardo's thorough corruption renders John Grady's vengeance just and guiltless (*Morality* 152). Yet the Catholic framing of this act by discussions with Magdalena, on the one hand, and Billy, on the other, suggests otherwise. John Grady knows what despair is and accepts what it entails. As he tells Billy, when he saw Magdalena's body at the morgue, he "didnt care to live no more" (*CP* 259). In fact, he declares to Eduardo, "I come to kill you or be killed" (248), and that the latter is his aim is demonstrated both by his twice refusing Eduardo's invitation to go home with his life (248, 250) and by the manner in which he takes Eduardo's own, exposing himself to yet another mortal blow—"He made no effort to step or to parry" (254)—in order to plunge his blade decisively into his foe's skull. Cole thus, as Arnold suggests, concludes his life by choosing a violence aimed at his own death as much as Eduardo's ("Last" 229). A refusal of faith having led him to despair of Magdalena, he breaks faith with her belief and with the law itself in order not just to kill another, but to effect a suicide that bespeaks his refusal of hope for himself in this world or any that might follow. His twofold failure of fidelity thus fuels his bloodiest assertion of autonomy yet and so exposes that ideal itself to judgment.

Yet if that ruling is damning, it is not quite final; if the trilogy ends hopelessly for Cole, a different conclusion awaits Parham. Though like his lost protégé in his devotion to Enlightenment precepts, Billy's end differs from the younger man's and does so as it is sustained by forms of fidelity John Grady deliberately rejects. Outliving Cole by fifty-nine years, Billy finds himself a lifelong drifter and septuagenarian itinerant. But if this course indicates his loyalty to the American creed of independence, the epilogue that brings his tale to its conclusion suggests this is not whole story. In his protracted roadside encounter with another wanderer, Parham meets with the last of his would-be spiritual guides, one who, again, preaches against the gospel of self-sufficiency that has wrought such harm for Billy, for John Grady, and for America itself. Insisting on a more Catholic perspective that views the world and every human life as that "which God has formed" (CP 285), this teacher inveighs against that mandate to mastery over self, others, and this providential Creation that has proved Cole's undoing. As he puts it, "Our waking life's desire to shape the world to our convenience invites all manner of paradox and difficulty" (283). Billy's own life testifies to this tragic and, for McCarthy, quintessentially American truth. Yet the way out of such trouble lies not in individuals' capacity to puzzle things out for themselves, but in their readiness to accept in faith their reliance on the Creator and to give themselves to charitable solidarity with humanity at large. As this final parabolist concludes, "Every man's death is a standing in for every other. And since death comes to all there is no way to abate the fear of it except to love that man who stands for us" (288). This last lesson, then, like those that preceded it, points away from the Enlightenment values that Cole insists on dying by and toward contrary, rather Catholic teachings on human finitude and obligation, on the need to recognize a universal dependence on God and strangers and to honor that truth with faith and charity.

That there is hope he might finally heed such a lesson is demonstrated in Billy's finding, after years of wandering, a home at last. Taken in and cared for by a New Mexico family, Billy shows himself, unlike Cole, ready to let himself be cared for and to hope for God's mercy by heeding the voice of a faithful, charitable other. Assured by the mother of the house that he will see his dead brother again (291), he is rescued in spiritual terms not just by this declaration of faith, but by Betty's grounding his dignity in participation in a common humanity owed each member's steadfast love. When Billy despairs of his own worth—"I aint nothing. I dont know why you put up with me"—she offers him the mercy in which John Grady could not believe: "I know who you are. And I do know why" (292). In the end, then, Billy is, as Cant argues, sustained by "that freely given hospitality that has been one of the cardinal virtues of Mc-Carthy's world" (235). More than this, he is redeemed from tragedy by forms of faithfulness resonant of McCarthy's Catholic heritage and critical of the Enlightenment underpinnings of Billy's idealized past and fallen present. Thus, both his end and John Grady's reveal, one more positively, one negatively, an affirmation of Ignatius of Antioch's definition of the path to eternal life: "life begins and ends with two qualities. Faith is the beginning, and love is the end; and the union of the two together is God" (Radice 65). If his ultimate experience of these qualities in a surrendering of sovereignty to loving care affords Billy a form of happy ending, then *The Road*, subject of my final chapter, will engage a still more profound meditation on these saving virtues in Eucharistic terms to derive divine comedy even out of dystopia.

CHAPTER 6

LIKE THE LAST HOST OF CHRISTENDOM

DEADLY PRAGMATISM, PROFANE COMMUNION, AND THE POWER OF EUCHARIST IN *THE ROAD*

One has only to consider what happens today . . . in order to measure at what point reason handed over to itself, to a pure objectivism, . . . can strike at what is most proper to the heart of man and threaten his "humanity," and at the same time humanity in its entirety.

—MICHEL HENRY, *Incarnation*

I am the food of full-grown men. Grow and you shall feed on me. But you shall not change me into your own substance, as you do with the food of your body. Instead you shall be changed into me.

—AUGUSTINE, *Confessions*

Prior to the 2022 release of *The Passenger* and *Stella Maris*, *The Road* stood as the capstone of McCarthy's oeuvre. Though followed by the publication, in 2006, of *The Sunset Limited* and, in 2013, of the screenplay for *The Counselor*, this novel seemed, as Frye maintains, "the pinnacle of McCarthy's popular and critical success" ("Life" 11), earning its author both the approbation of Oprah's Book Club and the 2007 Pulitzer Prize for Fiction. As the long-standing endpoint of the writer's novelistic career, *The Road* is remarkable, for my purposes, for two further reasons. First, in its relentlessly dismal post-apocalyptic milieu, it offers McCarthy's most thorough dismantling yet of an Enlightenment faith in the sure progress consequent on radical personal sovereignty and human mastery over nature, in that empire of "human utility and power" promised by such advocates as Bacon (164). Second, by punctuating this narrative, crafted under the working title of "The Grail" (Crews 12), with the language and imagery of the Eucharist, McCarthy also frames here what is arguably the most explicitly Catholic of his texts, one Cooper holds can even be read as a restaging of the Roman Catholic Paschal Vigil (*Cormac* 151). As such, *The Road* is a work that starkly illustrates my thesis and does so in a startlingly hopeful way. For despite Simon Schleusener's insistence that, in the novel's world, the "concept of the future seems to have almost completely vanished" (par. 15), it is rather the case that this apocalyptic tale is one that, through its Eucharistic critique of Enlightenment values, emerges as perhaps the author's most optimistic.[1]

This may seem counter-intuitive. Set on a frigid, ash-choked, and dying planet, one marked by an ostensibly terminal scarcity of life-giving goods, *The Road*'s narrative seems merely the prelude to an absolute extinction event. Indeed, its Hobbesian scenario gestures not simply toward the end of human life, but through the already accomplished dissolution of society, toward the eradication of the species' humanity. These dystopian valences are, I contend, central to the novel's critical assessment of Enlightenment thought. Not only does its animating vision of the world's end mark an inversion of confident forecasts of the progressive and beneficent humanization of nature; the prime fruit of this barren setting is humanity's widespread dehumanization via its deployment of enlightened forms of rationality. While Spinoza asserts that "true virtue is nothing other than to live by the guidance of reason" (175), McCarthy's text rather dramatizes the brutalizing malevolence to which ideals of personal autonomy and self-interested practical reasoning are prone. For confronted with the dwindling unto disappearance of other foodstuffs, the survivors of *The Road*'s comprehensive catastrophe pursue their own interests to the extent both of canceling the social contract and of nullifying others' humanity. Adopting a cannibalism that unmakes community and reduces human persons—both consumer and consumed—to functions of appetite, the murderous bands McCarthy's father-son duo flee pursue the dictates of Henry's reifying reason as a benighted surrender both of their humanity and of hope for a human future. These inhumane remnants thus represent, as Casey Jergenson observes, the "intersection of animal instinct and utilitarian, instrumental rationality" (126); by so doing, they indict not just themselves, but their mode of reasoning.

Even in their anthropophagy, however, McCarthy's marauders evoke a contrary model for self-governance and relationship. Forfeiting humanity in their reduction of others to flesh upon which to feed, these agents of self-interest enact a demonic perversion of the communion of Eucharist, a sacrament whose elements and symbolism distinguish the novel's cannibalism-eschewing protagonists. Eucharistic imagery abounds in *The Road*, framing not only the portrait of the cannibals' self-annihilating Enlightenment, but also the humanity preserved by McCarthy's unnamed father and son. In their fidelity and numberless acts of selfless love, this pair preserves genuine community precisely through their exemplification of Christian charity and their expanding communion. The faith and sacrificial love at the heart of the Catholic sacrament are shown to be central to this rescue of humanity, justifying Giemza's claim that "the unmediated encounter with the Eucharist . . . becomes a spiritual desideratum in McCarthy's world" (225). Indeed, to the extent that the man remains committed to prudential practical reasoning, to the good only of his own child, he stands in the way not just of enlarged community, but also of a humane fate for the son who will outlive him. As Griffis notes, the man's "survivalist mindset clashes with the boy's neighborly virtues" (89). Yet in what is McCarthy's most hopeful ending, the father takes a leap of faith by committing to that truly Eucharistic promise—of selfless, communion-forging charity, not community-annihilating rational self-interest—he has consistently identified with the son. In fact, the duo, at the boy's urging, pursue an ever-widening communion based in love and faith. This expansion of Eucharistic relations to include a properly human community finally trumps the father's fearful pragmatism and enables his taking the chance that delivers his son into the hands of the prayerful adoptive family of the novel's conclusion. Thus, the dead end of a rapacious, self-seeking Enlightenment is overcome by means of Augustine's different diet, the faith, love, and sacrifice that lie at the heart of the Eucharist.

ENLIGHTENMENT'S APOCALYPTIC HUNGER

The place to begin, however, is the ending McCarthy's tale presupposes. The cataclysmic event that has seemingly signed the death warrant for life on earth lies many years in the past. More than this, its true nature is left tantalizingly vague. All the reader is told is that, in the days prior to the boy's birth, his parents are shocked awake at 1:17 A.M. by "a long shear of light and then a series of low concussions," followed by a "dull rose glow in the windowglass" (R 52). Uncertain as this description remains, McCarthy has made it clear that such obscurity was his intention, refusing in interviews to offer any clarification of *The Road's* apocalypse and insisting that the specific cause "is not really important" to the book's concerns (Jurgenson). Yet this has done little to quell scholarly speculation on this matter, with critics naming as culprit everything from nuclear war to God-sent judgment.[2] Nonetheless, as McCarthy's refusal to elucidate suggests, it is less the source than the result of this disaster that matters here. For, whatever the cause of the world's descent into its utterly barren ice age, the effects of this apocalyptic event are such as to utterly overturn the kinds of material and moral progress envisioned by Western modernity. The future occupied by McCarthy's father and son is no Baconian utopia; its natural environment has not been directed by empirical science and practical reason to proliferating human goods. Instead, nature has been so utterly unmade as to leave what humans remain her abject victims, all but powerless to secure the barest necessities of food, warmth, and shelter in a world in which all things seem locked in a common death-march.

The novel opens with the father waking from nightmare to scan a landscape "barren, silent, godless" (R 4). Heading south in hopes of outpacing the killing cold, McCarthy's pair traverse a "cauterized terrain" (14), depopulated, burnt-out, and devoid of any life that might nourish them. This deathscape is no localized affair. Their quest for warmer climes concludes at a seashore that testifies to a global extermination: "At the tide line a woven mat of weeds and the ribs of fishes in their millions stretching along the shore as far as the eye could see like in an isocline of death. One vast salt sepulchre. Senseless" (222). The carnage extends beyond the seas and embraces more than this grim sepulchre's piscine remains. Towns and cities themselves are no mere ruins but open graves, plundered and profaned. Exploring an abandoned cityscape, father and son find "the mummied dead everywhere . . . discalced to a man like pilgrims of some common order for all their shoes were long since stolen" (24). In this resolutely hostile environment, McCarthy's protagonists are desperate foragers always on the verge of starvation. Repeatedly going days without food in this comprehensive waste, they look to themselves like fearsome aliens or pitiable victims. Plagued by bloody coughing and ravaged by hunger, the sickly father almost raises a pistol at his unrecognizable reflection in a mirror (132) and sees in his son's diminished form "something out of a deathcamp" (117). Such an attenuation of the flesh, in the face of a world that lacks both sanctuary and sustenance, threatens not simply physical death, but a more spiritual defeat, a despair that dogs McCarthy's man from the outset and torments him with visions of the "cold relentless circling of the intestate earth. Darkness implacable. . . . The crushing black vacuum of the universe" (130). Thus it is that, even in his steadfast efforts to secure their welfare, "some part of him always wished it to be over" (154).

Such a moribund planet itself stands as a frustration of Enlightenment expectations for a coming age improved by scientific progress and humanity's extended dominion over such natural foes as scarcity, disaster, and disease. This contradiction of modern hopes is even more forcefully expressed in *The Road*'s depiction of its human environment. Adeline Johns-Putra maintains that "the novel mourns the loss of human rather than nonhuman nature" (521); there is considerable justice in this claim. McCarthy's apocalypse has more to do with what is forfeited by humanity's response to the disappearance of natural goods than with environmental destruction per se, and the future depicted here counters Kant's claim that "men raise themselves . . . out of backwardness if one does not purposely invent artifices to keep them down" in no uncertain terms (138). The father recalls a swift collapse of modern civilization in the absence of the networks of power, production, and distribution upon which it relies: "Within a year there were fires on the ridges and deranged chanting. The screams of the murdered" (*R* 32). In months, post-apocalyptic America moves from a culture in which the bereaved erect cairns to their dead to one defined by the discarding of foundational taboos, "populated by men who would eat your children in front of your eyes" (181). This nation founded on Enlightenment principles becomes, in the face of radical scarcity, not just a territory without government, but a wilderness bereft of human community. Once "stores of food [have] given out and murder [is] everywhere upon the land" (181), society disperses into a wasteland peopled by refugees from a failed civilization, "creedless shells of men tottering down the causeways like migrants in a feverland" (28). What we see, then, is an unmaking of modern ideals and hopes, as the culture the Enlightenment has wrought disintegrates and the future realizes not progress, but devolution. As Monk observes, the novel discloses "the ultimate destination of the violence that accompanies modernity [in] the return of humanity to more rudimentary forms of violence" (80).

This regression threatens human survival at least as much as does the lack of food. Not simply the risk of violence from predatory others, but also the resulting despair noted above, undercuts both the possibility of preserving one's own humanity and the desire to persist in so hopeless a world. Given these conditions, the man's wife denies they have survived at all. Though not yet struck down by hunger or violence, their family is, for her, merely "the walking dead in a horror film" (*R* 55), animate, but robbed of all that constitutes a genuinely human life. After she has acted on this despair and taken her own life, the man adds her to his reckoning of griefs and failures: "He did not take care of her and she died alone somewhere in the dark" (32). The burden of such sorrow, added to the toll taken by stintless struggles against a wholly hostile environment, makes the mother's suicidal answer to their situation perhaps the greatest threat to the continuance of the human. Certainly, the man, taxed by the hardships his world imposes, wrestles with a rage and despair akin to his wife's. Looking at his son's gaunt face by firelight, he is shaken by the futility of his efforts: "He fought back the rage. Useless" (96). Moreover, faced with the real dangers posed by men who will eat his child, the father has, for all his work to keep them alive, schooled his son in suicide, in hopes of saving him from more terribly inhuman fates. "You put it in your mouth and point it up," he instructs the boy in the use of their revolver (113). Given the education offered by such lessons and by the deathscape which is the only world he has known, it is unsurprising that the son should himself despair, telling his widowed father, "I wish I was with my mom" (55). The man may admonish his son for such sentiments—"Dont say it. It's a bad thing to say" (55)—but he is keenly aware how grief for wife and world has fostered similar longings in himself: "the boy was all that stood between him and death" (29).

That the boy preserves him in this way, however much it may seem the man who safeguards his son, is crucially important, for it indicates the extent to which human survival, the survival of the human, is in this novel rooted not in an Enlightenment faith in the fruits of human mastery and rational self-interest, but in selfless, even irrational, love for others. For it is plainly the case that the mother's self-annihilating despair, the father's weary rage and thirst for death, are eminently rational responses to their situation. In a world where all human community seems irreparably shattered, all hope for nonviolent treatment at others' hands is deluded, and all (nonhuman) sources of nourishment are near exhaustion, surely suicide is the most reasonable of propositions. If to be modern is, as Gillespie notes, "to be self-liberating and self-making" (2), then such an utterly abject existence is an offense to such a self as American modernity has so prized. In the face of enforced powerlessness and radical, incurable vulnerability, the kind of autonomy valorized by Enlightenment thought can be best secured through self-destruction. Taking into account the terrible cost of simply persisting in this broken world, the certainty of no improvement in one's prospects, and the likelihood of an excruciating, dehumanizing end, a rational individual might well conclude that the good lies most in abjuring this living death. If one is guided by an essentially enlightened compass, the mother's choice to leave her family and end her own life is arguably the proper one. As Grace Hellyer puts it, "the mother's suicidal indifference is, technically speaking, the most rational position" (56).[3]

Such, certainly, is the mother's view. Before she departs to take her life with "a flake of obsidian" (R 58), she tells the man he cannot convince her to stay: "You have no argument because there is none" (57). From that perspective of rational self-interest advocated by Enlightenment, there is no reason to stay her hand. What she can reasonably look forward to is the utter negation not just of her personal advantage and autonomy, but of her dignity, humanity, and life. The trio's foreseeable fate is not just imminent death, but unconscionable suffering, violation, and dehumanization: "Sooner or later they will catch us and they will kill us. They will rape me. They'll rape him. They are going to rape us and kill us and eat us" (56). Nothing in the novel suggests this is an unreasonable expectation. In the face of such realities, the only shield she possesses is that of a preemptive, self-chosen, and painless demise. Through suicide, personal suffering is minimized, while individual sovereignty is maximally preserved. Indeed, it is precisely because the man no longer has bullets enough to promise such escape for all three of them that it has become urgent for the mother to act on her own behalf. No longer a reliable defender of her dignity, he is useless to her: "You cant protect us. You say you would die for us but what good is that?" (56). Seeking the practical maintenance of her autonomy, she spurns this spouse in favor of her "new lover," death (57): "my only hope is for eternal nothingness and I hope it with all my heart" (57). Certainly, the man's professions of love and fidelity, his calls that she think of the boy's feelings, fail to change her heart. Such appeals to the loving obligations of kin and covenant are, in the face of her certain loss of self-possession, utterly empty: "I don't care. It's meaningless" (56). The mother's suicidal desertion thus dramatizes an important link in this text between mere reason and despair, more specifically, between the rational self-interest of Enlightenment psychology and the loss of humanity itself. In her suicidal refusal of the bonds of blood, McCarthy offers a portrait of that paradox of self-love detailed by Michel Henry, whereby the modern ego, in making absolutely sovereign an inescapably fragile self, can come only to idolize its own limits and final erasure: "it is his own powerlessness that man loves, and it is to his own finitude and death that he entrusts himself" (234).

Now, the cannibals who prompt the mother to entrust herself to death may at first glance seem her perfect antithesis. Far from replicating her choice of self-destruction as an escape from a seemingly hopeless world, they will rather kill and consume others so as to ensure their own survival. We might see here the contrast that Broncano draws between the novel's father-son duo and its fearsome "bad guys," that "between those willing to sacrifice themselves before sacrificing others and those willing to sacrifice others in order to survive themselves" (127). However, the bad guys' chosen course is, much like the mother's, one that endorses both death and the radical severance of human ties. Further, they follow her in embracing nothingness—the annihilation of morals, taboos, others' lives—on the grounds of the rational pursuit of their self-interest. Confident in their power to be the rapists, murderers, and cannibals, and not victims of such, they take an alternate, but not irrational, course of unbridled consumption of what material goods their dying world yet affords. Indeed, as many have noted, the seemingly atavistic normalization of cannibalism is evocative of much more modern forms of consumerism. Cooper reads *The Road* as "a post-Anthropocene retrospective on the economic history of the US, from its use and consumption of people kept in slavery through its reckless consumption of fossil fuels" (*Cormac* 133), while Rikard more precisely insists that "cannibalism, like the fires that devour the landscape, becomes the final evidence of an unchecked consumerism" (217).[4] Certainly, the novel offers considerable grounds for treating its cannibals as quintessentially modern, both in their self-seeking and in the consumerist form it takes.

The text, then, places its characters in an environment still marked by pre-apocalyptic forms of consumerism. Following the vanished nation's network of highways, McCarthy's duo passes roadside notices for the consumer goods of a now defunct marketplace. The father remarks "billboards advertising motels. Everything as it once had been save faded and weathered" (R 8). Later, he notes "a log barn in a field with an advertisement in faded ten-foot letters across the roofslope. See Rock City" (21), which testifies to America's onetime power to monetize an obliterated natural beauty. But if such hieroglyphs suggest the disappearance of American consumerism, *The Road* makes clear that its survivors have not freed themselves from the goods and even the rationality that underlay that culture. With nature's bounty despoiled, human beings are left to haunt the malls and supermarkets of this ruined civilization, searching for what of its processed comestibles remains. The bad guys' role not simply as Hobbesian rivals in a world of absolute scarcity, but as demonic consumers in recognizably mercantile space, is demonstrated by the father's recollection of cityscapes overrun by scavengers "white of tooth and eye carrying charred and anonymous tins of food in nylon nets like shoppers in the commissaries of hell" (181). Indeed, as a world incapable of husbandry, McCarthy's dystopia is one given over altogether to consuming, and as its foodstocks dwindle, the nature of this consumption becomes ever more infernal. Thus, coming upon a ruined orchard, the man finds evidence, not of consumerism's end, but of its terrible extension: "He'd seen it all before. Shapes of dried blood in the stubble grass and gray coils of viscera where the slain had been field-dressed" (90). This rampant reduction of persons not just to commodities, but consumables, is evident in the old plantation house, where "chattel slaves had once trod" as servants (106) and where McCarthy's pair nearly meet their end. With its "great heap of clothing" stripped from earlier victims (107) and its great cauldron, "the kind once used for rendering hogs" (109), this manor discloses the horrible character of its ménage in a hellish cellar larder where human beings are kept to be eaten at their captors' leisure: "Huddled against the back wall were naked people, male and female. . . . On the mattress lay a man with his legs gone to the hip and the stumps of them blackened and burnt" (110).

In the wake of this terrible discovery, the traumatized boy asks his father, "Why do they have to do that?" (127). Certainly, the conduct of McCarthy's protagonist pair and of the suicidal mother indicates that this ghoulish consumerism, this insistence on one's own interests to the point of the other's assimilation, is far from inevitable. Yet the answer to this question is one that, in fact, points to a certain kinship with the mother's own desertion of others and destruction of life, precisely as it resonates with Enlightenment formulations of the individual's properly sovereign self-interest. On Spinoza's account, it is both true and right that "nobody, unless he is overcome by external causes . . . neglects to seek his own advantage, that is, to preserve his own being" (166). Far from a moral lapse, this conatus is a supreme good, such that "the more every man endeavors and is able to preserve his own being, the more he is endowed with virtue" (166). As Adorno and Horkheimer extrapolate, Enlightenment epistemology is not just materialist, but personal and pragmatic. It enjoins the self to an instrumental rationality aimed at empowering a manipulation of its environment that secures its own advantage and persistence: "Its principles are the principles of self-preservation. Immaturity is then the inability to survive" (83). Now, the mother, too, rejects the immature role of victim. Unable to realize her conatus, she nonetheless repudiates world and relationship so as to preserve her standing as an autonomous self. In so doing, she denies value even to her family and embraces death. The bad guys likewise deal in death and the annihilation of others' moral worth with an eye to preserving their own agency. The novel therefore emphasizes their instrumental intelligence. The father, remembering the roadrat who nearly took his boy, is haunted not just by his "gray and rotting teeth. Claggy with human flesh" (*R* 75), but by the "reptilian calculations in those cold and shifting eyes" (75). What the roadrat calculates is how best to claim this boy as meal and escape, his own survival trumping all other considerations.

Yet, as this description suggests, living by such calculation alone effects a profound dehumanization not only in those reduced to the status of nutriment, but in those who seek their good through such brutalizing means. Obviously, persons consumed as one might devour the contents of one of the novel's charred tins are being denied human dignity or any moral standing by their murderers. Penned up, as in the plantation house, like so much livestock, these victims are forcibly robbed of humanity, made nothing more than objects serving another's self-preservation. But as the roadrat's saurian reasoning reveals, such unfettered self-seeking corrodes the predators' own humanity. This it does by equating virtue and power, defining the good as individual persistence alone.

Through such an equation, the bad guys affirm the supremacy of meaningless-ness declared by the mother; with her, they deny any value to other persons, but also to such virtues as fidelity, reciprocity, hope, or love. As Erik Wielenberg puts it, they are undone as they reject the whole realm of the moral: "Bad guys are not people who strive to be moral and fail; they are people who have ceased to care about morality altogether" (9). But so to exist beyond moral reckoning is, the novel insists, to cease to be human, even if it secures one's survival. The threat of such a fate—not of being consumed or killing oneself, but of becoming a pointlessly perduring thing—looms over this text. It appears in the bestial-ization of captives like the "consort of catamites illclothed against the cold and fitted in dogcollars" driven down the road (R 92). It is evident in the ravening roadrat, whose gaze darts "like an animal inside a skull looking out of the eye-holes" (63). It haunts the boy, who wakes from nightmares of wind-up toys with a dread of an unmotivated mechanical persistence: "nobody had wound it up and it was really scary" (36). In fact, in the hellish world in which he spends his waking hours, this dream of inhuman pseudo-life has been realized, as the lords of the sex slaves described above are described as marching past "with a swaying gait like wind-up toys" (91).

DEMONIC COMMUNION, CHRISTLY EUCHARIST

In the end, the novel's cannibals enact, even if they cannot articulate, a nihilism more total than the mother's. Cooper even argues that they are comparably sui-cidal, their preying on the young revealing "a desire to cut short the degenerate and degenerating remains of the race" (*Cormac* 140). While I think this over-states the extent to which they weigh any objective beyond their own survival, it does indicate how their murderous pursuit of that end yields a similarly hope-less embrace of death in place of community or futurity. However, the predatory manner in which they pledge themselves to nothingness also evokes a powerful Catholic counterpoint to the destruction of communion their self-seeking ra-tionality effects. Their recourse to cannibalism, that is, points to a radically alternative mode of being human insofar as it is figured as a perverse Eucharist. As Justin Martyr testifies, the association of this sacrament with anthropophagy dates back to Roman persecutions of the second century (63). The Church has historically courted such confusion by insisting that, in partaking of the consecrated bread and wine, communicants are not simply restaging the Last Supper, but consuming the truly present Christ. The sacrament itself is predicated on the violence of the Passion and Crucifixion, and it involves participants' eating the flesh of the Son of God. As Marshall explains, for Roman Catholicism, "The Eucharist is the body and blood of Christ" (511); bloodshed and consumption are inextricable from it (512). Indeed, Nutt observes that the discrete consecration of bread and wine presents Christ's body and blood as sundered, emphasizing the sacrament's sacrificial character (86). This means that even the bad guys' violence can allude to this radically different model of communion.

Certainly, McCarthy's narrative is not shy about making such links. Ghastly and violent his man-eaters may be, but they are not divorced from ritual. The father speculates as to the fate of post-apocalyptic "bloodcults [that] must have all consumed one another" (*R* 16). Though he recalls the diaspora that attended the world's end in terms of "creedless shells of men" (28), the savagery such figures enact takes on at times a markedly ceremonial cast. Thus the duo comes upon a minatory palisade of victims' heads clearly constructed not just as warning, but as testimony, with the skulls' "crude tattoos etched in some homebrewed woad. . . . Spiders, swords, targets. A dragon. Runic slogans, creeds misspelled" (90). The most horrifyingly precise and murderous anti-Eucharist comes later. Father and son spy, then cautiously trail, another party on the road, a "wretchedlooking" foursome comprising three men and a single woman "waddling" with late pregnancy (195). Coming upon this group's hastily abandoned camp, the pair smell cooking and then gaze upon the novel's most grisly tableau: "What the boy had seen was a charred human infant headless and gutted and blackening on the spit" (198). This culmination of self-interest in filicidal anthropophagy represents not just the starkest antithesis to the father's devotion to his son's welfare, but a cannibalistic perversion of the Eucharist. Having delivered a child only to sacrifice it to their own appetites, this profane congregation would eat a son's body and blood, and in so doing, lay bare the humanity-destroying character of self-seeking rationality in this text. As Johns-Putra maintains, "Paedophagy—the most extreme and visceral opposite of parental care—lies at the heart of this inhuman world" (530). Yet in so powerfully evoking, even as anti-type, a different kind of communion, the blasphemously Eucharistic cast of this inhumanity points to the different, more Catholic community enacted and sought by McCarthy's protagonists.

Yet the father and son also remain consumers in a less than strictly sacramental sense. Donovan Gwinner highlights how they, too, are guided by instrumental reason and self-interest, to the extent that "from the father's perspective, that which is right depends only on the *actual* survival of his son" (138). While such an assessment, denying the pair any greater objective than their own welfare, is not, I will show, ultimately confirmed by the text, it is true that McCarthy's duo is largely governed by pressing physical needs and by the residual commodities that intermittently meet them. Indeed, their most emblematic accessory serves to identify them with the consumerism of the culture obliterated by the novel's mysterious catastrophe. Their few possessions—coats, tarps, cans of food—they carry in "the grocery cart" (R 5). So vital is this mobile storehouse to the father's commitment to their survival that its theft moves him to an uncharacteristic murderous rage. "You tried to kill us," he tells the thief; "You took everything" (257). As Susan Kollin argues, then, the shopping cart is more than a useful hold-all; it is proof of the pair's ongoing implication in the now collapsed consumer culture of pre-apocalypse America (160).[5] Moreover, as a vestige of that culture, it seems, as in the scene with the thief, to tempt the man to a violence evocative of the cannibals' own.

If, at minimum, this mechanical familiar casts the pair as shoppers, this is a role their tortuous journey has them fulfill. Their first roadside stop has them halt at a gas station and painstakingly harvest, from the dregs of discarded bottles, a half-quart of motor oil "for their little slutlamp to light the long gray dusks, the long gray dawns" (R 7). They are repeatedly drawn to the shops and supermarkets of ruined towns and cities, in hopes of turning up food to fuel another day on the road, apparel to shield them from their inimical environment. They scour long-pillaged department stores for ready-to-wear suitcoats that can serve as parkas (79), and their diet largely consists of the dwindling canned goods, relics of a vanished food industry, to be salvaged from similar venues. They dine on such fare as "crackers and a tin of sausage" (34) or "a can of white beans" (69). They delight in such processed consumer goods as a sachet of "grape flavored powder to make drinks with" uncovered in a ruined farmhouse (119). Yet their uncanny resemblance to shoppers of our own day is perhaps most visible in their treatment of what, as Jordan Dominy notes, is the only one of their finds be identified by its brand name (148). In the ruins of a suburban supermarket, the father retrieves a last can of Coca-Cola from an upended vending machine and makes of this iconic remnant of America's consumerist empire a gift of some moment to his son. "It's a treat. For you" (R 23), the father says, and the boy replies with a form of benediction: "It's really good" (23). That they should, in their starvation, savor so sweet a refreshment is no surprise, but that the barrenness of their world leaves them little but such processed goods to cherish and consume nonetheless underscores the extent to which they, too, are grounded in decidedly modern and materialist forms of consumption.

Now, Dominy reads the Coke scene—its relishing of a mass-produced, nutritionally inessential, and strictly consumerist commodity—as establishing "a link between anthropophagy and consumer capitalism" (148), one which could only implicate the father and son themselves. That their essential worldly consumption need not be similarly demonic, however, is indicated not just by the giving, rather than murderous taking, at the heart of this moment, but by other encounters with decidedly humanizing consumer goods. The most obvious of these occurs with their discovery of an intact, fully stocked bomb shelter soon after the horrors of the plantation house. Found just as the man is "beginning to think that death [is] finally upon them" (R 129), this sanctuary appears as a virtual godsend and does so precisely as a cornucopia containing "crate upon crate of canned goods" (138). These literally life-saving goods appear to the man himself as the abundance of an utterly eradicated economy: "Chile, corn, stew, soup, spaghetti sauce. The richness of a vanished world" (139). Yet far from effecting their atavistic regression, their time in "this tiny paradise" saves them from starvation (150), yields them ample provisions for the road, and restores, through its opportunity for washing and grooming, the outward marks of their human dignity. While they cannot stay here,[6] this interlude indicates that they embody, even as they are themselves driven by the urgent appetites that deform the novel's cannibals, even as they cling to the traces of a suspect modernity, a different ethic of consumption.

As their departure nears, the man discerns in the bunker's trapdoor an ambivalent omen: "The faintly lit hatchway lay in the dark of the yard like a grave yawning at judgment day in some old apocalyptic painting" (155). This image tellingly suggests both death and resurrection. The desperate need that the shelter meets can, as the wife and bad guys have both illustrated, make of life a living death, make living a murderous erasure of meaning and morals. But

McCarthy's pair emerge from this possible crypt because, while they scavenge hell's commissaries for what charred tins remain, their own consumption serves the maintenance, not the repudiation, of more than strictly self-interested ends. Their consuming affords Eucharistic communion precisely because there are goods they will not sacrifice to their own survival. As many have noted, supreme among these is a recognition of the other's and one's own human dignity in an absolute interdiction on anthropophagy.[7] Himself nearing death, the son is less troubled by his own hunger than by the traumatizing example of the plantation house. Prior to their discovery of the bomb shelter, he interrogates his father—"We wouldnt ever eat anybody, would we?" (128)—and presses him to be unqualified in his response: "No. No matter what" (128). It's worth noting that nothing in the text puts this declaration in doubt. The pair do not hunt those they spy on the road. They do not fall upon the helpless lightning-struck man to claim, as they might, his flesh (49–50); they do not partake of the abandoned infant whose life has already been taken, whose carcass is already cooked (198). Rather, both their travels and meals, marked by the same dire scarcity as faces the novel's cannibals, show them steadfast in upholding more than just material goods or personal interests. Thus, in the aftermath of their plantation house escape, they "set out upon the road again, slumped and cowled and shivering in their rags like mendicant friars sent forth to find their keep" (126), choosing the misery of beggars and the valuing of human dignity over marauders' annihilation of the latter in theft, murder, and desecration.

Now, Gwinner argues that, even for McCarthy's father and son, the dictates of decency remain secondary to the overriding imperative to survive (145). But, as Wood observes, and the mother's decision underlines, the novel's world is so bleak as to render such an objective itself highly questionable: "survival is the only thing that matters, but why bother surviving?" (46). The answer the duo provides is a challenge to the question's premise. As noted, the pair hold to goods that forbid them certain unconscionable, though life-saving, acts. Their very reason for surviving is the ongoing struggle to uphold values that trump mere survival. As their depiction as itinerant monks suggests, these have to do with more than physical subsistence, more than the Enlightenment's materialist universe and calls to sovereign individualism and practical reasoning. In fact, the pair comes to model a specifically Eucharistic alternative to the bad guys' carnage, as they uphold moral and spiritual ideals that provide both a reason to survive and limits on what is permissible in the name of survival. These ideals take on a decidedly Christian cast as they are expressed in a compassion clearly rooted in a faith that there are realities and relationships that transcend the temporal. As Crews puts it, "charity is precisely where McCarthy locates the religious life" (285). If, as Irenaeus insists, apostolic teaching is encapsulated in "the pre-eminent gift of love, which is more precious than knowledge, more glorious than prophecy" (390), then McCarthy's monkish protagonists are not simply, as Crews would have it, religious, but more specifically bearers of the gospel, as they pursue a life of love and charity guided by a persistent, if often questioning, belief in God.[8]

Though the father reflects, "On this road there are no godspoke men" (*R* 32), his own presence contradicts this statement. To be sure, his many invocations of God and Christ may not signify much. The "Jesus" and "Christ" he utters on uncovering the basement prisoners seem nothing more than idiomatic blasphemy (110); the more prayerful, and thankful, "Oh my God . . . Oh my God" with which he greets the bounty of the bomb shelter may likewise be a figure of speech (138). But, as we will see, the way in which he views his son suggests otherwise. Even at his most despairing, the man still challenges a God conceived in theistic and providential terms, even his angry doubts communicating a belief that someone hears and can be called to account: "Are you there? . . . Will I see you at the last? Have you a neck by which to throttle you? Have you a heart? Damn you eternally have you a soul?" (11–12). And despite Gwinner's claim that "the boy seems unable to embrace the holy fire of religion" (154), the son likewise strives, the ostensible godlessness of their setting notwithstanding, for relationship with just such a Creator. When the pair struggles in stormy darkness to find their camp, the father tells him to pray for lightning to guide them; lightning duly comes and reveals the boy making urgent petitions: "When the light broke over the beach again he saw that the boy was bent over and was whispering to himself" (*R* 235). Later, he is eager to have the father shoot a newfound flare-gun, less to signal other good guys than to reach out to God or "somebody like that" (246).

This enduring attempt to sustain belief in, and contact with, a Christian godhead is accompanied—in the boy, particularly—by a compassionate desire to play the role not simply of good neighbor, but of rescuer and even savior. The son consistently responds to those the pair encounters with empathy and charity, advocating to the father that they assist, adopt, or spare not just the needy, but those who have injured them. This willingness to sustain loss for others' welfare is extended even to the nonhuman, as the boy, starving though he is, makes the man promise they will not hunt down and eat a dog they have heard barking in a ruined town: "We wont hurt the dog, he said. I promise" (82). Sure that he has glimpsed another boy, the son begs that they should locate and adopt him. The son's yearning to protect this stranger is underwritten by a charity both generous and selfless: "I'd give that little boy half of my food," he tells his father (86). Nor is such a disposition to sacrifice impulsive, quickly forgotten; much later he laments, "I wish that little boy was with us" (131). After the discovery of the spitted infant, the boy similarly mourns not having been able to play savior to this helpless child: "If we had that little baby it could go with us" (200). Lest it be assumed that such empathy is elicited only by children in whom he sees himself, that such charity is merely a kind of self-concern, the text offers ample evidence of the boy's compassionate response to figures both unlike and inimical to himself. Elderly Ely—"smell[ing] terrible" (161) and looking "like a pile of rags fallen off a cart" (162)—is no obvious double, but the boy feels for him nonetheless, urging his father to treat this frightened old man with tenderness (162) and later scolding Papa for mocking him: "You shouldnt make fun of him . . . He's going to die" (175). The boy extends such concern even to the man who has robbed the pair of all their goods. Despite the fact that this thief has done them potentially deadly harm, the son offers him compassion and mercy, mitigating his offense—"He was just hungry, Papa" (259)—and identifying with his distress: "He's so scared" (259). This love for the enemy moves him to intercede on his behalf, in hopes of literally saving this offender's life: "Papa please dont kill the man" (256).

On the strength of such scenes, Cooper identifies the son as "the novel's moral center," insofar as he demonstrates "the capacity of compassion to triumph over fear" (*Cormac* 148). But that capacity itself reveals no small measure of faith, in himself and others; as Stacey Peebles states, then, if there is a sanctity in this boy, it lies in "his insistence on taking risks on people" (132). Indeed, this willingness to hazard himself, to suffer, so as compassionately to safeguard the other grants his goodness a rather more definite, holier form. Given his disposition to give, forgive, and save—even his foes, even at cost to himself—it is no wonder that father and critics both tend to view the son in

Christological terms.[9] The man's first reflections on his boy name him son of God: "He knew only that the child was his warrant. He said: If he is not the word of God God never spoke" (R 5). If the child justifies the man's persistence, he does, of course, play the role of life-saver and, metaphorically, of Savior. But the naming of the son here is much more forceful than that, identifying him with the Johannine Logos and so with the Son of God (see John 1:1–5).[10] That the father thus views his boy in messianic terms is only underscored after the roadrat's attack. Washing the slain marauder's gore from his son's hair, the man reflects, "All of this like some ancient anointing. So be it" (R 74). The father here both asserts the spiritual significance of his act and, in affirming his child's status as anointed, claims for him a literally Christ-like stature. Further, it is clear that the man is invested in this identification in more than a metaphorical sense. Speaking to Ely of the boy's goodness, he effectively declares its divinity: "What if I said that he's a god?" (172). Significantly, such declarations go beyond the loving perspective of the father; as the novel nears its end, the son's own words work to confirm his Christly status. The man deflects the boy's criticism of their treatment of the thief by saying, "You're not the one who has to worry about everything" (259), which garners this reply: "Yes I am, he said. I am the one" (259). This repeated "I am" recalls the answer to Moses's question of how he is to name God to the Israelites: "Thus shalt thou say unto the children of Israel, I AM hath sent me unto you" (Exod. 3:14).[11] Further, it echoes Christ's own response to Judas's confederates at Gethsemane. When asked where they may find Jesus of Nazareth, he twice replies "I am he," at which answer they are thrown to the ground (John 18:6-8).

Such hints at the boy's messianic stature are bolstered by, and themselves cue the reader to perceive, the ways in which McCarthy's duo enacts a Eucharistic rebuttal to the cannibals' anticommunion. As Schaub rightly notes, the boy becomes, in his Christliness, a "receptacle for any number of related ideas, including the consecrated elements of the Eucharist and the body of God" (163). Indeed, the very scene that reveals him to be anointed also establishes his link to the Catholic sacrament. Watching over his child's sleep, the man looks lovingly at the head of his fair-haired son and sees there a more than human good: "Golden chalice, good to house a god" (R 75). This language reaffirms the boy's messianic role, as the "god" the Roman Catholic chalice houses is the blood of Christ, but it also indicates that what sanctifies him is related to an altogether different form of life through consumption than that exemplified by the novel's benighted man-hunters. Nor is this association of the boy with the sacrament unique. Earlier, he welcomes snowfall in terms that point to his Eucharistic function by invoking the sacramental bread, the body of Christ, that complements the chalice that will follow: "A single gray flake sifting down. He caught it in his hand and watched it expire there like the last host of christendom" (16). If the fugitive character of this host might imply that, far from a Savior himself, the boy is condemned to an irredeemable and desacralized world, the recurrence of Eucharistic motifs later in the text suggests otherwise. The man on his deathbed experiences an epiphany that reveals the boy's sanctity to inhere in his status as the sacramental antithesis to, and hope for, his ruined and inhuman world, "standing there in the road looking back at him from some unimaginable future, glowing in that waste like a tabernacle" (273). Cast here as the receptacle for the consecrated host, for the real presence of Christ, the boy is once more identified with the Christian savior and the Catholic sacrament both, in such a way as to emphasize the essence of the latter to the novel's notion of salvation.

That this is a world bereft of churches or priests need not entail the dismissal of such scenes' Eucharistic messaging. As Ratzinger instructs, "the Eucharist . . . is not an isolated cultic act but a way of existence: life in sharing, in communion with Christ" (43). Built on faith in God, it also requires an active and community-forging love for neighbor. Moreover, this charity is, for Ratzinger, both powerful and profound, for "Communion means the fusion of existences" (37), not in the profane, cannibalistic sense of The Road's bad guys, but in terms of that pledging oneself wholly to the other's good frequently achieved by the boy. Eucharist is a repeated and ritualized act of faith, and for this reason, it involves blessing and thanksgiving. But it is also founded on, and realized in, a sacrificial love enacted in this world. This selfless love for the other is most clearly embodied in the relationship between father and son, who, "each the other's world entire" (R 6), enact that fusion of existences of which Ratzinger speaks. The man's custodial love for his child is literally the first thing we learn about him and his world. The novel's opening words detail his utter devotion to the son's welfare: "When he woke in the woods in the dark and the cold of the night he'd reach out to touch the child sleeping beside him" (3). The beginning and end of the man's tale is his absolute commitment to this life entrusted to his care. His confirmation of the child's continued presence, his anxious treasuring of "each precious breath" (3), is presented from the start as habitual, a ritual of loving concern in its own right. Nor does the ensuing narrative contradict that implication. Time and again, the man holds the child to himself to shield him, warm him, bear him up with a love made flesh. Thus, shivering under a quilt as their wet clothes dry, Papa presses "the boy's feet against his stomach to warm them" (36). This profoundly corporeal love is reiterated in much bleaker moments as well. When the boy falls sick with fever, the man's attendance only intensifies: "He held him all night, dozing off and waking in terror, feeling for the boy's heart" (247). After the scene at the plantation house, hiding from cannibal hunters, the man knows now is the time to use his last bullet to spare the boy that gruesome fate, foreseen by the mother, their capture promises, but love stays his hand. Instead of killing his son, he again embraces him, hiding him, comforting him, ultimately saving him through steadfast love: "Hold him in your arms. Just so. The soul is quick. Pull him to you. Kiss him" (114).

As Joakim Hermansson notes, the father exemplifies an ethics defined by "a focus on care, intimacy, responsibility, and unity" (50),[12] in other words, by communion in Ratzinger's sense. Notably, this is a communion which, though grounded in corporal works of mercy, extends past the life of the body. This is a love that reaches beyond the grave and trumps the goal of personal survival. Early on, the father promises plainly that death will not sever the bond of love that unites him to his child:

If you died I would want to die too.
So you could be with me?
Yes. So I could be with you. (R 11).

This vow is nearly realized at the plantation house, where the father cannot abandon his child, even if his doing so might draw danger away from the boy: "I was going to run. To try and lead them away. But I cant leave you" (113). Given their grim circumstances, this is, so far as the man knows, a decision to stay and die with his child. In fact, as they have only the one bullet for purposes of euthanasia, it effectively means offering himself up, for the sake of the son, to the fate of the basement-larder captives. Similarly, when the son is near death with fever, the father repeats his promise to stand by him, even if this means the man's laying down of his own life: "I will not send you into the darkness alone" (248). Nor is the boy solely the object of such devotion. When the man is felled by his final sickness, the boy emulates the father's care for him and refuses to abandon Papa, despite his repeated command, "You need to go on" (278). In fact, the boy remains faithful beyond death, sitting in famished mourning by the man's body for a full three days. Wielenberg is therefore right to observe that "the greatest fear of the man and the child is not death, but rather being alone" (14). Such faithfulness to the loving communion they share stands in stark contrast to the novel's profane communicants.

Again, that this difference derives from the Eucharistic character of their love is indicated not simply by its enduring beyond, and constituting something more cherished than, physical survival, but also by its repeated expression of constitutive features of the sacrament. These include the communion-forging charity illustrated above, but also notions of gift, thanks, and blessing that lie at the heart of the liturgy whose name is Greek for thanksgiving. Indeed, as Snyder notes, "humane generosity in an inhuman world where self-preservation seems paramount may constitute McCarthy's essential notion of goodness and grace" ("Hospitality" 70). Such generosity is first exhibited in the context of the duo's own relationship, specifically in the conduct of the father toward that son he identifies with the godliness and grace of Eucharist. The father gives the boy not simply his body, but whatever gifts he can salvage from their ruined world. He delights, therefore, in being able to offer his son the unique gift of the unlikely can of Coke (R 23). Despite the life-threatening cold, he is happy to burn precious fuel as a comforting nightlight for his son: "Can we leave the light on till I'm asleep? Yes. Of course we can" (10). Desperately fearful of discovery, the father nonetheless consents to potentially drawing attention to themselves by firing off their new-found flare gun, in response to the boy's suggestion that "it could be like a celebration" (241). Having had such generosity modeled for him, the boy responds in loving kind, insisting that the father likewise partake of their few goods. He refuses to drink the Coke himself—"You have some, Papa" (23)—and he scolds the man for attempting to pour all their remaining cocoa in the boy's cup: "I have to watch you all the time" (34). Similarly, having watched Papa craft makeshift snowboots for his own feet, the boy then insists that the man share in this same gift: "Now you, Papa" (100).

Indeed, the boy's loving insistence on communal sharing reveals in him a generosity that he expresses also by bestowing the gift of his blessing on his father and the etiolated gifts of their shared world. This characteristic gesture first appears when the pair halt for a time at a waterfall. The source of a cold, but joyous swim and a feast of harvested morels, this location wins from the boy an approval offered as benediction. If the mushrooms "are pretty good" (40), then the site of their persistence is likewise proclaimed "a good place" (41). Such blessings are acts of thanksgiving, in line with the sacramental action of Eucharist itself. Frequently, such thankfulness is directed expressly to the father. Thus, when his scavenging yields sere apples and clear cistern water, the man is welcomed with, "You did good Papa" (124); playing barber to his son in the bomb shelter, the father receives similar acclaim: "You did a good job, Papa" (152). But, in keeping with the Eucharistic framing of their relationship, these blessings, too, are shared. When, near death, they are saved by finding a deserted farmhouse and stores of home canning, the boy insists, "We did good, didnt we Papa?" (213). At the waterfall itself, the boy's blessings clearly address more than the father who has guided them to such boons as growing food and cascading currents. In naming the place and the mushrooms themselves as good, the son works to affirm, in sacramental fashion, the ongoing goodness of nearly unmade Creation; he expresses a thanks that already gestures toward a sense of superhuman providence. And while the man is less prone to spoken benediction, he is far from sparing in blessings of his own, expressing these more typically in the form of consecrating kisses bestowed on his son (see 114, 149). While such gestures might reveal his sense of communion to be more strictly worldly than the boy's, the fact that he understands himself to have been "appointed . . . by God" (77) to take care of this child indicates that these tender gifts express gratitude toward someone who has laid this duty upon him, as well as love for the child.

Site of communal sharing, thanksgiving, and blessing, the relationship between father and son not only counters the savagery of their antagonists, but amply conforms to the sacramental model suggested by the son's repeated ties to Christ. Yet their love is most clearly Eucharistic in its following the dictates of charity even to the end of radical selflessness. As Augustine indicates, central to the Church's understanding of Christ's redeeming gift is the notion of suffering offered up for the world. In his Passion and Crucifixion, as much as in the action of the Eucharist, Christ is both the subject and the object of a saving sacrifice, "both the Priest who offers and the Sacrifice offered" (*City* 325). That oblation is memorialized and reenacted in the Eucharist, in such a way as to make the faithful gathered for the sacrament part of this saving action: "The cup and bread signify Jesus' ultimate sacrifice [and] mysteriously incorporate his followers in this" (Humphrey 78). Made one in and through the Body of Christ, communicants are called to live in accordance with this example of self-giving love. Such gestures not just of sharing, but of sacrifice likewise characterize the duo's bond, particularly the love of the father. As Wilhelm asserts, the man's efforts on the boy's behalf "evoke the sense of the beautiful implicit in human sacrifice for moral ends" (138). Certainly, the man is eager to safeguard the boy's life, but also to model for him a morality grounded in such selflessness.[13] Thus, though "there [are] few nights lying in the dark that he [does] not envy the dead" (*R* 230), the man endures for the sake of the child's physical well-being, but also his moral education. As he tells the boy, "This is what the good guys do. They keep trying. They dont give up" (137). To safeguard the boy's morale, Papa takes the child's failings on himself, insisting, when the son has let their fuel run out, "It's not your fault. I should have checked" (176). Likewise, when the boy mislays their gun, the father offers him forgiveness: "I'm the one who's supposed to make sure we have the pistol and I didnt do it" (232). Moreover, when they are fired upon by a hidden bowman, the father is ready to lay down his life for the son: "he pushed the boy's head down and tried to cover him with his body" (263). This education by example proves efficacious, as the man's sacrifices for the boy are again reciprocated. Bringing a tin of peaches to Papa's sickbed, the boy is met with demurrals; his dying father wishes him to eat it all. Though this is the last of their food, however, the boy will not do so, but offers his hunger to the father: "I'll save your half" (277).

HOPE AND THE WIDENING EUCHARISTIC CIRCLE

In short, McCarthy's pair fulfill the promise represented by the boy's Christly attributes. Their love is not only a powerful rebuttal to the cannibals' inhumanity; it is, in its charitable gifts, blessings, and sacrifices, profoundly Eucharistic. As Josephs argues, "the divine becomes immanent in the love between the father and the boy" (143). However, their survival, and that of the communion they sustain, is imperiled by the man's own commitment to the self-seeking rationality granted so fearsome an aspect by the novel's bad guys. Cant maintains that, even in McCarthy's grimmest fictions, there remain two loci of genuine value: craftsmanship and hospitality (254). Certainly, the latter is celebrated. It is also fair to note, with Ellis, that McCarthy typically presents technical knowledge and practical resourcefulness as admirable ("Science" 186). The father's know-how, for instance, extends to such useful end-of-world talents as the ability to suture his own wounds (R 265–66). However, these practical skills bespeak more than a rugged self-reliance; as that term itself suggests, they are tied also to a stern devotion to autonomous self-interest over community. While capable of radical selflessness, the man's charity seems to extend only to his child. More parental care than agape, it can be read, as Johns-Putra contends, as selfishness, a "Darwinian" ethics concerned only for the survival of his offspring (532). There is certainly some truth to this, as the man's commitment to keeping his boy from harm leads him consistently to resist any expansion of their circle of regard in ways that endanger not just the boy's survival but the persistence into the future of the humanizing ethos he embodies.

That his fear for their lives leads the father to expose the duo to risk is revealed in his repeated insistence that they abandon those places of sanctuary the boy proclaims good. "Always" expecting trouble (R 151), Papa defines it as other people. His anxious scanning of the landscape, "watching for any sign of a fire or a lamp" (9), is a vigilance aimed at avoiding encounters with, or discovery by, other travelers. Given the example of the roadrat, such precaution is only reasonable. But that this reasonable foreclosure on broader communion can prove as deadly as the cannibals' or the mother's own is indicated by its dictating retreat from sites of humanizing shelter. Despite the delight his son takes in the waterfall, despite this spot's being the first to yield fruits of the earth to nourish them, the man insists they depart. This place must be abandoned because its goodness makes it a site of congregation and so of peril. The waterfall, he tells the boy, "is an attraction. It was for us and it will be for others and we dont know who they will be" (42). They must leave this place where natural goodness survives in the interest of survival, an over-riding good that the community-forging power of this good place puts at risk. Such retreat is repeated at the bomb shelter. This bunker literally saves McCarthy's pair and offers them more food than they can cart off and protection from an unforgiving environment. Yet, precisely because such goodness invites others, the duo is scarcely settled before the man starts the countdown to their departure: "They weren't going to be here that long" (144). Indeed, despite the boy's clear preference—"I wish we could live here" (151)—the certainty of encounter with others he can imagine only as enemies renders such a notion untenable for the father: "Anyone could see the hatch lying in the yard and they would know at once what it was" (144). The goodness of this place becomes, according to the self-seeking practical reasoning of the father, an unanswerable argument for its desertion.

Thus, the man's devotion to the pair's practical interests fosters a paranoia that has them repeatedly forfeiting obvious material goods. More, it repeatedly commits Papa to violations of charity that imperil the moral good he seeks to preserve. Potts maintains that the father's survivalist outlook "turn[s] all other humans into rivals to be dominated" (177). While this overstates the case—others, for the man, are better eluded than dominated—it is fair to observe, with Kunsa, that his fierce safeguarding of the son entails the commission of deeds "if not immoral and unethical . . . at least reprehensible" (59). The reprehensible nature of these acts lies in their contradiction of the very ethos the pair have themselves sought to enact, in their offering only indifference and hostility, not generous, self-forgetting love, to outsiders. Such failures of charity begin with the lightning-struck man. Watching this maimed figure, "as burntlooking as the country" (R 49), limp down the road ahead of them, the father passes him by, answering his son's reproachful tears with "No. We cant help him" (50). Later, in the ruins of a town, the son glimpses the face of the other little boy and implores Papa to look for and adopt this child: "What if that little boy doesnt have anybody to take care of him?" (85). Yet despite the son's weeping petition, the father is only fearful of any possible encounter—"There are people there. They were just hiding" (85)—and refuses any such search. The father's failure to extend concern to others is most starkly dramatized in the case of the thief. Having tracked down the man who absconded with all their goods, Papa compels him, at gunpoint, not just to return his booty, but to surrender the few rags that protect his nakedness. Far from the blessings, forgiveness, and selfless love he bestows upon his child, this command is wrathful and death-dealing. The father's rage is, again, fruit of his jealous regard for the duo's physical well-being, but it leads to a cruelty that not only betrays the son's moral example, but has little to do with the pair's survival. The two are no safer once the thief is exposed to the elements, after all.

The father's love-born devotion to a rationality committed to the pair's material advantage does more than lead them away from the novel's good places. It undermines the moral good they embody in at least two ways: first, it leads them to eschew any broadening of the community they themselves constitute, and second, it corrodes the father's ethical standing. If, however, it is the Christlike boy who, in his association with the sacrament, is most fully identified with the virtues of Eucharistic communion, then the father's commitment to reason over love also threatens the survival of this goodness itself. For his community-fleeing means for securing the boy's moral and physical survival work, in fact, to endanger both. Certainly, the boy's sense of their having repeatedly betrayed the standard of charity they uphold between themselves diminishes not simply his faith in their being the good guys of his father's tales—"in the stories we're always helping people and we dont help people" (268)—but also his hope for the future, his desire to survive at all. Thus, as he is dragged from the town site still weeping for the boy whom they will neither love nor protect, the son replies to his father's challenge, "Do you want to die?," with "I dont care" (85). Though he eventually prevails upon the father to return the thief's clothes, the boy, after they fail to locate their malefactor, reverses his typical habit of benediction to identify himself and Papa as bad guys: "But we did kill him" (260). Moreover, having witnessed the father abandon the material blessings of good places and violate the humanizing charity by which he himself yearns to live, the boy increasingly fails to see the point of their travails. After they quit the bomb shelter's obvious sanctuary, he questions their objectives, asking "What are our long term goals?" (160). The faltering faith in the father's guidance, the flagging hope for the future, that this question expresses is more desperately voiced later on, when the man doubts their finding good people on the road, and the boy replies, "I dont know what we're doing" (244). Such moments make clear that, in his pragmatic efforts to preserve their lives, the father is imperiling the boy's survival as something more than a body in the world, as that Christlike figure of faith and love Papa has taken the son to be.

In this way, as I have argued elsewhere, the man's refusal of encounter and outreach "destroys hope, precisely as it threatens love" (DeCoste, "A Thing" 80). But this strategy of self-reliance and instrumental reason also threatens the boy's chances to survive even in the sense this program privileges. *The Road* all but commences with a portrait that will recur, of the father "crouched coughing . . . for a long time" (*R* 11). As he admits to himself, after another fit of coughing, "I am going to die" (175). This imminent event will orphan his son in a world whose dire natural and human perils Papa knows all too well; without a caretaker, the boy's chances for physical, much less moral, survival are, if the fate of the babe on the spit is any indication, surely nonexistent. In other words, this boy who embodies Eucharistic faith and charity, and thus the hope of humane relations in the future, is threatened with annihilation by the father's choice of self-interest over communion. Guided by the conviction that they are unlikely "to meet any good guys on the road" (151), the father's long-term goals lead them to his deathbed and his son's rightly fearful question, "Who will find the little boy?" (281). The man's having shunned contact with others, it is clear from the words of the boy's ultimate adoptive father—"There was some discussion about whether to even come after you at all" (283)—that Papa has served as a deterrent to good guys who have tracked the duo but kept their distance. His example grants the son's question urgency, and his dying words indicate the extent to which his commitment to practical reasoning results in an absurdly self-defeating code: "You need to find the good guys but you cant take any chances. No chances" (278). Having hewed to the latter directive, the man has rendered the first unattainable, his refusal of risk, his lack of faith in any good guys beyond themselves, ultimately putting the son in gravest danger.

However, the pair demonstrate, in their Eucharistic bond, both that such good guys exist and how they are to be identified. As the son replies to the father's dismissal of other travelers, "We're on the road" (151). And they are so as still humane agents who make the discovery of a larger community of goodness possible by pursuing, at the boy's urging, a progressive expansion of their relationship. This campaign is a decidedly practical one, though not constrained, as is the father's pragmatism, by self-interest. The community the duo cultivates is not simply a matter of the father's perceptions of a Messiah in his son or of the narrator's fondness for liturgical imagery. Nor has it to do just with any kind of sacrifice undertaken for a beloved. The relationship that survives between, and grows out from, McCarthy's protagonists is built on a food-sharing suffused with charity, faith, and thanksgiving. In this way, it takes on a more decisively sacramental cast; in Yarbrough's words, this "ritualistic breaking of bread . . .

operates as a Eucharistic signifier, evoking yet repudiating the cannibalistic perversion of the sacrament" (*"The Road"* 187). Now, by the mid-second century, the Eucharist had already evolved from a communal meal to a religious ritual, "the central act in the weekly assembly of Christians" (Ferguson 130). Justin Martyr's description of early Church practice stresses both the sharing of food and its more than nutritional import. Communicants, he reports, congregate to share readings and prayers, before partaking of a Eucharist "which nourishes our flesh and blood" and is also "the flesh and blood of that Jesus who was made flesh" (106). Similarly, McCarthy's protagonists live out their love in repeated scenes of emotionally charged, even ceremonial, meal-taking. Wilhelm counts no fewer than forty scenes of the pair eating and drinking (134) and notes the ritual aspect of many of these repasts (132). Indeed, the novel opens with just such a meal. Having woken before his son, the father prepares a breakfast of "cornmeal cakes," "spread[ing] the small tarp they used as a table on the ground and la[ying] everything out" as he waits for the boy to wake (*R* 5). There is a striving here to make this humble meal something special, an instance of giving that fosters love and gratitude. Such an attempt is repeated in a later scene, first, in the father's working to elevate a simple meal by serving the boy "a last half packet of cocoa" (34), and second, in the boy's insistence on reciprocity: "You promised not to do that, the boy said" (34).

Potts asserts that such scenes convey sacramental reverence because of "the sheer gratitude with which food is given and received" (156). But the emphasis on ritual care and selfless sharing indicated in these early meals ramifies beyond a simply worldly gratitude. Indeed, contrary to Chris Danta's claim that goodness in *The Road* is restricted to the duo, "localized to the point of almost complete relativity" (16), the love sustained in the pair's food-sharing pushes beyond them, reaches past the grave and toward heaven, in ways that underscore the Eucharistic valences of their humanizing bond. This is clearest during their time at the shelter. First, despite their near-starvation, they take care to set a proper table for their first collation of canned pears and peaches, the father taking "two paperware bowls from a stack of them wrapped in plastic and set[ting] them out on the table" (*R* 140). This scene, an echo of the novel's first, again has love, sharing, and gratitude, not appetitive self-seeking, define the duo's communion. The next morning, however, sees the boy insisting that this communion be extended. The father again rises early to prepare a breakfast feast of "Coffee. Ham. Biscuits" (144). As before, he sets a proper table, dragging "a footlocker across the floor between the bunks and cover[ing] it with a towel and . . . plates and cups and plastic utensils" (145). Moved by the father's care and the providence manifest in this banquet, the boy longs to give thanks, and so to extend communal regard, to "the people who gave us all this" (145). This loving response, though in keeping with the relationship of father and son, expresses itself in a gesture of thanks that founds a much broader community, one inclusive not just of other people, not just of dead good guys understood as still persons, but of God himself. Thus, the boy's capacity for love and gratitude makes this meal a Eucharistic moment of thanksgiving and prayer, a communion expressive of faith, as much as selfless love: "Dear people, thank you for all this food and stuff . . . we're sorry that you didnt get to eat it and we hope that you're safe in heaven with God" (146).

In this prayer, the son does more than include others in the love he shares with the father; he makes plain the vertical aspiration of their communion, its rootedness in a belief in God and a conviction that death is not, as mother and cannibals maintain, the final answer to their predicament. This scene demonstrates, then, how the selfless love shared by father and son, and nourished by humanizing meals antithetical to their world's anthropophagous norm, is married to a vital faith. It bears out de Sales's claim that the Eucharist is "an ineffable mystery which contains within itself the abyss of divine charity" (95). But the pair's time in the bunker is short, and as they depart, their congregation numbers but two. Once again, though, the boy enacts a widening of their community, this time in horizontal terms, in the encounter with Ely. Ely is no obvious candidate for communion. Asserting that "it's better to be alone" (R 172), proclaiming "there is no God and we are his prophets" (170), he is a reluctant guest who offers nihilism in place of faith.[14] Indeed, in contrast to the boy, he offers no thanks for the "cans of vegetables and of fruit" the child's intercession has won for him (173). This makes the characteristically leery father reluctant to have dealings with this wretch, telling his son, "Dont hold his hand" (166), and maintaining, in response to the boy's pleas for charity, "I dont think he should have anything" (165). Nonetheless, at the son's insistence—"Maybe we could give him something to eat" (163)—the pair first offer Ely a can of fruit cocktail from their finite stores and then, at the child's suggestion that "he could eat with us" (165), dine with him. This is the first time we see the pair break bread with another living soul, such that this scene, too, constitutes a widening of their communion effected by the son's desire to have the love he shares with the father extended. Nor does this more horizontal growth strip this scene of its Eucharistic cast. This is a dinner that involves more than ingestion, fostering not just civil conversation, but extended discussion of spiritual matters even with the atheistic Ely.

It is worth noting that this unprepossessing figure fares better with the father than the lightning-struck man or the little boy has done. In fact, Griffis argues that the novel charts Papa's increasing willingness to submit to the boy's arguments for putting charity ahead of instrumental reason (91). Indeed, the father's treasuring of the boy's goodness—his faith, charity, and gratitude— progressively leads the man, for love of this child, to grow in these same virtues, in such a way as to enable a final broadening of the pair's communion that reaches hopefully toward a humane future. At death's door and aware that his pragmatism has failed to make the boy safe, the man is nonetheless as far from doubt or despair as he has been. Looking with undying tenderness at the child whose capacity for love outstrips his own—"You're the best guy. You always were" (R 279)—the father discards his long-held plan to save the boy from torment by killing him. Instead, his own loving regard for the boy's Eucharistic example leads him to an uncharacteristic leap of faith. Assuring the terrified son that "Goodness will find the little boy" (281), he releases his own little boy into this hostile world with his fullest benediction and an insistence that all will be well: "You dont know what might be down the road. We were always lucky. You'll be lucky again" (278). Astonishingly, given what we have learned of those who travel the road, the father's faith is all but immediately vindicated: the son is found, after a three-day vigil over the man's body, by the "veteran of old skirmishes" (281). Though fearsome, this man welcomes the boy to a new and wider community: "I think you should come with me" (282). As the son recognizes and the vet concedes, this invitation demands a profound act of faith: "How do I know you're one of the good guys? / You dont. You'll have to take a shot" (283). Yet the boy's habitual, love-born readiness to extend welcome in his turn, to take a shot on the goodness of others, combines with his father's dying ratification of such love and faith to lead him to embrace this chance.

What's more, that future, like the love that has enabled it, remains pointedly Eucharistic, only in a more realized way. The boy is welcomed into an intact family who "dont eat people" (284), who care for and do not prey upon their own boy and girl. Embraced by the mother, who exclaims "I am so glad to see you" (286), the orphan is made part of a larger community than he has ever known, one that, with its daughter, affords the possibility of new generations of good guys. He has, then, through the virtues of love, gratitude, and faith shared with his father found his way into a communion that heralds the growth and persistence through time of humanizing charity and reciprocity. As Hermansson notes, the father's last words, promising good guys to come, stress how humanizing endeavor is "always collaborative and shared in a community" (63), and his release of his son in faith allows such genuine community to be both found and fostered. Further, this new home effects the synthesis of this horizontal broadening with that vertical dimension of faith seen in the shelter. The boy ensures this marriage, first, by affirming that death will not undo the saving communion he has known with his father: "I'll talk to you every day" (R 286). Moreover, the adoptive family into whose care the man's love has delivered him sustains their charitable community through prayerful communion; hence the mother is eager to "talk to him sometimes about God" (286). Nor does such talk fall on deaf ears. The grieving boy prays to God, even if "the best thing was to talk to his father" (286). Far from the latter preference disproving the boy's faith,[15] it in fact demonstrates its persistently communal and Eucharistic tenor, keeping his relationship with the father alive as it forges deeper bonds with his new family and with God. As Ratzinger explains, from the Church's perspective, it is in communion sacramentally conceived that such intercourse with the dead becomes possible: "In the Body of Christ, death no longer works as a limit; in this Body, past, present and future interpenetrate" (99). Similarly, the woman reassures the boy that his prayers to his father are themselves a participation in holy communion: "She said that the breath of God was his breath yet though it pass from man to man through all of time" (R 286). In the novel's conclusion, then, we see the fruition in faith, hope, and love of the duo's Eucharistic refusal to accede to the nihilistic course of those in the novel who cleave to instrumental rationality and sovereign self-seeking.

Despite Kenneth Lincoln's claim that the duo "have no good way to think about beauty or goodness anymore" (170), *The Road* makes plain that even at the end of things goodness and beauty can be located and nurtured by answering a call to comprehensive charity and unflagging faith. It is that answer—serially, reciprocally, on the part of both father and son—that allows McCarthy's most hopeful ending to emerge from his most apocalyptic vision. That this conclusion caps the most sacramental and Catholic of McCarthy's narratives is significant. Certainly, *The Road's* depiction of the nihilism and savagery attendant on the idolization of the sovereign self recalls, even as it intensifies, portraits as old as 1968's *Outer Dark*. Yet after a twentieth-century career marked by cautionary tales of the corrosive power of Enlightenment ideals, McCarthy, in what seemed for so long to be his twenty-first century farewell, not only maintains, but intensifies the Catholic perspective from which he offers that critique. *The Road* is not simply adorned with the symbolism of the Mass. It is, at root, built around the substance of the Eucharist, its call to communion in charitable self-giving, communal thanksgiving, and prayerful faith. Its ethics reveal not simply the sacrilege embodied by the novel's bad guys, but by the materialist, self-seeking, instrumental rationality that guides them. In forming both the novel's metric of goodness and its means for communicating the most profound human evil, the sacrament in the end testifies to the enduring centrality of Catholic thought to the spiritual and ethical outlook of the McCarthy corpus and its critique of Enlightenment values' realization in American history.

THE UNIMAGINABLE PENITENT

PENANCE AND THE MYTH OF AMERICAN
INNOCENCE IN *THE COUNSELOR*, *THE PASSENGER*,
AND *STELLA MARIS*

A person cannot confess if from the very beginning he sees a chasm between himself and sin. He must be completely and truly convinced that he belongs to the realm of sin.

—ADRIENNE VON SPEYR, *Confession*

With a Rotten Tomatoes rating of 34 percent "fresh," Ridley Scott's 2013 production of *The Counselor* has, it is fair to say, failed to win many admirers. Dismissed by reviewers as "boilerplate pulp" (Buckwalter),[1] this adaptation of McCarthy's original screenplay floundered at the American box office. But it was not just the film that failed to find favor; McCarthy's script, published in the lead-up to the theatrical release, was also widely reviled. For Ellis, it represents "a great author's aesthetic nadir" ("Science" 189), while for Josyph, "it is not merely the worst thing Cormac McCarthy has done, it's one of the worst things *anybody* has done" ("What's Wrong" 203). Josyph scorns the text as "a story that is ethically and aesthetically bereft" (203). Yet I contend that such an assessment, certainly as regards the work's ethics, constitutes a profound misreading of *The Counselor*. In line with Hillier's insistence that the screenplay is "didactic and fiercely moralistic to the core" (*Morality* 162), I maintain that it reveals McCarthy at his most morally austere and that this austerity betrays, in its decidedly Catholic cast, the extent to which the author's childhood faith remains an ethical lodestone even in his latest work. As such, it serves as fitting prelude to the strikingly different texts that followed it in late 2022, namely the novelistic duology formed by *The Passenger* and *Stella Maris*.

First, as regards *The Counselor*, I take issue with Peebles's claim that the screenplay's treatment of the Roman Catholic confessional is "a joke that's largely incidental to the plot" (178). Instead, I argue that this tale of the twenty-first century drug trade, like *Outer Dark*, *Child of God*, and *Blood Meridian* before it, makes the sacrament of Penance central to a critique both of the modern market's reification of the person and of America's persistent understanding of itself as an innocent world actor. Emphasizing the script's stark dramatization of American responsibility for the sins of the cross-border drug trade, sacramental confession figures in this work as an alternative to the morally corrosive character of both the American economy's traffic in human lives and Americans' presumption that such traffic incurs for them no moral cost. By situating the scene of Malkina's visit to the confessional at the very heart of his tale, McCarthy underscores the moral depravity of the film's casually self-seeking investors and presents the radical possibility of conversion for even the blackest of its sinners. By so establishing the relevance of Catholic confession to its critique of American consumerism, *The Counselor*, I conclude, proffers the figure of the penitent as the proper American hero of our time.

It is in their similar foregrounding of modernity's need for contrition that McCarthy's final novels serve as apt sequels to this generically distinct precursor. For if this diptych's protagonists—lapsed Catholic children of a nuclear physicist—embody science's impact on the postwar world, they do so problematically. Bobby Western acknowledges himself a child of "Auschwitz and Hiroshima, the sister events that sealed forever the fate of the West" (P 165). As so fraught a pedigree suggests, the science pursued by Bobby's father on the Manhattan Project is cast here as something dangerous, as corrosive to the soul as threatening to the planet. Following in the footsteps of *The Counselor*'s meditations on the proper response to the potentially murderous works of modernity, *The Passenger* and *Stella Maris* offer, I argue, two alternative moral models to orient the post-Hiroshima West that Enlightenment science has wrought: one centered on a zero-sum game of knowledge/power, the other on the need to own an inescapable ignorance and guilt. Alicia Western, aiming, like Judge Holden, to "*wrest the secrets of creation from the gods*" (114), sees this quest for absolute knowledge as an attaining of Enlightenment sovereignty over nature's secrets. Imagining her probing of reality as a contest ending in either final mastery or utter futility, she ultimately chooses suicide over the humiliating defeat of unknowing. Bobby's different response to the tragic limits of Western epistemes hints at a less despairing conclusion, one that conforms rather to *The Counselor*'s call for an American penance. Burdened by grief and guilt, Bobby accepts, as Alicia will not, that "in the end you really cant know" (279). On this basis, he pursues, unlike his sister, a penitent's path. Accepting ignorance, he works at practicing forgiveness and prayer so as to offer penance for himself, his Western kin, and their common Enlightenment hubris. As such, his example serves as McCarthy's final, still rather Catholic, word on his culture's need to make that admission of fault and surrender of autonomy von Speyr's confessional demands.

Centered on the twin cities of Juarez and El Paso, *The Counselor* does not shrink from portraying the human costs of transactional relations in the form of illicit cross-border commerce. Nor does it balk at indicating which of two populations—American or Mexican—bears the bulk of such costs. A tale of the illegal drug trade, the script also signals early on its interest in the contemporary traffic in people. As the septic-tank truck bearing the drug shipment that will be the undoing of most of McCarthy's cast winds its way north, its driver watches "*a line of stragglers crossing through the chapparal, men and women, carrying suitcases, carrying laundrybags over their shoulders*" (C 13). Goods and services make their way daily across this contentious border, but the flow of such migrants, crossing with all they have, establishes from the outset whose profit such commerce serves. Such everyday desperation makes no impact on the consciousness of those who travel in the circles of McCarthy's counselor, but there remains nonetheless a demand for these exploitable laborers in America that keeps this trade in suffering profitable. The gruesome reality of America's morally indifferent market is only underscored by the discovery, upon the truck's arrival in Chicago, of a "free rider" (154), a dead body shipped in sewage across several international borders for "no reason. It is convenient" (155).

If this nameless victim evokes the many casualties of people-smuggling, he also indicates the cost of America's taste for recreational narcotics. However high the American street price for cocaine, this is a check largely paid by others. While the go-between Westray implies that any number of ostensibly respectable Americans profit from this trade—"You'd be surprised at the people who are in this business," he says (54)—he also insists on what such safely anonymous investors and their customers can largely afford to ignore: namely, that theirs is a business that feeds on Mexican misery. Westray informs the Counselor that Juarez reported three thousand, mostly cartel-related, murders the previous year (58), a testimony to the brutalization of that Mexican city that the Counselor himself corroborates when he crosses the border in search of his kidnapped fiancée, Laura. There he finds a war zone of bullet-riddled streets, police-taped crime scenes, and processional mourners carrying "*crosses of raw wood and crosses with wreaths*" for their disappeared, victims of the drug trade (153). That trade, for which America supplies the market, fosters violence visited disproportionately on those south of the border, those easily disregarded by American purchasers. The end toward which it tends is the destruction of human lives and the radical dehumanization of persons. This trafficking in drugs has become, as the free rider proves, a commerce in disposable human bodies. Among Juárez's three thousand, Westray reports, are girls bought and sold by cartel lords to be raped, murdered, and further commodified in snuff films (59). The logic of this business that peddles a deadly product to its consumers is to treat people themselves as fungible commodities, a point brought home to the viewer when Laura's decapitated body is sighted at the Juarez dump (174), and to the Counselor when he receives a DVD we understand records her violation and murder (165).

Cooper is correct, then, when she writes that *The Counselor* "critiques the ethical failures of late capitalism" (*Cormac* 62). Indeed, contrary to Josyph's claim that the film "begs sympathy for investors in the cartel" ("What's Wrong" 209), its focus on American culpability leads to a merciless indictment of the presumption and guilt of its frivolous protagonists. The script is at pains to demonstrate, as Agner insists, how McCarthy's protagonist "cannot see past his American privilege" (207). For the Counselor, this privilege equates to moral untouchability. He may indulge his tastes, consume what pleases, even break the law to these ends, but none of this can involve him in any moral responsibility or negatively impact his essential goodness. So convinced is he of his own untaintability that evil itself is, for him, but a titillating make-believe, something with which one may play because one knows it is merely myth. Hence the bedroom scene with which the film opens has him teasing Laura for her naughtiness. "How did you get to be such a bad girl?" he asks (C 7), before complimenting her on having "reached a whole new level of depravity" (9). A joke to add piquancy to their foreplay, "depravity" can serve such a role only because they are certain that it doesn't exist or, if it does, that it can never actually touch them or their choices.

Yet depravity is palpably real in this text and indeed fostered by the Counselor's faith in his own immunity to it. Though he is aware of the cartels' calling card—"Where's all this beheading shit come from?" he asks partner-in-crime Reiner (39)—he is convinced he can, for an easy payday, guiltlessly do business with these suppliers. This is, for him, a "one-time deal" (35), and he is confident that it can neither impact his moral character nor imperil anything he values. That the deal he sets in motion ultimately claims at least nine lives, including Laura's, suggests otherwise, but the text has been plain on this score throughout. McCarthy's protagonist does not want for warnings, but as Agner notes, "The central irony of the counselor is his inability to be counseled" (206). Reiner himself preaches caution: "You pursue this road that you've embarked upon and you will eventually come to moral decisions that will take you completely by surprise" (C 34). Yet the Counselor affirms he is all in, even after Westray details the evils of his "one-time" partners, men capable of buying, raping, and killing girls to expand their video library (59). He is in because, at root, he does not believe in such things and is certain that his easy life could never be impacted, its goodness never tainted, by them. This becomes clear when Westray discusses snuff films not just as a crime his new partners commit, but as a metaphor for the drug trade itself. Westray insists that the purchaser of such a commodity is as guilty as the murderous producer, "because the consumer of the product is essential to its production. You cant watch without being implicated in a murder" (112). Likewise, the buyer of narcotics cannot use or traffic without being implicated in the evils that attend their production and sale. To this, the Counselor replies, "I dont do drugs" (113), asserting that as a purveyor he can maintain both his innocence of the cartels' crimes and his superiority to stateside users.

This disastrous moral blindness is no idiosyncratic flaw of the Counselor's. As Malkina indicates when one of her operatives balks at payment after learning the man she has just betrayed may now, on account of her actions, be murdered, this moral prevarication operates in *The Counselor* as a national brand. "You know what I like about Americans?," Malkina asks: "You can depend on them" (164). What is dependable is their dishonest insistence upon their own uprightness, even as they profit from others' misery. This brand of self-deception extends even to the script's ostensibly good Catholic girl, Laura. Though dubbed "wholesome" by Cooper (*Cormac* 129), Laura, too, mistakes a morally suspect ignorance for innocence. Noting Malkina judges her worldview naïve, Laura asks, "Is that so bad?" (*C* 97). McCarthy's answer is an emphatic yes, for that naïveté is a form of culpable unknowing that allows her to sidestep moral maturity and to profit from evils to which she remains wilfully blind. Keen on a church wedding, Laura insists her faith is important to her (46). Yet it's clear what she seeks from her Catholicism is simply that presumption of innocence that characterizes her betrothed. She is demonstrably ignorant of the faith whose value she affirms, erroneously informing Malkina that the Counselor's previous divorce is no obstacle to their wedding because "the Church doesnt recognize other marriages" (46), and falsely stating that the damnation of non-Catholics is "pretty much what the Church teaches" (48).[2] Apart from indicating the unseriousness of her faith, such errors demonstrate that what she seeks from the Church is not mature moral reflection, but an affirmation of her own inalienable goodness. Confession, she admits, is "maybe not so much" her thing (46), and though she confirms that a resolution not to recommit sins confessed is central to the sacrament, she concedes that she does, "[u]sually" (48), recommit them. As the Counselor does with the drug trade, Laura embraces only those parts of Church teaching that serve her convenience and vanity, not those that would accuse her.

Thus, while Knepper identifies the grieving Counselor as "a sort of penitent" (44), it is rather the case that neither he nor the beloved whose death his acts precipitate ever engages in penitential self-scrutiny. Even when he reaches out to the cartel Jefe in hopes of bargaining for Laura's life, even when he declares he would swap places with her, he never acknowledges that his own heedless pursuit of profit has led to her torture and death. Yet as Laura's discussion of confession indicates, the question of penitence, of redemption through admission of guilt, is central to this text. Indeed, the question of penance is broached in just the Counselor's second scene. In Amsterdam to purchase a trophy diamond for his wife-to-be, he meets, in his jeweller, a character who foregrounds the perspective that empowers the film's critical scrutiny of America's moral obliviousness. Professing that "the heart of any culture is to be found in the nature of the hero" it promulgates (*C* 19), this merchant observes that if, in classical antiquity, this hero was "the warrior" (19), in the later West "it is the man of God. . . . The prophet. The penitent" (19), a figure "unimaginable" to the ancient Greeks (19). Yet if this is true, then *The Counselor* serves to illustrate that, in America, even among those, like Laura, who confess the living Christ, this Western hero has been displaced.

However, if McCarthy's characters shy away from the penitent's acceptance of evil and admission of fault, the text itself, in dwelling on confession, works to expose such evasions. Strikingly, the Catholic sacrament takes up—in Laura's description of confession and Malkina's subsequent visit to the confessional—eleven pages of the script. Placed next to the cold-blooded malice and moral dishonesty that abound in *The Counselor*, this emphasis indicates precisely the perspective that might oppose rather than facilitate the carnage the film's hijacked drug deal unleashes. According to the Catechism, Penance involves a turning away from one's sin and toward God, in a confession of guilt and a resolution to abjure the sins confessed (399). The sacrament thus requires of the penitent three things none of McCarthy's American innocents ever commits to: "contrition, confession, and satisfaction" (404). Chief among these is the first. In order properly to confess and be absolved, one must sorrowfully accuse and acknowledge oneself as a sinner. As von Speyr puts it, the penitent must first identify himself with sin. The sinner confesses so as to be absolved of guilt, but he first "binds himself to this guilt so that he will be released from it" (30). For forgiveness to be granted, he must not hold to that presumption of innocence to which both the Counselor and Laura, quintessential American consumers, cling. Sorrow over sin, the Church teaches, not certainty as to one's moral worthiness, permits the redemption confession affords. As von Speyr insists, the true confessant "does not anticipate absolution. It comes to him like a bolt of lightning" (68). Yet if the sacrament demands of sinners that they frankly acknowledge their own participation in evil, it also offers a promise of pardon at no higher cost. As Knox writes, the Church has always opposed sects that posited unpardonable sins (*Belief* 187); for it, "sorrow for sin combined with a purpose . . . of avoiding it in the future" is all that is required for absolution of the gravest crimes (188). In confession, innocence may be attained if one surrenders the illusion of one's impeccability; as von Speyr explains, it is "a completely new beginning, a divine pardon that takes everything away" (223).

Certain of their lack of responsibility for the crimes committed to serve their appetites, however, the Counselor and Laura never achieve such innocence. In fact, the film offers but one character genuinely attracted to the confessional's offer of renewal, and she is the gravest sinner of all. Malkina, whose initial theft of the shipment exposes all other partners to the cartel's murderous wrath, is also the character who best sees her own and others' corruption, and who seemingly experiences longing for an innocence she knows she has forfeited. To be sure, she is, as Monk has noted (207), a villain on par with *Blood Meridian's* notorious Judge Holden himself.[3] She betrays her lover Reiner, leaving him to the drug lords' vengeance, and arranges the hit on Westray, also a lover and implied father of the son she now carries. Indeed, while Hillier suggests she is motivated by her own desire for vengeance on Westray's fugitive attentions (*Morality* 242), the text suggests she seeks a more monstrously comprehensive revenge. "When the world itself is the source of your torment," she tells her escort at film's end, "then you are free to exact vengeance upon any least part of it" (*C* 182), going on to suggest that she has disrupted the drug deal precisely for the ramifying scope of harm, of vengeance, this act afforded.

Yet, however malign her own deeds and motives, Malkina is the text's most clear-eyed moral judge. While Hillier maintains that she is drawn to Laura's exemplification of purity and faith (*Morality* 243), it is rather true that she sees their vacuity; in response to Laura's complacent description of the certainty of absolution, Malkina can only marvel, "What a world" (*C* 49). Indeed, it is possible that it is Laura's presumption to innocence that is the real target of Malkina's crimes. The deal the Counselor enters into so as to pamper Laura is undone in such a way as to deny her not just the fairy-tale marriage to which she feels entitled, but her life itself. Further, Malkina's behavior in the confessional reveals a desire to expose the spuriousness of this sacrament that has provided consolation to a woman she despises. While there, she urges the priest to break the seal, taunts him with questions as to his sexual experience with girls or boys, and seeks to shock him with tales of sibling incest, finally driving him from the scene (*C* 82–86). In this rout, she may see further proof of the moral cowardice that she deems definitive of the American epoch. This age of carefree consumption is one exemplified by just that willed flight from implicating moral ugliness that has typified the Counselor's ruin. The Counselor and Laura certainly, the retreating priest arguably, wish in Malkina's words, "to draw a veil over all that blood and terror" upon which their own lifestyles rest (183); yet, she notes, willed ignorance does not dispel such terror but only "makes of it our destiny" (184).

However, McCarthy's priest never betrays the dignity of his office or the sacrament, refusing to rise to Malkina's taunts, break his vows, or dishonor the confessional. Similarly, whatever her own rage at embodiments of innocence true or false, Malkina evinces a genuine attraction to the sacrament's promise. It is she who first brings the topic up in conversations with Laura (46), and the fact that she then bothers on her own to investigate suggests motives less than altogether blasphemous. In the confessional, she is particularly interested in the priest's claim that, once she has taken Catholic instruction, she can indeed confess and have her sins forgiven. She asks, "What if they're unforgivable?" (82), and on hearing no sin is unpardonable, presses the point, asking whether this might extend even to murder, a crime she will soon commit, if she has not already done so (83). Before the scene closes, a seeming desperation creeps into her request that he hear her sins: "All you would have to do is listen. To the sins. You could even pretend I was lying. If you didnt like what you were hearing" (85). Again, all of this might still be counted further evidence of Malkina's wickedness. But the hunger for a hearing, the hope that her transgressions can be pardoned, suggests a sense of her sinfulness alien to the Americans she disdains and a longing for an honest path to a world more innocent than the bloody marketplace she inhabits.

Ultimately, the script's conclusion reveals this longing to be both real and repudiated. Reflecting on her few desires, Malkina lists one that indicates a moral self-knowledge that works to vindicate the perspective of the confessional as a moral counter to the American cult of innocence *The Counselor* ruthlessly dissects. Asked what it is she wants, Malkina replies, "There are times when I imagine that I would like my innocence back. . . . But I would never pay the price which it now commands on the market" (181–82). Though this essentially rehearses her earlier lashing out at priest and sacrament, it also, I submit, concedes their authority. Unlike McCarthy's protagonist, Malkina accuses herself, acknowledges her guilt, and confesses a longing for absolution. Yet what such pardon requires of her is that she become the penitent and submit to another's authority in faith; as von Speyr emphasizes, the confession that absolves is not simply a matter of self-expression, but of obedience (20). This, for Malkina, is too high a cost, and in her telling economic idiom, she confirms both her allegiance to the ethos that has damned her victims and the text's use of confession to highlight the dehumanizing power of that outlook. Thus, while Knepper insists that *The Counselor* deems "any prospect of redemption . . . chimeric" (48), the film instead asks its audience if they are ready to pursue a penitential path to renewal.

Strikingly, it is just this path—of contrition, confession, and attempted satisfaction—that is finally followed by Bobby Western in *The Passenger.* Yet his tale, too, begins with a rather darker portrait of the Enlightenment's fruit. McCarthy's 2022 diptych opens with the discovery of polymath prodigy Alicia Western dead by her own hand. One of the novels' two sibling inheritors of revolutionary science, she is found hanging from a tree, *"her eyes . . . frozen cold and hard as stones"* (P 3). If the end to which her pursuit of scientific inquiry has brought her is thus a grim one, it is not uniquely hers. Her mother and father before her, brought together by the Manhattan Project, both succumb to cancer, victims of their radioactive work (176). However, the threat constituted by Western science extends beyond the fates of the Westerns alone. As Bobby is acutely aware, breakthroughs in the physics he once studied have done more terrifying harm to people altogether ignorant of particle theory. As his foil, John Sheddan, explains, Western's own father collaborated in "the design and fabrication of enormous bombs for the purpose of incinerating whole citiesful of innocent people" (30). Himself haunted by visions of "burning people crawl[ing] among the corpses like some horror in a vast crematorium" (116), Bobby sees this Enlightenment nightmare still ramifying to effect a civilizational demise. Ending up in the Mediterranean, he sees in this locale a Western culture nearing its end: "Cradle of the west. A frail candle tottering in the darkness. All of history a rehearsal for its own extinction" (369). As his own family history so clearly testifies, this imminent apocalypse is something Enlightenment progress has itself helped realize.

Such historical judgments point back to *The Counselor*'s treatment of the question of the West's proper ethical stance in a postwar world. Specifically, the discourse of the screenplay's diamond merchant, I argue, articulates Bobby and Alicia's divergent responses to that challenge. His division of Western culture between the warrior and the penitent, I hold, maps neatly onto the Westerns' tale but in some perhaps counterintuitive ways. For by the criteria the jeweler lays out, the Enlightenment science that has shaped and imperiled the modern West is scarcely western at all. As embodied by Alicia, that modernity is classical and martial in its temperament. By contrast, the penitential path of Bobby, who ultimately rejects both physics and self-destruction, offers a measure of living heroism and hope. Suicidal Alicia openly identifies herself as a hero of antiquity. As she tells the Thalidomide Kid, "I wanted to be a warrior. . . . I was a born classicist and my heroes were never saints but killers" (*SM* 127). Like the physicists of the Manhattan Project, she pursues science as warfare, a struggle with the world aimed at isolating and grasping foundational truths. Her quest for knowledge establishes science as an all-or-nothing contest in which the heroic knower either prevails or is vanquished. As the idiom of war suggests, the wages of defeat here are death. Epistemological victory alone stands between the knower and nothingness. As she taunts her psychiatrist's attempts to solve her, "Devise a theory. The enemy of your undertaking is despair. Death" (52). Yet for all her warrior's confidence, she confesses that she "came to see the world as pretty much proof against any comprehensive description of it" (37). Committed to a science that demands conquest or annihilation, however, she deems such enduring unknowing to be untenable. It feeds in her a warrior's fury, the belief that the world that has humbled her attempt at omniscience is hateful. Thus, as her faith in the possibility of mastery through science falters, she becomes convinced that there is "an ill-contained horror beneath the surface of the world" (152). It is just this distillation of certainty from mystery that leads her, in her classical quest for mastery, to parallel the suicidal course upon which her culture itself seems set. As Alicia admits, rage at one's own failure cannot last, and "sorrow is what is left when rage is expended and found to be impotent" (164). From this sorrow at her epistemic defeat, emerges the death wish that grows in her from her early teens and finds its fulfillment in wintry Wisconsin woods.

Former physicist and child of the atomic age, Bobby inherits the same legacy of world-threatening scientific discovery as does his sister; what's more, in his search for knowledge he, too, achieves only incomprehension. More plainly than Alicia's, his is a story of unsolved puzzles. *The Passenger*'s mysteries abound. Who is the missing passenger? Why is Bobby hunted by government agents? Who has stolen his father's papers and why? Such questions and others go unanswered. Yet as my comments on Alicia should indicate, this is no matter of writerly oversight. Rather, such flamboyantly unresolved riddles underscore what Bobby's own abandoned career in physics has already taught him: namely, that no scientific model will decode reality's enduring enigma. Asked if he still believes in physics, Bobby replies, "I dont know that it actually explains anything" (*P* 156). But his response to this defeat differs from Alicia's and enables him to offer a less deadly response to the precipice to which Enlightenment science has brought modernity. For if Bobby is well aware of his epistemic failure, he is even more certain of his ethical shortcomings. When asked if he has faith in a Catholic God, Bobby replies agnostically to the ontological question, but more affirmatively to the implied moral one: "The best I can say is that I think he and I have pretty much the same opinions" (180). By the measure of such moral sentiments, too, he judges himself a failure. As he confesses to Kline, "I've failed everyone who ever came to me for help" (309). He is moved more by the problem of guilt—his own, which he must expiate, his father's, which he must forgive—than by the puzzles of science. Thus, on hearing of a friend's death, he takes his grief to St. Louis Cathedral, where he sits in silence, "bent forward like any other penitent" (116).

Though Bobby later comes to imagine himself "the last pagan on earth" (383), earlier descriptions of him as "liv[ing] like a monk" and roving New Orleans "like some wandering mendicant" are nonetheless significant (86, 210), for his response to the crimes committed in the name of an impossibly absolute Enlightenment mastery of nature is increasingly a spiritual one. Twice he retreats from pursuers into ascetic stateside isolation, the second time, crucially, after having finally abandoned his attempts to unravel the mystery of their persecution: "I dont know what they're up to and I never will. And now I dont care" (285). This surrender of the imperative to know helps enable a last retreat, not into his sister's nothingness, but into a strikingly monastic discipline. Installed on the Spanish island of Formentera, sleeping on "a sheet of plywood . . . laid over with a straw tick" (365), Bobby lives out his days in humble devotion, not importunate investigation. Through such means, he begins to find some measure of peace in and with the world, and to move beyond his sister's fatal rejection of a reality that will not submit to her Enlightenment ambitions. Sitting "sometimes in the little church at San Javier" (368), Bobby presumes to no certainty and avows no doctrine. He refuses even the title of atheist on such grounds; as he corrects a visitor, "I dont have any religion" (374). What he has in place of settled doctrine or the self-destructive sorrow of his warrior sister is a practice of appeal and atonement: "I light candles for the dead and I'm trying to learn how to pray" (374). His tale concludes, then, not in a commitment to those Enlightenment paths that lead to Hiroshima or Alicia's ghastly tree, but in the penitent's uncertain search for absolution. Bobby's rituals target forgiveness, not knowledge or power, forgiveness for his own sins and forgiveness in his heart for those, like his physicist father, who have done great harm in knowledge's name. Contrite, he tentatively schools himself in practices, not theorems, aimed not at comprehension, but mercy. This, he realizes, is a life's task. "Mercy," he reflects, "is the province of the person alone . . . there is no mass forgiveness. There is only you" (381). But by surrendering the Enlightenment commandment to achieve lordship through knowledge, mercy becomes a task that can foster life, communion, even peace. As such, it offers the diptych's, and McCarthy's, final, unsure, but still resonantly Catholic answer to the maelstrom unleashed by the Enlightenment's too certain science.

These final three works, then, confess the darkness of America's enlightened culture, both in its commonly dehumanizing transactional norms and in the deadly threats established by its weaponized science. More than this, however, and despite their differences in genre, mode, cast, and plot, these works all proffer the path of the penitent as the surest start toward the light. Indeed, their elaboration of the character of, and need for, a decidedly unmodern contrition becomes a chief means by which they reveal the spuriousness of a self-interested modernity's righteousness and the brutalizing potential of its scientific progress. By so advocating for an American examination of conscience, these works of the past decade confirm, as have others reaching back some sixty years, the ongoing relevance to McCarthy's thought and art of the sacramental faith in which he was raised.

NOTES

INTRODUCTION. THE ONLY WORDS I KNOW ARE THE CATHOLIC ONES:
MCCARTHY'S CHRISTIAN CRITIQUE OF AMERICAN ENLIGHTENMENT

1. As Cant's 2008 claim indicates, such assessments reach beyond Bell's 1980s. Phillips himself reiterates them in his 2011 dismissal of God-centered readings of an author in whose oeuvre "realities, and not deities, are the plenipotentiary entities" ("He ought" 179). Similarly in line with Bell's approach is Timothy Parrish's more recent declaration that McCarthy's Westerns are "beyond good and evil" ("History" 77) and David Cowart's claim that the writer is "indifferent to questions of Meaning even as his gravid style seems paradoxically fraught with import" (399). Indeed, Robert Metcalf maintains that McCarthy's erstwhile valediction, *The Road*, narrates "the death of God—at least, the providential God of traditional theism" (141).

2. Other critics have identified a similar ambivalence but questioned its appeal. Thus, Amy Hungerford reads McCarthy as participating, along with such writers as Toni Morrison, Thomas Pynchon, and Don Delillo, in a distinctly postsecular trend in American letters, seeking, like such peers, to re-enchant both world and art by deploying religious symbols without affirming any belief in what they signify. For Hungerford, this bespeaks a suspect desire for "the fruits of religious power" wedded to a reluctance to stand accountable for "the assumptions about the world . . . upon which such visions are built" (133). Derek J. Thiess expresses a cognate frustration with McCarthy's deployment of the complexity theory favored by his peers at the Santa Fe Institute, accusing *The Road* of using such thought to grant its spiritual preoccupations a spurious scientific imprimatur (535), a tactic that, he complains, "moves us away from science and toward metaphysics" (545).

3. Writing seven years later, Cant takes this critical project to be central. For him, then, "McCarthy writes in mythic form in order to deconstruct American mythology" itself (10), a claim echoed that same year by Christopher Walsh, who contends that, to this critical end, all of McCarthy's characters "experience the denial of foundational American myths of progress, prosperity, and mobility" (20). More recently, both Ty Hawkins and Hillier have argued for the fiction's status as an indictment of modern materialism, in both an ontological and economic sense. For Hawkins, McCarthy is consistently skeptical of the quintessential Enlightenment belief "that the advance of the scientific method, as applied to the manipulation of the natural world, including man, will lead to progress" (7), while Hillier deems the work an indictment of the "remorseless industrial-technological progress, uncontainable social fragmentation, and uninhibited economic greed" characteristic of the modernity framed

by Enlightenment thought (*Morality* 103). Most recently, Cooper stresses the importance particularly of misguided economics, proposing "a fundamental critique of late capitalist consumption" lies at the heart of McCarthy's work (*Cormac* 19).

4. As early as 1997, Robert Jarrett could speak of scholarship in which McCarthy's fiction had been "variously termed nihilistic, existential, or gnostic" (*Cormac* 121), and this latter label has enjoyed critical favor to this day. Thus, 2013 saw Brian Evenson argue that McCarthy's work marries twentieth-century existentialism to "earlier Gnostic ideas of the world having been formed . . . by an imperfect and perhaps evil demiurge" ("Uses" 54) and Frye list "ancient Gnosticism" as a foundational philosophical schema for the writer ("Histories" 5). Five years later, Dennis Sansom identifies that same "ancient Gnosticism" as orienting one of McCarthy's three species of parabolists in the Border Trilogy (75), while Benjamin West, in 2020, insists that Gnostic themes are discernible "in practically every work" (132). Indeed, even James Dorson, charged with charting the impact of Judeo-Christian thought on McCarthy's work, concludes that it is such "heterodox offshoots of this tradition [that] interest him the most" ("Judeo-Christian" 125).

5. See DeCoste, "'When You Stop Pretending That You Know': Gnosis, Humility, and Christian Charity in Cormac McCarthy's *The Stonemason.*"

1. DISENCHANTMENT AND DEPENDENCE: THE CONTENDING CREEDS OF ENLIGHTENMENT AND CATHOLICISM

1. Often gendered as a call to manhood, this equation of independent thinking with adulthood resonates in writings of the philosophes' forebears and descendants. Thus, Bacon dismisses both the inherited "wisdom" of the ancients and the empiricism of nonexperimental observation as "childish" (156, 243); indeed, the speculations of Greek philosophy are contrasted to his new practical science for being "but like the boyhood of knowledge: . . . it can talk, but it cannot generate" (156). Some four hundred years later, Sigmund Freud similarly treats belief in received religion as an "infantilism . . . destined to be surmounted" by humanity's inevitable growth in reason and courage (49).

2. See Book IV, Chapter II, of *The Wealth of Nations,* where Smith argues that the individual marketplace actor will, even in seeking only his own gain, be "led by an invisible hand to promote an end which was no part of his intention. . . . By pursuing his own interest he frequently promotes that of the society more effectually than when he really intends to promote it" (423).

3. This equation of the term with Catholicism's seven sacraments—Baptism, Penance, Confirmation, Eucharist, Ordination, Marriage, and Anointing of the Sick—was itself, Boyd Taylor Coolman reports, only effected in the thirteenth century (202). These sacraments, the Church holds, were established by Christ during his worldly ministry and left to the Apostles as their chief commission (see Knox, *Belief* 129). They are rituals and present their actions as signs, but central to the Church's understanding of their signifying is the notion of efficacy. While Edith Humphrey is right to note that "sacraments partake of the physical world and . . . point to the divine world" (69), they also, on the Catholic account, make the divine actively present in such a way as to effect the spiritual change the physical signs indicate. As Nutt puts it, sacraments "effect the grace that they signify" (66).

4. As Eusebius reports, this leniency reaches back at least to the third century. The Novatians argued that Christians who had apostatized under the persecutions of Emperor Decius could not be

readmitted to the Church; for them, "there was no hope of salvation" (214). Yet a synod of bishops rejected such "inhumanity" and declared it heretical, teaching instead that "those brothers who had had the misfortune to fall should be treated and cured with the medicine of repentance" (215).

5. According to David Lincicum, Pauline epistles indicate the formalization of this rite "within two decades of the early Christian movement's beginnings" (97), and Everett Ferguson adduces evidence for the Eucharist's status as "the central act in the weekly assembly of Christians" by the middle of the second century (130). Catholic tradition professes that in its reenactment of the Last Supper, Christ's person and sacrifice are made truly present as those agencies which permit a sanctifying communion. For Bruce D. Marshall, then, Catholicism insists that "[t]he Eucharist is the Body and Blood of Christ" themselves (511), and by presenting them as sundered, it also re-presents Christ as the founding sacrifice for his Church (515).

2. IN THIS LUSH WASTE: COMMODIFICATION, COMMUNION, AND THE SACRAMENTAL MARGINS IN *SUTTREE*

1. Lamenting critics' supposed neglect of the text, Josyph claims *Suttree* should be "ranked as one of the greatest of the greats" (*Adventures* 39). McCarthy scholars have, however, been far from reluctant in their praise. For Walsh, it "rivals *Blood Meridian* as his finest achievement" (212), a view of McCarthy's twin peaks echoed by J. Douglas Canfield ("Dawning" 664) and Michael Crews (46).

2. This Joycean influence was a critical truism by 1992 (Woodward), and the past thirty years have not changed matters. Thus, for Marius, *Suttree's* "Knoxville becomes [McCarthy's] Dublin and he its Joyce" (3). Such sentiment has been seconded by Cant, who notes the novel's inclusion of characters named Ulysses and Joyce (104), Josyph (*Adventures* 41), Yarbrough, who reads Suttree as McCarthy's Stephen Dedalus ("South" 22), Crews (95), and Cowart, who sees McCarthy's novel as steeped in the whole of Joyce's *oeuvre* (403).

3. This library of identified intertexts reaches as far back as Dante (Giemza 198). A more critically popular source text may, however, be found in Twain's *Adventures of Huckleberry Finn,* a precursor emphasized by Bryan Vescio (74), Crews (255), Evenson, who names Twain with Jack Kerouac as signal influences on *Suttree* ("Uses" 62), and O'Gorman, who treats the novel as a fusion of *Huckleberry Finn, Ulysses,* and Flannery O'Connor's *Wise Blood* (123). Richard B. Woodward, Evenson ("Uses" 62), Polk (10), and Yarbrough ("South" 22) all testify to Faulkner's impact on the novel's prose style, while Josyph echoes Evenson to name not just Kerouac, but Ginsberg and William S. Burroughs as models (*Adventures* 41).

4. Though Cooper resists the idea that *Suttree* is either an autobiographical or a confessional text (*Heroes* 57), Josyph reports having met three different Knoxville men, one-time associates of McCarthy, whom he takes as originals for characters from the novel (*Adventures* 21). Wesley G. Morgan goes further, identifying a slew of the novel's McAnally Flats casualties with real-life acquaintances from McCarthy's Knoxville years, links, he concludes, that "strengthen the position of those who would hold that *Suttree* is at least partially an autobiographical work" ("Suttree's Dead" 102).

5. Cant, for one, maintains that the novel identifies Christianity with death (106), and Cowart balks at arguments for any "element of stealth religiosity" (392). Walsh, like Luce, argues that protagonist and tale reject "the false and chimerical promise of religious consolation offered by the Roman

Catholic Church" (229). Less dismissive, Watson holds that the novel presents Catholic sacraments as genuinely efficacious, not as portals to the divine, but as agents of existential enlightenment (22). Critics are not unanimous on this point, however. Beavers, going a step further than Watson in my own direction, holds that the novel, for all its seeming irreverence, "take[s] sacraments and religious questions seriously" as such (96).

6. Neither this existentialist reading nor Shelton's reliance on Camus's *Myth of Sisyphus* is a rarity in criticism of the novel. Bell, mobilizing a more Sartrean idiom, reads *Suttree* as establishing that, notwithstanding the "ontological anxiety" of its protagonist (*Achievement* 89), "existence precedes essence" (114). Meanwhile, Walsh echoes Shelton by reading Suttree as a Camusian hero waging an "existential battle to transcend his fear of death in an increasingly absurd and godless world" (181), and William Prather deploys Camus to argue that, while confronting the challenge of an absurd existence, Suttree "clearly rejects the recourse of religion" (106). As will become clear, I depart from such readings by seeing the novel as revealing, in the end, a nature and a human condition far less absurd than sacramental.

7. Harrogate's role as the novel's American dreamer par excellence has been widely remarked. Walsh, for one, notes that most of his energy and all of his faith are bound up in his attempts to "fulfill the Horatio Alger myth" (207), while Hall reads his many get-rich-quick schemes as a "travesty of the American dream of easy wealth" ("Comedy" 55). More sympathetically, Chollier speaks of Harrogate as a victim of a reigning ideology, "prey to the American Dream of success which takes the form of easy money" ("I aint" 173).

8. Not surprisingly, given the corpses and bodily fluids that bestrew the text, critics have been eager to read *Suttree* through the lens of Kristeva. Beatrice Trotignon, for one, reads the novel as a master class in the Kristevan abject, a catalog of things and experiences inassimilable to a self-sufficient subjectivity (89). Canfield himself presents Suttree as a paradigmatic Kristevan subject, terrified of the destabilizing potential of abjection and maternal power ("Dawning" 676), though he sees the novel as ultimately countering this view of embodiment with an affirmation of Bakhtinian humor (694). Though I will be taking this in a more sacramental direction, I concur. The body celebrated by Mikhail Bakhtin's grotesque is so as it founds communion—"something universal, representing all the people" (19)—and represents enduring life, as "the condition of constant renewal and rejuvenation" (50). Similarly, the often abject body of *Suttree*, when embraced as the locus of communion, and not simply as commodity, emerges as means to Suttree's own rejuvenation.

9. Cant concurs. For him, T. S. Eliot's depiction of the Waste Land functions in *Suttree*, and elsewhere, as the dominant view of modern America itself (107).

10. The notable exception to these demurrals is Suttree's acceptance of an invitation to partake of turtle stew prepared by Native American Michael (234), but this bond, too, seems fleeting, and Suttree ultimately abandons the charm Michael bequeaths him at this meal (see 468).

11. Such a reading of a Joyce ill-used by McCarthy's protagonist would meet with disagreement from certain critics. Jillett presents Joyce as something of a snare for Suttree, the source of a wallowing in commodities that breeds in him "stasis and stultification" (154). Anthony Uhlman likens her to Homer's Circe, an enchantress who waylays Suttree for a time and to his cost (165), while Watson, more negatively still, dubs her "the very incarnation of Mammon" (18). Though Potts may be correct that *Suttree* "undoubtedly has a gender problem," a tendency to misogynistic representations of its women (82), I think that, in the case of Joyce, such problematic antipathy is more the critics' than the text's. While Jillett's

claim concerning Suttree's entrapment might find support in the image of his being "brailed in the soft and springshot bed" he shares with Joyce (*S* 394), the pathos of her presentation, the shame Suttree feels over his dishonesty in the relationship (402), and his established attraction to both aloofness and the goods of the marketplace all powerfully suggest that he is more the victimizer than she.

12. Its protagonist's conflicted response to human embodiment has, in fact, fostered a common reading of *Suttree* as exemplifying Gnosticism's "unequivocally negative evaluation of the visible world and its creator" (Rudolph 60). Luce, who discerns in all of McCarthy's work "a markedly antimaterialistic stance" (*Reading* ix), presents *Suttree*'s Knoxville as a "gnostic netherworld" and the sinister figure of the prologue as an "archontic huntsman," deadly minion of Gnosticism's malevolent creator (197). Frye agrees, presenting the novel, alongside *Blood Meridian* and *Outer Dark*, as clear evidence of McCarthy's attachment to Gnostic thought ("Histories" 5), and West reports that references to that thought appear in McCarthy's working notes for *Suttree* (135). That the latter is the case is no surprise, as the novel explicitly references Gnostic cosmology, but it does so in a manner that renders claims to the author's Gnosticism dubious. At novel's end, Suttree witnesses the demolition of McAnally Flats and the construction of the new Interstate by "Gnostic workmen who would have down this shabby shapeshow that masks the higher world of form" (464). But Suttree, who cherishes in memory "another McAnally, good to last a thousand years" (463), seems committed to the earthy material world these agents of progress assail. Given what I take to be the sacramental stance of the novel toward material Creation, I concur rather with Potts in reading *Suttree* as "a critique of the spiritual rejection . . . of material reality" (87), and so "an extended *critique* of the Gnostic impulse" (107).

13. So pronounced is this religious aura about Suttree that some critics have taken him to function as a Christ figure in the novel. While Beavers states the novel's "Christology is anemic at best" (97) and Cooper insists "Suttree is no savior, literally or symbolically" (*Cormac* 208), Cant takes the life of Christ as the mythic subtext for the novel (104), and O'Gorman points to Suttree's consorting with the outcast as evidence of his serving as "a sort of stand-in for Christ in the novel" (126). John Rothfork concurs but, pointing to the text's focus on human suffering, argues that he plays the part, specifically, of "Christ crucified" ("Redemption" 389).

14. One might add to such proofs the novel's two fulfilled omens. Long before he meets his doomed young lover, Suttree sees her end foretold in a tattoo worn by a prostitute named Ethel: "a wreath with the name Wanda and the words Rest In Peace 1942" (75). Similarly, the death of Billy Callahan is prophesied when blind Richard reads his name incised on one of Ab's gravestone tables (371).

15. Beavers, too, takes Suttree's ostensibly flip reply to the priest's asking if he wishes to confess—"I did it" (*S* 461)—as a valid confession (108).

16. Shelton likewise deems Suttree's charitable acts, though undeniable, often reluctant and frequently withheld (78). Canfield, however, emphasizes the character-defining importance of such compassion (666), and both he and Prather read the concluding generosity shown him by the waterboy and driver as a reward for his own comparable deeds (Canfield, "Dawning" 684, Prather 112). It is true that Suttree is shown to check in on, and extend aid to, a wide range of needy neighbors. He gives four cents to the blind beggar of the marketplace (*S* 68), undertakes to help Michael find his stolen boat (223), and offers the junkman a bed (266). His charity extends, above all, to Harrogate, whom he fights to defend in the workhouse (52), treats to dinner on a frosty Thanksgiving (172), and rescues from his cloacal grave beneath the city (276). Yet while he is happy to play the giver, he is less at ease in more reciprocal

relations, and feeling, for much of his tale, no bond of solidarity with the recipients of his charity, he can as readily spurn beggars (245) and scorn the needy as, for example, in his doling out food, during his workhouse days, to the indigent: "To Suttree they seemed hardly real" (59).

3. A FIGURE OF WRETCHED ARROGANCE: REIFYING AUTONOMY, DEHUMANIZING SCIENCE, AND THE HOPE OF CONVERSION IN *OUTER DARK* AND *CHILD OF GOD*

1. Despite its inclusion in such studies of McCarthy's Tennessee period as Luce's *Reading the World* (62–133) and Walsh's *In the Wake of the Sun* (97–141), *Outer Dark*'s status as a Tennessee novel has been questioned. Christopher Metress claims its "events occur in a setting that cannot be fixed with certainty" (151), Arnold contends its milieu derives more from folklore than history ("Mosaic" 20), and Berry argues Culla haunts "a land that could be any place at any time" (67). I agree, however, with Gabe Rikard that the evidence points to a southern scene; on Rikard's account the murkiness Metress notes derives from the novel's splicing, as does a cartoon of the South dear to the popular imagination, features of Appalachia with the swampier environment of the deep South (195).

2. Several critics have heard echoes of Genesis 3 in the opening pages of *Outer Dark*. Ellis, for one, dubs the Holmes's secluded cabin "their own fallen Eden" (*No Place* 115), while Cant reads Culla and Rinthy as inversions of Adam and Eve, sharing the latter's ignorance, not their innocence (76). Likewise emphasizing such fallenness, Walsh treats their rural setting as antipastoral, "hardly an Edenic sanctuary" (105). As I will show, both this text and *Child of God* do more than subvert Edenic transcriptions of their backwoods locales; they also dramatize the expulsion of their protagonists through sinfulness into a fallen world.

3. Luce has done fine work in tracing the materials that went into the genesis of Lester Ballard. She argues he derives from two notorious cases, those of James Blevins and of Ed Gein, inspiration for Norman Bates in Robert Bloch's 1959 novel *Psycho* and Alfred Hitchcock's subsequent film adaptation. Blevins confessed to spying on parked lovers, as Ballard commences his career by doing, and was charged but ultimately acquitted of the murder of one object of his voyeuristic attention. Gein, grave robber and murderer, anticipated Ballard's own transvestism, keeping of human trophies, and wearing of human skins (*Reading* 136–44).

4. The question of Ballard's responsibility for the crimes he commits remains contested, with some critics insisting he is the product not of his moral choices, but of society's mistreatment. Cooper asserts he "at no time demonstrates any sort of moral consciousness" (*Heroes* 43). Others, too, echoing Ashley Craig Lancaster's recommendation that *Child of God* be read as "an updated version of Mary Shelley's *Frankenstein*" (132), have viewed Ballard's monstrousness as others' creation. Thus, Ellis maintains Ballard is "*made* a necrophilic murderer by the circumstances and forces of the society that refuses, repeatedly, to claim him" (*No Place* 80). Hillary Gamblin reads his "misogynistic tendencies" as deriving from "an unfortunate circumstance of alienation" that Ballard himself has not elected (35), and Rikard offers a still more forceful indictment of Sevier County, stating that its "society creates him and then uses him to keep potentially subversive members on the periphery" (137). While it is true both that social forces initiate Ballard's Fall and that his crimes mirror his society's diseased values, it is clear, in scenes I analyze, that Ballard remains a moral agent, and no simple artifact.

5. For an extended analysis of homelessness in McCarthy's first nine novels, see Ellis, *No Place*.

6. Augustine is clear on this point: "the man who does not believe that sins are forgiven in the Church and therefore scorns this great largess of divine bounty . . . is guilty of the unpardonable sin against the Holy Spirit" (*Faith* 82). In *City of God,* he identifies such despairing presumption as the sin that finally damned Judas (22), a claim echoed centuries later by Catherine of Siena, whose God calls such despair the sin "which is neither pardoned here nor there, because the soul would not be pardoned, depreciating My mercy" (49).

7. This fact has elicited much critical admiration. For Crews, "McCarthy, in one of the great tight-rope acts of American fiction, manages to create both pathos and moral revulsion" in his portrait of Ballard (34). Luce praises the novel for achieving a "compassionate portrayal of one of the most offensive criminals in all of serious literature" (*Reading* 134); she is seconded in this by Walsh (155). While both Nell Sullivan ("Evolution" 74) and Harriet Poppy Stilley call attention to the abhorrent nature of Ballard's "murderous misogyny" (Stilley 103), then, many have agreed with John Lang that the construction of *Child of God* makes impossible any simple denial of Ballard's "fundamental human-ity" (88). I agree and note that one source of such sympathy is the less culpable version of the Fall we witness Ballard undergo.

8. The resolute nature of the rejection of this orphaned boy is such as to imply not just the moral failings of individuals, but the pursuit of community consolidation through scapegoating. Certainly, *Child of God* suggests that the monstrous Ballard is somehow desired by his society. Thus, when, his mur-ders discovered, Ballard struggles to elude pursuers, McCarthy's narrator directs the reader, "See him. You could say that he's sustained by his fellow men, like you. . . . A race that gives suck to the maimed and the crazed, that wants their wrong blood in its history and will have it" (156). As Boguta-Marchel notes (131–32), this recalls René Girard's roughly contemporary delineation of the scapegoat as a means by which cultures defuse ramifying internal strife by electing a single victim to be the legitimized object of unanimous violence: "the fearful transgression of a single individual is substituted for the universal onslaught of reciprocal violence" (Girard 77). This mechanism, Girard argues, forges social cohesion by translating proliferating violence between individuals into a contained violence against an arbitrary but unanimously accepted target. Indeed, on his account, this is the source of religion and ritual, "the very basis of cultural unification" (302). While Ballard is not, as Ciuba suggests, the blameless Girardian victim (83), the role played by communal antipathy in his fate helps indicate links between his extreme crimes and the more mainstream values of his society.

9. Fate is an apt spokesperson for his community. The retrospective first-person accounts of Lester's development offered by neighbors over the course of Part I of the novel are largely etiological, seeking to explain Ballard's terrible crimes in ways that exculpate Sevier County. Thus, he is presented as decisively compromised after the blow to his head (9), as a bully by nature (17–18), as traumatized at an early age by his father's suicide (21), or as simply the latest in a degenerate line of Ballards: "They wasn't none of em any account that I ever heard of" (80). Such accounts do more than exonerate the community. They deny meaningful agency to Ballard himself, treating him as a determined object of scientific scrutiny and cuing readers to the novel's treatment of the dehumanizing potential of this modern episteme.

10. Indeed, their very status as profanations is indicated by what many have taken to be their blas-phemous mirroring of the triune God of Christian theology. While Crews describes them, in classical imagery, as "Furies summoning Culla to a reckoning" (26), and Bell, in more Christian language, dubs them "spectral magi" (*Achievement* 41), others have followed Luce in reading this trio "as a grim parody

of the Christian trinity" (*Reading* 88). For Spencer, they are not simply to be understood as "evil incar-
nate" ("Unholy" 69), but as a "three-personed principle of destruction in brilliant counterpoint to the
concept of a tripartite creator" (73). Hillier, too, describes them as "an anti-Trinity" ("In a Dark" 56), and
he follows Spencer in identifying each member as a perversion of a specific person of the Christian Godhead: the bearded spokesman of God the Father, belligerent Harmon of Christ the Son, and the nameless mute of the Holy Spirit (56; Spencer, "Unholy" 74–75). These convincing observations serve to underscore again the pervasive presence of Christian thought and iconography in McCarthy's dark parable.

11. There has been considerable comment on the identity of this odd trio. Ellis treats them as "a
magical force deeply connected to Culla's guilt" (*No Place* 114), while Rikard argues—in the teeth, I
hold, of the Cheatham interlude—that they have no real existence: "[Culla] commits all the crimes
attributed to them" (202). More typically, Erik Hage dubs them "shadow figures from his psyche" (93),
outer manifestations of Culla's inner darkness (130). Spencer concurs ("Unholy" 73), as does Luce,
who reads them as "projections of [Holme's] inner dark, forecasting or representing his own dark
impulses" (*Reading* 63). Such readings, accord with McCarthy's intentions, as in a marginal note to the
manuscript, he writes: "The triune kill all that Holme *wants* to kill" (qtd in Crews 27). I would only
add that the biblical presentation of Holme and the triune renders this externalization a matter less of
psyches and impulses than of souls and sins.

12. Boguta-Marchel likewise remarks the bearded one's "particular affinity with this satanic element" (169); moreover, this passage's wedding of the fiery and frigid clearly evokes Dante's vision of
an icebound Satan (34.28–36).

13. Ellis makes a similar claim, asserting that having been dispossessed by the county's sale of his
land, Ballard is motivated always by the desire to re-establish a home for himself (*No Place* 70).

14. Ballard's status as mirror to the American mainstream has been widely discussed. While Evenson emphasizes how he "kills without motivation and without plan" ("Wanderers" 43), most critics have
identified in the values of his wider society the seeds for his crimes. Stilley herself reads his necrophilia
as an extended metaphor for American consumerism and its embedded misogyny, concluding that, in
Ballard, there is "no discrepancy between normality and abnormality" (110), a conclusion anticipated by
Bell, who dubs Ballard "an aberration and a norm at the same time" (*Achievement* 55). Cooper likewise
sees Ballard's brutishness as only an intensified manifestation of social norms (*Heroes* 44), and Luce
asserts that he is merely "emblematic of the society from which he arises" ("Cave" 177). Both Nash
and Ciuba fairly observe that even the unspeakable nature of his offenses echoes the culture of Sevier
County, with Nash remarking how his necrophiliac desire is by no means beyond his peers' imagination
(Ciuba 81: Nash, "News" 78; see *CG* 182).

15. Despite this disavowal, the blind man has commonly been identified as the text's truest
preacher. Thus, Metress argues that he represents the *via negativa* of the apophatic theology central to
the novel's vision (152), Cooper reads him as articulating the intimate link "between life (flesh) and
language (word)" McCarthy strives to delineate (*Heroes* 24), and Giles treats him as "an actual prophet"
bearing "a promise of redemption" (96).

16. Blair, for one, reads this return to custody as an interpellated Ballard's capitulation to the
institutional control of the state, a demonstration "that subjection to power is what makes us human
in modern society" (103). Rikard concurs, arguing that, by turning himself in, Lester "has policed
himself and commits himself to a perpetual examination" (159). Such readings, to my mind, miss how

profoundly at odds, not just with Ballard's established character, but with the fiercely individualist norms of his society, this surrender really is.

4. PROPERLY SUZERAIN OF THE EARTH: AUGUSTINIAN EVIL AND THE UNMAKING OF DIABOLICAL ENLIGHTENMENT IN *BLOOD MERIDIAN*

1. Phillips terms it McCarthy's "most noteworthy book" ("Ugly" 18), while Canfield dubs it "an acknowledged masterpiece" ("Dawning" 664). Echoing Bloom, Cooper hails it as "one of the great novels of American Literature" ("Southwest" 24). Emphasizing its American pedigree, Parrish describes *Blood Meridian* as an "unholy combination of *Huckleberry Finn* and *Moby Dick*" ("Killer" 33), while Steven Shaviro asserts that, among American masterworks, only *Moby Dick* rivals it (146).

2. Wallach reads the novel as exposing America's "genocidal appropriation" of the Southwest ("Judge" 135), Mark Eaton dubs *Blood Meridian* and the Border Trilogy "not so much Westerns as anti-Westerns" (156), and Cant asserts they enact a wholesale deconstruction of Manifest Destiny (252). Similarly, Sara Spurgeon speaks of McCarthy's "antimyth of the West" ("Sacred" 76), and Ronja Vieth discusses its "mythoclastic counternarrative" (63). Thus, while Liana Andreasen maintains that McCarthy "is not interested in rewriting history" (25), most critics have argued otherwise and agreed with Dan Moos that it is "a Western, but . . . a Western in which we would rather not believe" (23). This approach has also yielded readings of *Blood Meridian* as a critique of later American colonialism. For Jonathan Imber Shaw, the novel "dramatizes the consequences of an American foreign policy undergirded by a marriage of philo-theological abstraction and physical force" (226), and more especially, the bloody results of the Reagan administration's interference in Central America (209), while Megan Riley McGilchrist argues that McCarthy's unsentimental exposé of American nation building offers a critical gloss on the disillusion of the Vietnam War (130).

3. Others have taken this denomination further and in different directions. Wallach, rejecting Josyph's antithesis, takes the novel to be "McCarthy's epic antiwestern" ("*Beowulf*" 199). Justin Evans concurs, tracing in *Blood Meridian* such hallmarks of the epic as its reliance on parataxis and simile (410–11), but judging it to be a "critical epic" (405), working "to disenchant the idea of the epic and of the society of which that idea is a part" (415). Gareth Cornwell contends that the text is a less deconstructive instance of the genre. Calling attention to the same traits as Evans (535–36), he argues for the novel's status as an unironic epic of nation-founding, in which "McCarthy is paying an ambivalent tribute to the United States by *remythologizing* the frontier" (539). As will become clear, my understanding of Judge Holden's embodiment of knowledge/power as annihilating evil places me in Evans's camp rather than Cornwell's.

4. Taking up this search for models in earlier periods, Broncano treats *Blood Meridian* as a mélange of such medieval and early modern forms as "the epic narrative, the sermon, the parable, the moral tale, the spiritual (auto)biography, and . . . the allegorical journey" (36). Vieth sees the novel as splicing later genres so as to craft a Frontier Gothic aimed at countering "the official, mythologized history with the eclipsed reality of violence" (55). Sullivan, by contrast, claims the text springs from more theoretical soil, judging it a Barthesian text of amoral *jouissance* ("Cormac" 120).

5. While Josyph likewise sees Conrad as one of the novel's intertexts (*Adventures* 63), Spurgeon goes further, identifying both Holden and Conrad's Kurtz "as the ultimate expression of Euro-American

manhood (poet/scholar/warrior) and as the primitive savage" ("Sacred" 84). Certainly, Conrad's "universal genius" (Conrad 91), with his preeminent "gift of expression" (113), does resemble the polymathic Holden, both in the comprehensiveness of his talents and in his pursuit of bloody trophies (125). Yet the Judge, I argue, offers a more radical critique of progress even than Kurtz. Kurtz, having begun as one of "the gang of virtue" (88), is corrupted and experiences a mighty Fall. But Holden has no belief in moral progress of any kind. He thus reveals the Enlightenment culture he exemplifies as not simply vulnerable to, but essentially at one with, a diabolical pursuit of mastery through unmaking. This being the case, I agree with Bell that Holden is the "more terrifying figure" (*Achievement* 119).

6. While Wallach has argued that the novel "cannot be considered nihilistic" ("*Beowulf*" 199), many have disagreed, particularly if the bulwark against nothingness is understood to be some theistic divinity. For Cornwell, McCarthy makes plain that "there is no intelligent or intelligible design" at work in his historical setting (540), and Phillips argues that this milieu is one in which "salvation history, which understands the world and man's travails in it as symbols of the spirit, has long since been played out" ("Ugly" 34). Robert Hamilton concurs, affirming the novel's "post-Christian, even posthuman setting" (140), while Cooper argues *Blood Meridian* offers "an explicitly anticonfessional account of savagery" (*Heroes* 73). Daugherty offers a dissenting opinion, claiming for the novel a clear creedal position; his *Blood Meridian* takes its stand with a dualistic Gnosticism. For the Gnostics, Daugherty explains, "evil was simply everything that *is*. [. . .] And what they saw is what we see in the world of *Blood Meridian*" (162). This position, as my introduction indicates, has been much echoed, most notably by Mundik (see *Bloody*, chapters 1–4). While the text indicates a world where faith is under siege, the novel's Augustinian understanding of evil, and of the role of penance and charity in counteracting it, suggest that *Blood Meridian* is far from a post-Christian reflection on the Enlightenment and far, too, from a Gnostic equation of evil with Creation.

7. Patrick Shaw sees Holden's deification of war as restating McCarthy's own conviction that "there's no such thing as life without bloodshed" (Woodward); for Shaw, Holden clearly speaks for a writer whose "advocacy of violence is deliberate and fundamental" ("Kid's Fate" 104). While Hillier seeks to counter such an identification, insisting that, in contrast to the Judge, McCarthy's work "conveys an impassioned and consistent moral vision" (*Morality* 6), Parrish suggests that this may argue in the Judge's favor, since he "represents the most coherent statement in McCarthy's novels of any moral order" ("Killer" 35). Sepich agrees with Ellis and Shaviro, noting that the novel presents "a portrait of Holden as an artist working in the wildest mixed medium of all—the world," and so as a double for his creator (*Notes* 138). Wallach, on the other hand, insists that "Holden's voice is not the narrator's" ("*Beowulf*" 200). As regards Sepich's point, Wallach argues more persuasively that the Judge and narrator, however akin as wordsmiths, are fundamentally at odds, because Holden "effaces the physical subjects of his journal as he records them," erasing the sites of injury *Blood Meridian* is at pains to render (212).

8. Others have made this connection between Holden and the Enlightenment. Thus, Bell describes the Judge as an "only slightly demented revival of Enlightenment philosophy" (*Achievement* 124). A decade later, Jarrett likewise sees the Judge's lectures as indebted to the Enlightenment emphasis on reason as the source of power over nature (*Cormac* 78). More recently, Monk has dubbed Holden "the supreme avatar of the European Enlightenment in modern fiction" (37), and Frye has seen McCarthy as using this character to argue "against the Enlightenment conception of human perfectibility" ("*Blood Meridian*" 109).

9. Even though Holden's pursuit of science entails the annihilation of its objects, few readers have related *Blood Meridian* and its chief villain to Augustine's formulation of evil as the corruption of an innately good Creation. Wallach mentions the novel's evoking "the Augustinian double bind of western theodicy" ("Judge" 134), but fails to elaborate what this evocation signifies. Potts mobilizes Augustine in his study of the sacramental outlook of McCarthy's work, but only for a definition of "sacrament" (11–12). Indeed, in her reading of *All the Pretty Horses*, Mundik states that McCarthy's concept of evil clearly rejects the Augustinian view (*Bloody* 108). Rachel Griffis deploys an Augustinian understanding of evil in her reading of *Outer Dark* and *The Road* as both depicting "sin as a perversion of virtue" (84), but when it comes to *Blood Meridian* itself, Dorson, though he neglects to mention the author of *Confessions*, best approximates my argument by observing that Holden's is an "evil without an essence" ("Demystifying" 114).

10. Potts concurs, noting that "nearly every church or mission depicted in the novel lies in ruins" (21), and argues that this motif indicates how McCarthy offers a "critique of Christianity" as utterly incapable of offering "any practical protection to the persecuted" (19, 20). While the Church in *Blood Meridian* has failed to provide worldly sanctuary from bloody progress, I argue that the novel's critique is centered instead on the forces that assail it and is animated by an ongoing commitment to core Christian concepts.

11. Like Holden, Tobin derives from Samuel Chamberlain's *My Confession: Recollections of a Rogue*, "the only personal narrative written by a member of Glanton's gang" (Sepich, *Notes* 14). Chamberlain describes him thus: "Ben Tobin was one of the best fellows in the world. Son of a Irish gentleman [*sic*], he was sent to Maynooth College to be educated for the Priesthood, was expelled, came to America, and was now the wild rolicking [*sic*] Texas Ranger" (136).

12. Historically, filibusters were "private military expeditions . . . whose aim was to use American manpower and firepower to achieve victory" for embattled or exiled Latin American partisans (Slotkin, *Fatal* 243). As Sepich notes, White's filibuster is unattested and comes earlier than the commonly identified inauguration of Anglo-American filibustering with William Walker's Sonora expedition of 1853 (*Notes* 20). Yet Luce demonstrates McCarthy's abiding interest in historical filibustering by tracing the echoes of Henry Crabb's 1857 assault on the Mexican town of Caborca in *The Crossing* (see "Doomed Enterprise").

13. Spurgeon is not alone in highlighting how McCarthy's depiction of Holden as scientist makes of him "a mythical being" (Andreasen 20), evocative of the supernatural thinking he works to displace. Many critics have called attention to the manner in which his pursuit of domination grants him godlike status. Daugherty, treating him as a Gnostic archon, dubs him the governing force in the world of the novel (163), and Frye, pursuing this same Gnostic tack, identifies him as the Demiurge, the fallen creator of the material universe ("Histories" 6; see also, Mundik, *Bloody* 35). Similarly, Broncano likens him to the Old Testament Creator, as he "who decides what exists and what does not" (18), and Masters argues the Judge's power to name and to interpret the world is presented as "absolute" (28). This paradox, I maintain, is explained by Holden's clear ambition to conquer and replace the offensively preexisting Creator.

14. Sepich traces such depictions of Holden as ornithologist to two generations of America's most famous family of painter-naturalists. John James Audubon (1785–1851) worked, Sepich reports, much as Holden does, shooting and stuffing avian specimens he then painted in detail (*Notes* 138). Sepich notes also a kinship between Holden and John James's son, John Woodhouse Audubon (1812–1862),

writer, painter, and naturalist, who traveled the Southwest in the mid-nineteenth century and whose journal entry for June 13, 1849, records an encounter Sepich takes as the source for the tarot reading scene of McCarthy's chapter 6 ("What Kind" 132).

15. According to Slotkin, such sentiment was historically directed at American soldiers, not just mercenaries like Glanton. U.S. troops committed numerous atrocities during the Mexican War, such that "some Mexicans are reported to have fled to the Comanches for protection from the Americans" (*Fatal* 190).

16. For elaboration of one brand of bestializing, specifically of how the novel "repeatedly conjoins canine and man" (113), see Sanborn, chapter 6.

17. Many, like Rothfork ("McCarthy" 202), have identified a kinship between Holden and this thinker whom Adorno and Horkheimer adduce as proof of the Enlightenment's totalitarian trajectory (86–119), and Crews confirms McCarthy was reading Nietzsche's *Twilight of the Idols* while at work on *Blood Meridian* (200). Cant reads Holden's marriage of reason and appetite as a Nietzschean fusion of the Apollonian and Dionysian (173), Ellis suggests the Judge be understood as "a darker precursor to Nietzsche" (*No Place* 9), and Frye sees *Blood Meridian* as offering Nietzsche's ideas, through Holden, "as potentially accurate descriptions of the world" ("Histories" 8). Potts similarly sees in McCarthy's novel an endorsement of Nietzschean thought but maintains that Holden "embodies a corrupted version of the Nietzschean philosophical and moral position" (30). Certainly, Holden's advocacy of will to power justifies such readings, but his philosophical pedigree, and the cultural currents he allows the novel to scrutinize, extend beyond this one thinker, just as the abhorrence of his deeds serves to place such modern philosophy under radical moral question.

18. The novel consistently associates Holden not just with gratuitous violence—as in his purchase of two pups only to toss them in the river to drown (*BM* 200–201)—or with falsehood (as Tobin's "bloody old hoodwinker" [263]), but with flames. He passes through a campfire "and the flames delivered him up as if he were in some way native to their element" (101). Responding to such cues, many have read Holden as diabolic. Thus Dorson dubs him "a personification of evil" ("Demystifying" 114), Hamilton speaks of his "infernal rites" (143), Mundik judges him "demonic" (*Bloody* 32), and Masters calls him "a Mephistophelean figure" (25). For Sepich, Holden's pride, eloquence, and love of legalism cast him in the role of Satan (*Notes* 122–23), a role affirmed by Boguta-Marchel (122, 125). This identification receives scriptural warrant in Jordan Carson's reading of the Judge's desert showdown with Tobin and the kid as an adaptation of the Lukan rendering of Christ's temptations (23). Such an identification is given a more literary pedigree by Hillier and Evans, who see Holden's creation of gunpowder in chapter 10 as modeled on the arms-making work of Milton's Satan in Book VI of *Paradise Lost* (Hillier *Morality* 22; Evans 412); indeed, Mark Steven, adducing the same evidence, argues "Holden embodies the literary-historical rebirth of the Miltonic Satan" (151).

19. Sepich all but uniquely claims of Holden's violence against children that "there is not a single hint of sexuality in these events" (*Notes* 15). Hillier, by contrast, speaks of Holden "sometimes scalping, frequently raping . . . disappearing children" (*Morality* 19–20), and Patrick Shaw, though mistakenly asserting all his victims are male, sees sexual violence as key to Holden's relationship with the kid and as typifying his other encounters with children ("Kid's Fate" 110). The nakedness of the "halfbreed" boy and of the girl at Yuma in my view makes plain the Judge's intent with these victims, even if no rape is ever described by the text.

20. The precise nature of the kid's fate is uncertain; we know only that whatever is left in the jakes is an object of horror even for the jaded clientele of a frontier saloon (347–48). This has led to a variety of accounts. Ellis suggests the kid dies a victim of sodomy, murder, and cannibalism (*No Place* 166), and Mundik echoes the final two of these claims (*Bloody* 92). Patrick Shaw emphasizes the first, insisting "the judge's essential motivation is to assault the kid sexually" ("Kid's Fate" 103). Sepich reads the kid's end as foretold in the tarot reading of chapter 6 ("Dance" 18), and as the fruit of his there representing "mercy" to the Judge's "war" (18–19; 22).

21. Parrish's assessment is more damning still, calling the kid "a collaborator whose will was only strong enough to throw him in with bad and vicious companions" ("History" 72). Similarly, Wallach sees no evidence of the kid's supposed "clemency" ("Judge" 133), a perspective shared by Sepich (*Notes* 105). For Cooper, even the kid's refusal to shoot an unarmed Holden stands to his discredit, revealing an inability to resist evil (*Heroes* 73). Many, however, have countered this view. Mundik goes so far as to dub the kid "a messianic figure," though of a Gnostic, not orthodox Christian, cast (*Bloody* 72). More modestly, Josyph records Harold Bloom as crediting him with "considerable moral force and courage" (*Adventures* 83), and Lauren Brown argues he "*alone* remains autonomous" in the face of Holden's attempts to make true believers of all Glanton's men (77), a case seconded by Carson (21). Likewise, Linda Woodson insists upon the kid's "refusal to act fully on the will to power" ("Leaving" 271), Hillier affirms his "innate capacity for pity" (*Morality* 54), for minor acts of mercy that shine, in the novel's bleak world, like "small miracles" (73), and Kirk Essary contends that this attenuated protagonist none-theless "serves as a sort of ethical foil to the judge's attempts at self-deification" (282). Though the kid's compassionate gestures are largely robbed of efficacy, I agree with Hillier that he represents a counter to, and a Christian lens through which to perceive, the Judge and his works.

22. It is significant in this regard that the novel, as Brad Bannon observes, suggests it is the kid's return to bloodshed that fatally invites Holden back into his life: the Judge reappears, after all, just after the kid has shot down the young Elrod on the outskirts of Fort Griffin (89).

23. Dubbed by Sepich "a description of digging postholes using a throw-down tool" (*Notes* 66), this enigmatic conclusion has often been taken as a chastening rejoinder to the triumphant Judge dancing deathlessly at novel's end. Daugherty reads this digger as a Gnostic liberator, freeing the divine spark imprisoned in Holden's benighted material domain (169), a claim seconded by Mundik (*Bloody* 95). Similarly, Frye sees the episode as envisioning a future order "in which the judge does not wholly reign" ("*Blood Meridian*" 119), and Carson speaks of its dramatizing the forging of alternative moral narratives (31). Potts likewise views this digger as offering an ethical riposte to Holden's seeming victory (69). Nonetheless, I hold that the novel's depiction of American settlement militates powerfully against such hopeful interpretations.

5. LA FE ES TODO: FALSE INNOCENCE AND BROKEN FAITH IN THE BORDER TRILOGY

1. Cooper similarly deems both characters "cast in the heroic mold" ("Southwest" 27), yet critics have fixated more on Cole's heroism. Hillier dubs him McCarthy's "most sustained fictional portrayal of virtue" (*Morality* 96), and Gail Morrison repeatedly affirms his hero status (178, 182). Cant reads John Grady as a tragic hero, noble victim of the "myth of the pastoral and the exceptionalism" of America (229). Others have expressed skepticism. For McGilchrist, Cole embodies McCarthy's "critique of the

hero of the traditional 'western'" (117); Husband, taking a more Marxian tack, likewise presents an unsympathetic John Grady, one "imprisoned within the rigid boundaries of his former class status" (74). For Lucy Neave, his tale charts his "transformation from being a boy with a strong moral code to a man who takes a brutal form of revenge" (26). While I judge Cole an appealing character, I concur with these more critical readers in detecting an interrogation of the cultural norms he exemplifies.

2. Most prominent in *The Crossing*, a narrative punctuated by the tales of "wise anchorites" (Mundik, "Clamorous" 209), extended scenes of storytelling characterize the trilogy throughout, from Dueña Alfonsa's history of the Madero brothers in *All the Pretty Horses* (230–39) to the itinerant's tale of his dream within a dream in the epilogue to *Cities of the Plain* (270–89). Sansom numbers fully thirteen of these teacher figures, each aimed, he claims, at cuing reflection on theological and moral questions (68).

3. The Comanches had long ceased to range freely in west Texas by John Grady's 1949. While estimated to number some 40,000 in the late 1780s (Hämäläinen 102), the Comanches were reduced by drought, famine, disease, and encroachment to a population of roughly 1,500 by 1875 (340). Yet Comanche raids took "a heavy toll in Texan lives and livestock [from] the late 1850s" on (333). This ultimately resulted in a policy of total war on the part of the American state (332–33), one which ended with the surrender, and relocation to reservation lands, of the last Comanche hostiles in 1875 (341).

4. Arnold argues that this equation is bolstered by the ending of *All the Pretty Horses*. Observing that Cole passes before the gaze of Indians camped on the plains (see *APH* 301), Arnold reads this as a deliberate echo of his opening vision of the Comanches ("'Go to sleep'" 50). King accuses McCarthy, through such means, of "suggest[ing] that the marginalization experienced by these two groups is commensurate" (73). While John Grady and his father may believe as much, the trilogy, I argue, underlines these ranchers' implication in crimes against wilderness and Native Americans both in such a way as to acquit McCarthy himself of any such charge.

5. While some critics have praised the plot-centrality of Alfonsa (Hage 170) or the initiative of Alejandra (Morrison 181; Hillier, *Morality* 105), or both (Woodson, "This is another" 42), many have read the trilogy's women as evidence of McCarthy's penchant for stereotype. Hage deems this definitive of his work: "women are rarely the focus of his novels [and] are not as fleshed out and complex as the male characters" (169). Sullivan charges the Border Trilogy specifically with the "narrative expulsion or containment of women" ("Boys" 228). Barcley Owens likewise speaks of "two-dimensional figures kept off to the side" (65), and Patrick Shaw accuses these texts of trafficking in racial, as well as sexual stereotypes ("Female" 259), a critique echoed by Jennifer Reimer's denunciation of McCarthy's "stereotypical and often violent representation of Mexican women" (423). For Meg King, such renderings derive from the novels' demand "that the reader mourn white men's waning privilege" (81). While McCarthy's fiction is indeed androcentric, readings of the trilogy as furthering the dehumanization of women strike me as off the mark.

6. See Arnold, "McCarthy and the Sacred" 232. As he notes, this first atomic blast occurred in the early hours of July 16, 1945. While Sansom argues that, in McCarthy's hands, "the bomb's light reflects the senselessness of presuming a purpose in a dark world" (74), and Mundik sees in it "the profound alienation that underlies human existence" ("Right" 30), I maintain that its demonstration of a destructive Enlightenment underscores the vital importance of human purposes aimed at countering alienation through faith and fidelity.

7. Of course, McCarthy's Mexico is far from Eden. Daniel Cooper Alarcón has, in fact, read *All the Pretty Horses* in the light of prior English-language texts, by such figures as Graham Greene and Malcolm Lowry, which established the trope of Mexico as an Infernal Paradise (142). McCarthy's Mexico, he argues, conforms to this template by "function[ing] as a symbolic backdrop, juxtaposing the paradise of the hacienda with the hell of the prison at Saltillo" (145).

8. It is clear that it is this drifter, led by Billy to the Parhams' home, who later kills his parents and makes off with the horses. The sheriff tells Billy there were two assailants, likely Indians (*TC* 167). Boyd further informs him that, while he hid, he heard the attackers call his name (173); earlier Billy thrice names Boyd in front of this stranger (7–8).

9. John Grady's participation in such a conventional love story has been widely remarked. Thus, Charles Bailey dubs *All the Pretty Horses* "a courtly romance" (294). Others have more specifically related its tale to *Don Quixote*'s parody of that genre. Indeed, Broncano argues "we can read the trilogy as a rewriting of the Spanish classic" (75). While describing Cole as "chivalrous, resourceful, passionate" (190), Cant sees the first volume of the trilogy as emulating *Quixote* in a "mythoclasm" aimed at interrogating such traits (186). Mundik discerns a similar debt and critical concern. Noting that Don Hector addresses John Grady in language that casts the young cowboy in the role of Cervantes's knight of woeful countenance, she argues this allusion "marks his quest as hopelessly quixotic" (*Bloody* 104).

10. Some have suggested that such posing has McCarthy's cowboys function more as products of, than rebels against, postwar mass culture. Thus, John Dudley argues that *All the Pretty Horses* is "as much *about* nostalgic longing for earlier narrative form as it is an example of this form" (176). McGilchrist echoes such sentiments, holding that John Grady's is "a quest for what is actually a simulacrum" (119). Similarly, Holloway contends that Cole and Parham traffick in cowboy clichés (*Late* 72), a "pastiche behavior that the reader is encouraged to view with increasing skepticism" (*Late* 77). The trilogy's setting lends credence to such readings. According to Slotkin, the Western was an established cinematic genre by 1908 (*Gunfighter* 231), but enjoyed its heyday after World War II. From 1945 to 1973, it was "pre-eminent among American mass-culture genres as a field for the making of public myths" (278). Thus, the longing of McCarthy's protagonists can be understood as entangled not just with the social norms of their present, but in that moment's own myth of the cowboy.

11. As Steven L. Davis remarks, Quijada, like *Blood Meridian*'s Glanton, is drawn from history. Lupe Quijada, "a full blooded Yaqui Indian," did indeed, in the late 1930s, serve as manager of the Nahuerichic section of the Hearst family's sprawling Babícora ranch (54).

12. See Holden's own manual appropriation: "The judge placed his hands on the ground. . . . This is my claim, he said. And yet everywhere upon it are pockets of autonomous life" (*BM* 207).

13. Noting the Pietà imagery at the conclusion of *Cities of the Plains* (*Heroes* 77), Cooper argues that such a rendering elevates John Grady's end "from a meaningless act to a potentially redemptive, even Christological sacrifice" (77). Hillier concurs, reading his efforts on Magdalena's behalf as "a Christ-like *kenosis* or self-emptying for others" (*Morality* 145). Broncano also names Cole the trilogy's messiah (77). However sympathetic John Grady's concern for Magdalena, though, I agree with Jarrett that Cole's death does not successfully function as sacrifice, Christ-like or otherwise ("Sense" 322).

14. Monk himself elaborates, noting how horses "signify the romance of the premodern" (123). Such sentiments are echoed by Pilkington, who describes the trilogy's horses as "pristine and unfallen

nature" (319); Cooper, who reads them as victims of a commodifying modernity (*Cormac* 59); and Holloway, for whom they represent "a precapitalist enclave" (*Late* 62).

15. Joey Isaac Jenkins argues that such violence against animals results from their becoming objects for characters' displaced and inadmissible queer desire (23). Jenkins is not alone in calling attention to such queer undercurrents. For Sullivan, the trilogy's marginalization of women "creates a closed circuit for male desire" ("Boys" 230), discernible specifically in Billy's "homoerotic desire for John Grady" (246). Arnold, too, remarks a "sexual ambivalence" in this relationship ("Last" 237), but affirms its "forthright presentation of friendship and affection between heterosexual men" (237).

16. The number of such tales has led some to take storytelling itself to be the trilogy's overriding concern. Thus, while James Christie reads them as expressing McCarthy's faith in a supratextual reality that outstrips human expression (131), others have insisted on the inescapability of narrative in these works. Christopher White sees the trilogy foregrounding its status "as itself the dream of its author" and so insisting that readers confront the power of story (122). Focusing more exclusively on *The Crossing*, Cant maintains McCarthy argues that humanity achieves knowledge only through narrative (201), a claim echoed by Luce ("Road" 208) and Holloway (*Late* 27). Though such a tack has Cameron MacKenzie assert that "the delimiting agent of *The Crossing* is not, in fact, a transcendent God, but . . . an act of artistic creation" (102), it is clear, rather, that that novel's interpolated narratives themselves insist on God's remaining an eminently live consideration.

17. Such protests, paired with ample foreshadowing of John Grady's demise, have prompted many to read the trilogy as depicting a deterministic world. As Boguta-Marchel puts it, McCarthy's most self-aware characters "perceive their own past, present, and future as inextricably intertwined and predetermined" (67). Luce endorses such a reading of Billy, a character she insists is largely borne along by events and in no way responsible for the losses he suffers ("Road" 197), while Mundik extends such a judgment to John Grady as well, arguing that both cowboys lack "any power to change the course of their destinies" (*Bloody* 209). For Hage, fate persistently trumps these men's narrative construction of their identities and futures: "Myths don't hold up, but destiny is unwavering" (62). I side more with Marty Priola, who, in a reading of the role of games in the trilogy, maintains that, whatever the constraints under which they act, John Grady and Billy are consistently presented as genuine agents, presented with alternatives and knowingly pursuing self-determined courses. Of John Grady, in particular, he cogently notes, "he walks willingly and with no little premeditation into his own death" (271).

18. See also Cant 202.

19. Remarking John Grady's moral maturation, several critics have read *All the Pretty Horses* as an exemplary *Bildungsroman*. For Morrison, this text is "fundamentally a *Bildungsroman*" in the tradition of such nineteenth-century American novelists as Melville, Twain, and James (178). Similarly, Luce and Mundik treat the novel as tracking the spiritual growth of its protagonist, with Luce describing Cole as "the romantic dreamer who gradually awakens to reality" ("When You Wake" 155), and Mundik defining the plot in terms of his "painful initiation into an awareness of evil, suffering, and death" (*Bloody* 101). While there is some truth to this, I agree with Christie that the trilogy as a whole invokes conventions of this genre only, ultimately, to frustrate them (131), certainly so far as John Grady Cole is concerned.

20. Others have remarked the more profound solitude of McCarthy's elder cowboy. Cant, for one, notes his isolation through much of the trilogy (196), while Arnold speaks of Billy's "removal from emotional commitment and desire in general" ("Last" 238). James Keegan, seeing this loneliness as

Parham's own doing, speaks of "the border he has created between himself and the world" (47). Finally, Cooper maintains that "Billy's utter dispossession as a homeless, itinerate wanderer poses a stunning counter to the myth of the self-made man" (*Cormac* 60), highlighting, as I wish to do, the critique to which the trilogy exposes American ideals of personal sovereignty and independence.

21. For cognate readings of the novel as charting the progressive loss of faith, see Hillier (*Morality* 110) and Mundik (*Bloody* 116).

22. To be precise, Hall sees this as a penance offered for that community capable of the cruelty that forced him to euthanize the wolf ("Hero" 192). I read this as a rather more self-punishing gesture, an attempt at self-absolution akin to John Grady's interview with the judge.

6. LIKE THE LAST HOST OF CHRISTENDOM: DEADLY PRAGMATISM, PROFANE COMMUNION, AND THE POWER OF EUCHARIST IN *THE ROAD*

1. The novel's outlook has been much debated. Shelley Rambo claims it testifies to hopeless human suffering in a world "in which life and death can no longer be distinguished" (115). Stacey Peebles sees its final paragraph as deflating any optimism the boy's concluding adoption might underwrite (123), a view seconded by Tim Edwards (60). But while Monk (204) and Rikard (209) likewise maintain that *The Road*'s setting is devoid of hope, many have discerned in its grim tale a "deeply life-affirming" narrative (Crews 243). Hawkins dubs it McCarthy's "most-utopian novel" (129), Hage terms it "a story of redemption" (104), and Broncano asserts it offers a sense "of renewal and hope . . . never so explicit in McCarthy's canon" (2). For L. Lamar Nisly, this sense is rooted in "hints and possibilities that . . . point toward a hidden God" (313), while Ashley Kunsa insists that hope, grace, and redemption "fundamentally drive the narrative" (58), which she reads as "proto-Edenic" and rife with the potential for re-creation (64). In line with these optimistic readings, I argue that the development of kin-love into a charity that affords humanizing communion with neighbor and God makes this McCarthy's most affirmative tale.

2. Snyder, for example, describes McCarthy's protagonists as "moving through nuclear winter" ("Hospitality" 69); Edwards does likewise (56). Allen Josephs, by contrast, suggests that the novel's catastrophe may be truly apocalyptic and divine in origin (135). Some have seen the novel not simply as a warning against climate change, but as "one of the most important environmental novels of the last 50 years" (Spurgeon, "Introduction" 19), notwithstanding Adeline Johns-Putra's insistence that the particulars of McCarthy's dying planet make it plain that *The Road* "is no global warming jeremiad" (520). More commonly, critics have followed Dana Phillips in seeing the end as brought about by a meteor strike ("He ought" 177). Thus, Thiess speaks of a globe "scorched by a meteorite" (532), and Mundik sees the inherent evil of Gnosticism's Creation revealed by the fiery blow of a meteor (*Bloody* 287), a physical, if not metaphysical, culprit also endorsed by Richard Rankin Russell (129).

3. Other critics are less eager to concede the mother's wisdom. For Randall Wilhelm her decision "embodies the human mentality that succumbs to fear and doubt and deprivation because it cannot think beyond the limited scope of the self" (135). Hawkins, while willing to grant Hellyer's claim, sees the novel as using the mother's character to align mere reason with nihilism and death (131). I have argued elsewhere that the mother demonstrates how, for McCarthy, "despair is the dark child of love's failure" (DeCoste, "A Thing" 77). That there is a kind of reason upheld by her decision is I think clear;

that this brand of rationality is itself upheld by McCarthy's chronicle of parental love and charitable longing is dubious.

4. While Inbar Kaminsky speaks of "the non-consumerism of the wasteland" (par. 23), most commentators have understood McCarthy's apocalypse as drawing parallels "between the cannibalistic bands roaming the desolated countryside and the processes of capitalistic production and consumption" (Jergenson 118). Thus, Dominy reads the novel's nightmarish world as the logical end-point of market economics, the "realization of the religion of consumer capitalism" (149), Schleusener dubs it a "Hobbesian 'state of nature' extrapolated from the basis of our own experience of dog-eat-dog capitalism" (par. 12), and Broncano takes it as dramatizing the fruit of America's unbridled devotion to Mammon (136). Kollin extends this beyond a reading of the novel's cannibals, arguing that McCarthy's landscape, littered with the detritus of consumer culture, forcibly references "the excess and waste that marks daily life for many Americans" (160), and Paul Sheehan proffers the road itself as a critical metonymy, evoking as it does the automotive industry and Fordist consumerism that fuelled postwar America's economic preeminence (95). While the pair's own implication in the novel's economy of literal consumption complicates such readings, I agree with such critics that the novel is concerned to critique the pragmatic and Enlightenment values that underlie American modernity, its consumerism very much included.

5. Others have seconded this idea. Dominy, for example, concurs that this device identifies them as consumers on the model of the readers' own late capitalist moment (151). Wilhelm echoes this claim but reads the cart as a more ironic reminder of "the once prosperous society by which it was created . . . to carry groceries in abundance" (132). Along these lines, the fact that the pair must ultimately abandon the cart before the boy can find goodness in his adopted family indicates the protagonists' allegiance to communion over this vestigial mercantile consumerism.

6. Perhaps for this reason, some readers have taken a less positive view of this episode. Potts, for one, notes a disturbing juxtaposition between this life-saving subterranean pantry and the basement larder at the plantation house (160). Certainly, the boy sees, and is terrified by, such parallels. "Don't open it, Papa," he begs (*R* 134). Tore Rye Andersen further notes that the duo cannot halt at this place of plenty and seeming safety, arguing that to do so would mean their forfeiting the father's purpose-generating narrative of a better world on the southern coast (77).

7. Wielenberg, for example, identifies this prohibition as the chief moral imperative among the six points he sees as defining the good guys' code that the father seeks to teach the son (5-6), and Peebles holds that, for McCarthy's protagonists, the recourse to cannibalism is paramount to the loss of one's soul (121). See also, Kunsa (59) and Gwinner (147).

8. Critics have been quick to deny both that McCarthy's pair are themselves believers and that his novel takes seriously the possibility of God's existence. Broncano argues that *"The Road* heralds the death of God" (137), and Metcalf concurs, seeing in the novel a repudiation of "virtually the entirety of religious tradition" (136). Similar claims are put forth by Hage (52), Spurgeon ("Introduction" 17), Rikard (209), and Monk, who holds that "the notion of a benign deity and a continuing spiritual existence are inconsistent" with the world the novel depicts (204). On similar grounds, Phillips concludes the novel's milieu is "better suited to archaeological than theological treatment" ("He ought" 184). Indeed, Hellyer insists that the book's allusions to Christian belief represent a despairing and dubious defense mechanism, "melancholy traces manipulated by an allegorizing consciousness ambiguously positioned

between the man and the narrator" (46). Josephs, by contrast, points to the boy's implausible rescue at the novel's conclusion, a validation of the father's faith that "goodness will find the little boy" (*R* 281), and poses a compelling question: "Why drag out a deliberate and undisguised deus ex machina . . . if what you want is to deny any sort of deus?" (140). Moreover, if, as Taylor maintains, religion, "in a strong sense," can be defined as "the belief in transcendent reality, on one hand, and the connected aspiration to a transformation which goes beyond ordinary human flourishing on the other" (510), then it is, I argue, clear that protagonists and narrative may both be deemed genuinely religious.

9. While Nisly declares that McCarthy's boy "on some basic level connects with and reflects radical, divine love" (318), most readers have been more definite in their characterization of this divinity. For Kunsa, it is clear that the son is "a messiah not unlike Christ himself" (65). Similarly, Frye notes the boy's "Christ-like" concern for strangers ("Life" 12), Russell remarks his "Christological connotations" (133), and Josephs affirms that *The Road* depicts the son "in unmistakably Christ-like iconography" (139). There have also been dissenters. Phillips dismisses such messianic readings, insisting that "the boy is just a boy: one of the last boys on earth, and therefore precious, but just a boy for all that" ("He ought" 182). More sensitive to the novel's undeniable clothing of this character in savior's attire, Schleusener reads such traits as projections of the father's desperate love, treating "the messianic solution merely as a way of compensating for the absence of any solution" in their dying world (par. 16).

10. This passage and others open up less Christological possibilities. In line with Schleusener's treatment of the boy's apparent Christ status in the previous note, *The Road* invites a reading of his messianic identity as a survival strategy of the father. Requiring a warrant for his life, he finds one by making of the boy a transcendent good he must live to serve. Such an interpretation finds its basis in words offered the man by his wife prior to her suicide: "you wont survive for yourself. . . . A person who had no one would be well advised to cobble together some passable ghost. Breathe it into being and coax it along with words of love. Offer it each phantom crumb and shield it from harm with your body" (57). The father is haunted by this counsel. Washing his son's hair, a form of baptism, he thinks, "Evoke the forms. Where you've nothing else construct ceremonies out of the air and breathe upon them" (74). It is noteworthy, too, that he does the last three things the mother suggests, offering words of love, each last crumb, and even his own body for the boy. Thus, when they are targeted by a hidden bowman, "he pushe[s] the boy's head down and trie[s] to cover him with his body" (263). However, the son's role as the bearer of a future-founding Eucharistic ethos suggests that his goodness, and its specifically Christ-like and Catholic cast, are far from chimerical.

11. See Josephs, 138.

12. This ethic of care has led to the father's being viewed as a challenge to gender norms. For Cooper, his caretaking represents a "feminine masculinity in which nurture and violence contend for dominance" (*Cormac* 43). Sullivan reads the text, with its absent, suicidal mother and its relocation of traditional maternal virtues to an all-male community, as dissolving a "matriarchal power structure, recouping for 'the good guys' the power traditionally ascribed to the feminine" ("Good Guys" 89).

13. Many critics, guided by mention of the father sharing "old stories of courage and justice as he remembered them" (*R* 41), have emphasized narrative as the man's chief means of moral instruction. Andersen views the father as effectively a novelist, constructing, in the pair's quest for the sea, a humanizing purpose through story (68). Hawkins opposes the meaning-generating power of the father's tales to the nihilism exemplified by the mother (131), and both Wilhelm (138) and Hillier (*Morality* 276)

insist that the boy's moral qualities survive because of the father's rehearsal of stories of heroic virtue. Cooper even argues that these stories are "the sacraments and rites of a new religious order" (*Heroes* 133). As I have argued elsewhere, such claims overstate the evidence (the novel does not actually share any of the man's bedtime stories) and miss how the boy learns from the father's own example; in other words, the boy survives as a moral being "by believing not just in his [father's] . . . words, but in the proof of his life" (DeCoste, "A Thing" 86).

14. Despite this, Snyder uses his name to associate Ely with the biblical Elijah, specifically in his role as the promised guest of the Jewish Passover Seder ("Hospitality" 81), an identification seconded by Wielenberg (2). As Mundik notes, however, the name "Ely" also evokes Eli the high priest from I Samuel (*Bloody* 320). This latter figure presides at Shiloh over his two sons, failing to intervene as they profane proper sacrifice and "[lie] with the women that [assemble] at the door of the tabernacle" (1 Sam. 2:22). For this prizing of kin over righteousness, Eli and his family are punished by God, his sons killed in battle with the Philistines, Eli himself struck dead on hearing this news (1 Sam. 4:17–18). Given that Ely shares—"I cant see good" (*R* 166)—his namesake's blindness (see 1. Sam. 3:2), this identification seems the more persuasive. In any event, I agree with Mundik that the fact that "Ely" is an alias (see *R* 171) indicates that he is, whether prophet or priest, a fraud in either role (*Bloody* 320).

15. Wielenberg, for one, takes the boy's discomfort in praying to God as demonstrating that, from the novel's perspective, "Christian morality is flawed" (18). Similarly, Rikard sees here a wholesale displacement of orthodoxy, as the father becomes the boy's God (222). Yet as Augustine explains in *City of God*, the Church has always taught that prayers to the saintly dead are licit, not as entreaties to people taken for gods, but as petitions to those whose exemplary love for the one true God now enable them in heaven to advocate to Him on our behalf (832–33).

CODA. THE UNIMAGINABLE PENITENT: PENANCE AND THE MYTH OF AMERICAN INNOCENCE IN *THE COUNSELOR*, *THE PASSENGER*, AND *STELLA MARIS*

1. Other critics have discerned a more flattering pedigree for McCarthy's script. For Cooper, both *The Counselor* and *No Country for Old Men* function as "classic tragedies" (*Cormac* 104). Steven Knepper maintains, more precisely, that this drama seemingly conforms to Aristotelian prescription for tragedy (38), and Peebles similarly reads the character of the Counselor as a tragic hero in Aristotle's terms (165). Though more positive in his assessment of script and movie than many first reviewers, Jacob Agner quarrels with such readers and argues that both film and script are better understood as instances of "neo-noir" rather than Attic tragedy (205).

2. As regards matrimony, Laura is certainly mistaken. Citing Jesus's teachings (Matt. 19:3–12), the *Catechism* asserts that "the matrimonial union of man and woman is indissoluble: God himself has determined it" (450). Nor does this apply only to sacramentally married Catholics. Rather, as the United States Conference of Catholic Bishops makes plain, "The Catholic Church respects the marriages of non-Catholics and presumes that they are valid [and] binding for life" ("Annulment"). This being the case, the Counselor's prior marriage would, absent a declaration of nullity, bar the wedding she dreams of. Likewise, though the Catholic Church does famously maintain that there is no salvation outside the Church, it also understands its membership ultimately to include not just faithful Catholics, but "others who believe in Christ, and finally all mankind, called by God's grace to salvation" (*Catechism*

241). Thus, while affirming that "all salvation comes from Christ the Head through the Church which is his Body" (244), this does not condemn, as Laura suggests, all non-Catholics, but may offer salvation to those "who nevertheless seek God with a sincere heart, and, moved by grace, try in their actions to do his will as they know it through the dictates of their conscience" (244).

3. Monk is seconded in this view by Agner, who ranks Malkina with Judge Holden and Anton Chigurh from *No Country for Old Men* (218). Peebles concurs, noting that her sexual appetite also casts her in another, more stereotypical role, that of femme fatale (178), while Ellis, more critically, characterizes Malkina as "a misogynistic gender twist on Holden and Chigurh" ("Science" 189).

WORKS CITED

Adorno, Theodor, and Max Horkheimer. *Dialectic of Enlightenment.* Translated by John Cumming. Verso, 1997.

Agner, Jacob. "Salvaging *The Counselor:* Watching Cormac McCarthy and Ridley Scott's Really Trashy Movie." *Cormac McCarthy Journal,* vol. 14, no. 2, 2016, pp. 204–26.

Akinwale, Anthony, O.P. "Reconciliation." *The Oxford Handbook of Sacramental Theology.* Edited by Hans Boersma and Matthew Levering. Oxford University Press, 2018, pp. 545–57.

Alarcón, Daniel Cooper. "All the Pretty Mexicos: Cormac McCarthy's Mexican Representations." *Cormac McCarthy: New Directions.* Edited by James D. Lilley. University of New Mexico Press, 2002, pp. 141–52.

Andersen, Tore Rye. "Storytelling after the End: Plotting a Course through Cormac McCarthy's *The Road.*" *Cormac McCarthy Journal,* vol. 19, no. 1, 2021, pp. 67–84.

Andreasen, Liana Vrajitoru. "*Blood Meridian* and the Spatial Metaphysics of the West." *Southwestern American Literature,* vol. 36, no. 3, 2011, pp. 19–30.

"Annulment." *United States Conference of Catholic Bishops.* https://www.usccb.org/topics /marriage-and-family-life-ministries/annulment. Accessed February 9, 2022.

Aquinas, Thomas. *Selected Writings.* Edited and translated by Ralph McInerny. Penguin, 1998.

Arnold, Edwin T. "Cormac McCarthy's *The Stonemason:* The Unmaking of a Play." *Southern Quarterly,* vol. 33, no. 2, 1995, pp. 117–29.

———. "'Go to sleep': Dreams and Visions in the Border Trilogy." *A Cormac McCarthy Companion: The Border Trilogy.* Edited by Edwin T. Arnold and Dianne C. Luce. University Press of Mississippi, 2001, pp. 37–72.

———. "The Last of the Trilogy: First Thoughts on *Cities of the Plain.*" *Perspectives on Cormac McCarthy.* Revised Edition. Edited by Edwin T. Arnold and Dianne C. Luce. University Press of Mississippi, 1999, pp. 221–47.

———. "McCarthy and the Sacred: A Reading of *The Crossing.*" *Cormac McCarthy: New Directions.* Edited by James D. Lilley. University of New Mexico Press, 2002, pp. 215–38.

———. "The Mosaic of McCarthy's Fiction." *Sacred Violence: A Reader's Companion to Cormac McCarthy.* Edited by Wade Hall and Rick Wallach. Texas Western Press, 1995, pp. 17–23.

———. "Naming, Knowing, and Nothingness: McCarthy's Moral Parables." *Perspectives on Cormac McCarthy*. Revised Edition. Edited by Edwin T. Arnold and Dianne C. Luce. University Press of Mississippi, 1999, pp. 45–69.

Athanasius. *On the Incarnation*. Translated and introduced by John Behr. St. Vladimir's Seminary Press, 2011.

Auden, W. H. *The Dyer's Hand and Other Essays*. Vintage, 1968.

Augustine. *The City of God*. Translated by Marcus Dods, introduced by Thomas Merton. Modern Library, 1993.

———. *Confessions*. Translated by R. S. Pine-Coffin. Penguin, 1986.

———. *Faith, Hope and Charity*. Translated by Louis A. Arand. Newman Bookshop, 1947.

Ayres, Lewis, and Thomas Humphries. "Augustine and the West to AD 650." *The Oxford Handbook of Sacramental Theology*. Edited by Hans Boersma and Matthew Levering. Oxford University Press, 2015, pp. 156-169.

Bacon, Francis. *The Complete Essays of Francis Bacon*. Introduced by Henry LeRoy Finch. Washington Square, 1963.

Bailey, Charles. "The Last Stage of the Hero's Evolution: Cormac McCarthy's *Cities of the Plain*." *Myth, Legend, Dust: Critical Responses to Cormac McCarthy*. Edited by Rick Wallach. Manchester University Press, 2000, pp. 293–301.

Bakhtin, M. M. *Rabelais and His World*. Translated by Helene Iswolsky. MIT Press, 1968.

Bannon, Brad. "Divinations of Agency in *Blood Meridian* and *No Country for Old Men*." *Cormac McCarthy Journal*, vol. 14, no. 1, 2016, pp. 78–95.

Bartlett, Andrew. "From Voyeurism to Archeology: Cormac McCarthy's *Child of God*." *Southern Literary Journal*, vol. 24, no. 1, 1991, pp. 3–16.

Beavers, Jay Aaron. "'Stairwell to nowhere': The Darkness of God in Cormac McCarthy's *Suttree*." *South Atlantic Review*, vol. 80, no. 1–2, 2015, pp. 96–114.

Bell, Vereen M. *The Achievement of Cormac McCarthy*. Louisiana State University Press, 1988.

———. "The Ambiguous Nihilism of Cormac McCarthy." *Southern Literary Journal*, vol. 15, no. 2, 1983, pp. 31–41.

Berry, K. Wesley. "The Lay of the Land in Cormac McCarthy's Appalachia." *Cormac McCarthy: New Directions*. Edited by James D. Lilley. University of New Mexico Press, 2002, pp. 47–73.

Blair, Alexandra. "'The Wanted Stared Back': Biopolitics, Genre, and Sympathy in Cormac McCarthy's *Child of God*." *Southern Literary Journal*, vol. 47, no. 2, 2015, pp. 89–106.

Bloom, Harold. Introduction. *Cormac McCarthy*. Edited by Harold Bloom, Bloom's Modern Critical Views. Infobase, 2009, pp. 1–8.

Boethius. *The Consolation of Philosophy*. Translated and introduced by Victor Watts. Penguin, 1999.

Boguta-Marchel, Hanna. *The Evil, the Fated, the Biblical: The Latent Metaphysics of Cormac McCarthy*. Cambridge Scholars Publishing, 2012.

Bourassa, Alan. "Riders of the Virtual Sage: Zane Grey, Cormac McCarthy, and the Transformation of the Popular Western." *Criticism*, vol. 48, no. 4, 2006, pp. 433–52.

Brewer, Mary. "'The light is all around you, cept you dont see nothin but shadow': Narratives of Religion and Race in *The Stonemason* and *The Sunset Limited*." *Cormac McCarthy Journal*, vol. 12, 2014, pp. 39–54.

Broncano, Manuel. *Religion in Cormac McCarthy's Fiction: Apocryphal Borderlands*. Routledge, 2014.

Brown, Lauren. "Existing without Consent: American History and the Judge in Cormac McCarthy's *Blood Meridian*." *Cormac McCarthy Journal*, vol. 16, no. 1, 2018, pp. 73–94.

Buckwalter, Ian. "'The Counselor' Can't Make the Case for Itself." *NPR*, October 24, 2013, https://www.npr.org/2013/10/21/239143659/the-counselor-cant-make-the-case-for-itself. Accessed November 10, 2022.

Busby, Mark. "Into the Darkening Land, the World to Come: Cormac McCarthy's Border Crossings." *Myth, Legend, Dust: Critical Responses to Cormac McCarthy*. Edited by Rick Wallach. Manchester University Press, 2000, pp. 225–48.

Buttersworth, D. S. "Pearls as Swine: Recentering the Marginal in Cormac McCarthy's *Suttree*." *Sacred Violence: A Reader's Companion to Cormac McCarthy*. Edited by Wade Hall and Rick Wallach. Texas Western Press, 1995, pp. 95–101.

Calhoun, Craig, Mark Juergensmeyer, and Jonathan Van Antwerpen. Introduction. *Rethinking Secularism*. Edited by Craig Calhoun, Mark Juergensmeyer, and Jonathan Van Antwerpen. Oxford University Press, 2011, 3–30.

Canfield, J. Douglas. "Crossing from the Wasteland into the Exotic in McCarthy's Border Trilogy." *A Cormac McCarthy Companion: The Border Trilogy*. Edited by Edwin T. Arnold and Dianne C. Luce. University Press of Mississippi, 2001, pp. 256–69.

———. "The Dawning of the Age of Aquarius: Abjection, Identity, and the Carnivalesque in Cormac McCarthy's *Suttree*." *Contemporary Literature*, vol. 44, no. 4, 2003, pp. 664–96.

Cant, John. *Cormac McCarthy and the Myth of American Exceptionalism*. Routledge, 2008.

Carson, Jordan. "Drawing Fire from the Text: Narrative and Morality in *Blood Meridian*." *Cormac McCarthy Journal*, vol. 12, 2014, pp. 20–38.

Casanova, José. "The Secular, Secularizations, Secularisms." *Rethinking Secularism*. Edited by Craig Calhoun, Mark Juergensmeyer, and Jonathan Van Antwerpen. Oxford University Press, 2011, pp. 54–74.

Casarella, Peter J. "Catholic Sacramental Theology in the Twentieth Century." *The Oxford Handbook of Sacramental Theology*. Edited by Hans Boersma and Matthew Levering. Oxford University Press, 2018, pp. 417–432.

Catechism of the Catholic Church. Doubleday, 1995.

Catherine of Siena. *The Dialogue of Saint Catherine of Siena, Seraphic Virgin and Doctor of Unity*. Translated by Algar Thorold. Eremitical Press, 2009.

Chamberlain, Samuel. *My Confession: Recollections of a Rogue.* Edited and introduced by William H. Goetzmann. Texas State Historical Association, 1996.

Chollier, Christine. "Autotextuality, or Dialogic Imagination in Cormac McCarthy's Border Trilogy." *A Cormac McCarthy Companion: The Border Trilogy.* Edited by Edwin T. Arnold and Dianne C. Luce. University Press of Mississippi, 2001, pp. 3–36.

———. "'I aint come back rich, that's for sure,' or the Questioning of Market Economies in Cormac McCarthy's Novels." *Myth, Legend, Dust: Critical Responses to Cormac McCarthy.* Edited by Rick Wallach. Manchester University Press, 2000, pp. 171–76.

Christie, James Williams. "'He could not call to mind his father's face': Oedipal Collapse and Literary Decline in the Border Trilogy." *Cormac McCarthy Journal,* vol. 15, no. 2, 2017, pp. 128–51.

Ciuba, Gary M. "McCarthy's Enfant Terrible: Mimetic Desire and Sacred Violence in *Child of God.*" *Sacred Violence: A Reader's Companion to Cormac McCarthy.* Edited by Wade Hall and Rick Wallach. Texas Western Press, 1995, pp. 77–85.

The Cloud of Unknowing and Other Works. Translated and introduced by Clifton Wolters. Penguin, 1983.

Conrad, Joseph. *Heart of Darkness.* Edited by D. C. R. A. Goonetilleke. Broadview, 1995.

Coolman, Boyd Taylor. "The Christo-Pneumatic-Ecclesial Character of Twelfth-Century Sacramental Theology." *The Oxford Handbook of Sacramental Theology.* Edited by Hans Boersma and Matthew Levering. Oxford University Press, 2018, pp. 201–17.

Cooper, Lydia R. *Cormac McCarthy: A Complexity Theory of Literature.* Manchester University Press, 2021.

———. "McCarthy, Tennessee, and the Southern Gothic." *The Cambridge Companion to Cormac McCarthy.* Edited by Steven Frye. Cambridge University Press, 2013, pp. 41–53.

———. *No More Heroes: Narrative Perspective and Morality in Cormac McCarthy.* Louisiana State University Press, 2011.

———. "The Southwest." *Cormac McCarthy in Context.* Edited by Steven Frye. Cambridge University Press, 2020, pp. 23–32.

Cornwell, Gareth. "Ambivalent National Epic: Cormac McCarthy's *Blood Meridian.*" *Critique: Studies in Contemporary Fiction,* vol. 56, no. 5, 2015, pp. 531–44.

Cowart, David. "Death and the Wastrel: McCarthy's *Suttree.*" *Modern Philology,* vol. 115, no. 3, 2018, pp. 391–411.

Crews, Michael Lynn. *Books Are Made Out of Books: A Guide to Cormac McCarthy's Literary Influences.* University of Texas Press, 2017.

Curtis, Diana. "McCarthy's *Blood Meridian.*" *Explicator,* vol. 63, no. 2, 2005, pp. 112–14.

Danta, Chris. "'The cold illucid world': The Poetics of Gray in Cormac McCarthy's *The Road.*" *Styles of Extinction: Cormac McCarthy's The Road.* Edited by Julian Murphet and Mark Steven. Continuum, 2012, pp. 9–26.

Dante Alighieri. *Inferno.* Translated by Anthony Esolen. Modern Library, 2005.

Daugherty, Leo. "Gravers False and True: *Blood Meridian* as Gnostic Tragedy." *Perspectives on Cormac McCarthy*. Revised Edition. Edited by Edwin J. Arnold and Dianne C. Luce. University Press of Mississippi, 1999, pp. 159–74.

Davis, Steven L. "Mining Dobie: Cormac McCarthy's Debt to J. Frank Dobie in *The Crossing*." *Southwestern American Literature*, vol. 62, no. 5, 2013, pp. 52–57.

DeCoste, D. Marcel. "'One Among and not Separate From': Fallen Communion and Forfeit Community in Cormac McCarthy's *The Crossing*." *Christianity and Literature*, vol. 69, no. 3, 2020, pp. 439–58.

———. "'A Thing That Even Death Cannot Undo': The Operation of the Theological Virtues in Cormac McCarthy's *The Road*." *Religion & Literature*, vol. 44, no. 2, 2012, pp. 67–91.

———. "'When You Stop Pretending That You Know': Gnosis, Humility, and Christian Charity in Cormac McCarthy's *The Stonemason*." *Religion and the Arts*, vol. 25, nos.1–2, 2021, pp. 125–46.

De Sales, Francis. *Introduction to the Devout Life*. Edited and introduced by Allan Ross. Dover, 2009.

Descartes, René. *Discourse on Method and Meditations*. Translated and introduced by Laurence J. Lafleur. Macmillan, 1960.

Dominy, Jordan J. "Cannibalism, Consumerism, and Profanation: Cormac McCarthy's *The Road* and the End of Capitalism." *Cormac McCarthy Journal*, vol. 13, no. 1, 2015, pp. 143–58.

Dorson, James. "Demystifying the Judge: Law and Mythical Violence in Cormac McCarthy's *Blood Meridian*." *Journal of Modern Literature*, vol. 36, no. 2, 2013, pp. 105–21.

———. "The Judeo-Christian Tradition." *Cormac McCarthy in Context*. Edited by Steven Frye. Cambridge University Press, 2020, pp. 121–31.

Dudley, John. "McCarthy's Heroes: Revisiting Masculinity." *The Cambridge Companion to Cormac McCarthy*. Edited by Steven Frye. Cambridge University Press, 2013, pp. 175–87.

Eaton, Mark A. "Dis(re)membered Bodies: Cormac McCarthy's Border Fiction." *Modern Fiction Studies*, vol. 49, no. 1, 2003, pp. 155–80.

Edwards, Tim. "The End of the Road: Pastoralism and the Post-Apocalyptic Waste Land of Cormac McCarthy's *The Road*." *Cormac McCarthy Journal*, vol. 6, no. 1, 2008, pp. 55–61.

Ellis, Jay. *No Place for Home: Spatial Constraint and Character Flight in the Novels of Cormac McCarthy*. Routledge, 2006.

———. "Science and Technology." *Cormac McCarthy in Context*. Edited by Steven Frye. Cambridge University Press, 2020, pp. 180–193.

Elmore, Jonathan, and Rick Elmore. "'He wondered why a road should come to such a place': Community and Posthumanism in Cormac McCarthy's *Outer Dark*." *Cormac McCarthy Journal*, vol. 17, no. 2, 2019, pp. 116–33.

Essary, Kirk. "'We Languish in Obscurity': The Silence of God as Atavistic Calvinism in Cormac McCarthy's Fiction." *Soundings: An Interdisciplinary Journal*, vol. 97, no. 3, 2014, pp. 265–96.

Eusebius. *The History of the Church*. Translated by G. A. Williamson. Penguin, 1989.

Evans, Justin. "To Disenchant and Disintoxicate: *Blood Meridian* as Critical Epic." *Modern Philology*, vol. 112, no. 2, 2014, pp. 405–26.

Evenson, Brian. "McCarthy and the Uses of Philosophy in the Tennessee Novels." *The Cambridge Companion to Cormac McCarthy*. Edited by Steven Frye. Cambridge University Press, 2013, pp. 54–64.

———. "McCarthy's Wanderers: Nomadology, Violence, and Open Country." *Sacred Violence: A Reader's Companion to Cormac McCarthy*. Edited by Wade Hall and Rick Wallach. Texas Western Press, 1995, pp. 41–48.

Ferguson, Everett. "Sacraments in the Pre-Nicene Period." *The Oxford Handbook of Sacramental Theology*. Edited by Hans Boersma and Matthew Levering. Oxford University Press, 2018, pp. 125–39.

Fisher-Wirth, Ann. "Abjection and 'the Feminine' in *Outer Dark*." *Cormac McCarthy: New Directions*. Edited by James D. Lilley, University of New Mexico Press, 2002, pp. 125–140.

Foucault, Michel. "What Is Enlightenment?," translated by Catherine Porter. *The Foucault Reader*. Edited by Paul Rabinow. Pantheon Books, 1984, pp. 32–50.

Freud, Sigmund. *The Future of an Illusion*. Translated and edited by James Strachey. Norton, 1961.

Frye, Steven. "*Blood Meridian* and the Poetics of Violence." *The Cambridge Companion to Cormac McCarthy*. Edited by Steven Frye. Cambridge University Press, 2013, pp. 107–20.

———. "Histories, Novels, Ideas: Cormac McCarthy and the Art of Philosophy." *The Cambridge Companion to Cormac McCarthy*. Edited by Steven Frye. Cambridge University Press, 2013, pp. 3–11.

———. "Life and Career." *Cormac McCarthy in Context*. Edited by Steven Frye. Cambridge University Press, 2020, pp. 3–12.

———. *Understanding Cormac McCarthy*. University of South Carolina Press, 2009.

Gamblin, Hillary. "Discovering the Romantic in a Necrophile: The Question of Misogyny in *Child of God*." *Cormac McCarthy Journal*, vol. 9, no. 1, 2011, pp. 28–37.

Gay, Peter. *The Enlightenment: An Interpretation—The Rise of Modern Paganism*. Knopf, 1967.

Giemza, Bryan. *Irish Catholic Writers and the Invention of the American South*. Louisiana State University Press, 2013.

Giles, James R. "*Outer Dark* and Romantic Naturalism." *The Cambridge Companion to Cormac McCarthy*. Edited by Steven Frye. Cambridge University Press, 2013, pp. 95–106.

Gillespie, Michael Allen. *The Theological Origins of Modernity*. University of Chicago Press, 2008.

Gilson, Etienne. *God and Philosophy*. Yale University Press, 1941.

Girard, René. *Violence and the Sacred*. Translated by Patrick Gregory. Johns Hopkins University Press, 1979.

Goetzmann, William H. Introduction. *My Confession: Recollections of a Rogue,* by Samuel Chamberlain. Edited by William H. Goetzmann. Texas State Historical Association, 1996, pp. 1–25.

Griffis, Rachel B. "Inverting the 'Gracelorn' Father: Augustinian Notions of Evil and Goodness in Cormac McCarthy's *Outer Dark* and *The Road*." *Literature and Theology*, vol. 36, no. 1, 2022, pp. 79–95.

Gugin, David. "The Blood of a Nomad: Environmental Stylistics and *All the Pretty Horses*." *Cormac McCarthy's Borders and Landscapes*. Edited by Louise Jillett. Bloomsbury Academic, 2016, pp. 83–93.

Guillemin, George. "'As of some site where life had not succeeded': Sorrow, Allegory, and Pastoralism in Cormac McCarthy's Border Trilogy." *A Cormac McCarthy Companion: The Border Trilogy*. Edited by Edwin T. Arnold and Dianne C. Luce. University Press of Mississippi, 2001, pp. 92–130.

———. "'See the Child': The Melancholy Subtext of *Blood Meridian*." *Cormac McCarthy: New Directions*. Edited by James D. Lilley. University of New Mexico Press, 2002, pp. 239–65.

Guinn, Matthew. "Ruder Forms Survive: Cormac McCarthy's Atavistic Vision." *Myth, Legend, Dust: Critical Responses to Cormac McCarthy*. Edited by Rick Wallach, Manchester University Press, 2000, pp. 108–15.

Gwinner, Donovan. "'Everything uncoupled from its shoring': Quandaries of Epistemology and Ethics in *The Road*." *Cormac McCarthy: All the Pretty Horses, No Country for Old Men, The Road*. Edited by Sara L. Spurgeon. Continuum, 2011, pp. 137–56.

Hage, Erik. *Cormac McCarthy: A Literary Companion*. McFarland, 2010.

Hall, Wade. "The Hero as Philosopher and Survivor: An Afterword on *The Stonemason* and *The Crossing*." *Sacred Violence: A Reader's Companion to Cormac McCarthy*. Edited by Wade Hall and Rick Wallach. Texas Western Press, 1995, pp.189–94.

———. "The Human Comedy of Cormac McCarthy." *Sacred Violence: A Reader's Companion to Cormac McCarthy*. Edited by Wade Hall and Rick Wallach. Texas Western Press, 1995, pp. 49–60.

Hämäläinen, Pekka. *The Comanche Empire*. Yale University Press, 2008.

Hamilton, Robert. "Liturgical Patterns in Cormac McCarthy's *Blood Meridian*." *The Explicator*, vol. 71, no. 2, 2013, pp. 140–43.

Hanssen, Ken R. "'Men are made of the dust of the earth': Time, Space, Matter, and Meaning in Cormac McCarthy's *Blood Meridian*." *Cormac McCarthy Journal*, vol. 15, no. 2, 2017, pp. 177–92.

Harper, Julia Tulloh. "Affect and Gender in Cormac McCarthy's *Outer Dark*." *European Journal of American Studies*, vol. 12, no. 3, 2017, pp. 1–16.

Harris, Elizabeth A. "Early Cormac McCarthy Interviews Rediscovered." *New York Times*, September 30, 2022, https://www.nytimes.com/2022/09/30/books/early-cormac-mccarthy-interviews-rediscovered.html. Accessed October 24, 2022.

Hawkins, Ty. *Cormac McCarthy's Philosophy*. Palgrave Macmillan, 2017.

Heidegger, Martin. *The Question Concerning Technology and Other Essays*. Translated and introduced by William Lovitt. Harper & Row, 1977.

Hellyer, Grace. "Spring Has Lost Its Scent: Allegory, Ruination, and Suicidal Melancholia in *The Road*." *Styles of Extinction: Cormac McCarthy's The Road*. Edited by Julian Murphet and Mark Steven. Continuum, 2012, pp. 45–62.

Henry, Michel. *Incarnation: A Philosophy of Flesh*. Translated by Karl Hefty. Northwestern University Press, 2015.

Hermansson, Joakim. "Okay: *The Road* and the Good Guys' Adulthood Code." *Cormac McCarthy Journal*, vol. 19, no. 1, 2021, pp. 46–66.

Hickman, Trenton. "McCarthy's Blood Matrix in the Border Trilogy." *Southwestern American Literature*, vol. 25, no. 1, 2002, pp. 19–29.

Hillier, Russell M. "'In a Dark Parody' of John Bunyan's *The Pilgrim's Progress*: The Presence of Subversive Allegory in Cormac McCarthy's *Outer Dark*." *ANQ*, vol. 19, no. 4, 2006, pp. 52–59.

———. *Morality in Cormac McCarthy's Fiction: Souls at Hazard*. Palgrave Macmillan, 2017.

Holloway, David. *The Late Modernism of Cormac McCarthy*. Greenwood, 2002.

———. "Modernism, Nature, and Utopia: Another Look at 'Optical Democracy' in Cormac McCarthy's Western Quartet." *Southern Quarterly*, vol. 38, no. 3, 2000, pp. 186–205.

The Holy Bible, King James Version. Zondervan, 2000.

Humphrey, Edith M. "Sacrifice and Sacrament: Sacramental Implications of the Death of Christ." *The Oxford Handbook of Sacramental Theology*. Edited by Hans Boersma and Matthew Levering. Oxford University Press, 2018, pp. 68–82.

Hungerford, Amy. *Postmodern Belief: American Literature and Religion since 1960*. Princeton University Press, 2010.

Husband, Andrew. "McCarthy's Multitude(s): *All the Pretty Horses* and Los Hombres del Pais." *Cormac McCarthy: All the Pretty Horses, No Country for Old Men, The Road*. Edited by Sara L. Spurgeon. Continuum, 2011, pp. 58–74.

Irenaeus, Saint. *Against Heresies*. Beloved Publishing, 2015.

Jarrett, Robert L. *Cormac McCarthy*. Twayne, 1997.

———. "Cormac McCarthy's Sense of an Ending: Serialized Narrative and Revision in *Cities of the Plain*." *Cormac McCarthy: New Directions*. Edited by James D. Lilley, University of New Mexico Press, 2002, pp. 313–42.

Jenkins, Joey Isaac. "'The carnage in the woods': Queerness and Interspecies Violence in Cormac McCarthy's Border Trilogy." *Cormac McCarthy Journal*, vol. 19, no. 1, 2021, pp. 21–45.

Jergenson, Casey. "'In what direction did lost men veer?': Late Capitalism and Utopia in *The Road*." *Cormac McCarthy Journal*, vol. 14, no. 1, 2016, pp. 117–32.

Jillett, Louise. "Flânerie, Vagrancy, and Voluntary Exile in *Suttree*." *Cormac McCarthy's Borders and Landscapes*. Edited by Louise Jillett. Bloomsbury Academic, 2016, pp. 143–62.

John of the Cross. *Dark Night of the Soul*. Translated by E. Allison Peers. Dover, 2003.

Johnson, Luke Timothy. "Sacramentality and Sacraments in Hebrews." *The Oxford Handbook of Sacramental Theology.* Edited by Hans Boersma and Matthew Levering. Oxford University Press, 2018, pp. 109–22.

Johns-Putra, Adeline. "'My Job Is to Take Care of You': Climate Change, Humanity, and Cormac McCarthy's *The Road.*" *Modern Fiction Studies,* vol. 62, no. 3, 2016, pp. 519–40.

Josephs, Allen. "The Quest for God in *The Road.*" *The Cambridge Companion to Cormac McCarthy.* Edited by Steven Frye. Cambridge University Press, 2013, pp. 133–45.

Josyph, Peter. *Adventures in Reading Cormac McCarthy.* Scarecrow, 2010.

———. "Blood Music: Reading *Blood Meridian.*" *Sacred Violence: A Reader's Companion to Cormac McCarthy.* Edited by Wade Hall and Rick Wallach. Texas Western Press, 1995, pp. 169–88.

———. "What's Wrong with What's Wrong with *The Counselor.*" *Cormac McCarthy's Borders and Landscapes.* Edited by Louise Jillett. Bloomsbury Academic, 2016, pp. 203–22.

Juergensmeyer, Mark. "Rethinking the Secular and Religious Aspects of Violence." *Rethinking Secularism.* Edited by Craig Calhoun, Mark Juergensmeyer, and Jonathan Van Antwerpen. Oxford University Press, 2011, pp. 185–203.

Jurgenson, John. "Everyone's Favorite Cowboy." *Wall Street Journal,* November 13, 2009. *ProQuest,* https://login.libproxy.uregina.ca:8443/login?url=https://www-proquest-com.libproxy.uregina.ca/docview/399070032?accountid=13480. Accessed September 23, 2020.

Justin Martyr. *The First Apology, The Second Apology, Dialogue with Trypho, Exhortation to the Greeks, Discourse to the Greeks, The Monarchy of the Rule of God.* Translated by Thomas B. Falls, vol. 2, *Fathers of the Church: A New Translation.* Catholic University of America Press, 1948.

Kaminsky, Inbar. "The Eternal Night of Consumer Consciousness: The Metaphorical Embodiment of Darkness in Cormac McCarthy's *The Road.*" *European Journal of American Studies,* vol. 13, no. 2, 2018, doi: 10.4000/ejas.1310.

Kant, Immanuel. "What Is Enlightenment?," *The Philosophy of Kant: Immanuel Kant's Moral and Political Writings.* Translated and edited by Carl J. Friedrich. Modern Library, 1977, pp. 132–39.

Keegan, James. "'Save Yourself': The Boundaries of Theodicy and the Signs of *The Crossing.*" *Cormac McCarthy Journal,* vol. 1, no. 1, 2001, pp. 44–61.

Kellogg, Carolyn. "Cormac McCarthy, 89, has a new novel—two, actually. And they're almost perfect." *Los Angeles Times,* October 21, 2022, https://www.latimes.com/entertainment-arts/books/story/2022-10-21/cormac-mccarthy-89-has-a-new-novel-two-actually-and-theyre-almost-perfect. Accessed October 24, 2022.

Kiefer, Christian. "The Morality of Blood: Examining the Moral Code of *The Crossing.*" *Cormac McCarthy Journal,* vol. 1, no. 1, 2001, pp. 26–37.

King, Meg. "'Where is your country?': Locating White Masculinity in *All the Pretty Horses.*" *Cormac McCarthy Journal,* vol. 12, 2014, pp. 69–88.

Knepper, Steven Edward. "*The Counselor* and Tragic Recognition." *Cormac McCarthy Journal*, vol. 14, no. 1, 2016, pp. 37–54.

Knox, Ronald. *The Belief of Catholics*. Ignatius, 2000.

———. *God and the Atom*. Sheed & Ward, 1945.

Kollin, Susan. "'Barren, silent, godless': Ecodisaster and the Post-abundant Landscape in *The Road*." *Cormac McCarthy: All the Pretty Horses, No Country for Old Men, The Road*. Edited by Sara L. Spurgeon. Continuum, 2011, pp. 157–71.

Kristeva, Julia. *Powers of Horror: An Essay on Abjection*. Translated by Leon S. Roudiez. Columbia University Press, 1982.

Kunsa, Ashley. "'Maps of the World in Its Becoming': Post-Apocalyptic Naming in Cormac McCarthy's *The Road*." *Journal of Modern Literature*, vol. 33, no. 1, 2009, pp. 57–74.

Lancaster, Ashley Craig. "From Frankenstein's Monster to Lester Ballard: The Evolving Gothic Monster." *Midwest Quarterly*, vol. 49, no. 2, 2008, pp. 132–48.

Lang, John. "Lester Ballard: McCarthy's Challenge to the Reader's Compassion." *Sacred Violence: A Reader's Companion to Cormac McCarthy*. Edited by Wade Hall and Rick Wallach. Texas Western Press, 1995, pp. 87–94.

Lehner, Ulrich L. *The Catholic Enlightenment: The Forgotten History of a Global Movement*. Oxford University Press, 2016.

Lilley, James D. "'The hands of yet other puppets': Figuring Freedom and Reading Repetition in *All the Pretty Horses*." *Myth, Legend, Dust: Critical Responses to Cormac McCarthy*. Edited by Rick Wallach. Manchester University Press, 2000, pp. 272–87.

Lincicum, David. "Sacraments in the Pauline Epistles." *The Oxford Handbook of Sacramental Theology*. Edited by Hans Boersma and Matthew Levering. Oxford University Press, 2018, pp. 97–108.

Lincoln, Kenneth. *Cormac McCarthy: American Canticles*. Palgrave Macmillan, 2009.

Luce, Dianne C. "Ballard Rising in *Outer Dark*: The Genesis and Early Composition of *Child of God*." *Cormac McCarthy Journal*, vol. 17, no. 2, 2019, pp. 87–115.

———. "The Cave of Oblivion: Platonic Mythology in *Child of God*." *Cormac McCarthy: New Directions*. Edited by James D. Lilley. University of New Mexico Press, 2002, pp. 171–98.

———. "Doomed Enterprise at Caborca: The Henry Crabb Expedition of 1857 and McCarthy's Unquiet American Boys." *Cormac McCarthy's Borders and Landscapes*. Edited by Louise Jillett. Bloomsbury Academic, 2016, pp. 3–17.

———. "On the Trail of History in McCarthy's *Blood Meridian*." Rev. of *Notes on Blood Meridian* by John Sepich, *Mississippi Quarterly*, vol. 49, no. 4, 1996, pp. 843–49.

———. *Reading the World: Cormac McCarthy's Tennessee Period*. University of South Carolina Press, 2009.

———. "The Road and the Matrix: The World as Tale in *The Crossing*." *Perspectives on Cormac McCarthy*. Revised Edition. Edited by Edwin T. Arnold and Dianne C. Luce. University Press of Mississippi, 1999, pp. 195–219.

———. "'When You Wake': John Grady Cole's Heroism in *All the Pretty Horses*." *Sacred Violence: A Reader's Companion to Cormac McCarthy*. Edited by Wade Hall and Rick Wallach. Texas Western Press, 1995, pp. 155–67.

MacKenzie, Cameron. "A Song of Great Order: The Real in Cormac McCarthy's *The Crossing*." *Cormac McCarthy Journal*, vol. 13, no. 1, 2015, pp. 100–120.

Malewitz, Raymond. "Narrative Disruption as Animal Agency in Cormac McCarthy's *The Crossing*." *Modern Fiction Studies*, vol. 60, no. 3, 2014, pp. 544–61.

Mancusi, Nicholas. "Cormac McCarthy's First Books in 16 Years Are a Genius Reinvention." *Time*, October 24, 2022, https://time.com/6223619/cormac-mccarthy-the-passenger-stella-maris-review/. Accessed March 28, 2023.

Marius, Richard. "*Suttree* as Window into the Soul of Cormac McCarthy." *Sacred Violence: A Reader's Companion to Cormac McCarthy*. Edited by Wade Hall and Rick Wallach. Texas Western Press, 1995, pp. 1–15.

Marshall, Bruce D. "What Is the Eucharist? A Dogmatic Outline." *The Oxford Handbook of Sacramental Theology*. Edited by Hans Boersma and Matthew Levering. Oxford University Press, 2018, pp. 500–516.

Masters, Joshua J. "'Witness to the Uttermost Edge of the World': Judge Holden's Textual Enterprise in Cormac McCarthy's *Blood Meridian*." *Critique: Studies in Contemporary Fiction*, vol. 40, no. 1, 1998, pp. 25–37.

McCarthy, Cormac. *All the Pretty Horses*. Vintage, 1993.

———. *Blood Meridian, or The Evening Redness in the West*. Vintage, 1992.

———. *Child of God*. Vintage, 1993.

———. *Cities of the Plain*. Vintage, 1998.

———. *The Counselor: A Screenplay*. Vintage, 2013.

———. *The Crossing*. Vintage, 1994.

———. *The Orchard Keeper*. Vintage, 1993.

———. *Outer Dark*. Vintage, 1993.

———. *The Passenger*. Knopf, 2022.

———. *The Road*. Vintage, 2006.

———. *Stella Maris*. Knopf, 2022.

———. *The Stonemason: A Play in Five Acts*. Vintage, 1995.

———. *Suttree*. Vintage, 1992.

McCarthy, Dennis. "Myth, Legend, Destiny: The Resilient Narratives of the Outlaw in Dennis McCarthy's *The Gospel According to Billy the Kid*." Cormac McCarthy Society Conference, September 23, 2022, DeSoto Hotel, Savannah, GA. Panel Discussion.

McGilchrist, Megan Riley. *The Western Landscape in Cormac McCarthy and Wallace Stegner*. Routledge, 2010.

Metcalf, Robert. "Religion and the 'Religious': Cormac McCarthy and John Dewey." *Journal of Speculative Philosophy*, vol. 31, no. 1, 2017, pp. 135–54.

Metress, Christopher. "*Via Negativa:* The Way of Unknowing in Cormac McCarthy's *Outer Dark.*" *Southern Review,* vol. 37, no. 1, 2001, pp. 147–54.

Mitchell, Jason P. "Louise Erdrich's *Love Medicine,* Cormac McCarthy's *Blood Meridian,* and the (De)Mythologizing of the American West." *Critique,* vol. 40, no. 3, 2000, pp. 290–304.

Monk, Nicholas. *True and Living Prophet of Destruction: Cormac McCarthy and Modernity.* University of New Mexico Press, 2016.

Moos, Dan. "Lacking the Article Itself: Representation and History in Cormac McCarthy's *Blood Meridian.*" *Cormac McCarthy Journal,* vol. 2, no. 1, 2002, pp. 23–39.

Morgan, Wesley G. "The Route and Roots of *The Road.*" *Cormac McCarthy Journal,* vol. 6, no. 1, 2008, pp. 39–47.

———. "Suttree's Dead Acquaintances and McCarthy's Dead Friends." *Cormac McCarthy Journal,* vol. 11, no. 1, 2013, pp. 96–104.

Morrison, Gail Moore. "*All the Pretty Horses:* John Grady Cole's Expulsion from Paradise." *Perspectives on Cormac McCarthy.* Revised Edition. Edited by Edwin T. Arnold and Dianne C. Luce. University Press of Mississippi, 1999, pp. 175–94.

Mundik, Petra. *A Bloody and Barbarous God: The Metaphysics of Cormac McCarthy.* New Mexico University Press, 2016.

———. "'A Clamorous Tide of Unseen Consequence': *Heimarmene* in Cormac McCarthy's Border Trilogy." *Cormac McCarthy's Violent Destinies: The Poetics of Determinism and Fatalism.* Edited by Brad Bannon and John Vanderheide. University of Tennessee Press, 2018, pp. 207–42.

———. "'The Right and Godmade Sun': Fate, Death, and Salvation in Cormac McCarthy's *The Crossing:* Book IV." *Southwestern American Literature,* vol. 37, no. 2, 2012, pp. 10–37.

———. "Terra Damnata: The Anticosmic Mysticism of *Blood Meridian.*" *Cormac McCarthy's Borders and Landscapes.* Edited by Louise Jillett. Bloomsbury Academic, 2016, pp. 29–43.

Nash, Woods. "'Like a Caravan of Carnival Folk': *Child of God* as Subversive Carnivalesque." *Cormac McCarthy Journal,* vol. 11, no. 1, 2013, pp. 80–95.

———. "News Madder Yet: Sources and Significance of Cormac McCarthy's Portrayals of a State Psychiatric Hospital in *Child of God* and *Suttree.*" *Cormac McCarthy Journal,* vol. 13, no. 1, 2015, pp. 72–85.

Neave, Lucy. "Creatureliness and Justice in Cormac McCarthy's *All the Pretty Horses.*" *Cormac McCarthy's Borders and Landscapes.* Edited by Louise Jillett. Bloomsbury Academic, 2016, pp. 19–28.

Nietzsche, Friedrich. *Beyond Good and Evil: Prelude to a Philosophy of the Future.* Translated by Walter Kaufmann. Vintage, 1966.

Nisly, L. Lamar. "'The sacred idiom shorn of its referents': An Apophatic Reading of *The Road.*" *Christianity and Literature,* vol. 68, no. 2, 2019, pp. 311–24.

Nutt, Roger W. *General Principles of Sacramental Theology.* Catholic University of America, 2017.

O'Gorman, Farrell. "Joyce and Contrasting Priesthoods in *Suttree* and *Blood Meridian*." *Cormac McCarthy Journal*, vol. 4, no. 1, 2004, pp. 123–44.

Owens, Barcley. *Cormac McCarthy's Western Novels*. University of Arizona Press, 2000.

Paine, Thomas. *Common Sense*. Edited and introduced by Isaac Kramnick. Penguin, 1986.

Parkes, Adam. "History, Bloodshed, and the Spectacle of American Identity in *Blood Meridian*." *Cormac McCarthy: New Directions*. Edited by James D. Lilley. University of New Mexico Press, 2002, pp. 103–24.

Parrish, Timothy. "History and the Problem of Evil in McCarthy's Western Novels." *The Cambridge Companion to Cormac McCarthy*. Edited by Steven Frye. Cambridge University Press, 2013, pp. 67–78.

———. "The Killer Wears the Halo: Cormac McCarthy, Flannery O'Connor, and the American Religion." *Sacred Violence: A Reader's Companion to Cormac McCarthy*. Edited by Wade Hall and Rick Wallach. Texas Western Press, 1995, pp. 25–39.

Peebles, Stacey. *Cormac McCarthy and Performance: Page, Stage, Screen*. University of Texas Press, 2017.

Phillips, Dana. "'He ought not have done it': McCarthy and Apocalypse." *Cormac McCarthy: All the Pretty Horses, No Country for Old Men, The Road*. Edited by Sara L. Spurgeon. Continuum, 2011, pp. 172–88.

———. "History and the Ugly Facts of *Blood Meridian*." *Cormac McCarthy: New Directions*. Edited by James D. Lilley. University of New Mexico Press, 2002, pp. 17–46.

Pilkington, Tom. "Fate and Free Will on the American Frontier: Cormac McCarthy's Western Fiction." *Western American Literature*, vol. 27, no. 4, 1993, pp. 311–22.

Polk, Noel. "A Faulknerian Look at *Suttree*." *Cormac McCarthy Journal*, vol. 4, no. 1, 2004, pp. 10–38.

Potts, Matthew L. *Cormac McCarthy and the Signs of Sacrament: Literature, Theology, and the Moral of Stories*. Bloomsbury Academic, 2015.

Prather, William. "Absurd Reasoning in an Existential World: A Consideration of Cormac McCarthy's *Suttree*." *Sacred Violence: A Reader's Companion to Cormac McCarthy*. Edited by Wade Hall and Rick Wallach. Texas Western Press, 1995, pp. 103–14.

Priola, Marty. "Games in the Border Trilogy." *Myth, Legend, Dust: Critical Responses to Cormac McCarthy*. Edited by Rick Wallach. Manchester University Press, 2000, pp. 269–71.

Pugh, Marie-Reine. "'There is no God and we are his prophets': The Visionary Potential of Memory and Nostalgia in Cormac McCarthy's *No Country for Old Men* and *The Road*." *Cormac McCarthy Journal*, vol. 15, no. 1, 2017, pp. 46–65.

Radice, Betty, ed. *The Apostolic Fathers: Early Christian Writings*. Translated by Maxwell Stanforth (revised translation, introduction, and notes by Andrew Louth). Penguin, 1987.

Rambo, Shelly L. "Beyond Redemption? Reading Cormac McCarthy's *The Road* after the End of the World." *Studies in the Literary Imagination*, vol. 41, no. 2, 2008, pp. 99–120.

Ratzinger, Joseph. *Called to Communion: Understanding the Church Today.* Translated by Adrian Walker. Ignatius, 1996.

Rebman, Katja. "Cormac McCarthy's Topologies of Violence." *Cormac McCarthy's Borders and Landscapes.* Edited by Louise Jillett. Bloomsbury Academic, 2016, pp. 107–19.

Reimer, Jennifer A. "All the Pretty Mexican Girls: Whiteness and Racial Desire in Cormac McCarthy's *All the Pretty Horses* and *Cities of the Plain.*" *Western American Literature*, vol. 48, no. 4, 2014, pp. 422–42.

Rikard, Gabe. *Authority and the Mountaineer in Cormac McCarthy's Appalachia.* McFarland, 2013.

Rothfork, John. "Cormac McCarthy as Pragmatist." *Critique*, vol. 47, no. 2, 2006, pp. 201–16.

———. "Redemption as Language in Cormac McCarthy's *Suttree.*" *Christianity and Literature*, vol. 53, no. 3, 2004, pp. 385–97.

Rudolph, Kurt. *Gnosis: The Nature and History of Gnosticism.* Translated and edited by Robert McLaughlin Wilson. Harper & Row, 1987.

Russell, Richard Rankin. "'God's own firedrake': McCarthy's Allusion to Joyce's *Ulysses* in *The Road.*" *Cormac McCarthy Journal*, vol. 19, no. 2, 2021, pp. 128–37.

Sanborn, Wallis R., III. *Animals in the Fiction of Cormac McCarthy.* McFarland, 2006.

Sansom, Dennis L. "God, Evil, Suffering, and Human Destiny in the Border Trilogy." *Cormac McCarthy's Violent Destinies: The Poetics of Determinism and Fatalism.* Edited by Brad Bannon and John Vanderheide. University of Tennessee Press, 2018, pp. 67–91.

Schaub, Thomas. "Secular Scripture and Cormac McCarthy's *The Road.*" *Renascence*, vol. 61, no. 3, 2009, pp. 153–67.

Schleusener, Simon. "The Dialectics of Mobility: Capitalism and Apocalypse in Cormac McCarthy's *The Road.*" *European Journal of American Studies*, vol. 12, no. 3, 2017, doi: 10.4000/ejas.12296.

Scoones, Jacqueline. "The World on Fire: Ethics and Evolution in Cormac McCarthy's Border Trilogy." *A Cormac McCarthy Companion: The Border Trilogy.* Edited by Edwin T. Arnold and Dianne C. Luce. University Press of Mississippi, 2001, pp. 131–60.

Sepich, John Emil. "The Dance of History in Cormac McCarthy's *Blood Meridian.*" *Southern Literary Journal*, vol. 24, no. 1, 1991, pp. 16–31.

———. *Notes on Blood Meridian.* Revised and Expanded Edition. University of Texas Press, 2008.

———. "'What Kind of Indians Was Them?': Some Historical Sources in Cormac McCarthy's *Blood Meridian.*" *Perspectives on Cormac McCarthy.* Revised Edition. Edited by Edwin J. Arnold and Dianne C. Luce. University Press of Mississippi, 1999, pp. 123–43.

Shaviro, Steven. "'The Very Life of the Darkness': A Reading of *Blood Meridian.*" *Perspectives on Cormac McCarthy.* Revised Edition. Edited by Edwin J. Arnold and Dianne C. Luce. University Press of Mississippi, 1999, pp. 145–58.

Shaw, Jonathan Imber. "Evil Empires: *Blood Meridian*, War in El Salvador, and the Burdens of Omniscience." *Southern Literary Journal*, vol. 40, no. 2, 2008, pp. 207–31.

Shaw, Patrick W. "Female Presence, Male Violence, and the Art of Artlessness in the Border Trilogy." *Myth, Legend, Dust: Critical Responses to Cormac McCarthy*. Edited by Rick Wallach. Manchester University Press, 2000, pp. 256–68.

——. "The Kid's Fate, the Judge's Guilt: Ramifications of Closure in Cormac McCarthy's *Blood Meridian*." *Southern Literary Journal*, vol. 30, no. 1, 1997, pp. 102–19.

Sheehan, Paul. "Road, fire, trees: Cormac McCarthy's post-America." *Styles of Extinction: Cormac McCarthy's The Road*. Edited by Julian Murphet and Mark Steven. Continuum, 2012, pp. 89–108.

Shelton, Frank W. "Suttree and Suicide." *Southern Quarterly*, vol. 29, no. 1, 1990, pp. 71–83.

Slotkin, Richard. *The Fatal Environment: The Myth of the Frontier in the Age of Industrialization 1800–1890*. University of Oklahoma Press, 1998.

——. *Gunfighter Nation: The Myth of the Frontier in Twentieth-Century America*. University of Oklahoma Press, 1998.

Smith, Adam. *The Wealth of Nations*. Edited by Edwin Cannan. Ixia Press, 2019.

Snyder, Phillip A. "Cowboy Codes in Cormac McCarthy's Border Trilogy." *A Cormac McCarthy Companion: The Border Trilogy*. Edited by Edwin T. Arnold and Dianne C. Luce. University Press of Mississippi, 2001, pp. 198–227.

——. "Hospitality in Cormac McCarthy's *The Road*." *Cormac McCarthy Journal*, vol. 6, no. 1, 2008, pp. 69–86.

Spencer, William C. "Cormac McCarthy's Unholy Trinity: Biblical Parody in *The Outer Dark*." *Sacred Violence: A Reader's Companion to Cormac McCarthy*. Edited by Wade Hall and Rick Wallach. Texas Western Press, 1995, pp. 69–76.

——. "The Seventh Direction, or Suttree's Vision Quest." *Myth, Legend, Dust: Critical Responses to Cormac McCarthy*. Edited by Rick Wallach. Manchester University Press, 2000, pp. 100–107.

Spinoza, Baruch. *The Ethics and Selected Letters*. Translated by Samuel Shirley, edited and introduced by Seymour Feldman. Hackett Publishing, 1982.

Spurgeon, Sara L. "Introduction." *Cormac McCarthy: All the Pretty Horses, No Country for Old Men, The Road*. Edited by Sara L. Spurgeon. Continuum, 2011, pp. 1–22.

——. "The Sacred Hunter and the Eucharist of the Wilderness: Mythic Reconstructions in *Blood Meridian*." *Cormac McCarthy: New Directions*. Edited by James D. Lilley. University of New Mexico Press, 2002, pp. 75–101.

Steven, Mark. "High Road to Hell: Milton, Blake, McCarthy." *Cormac McCarthy Journal*, vol. 14, no. 2, 2016, pp. 149–67.

Stilley, Harriet Poppy. "'White pussy is nothin but trouble': Hypermasculine Hysteria and the Displacement of the Feminine Body in Cormac McCarthy's *Child of God*." *Cormac McCarthy Journal*, vol. 14, no. 1, 2016, pp. 96–116.

Sullivan, Nell. "Boys Will Be Boys and Girls Will Be Gone: The Circuit of Male Desire in Cormac McCarthy's Border Trilogy." *A Cormac McCarthy Companion: The Border Trilogy*.

Edited by Edwin T. Arnold and Dianne C. Luce. University Press of Mississippi, 2001, pp. 228–55.

———. "Cormac McCarthy and the Text of Jouissance." *Sacred Violence: A Reader's Companion to Cormac McCarthy*. Edited by Wade Hall and Rick Wallach. Texas Western Press, 1995, pp. 115–23.

———. "The Evolution of the Dead Girlfriend Motif in *Outer Dark* and *Child of God*." *Myth, Legend, Dust: Critical Responses to Cormac McCarthy*. Edited by Rick Wallach. Manchester University Press, 2000, pp. 68–77.

———. "The Good Guys: McCarthy's *The Road* as Post-9/11 Male Sentimental Novel." *Genre*, vol. 46, no. 1, 2013, pp. 79–101.

Taylor, Charles. *A Secular Age*. Belknap, 2007.

Thérèse of Lisieux. *The Story of a Soul*. Translated and edited by Roger J. Edmonson. Paraclete Press, 2012.

Thiess, Derek J. "On *The Road* and Santa Fe: Complexity in Cormac McCarthy and Climate Change." *Interdisciplinary Studies in Literature and Environment*, vol. 20, no. 3, 2013, pp. 532–52.

Tocqueville, Alexis de. *Democracy in America, and Two Essays on America*. Translated by Gerald Bevan, introduced by Isaac Kramnick. Penguin Books, 2003.

Trotignon, Beatrice. "Detailing the World in *Suttree*." *Myth, Legend, Dust: Critical Responses to Cormac McCarthy*. Edited by Rick Wallach. Manchester University Press, 2000, pp. 89–99.

Turner, Frederick Jackson. *The Frontier in American History*. Introduced by Allan G. Bogue. Dover, 2010.

Uhlmann, Anthony. "*Suttree*, Joyce, and Flaubert." *Cormac McCarthy's Borders and Landscapes*. Edited by Louise Jillett. Bloomsbury Academic, 2016, pp. 163–73.

Vanderheide, John. "Varieties of Renunciation in the Works of Cormac McCarthy." *Cormac McCarthy Journal*, vol. 5, no., 1, 2005, pp. 30–35.

Van Zeller, Hubert. *The Mystery of Suffering*. Foreword by Al Kresta. Christian Classics, 2015.

Vescio, Bryan. "Strangers in Everyland: Suttree, Huckleberry Finn, and Tragic Humanism." *Cormac McCarthy Journal*, vol. 4, no. 1, 2004, pp. 74–88.

Vieth, Ronja. "A Frontier Myth Turns Gothic: *Blood Meridian, or The Evening Redness in the West*." *Cormac McCarthy Journal*, vol. 8, no. 1, 2010, pp. 55–71.

Voltaire. *Candide, or Optimism*. Translated and edited by Theo Cuffe, introduction by Michael Wood. Penguin, 2005.

Von Speyr, Adrienne. *Confession*. Translated by Douglas W. Stott, second edition, Ignatius, 2017.

Wallace, Garry. "Meeting McCarthy." *Southern Quarterly*, vol. 30, no. 4, 1992, pp. 134–39.

Wallach, Rick. "From *Beowulf* to *Blood Meridian*: Cormac McCarthy's Demystification of the Martial Code." *Cormac McCarthy: New Directions*. Edited by James D. Lilley. University of New Mexico Press, 2002, pp. 199–214.

———. "Judge Holden: *Blood Meridian's* Evil Archon." *Sacred Violence: A Reader's Companion to Cormac McCarthy.* Edited by Wade Hall and Rick Wallach. Texas Western Press, 1995, pp. 125–36.

Walsh, Christopher J. *In the Wake of the Sun: Navigating the Southern Works of Cormac McCarthy.* Newfound Press, 2009.

Walter, Peter. "Sacraments in the Council of Trent and Sixteenth-Century Catholic Theology." Translated by David L. Augustine. *The Oxford Handbook of Sacramental Theology.* Edited by Hans Boersma and Matthew Levering. Oxford University Press, 2018, pp. 313–28.

Watson, James. "'The only words I know are the Catholic ones': Sacramental Existentialism in Cormac McCarthy's *Suttree.*" *Southwestern American Literature,* vol. 62, no. 5, 2013, pp. 7–24.

Wawrykow, Joseph P. "The Sacraments in Thirteenth-Century Theology." *The Oxford Handbook of Sacramental Theology.* Edited by Hans Boersma and Matthew Levering. Oxford University Press, 2018, pp. 218–234.

West, Benjamin S. "Gnosticism." *Cormac McCarthy in Context.* Edited by Steven Frye. Cambridge University Press, 2020, pp. 132–42.

White, Christopher T. "Dreaming the Border Trilogy: Cormac McCarthy and Narrative Creativity." *Cormac McCarthy Journal,* vol. 13, no. 1, 2015, pp. 121–42.

Wielenberg, Erik J. "God, Morality, and Meaning in Cormac McCarthy's *The Road.*" *Cormac McCarthy Journal,* vol. 8, no. 1, 2010, pp. 1–19.

Wilhelm, Randall S. "'Golden chalice, good to house a god': Still Life in *The Road.*" *Cormac McCarthy Journal,* vol. 6, no. 1, 2008, pp. 129–46.

Wood, James. "Getting to the End." Review of *The Road,* by Cormac McCarthy. *New Republic,* May 21, 2007, pp. 44–48.

Woodson, Linda. "Leaving the Dark Night of the Lie: A Kristevan Reading of Cormac McCarthy's Border Fiction." *Cormac McCarthy: New Directions.* Edited by James D. Lilley. University of New Mexico Press, 2002, pp. 267–84.

———. "'This is another country': The Complex Feminine Presence in *All the Pretty Horses.*" *Cormac McCarthy: All the Pretty Horses, No Country for Old Men, The Road.* Edited by Sara L. Spurgeon. Continuum, 2011, pp. 25–42.

Woodward, Richard B. "Cormac McCarthy's Venomous Fiction." *New York Times Magazine,* April 19, 1992, https://www.nytimes.com/1992/04/19/magazine/cormac-mccarthy-s-venomous-fiction.html. Accessed October 15, 2020.

Yarbrough, Scott D. "*The Road,* Consumerism, and Consumption." *Approaches to Teaching the Works of Cormac McCarthy.* Edited by Stacey Peebles and Benjamin West. Modern Languages Association, 2022, pp. 182–91.

———. "The South." *Cormac McCarthy in Context.* Edited by Steven Frye. Cambridge University Press, 2013, pp. 13–22.

INDEX

Page numbers followed by "n" refer to endnotes.

Printed in the USA
CPSIA information can be obtained
at www.ICGtesting.com
CBHW021306150624
10131CB00011BA/93/J